A Concept Approach TO SPANISH

Under the Editorship of Eduardo Neale-Silva

A Concept Approach to SPANISH

Zenia Sacks Da Silva
HOFSTRA UNIVERSITY

Gabriel H. Lovett
NEW YORK UNIVERSITY

SECOND EDITION

HARPER & ROW, PUBLISHERS

New York, Evanston, and London

 For information address Harper & Row, Publishers, Incorporated, 49 East 33rd Street, New York, N.Y. 10016

Library of Congress Catalog Card Number: 65-11707

C-1

TO

A. I. D. and Pat

CONTENTS

V / PERSONAL PRONOUNS (*CONTINUED*): THE REFLEXIVES 55

VI / DEMONSTRATIVES AND POSSESSIVES 67

VII / THE SUBJUNCTIVE 79

PREFACE

The story is told of Fray Luis de Leon who, after five years of imprisonment, returned to his classroom at the University of Salamanca, stood up before the assembled students, and began: "As I was saying. . . ."

Ours has not been exactly an imprisonment, but some five years have elapsed since last we had the opportunity to speak to you, to introduce for the first time the "concept approach," and to await your reaction. Happily, your verdict has been for the most part favorable, and so, we have taken that "most part," and reviewed it and elaborated upon it. And then we took the "least part," and reworded and reshaped it so that it too might, with fortune, fall within the realm of your approval.

As we were saying. . . . The concept approach is a means to the command of a today-filled language. It applies to conversation, reading, and structural materials, and to every aspect of classroom and laboratory teaching. Its focus is always the *idea*, the *meaning* that one person is trying to communicate to another. Its view of grammar is one which de-emphasizes, even eliminates formal terminology wherever possible, and which substitutes in its stead an understanding of what the spoken or written word would imply. (For example, the use of the subjunctive is reduced to three basic concepts, without need for reference to types of subordinate clauses, or for memorized lists of verbs, conjunctions, or expressions. **Ser** and **estar**, imperfect and preterite, **por** and **para**, passive and active voice, and other "problem points" are explained with minimum wordage, and with emphasis always on their connotations.) The concept approach seeks also to order the presentation of grammatical structure by association of related ideas. It stresses active conversation, in context, and based on subjects that are meaningful to the student. It introduces current, lively reading (in this instance, items adapted from Spanish and Spanish-American periodicals) to illustrate grammar points and as departures for oral participation. It provides varied and numerous exercises (almost three times as many as in the original edition), ranging from audio-lingual pattern, substitution, and response drills, to controlled translation, free discussion, and original composition. Its many Reference Guides include a glossary of grammatical terms and a *What's the Difference Between . . . ?* section now expanded to one hundred and fifty entries. And finally, it now offers a laboratory program that (1) uniquely involves the student in actual conversation with the speakers, (2) adds the dimension of twelve native voices from Spain and seven countries of Spanish America, (3) supplements the text with drills, reviews, and a variety of vocabulary building exercises, (4) devotes two separate tapes to the analysis and practice of authentic pronunciation, and (5) presents a students' workbook and teacher's manual that coordinate the classroom and laboratory into a single orientation.

We beg you to notice once again that *A Concept Approach to Spanish* may span all levels from early intermediate through advanced. For this reason, lessons are generally divided into Parts A and B. *Only Part A is intended for second year classes.* Part A gives a brief synopsis of fundamental usages and amplifies them through conversational application. It may be used intensively for one semester as a grammar review course, or, more advisedly, for a whole year, with additional reading or composition materials. Part A of each lesson can be divided into units, since exercises immediately follow every point of grammar and each lesson concludes with a review exercise that brings together all the important structures just studied. Part B (plus Part A of Lessons VII and VIII—the subjunctive) is designed for advanced courses in syntax and composition. It delves into the subtle nuances, the exceptions and current idiomatic turns of the language, both oral and written. It may well be the student's first experience on a level of expression that approximates that of the native speaker.

In short, these some five years past have hardly been for us a time of incarceration—but indeed they have been, of inquisition. We have enjoyed the freedom to challenge our every conclusion, to experiment with new techniques, and to develop and improve what we consider our own, ever mindful that our offering will be shaped by your personality and your needs.

May we offer special thanks to Professor Leonardo C. De Morelos of Columbia University for the generous time and heart he has given to this project, and to you, as always, for the talent, skill, and enthusiasm with which you undertake it.

Z. S. D.
G. H. L.

A Concept Approach
TO
SPANISH

LECCIÓN PRIMERA

THE PRESENT, IMPERFECT, AND PRETERITE TENSES

Adaptado de

PUEBLO

Madrid, 3 de julio de 1963

Tres Estudiantes Suspendidos

Era la semana de exámenes en el Instituto de Segunda Enseñanza de Lamego. En la sala de matemáticas, un estudiante parecía tener ciertas dificultades en realizar sus ejercicios porque llevaba vendada una oreja. El muchacho, mientras escribía, monologaba en voz baja, detalle que no chocó demasiado, pues frecuentemente los que estudian en voz alta tienen la costumbre de interrogarse a sí mismos.

De repente se presentó un señor, diciendo que quería hablar al director con urgencia. Declaró que había escuchado a través de un receptor portátil un diálogo sostenido desde una de las salas de examen con un local que distaba cerca de diez minutos del edificio. La conversación versaba sobre los temas del examen. El alumno preguntaba los puntos que le resultaban difíciles y dos personas le transmitían la explicación.

El director no podía creerlo hasta que el radioyente le trajo su aparato de radio y el director oyó el diálogo. Ya no cabía la menor duda: un alumno recibía la chuleta por medio de un transmisor de radio.

Discretamente el director entró en la sala, y como es lógico, despertó su atención el muchacho de la venda en la oreja, que continuaba monologando inocentemente. Llamado al despacho del director, el estudiante dijo que tenía una herida en el oído y que por esa razón llevaba la venda. Le quitaron la venda y bajo un buen trozo de algodón, había un minúsculo receptor. Un emisor, colocado en el reloj de pulsera, funcionaba con idéntica precisión. Allí estaba la ingeniosísima obra de sus dos hermanos, técnicos de radio por vocación. Por supuesto, los tres hermanos fueron suspendidos.

Aunque el episodio ocurrió hace casi un mes, no se dio a conocer hasta el sábado pasado. Las repercusiones fueron inmediatas. Hace ya tres días que el asunto apasiona a la opinión pública. La inmensa mayoría parece creer que los tres no sólo merecen benevolencia, sino becas para ampliar y perfeccionar sus conocimientos científicos. En cambio, respecto al "soplón" que denunció la estratagema estudiantil, no se oyen más que amargas censuras.

PREGUNTAS

1. ¿Qué semana era en el Instituto de Segunda Enseñanza de Lamego?
2. ¿Por qué parecía tener ciertas dificultades un estudiante?
3. ¿Quién se presentó de repente?
4. ¿Cómo había escuchado el diálogo?
5. ¿Cómo realizaban la chuleta el estudiante y sus hermanos?
6. ¿Qué dijo el estudiante cuando le llevaron al despacho del director?
7. ¿Qué descubrieron al quitarle la venda?
8. ¿Dónde estaba el emisor?
9. ¿Cuándo ocurrió el episodio? ¿Cuándo se dio a conocer?
10. ¿Cómo reaccionó el público a la suspensión de los tres hermanos?

CONVERSACIÓN

1. ¿Qué le parece a Ud. el caso de los tres hermanos? ¿Cree Ud. que hizo bien o mal el director al suspenderlos?
2. ¿Qué piensa Ud. del "soplón"? ¿Qué habría hecho Ud. en su lugar?
3. ¿Cómo explica Ud. la reacción del público? ¿Está Ud. de acuerdo?
4. ¿Recuerda Ud. un caso de chuletas en su experiencia personal?
5. En su opinión, ¿debe haber exámenes finales? ¿Por qué?
6. ¿Cree Ud. que habría más o menos chuletas si tuviéramos un "sistema de honor"?

PART A

1. The Present Tense

A. The simple present tense in Spanish describes an action that *is happening now* or that occurs as a general rule. It has three translations in English:

Comes demasiado.	(1) You eat too much (generally).
	(2) You are eating too much (now).
Sí, como mucho.	(3) Yes, I do eat a lot. (Emphatic)

In questions and in negative statements, English must use an auxiliary verb (is, does, etc.). Spanish maintains the simple present and indicates the question by placing the verb before the subject, the negative by putting **no** before the verb.

¿Trabaja Juan?	Does John work? Is John working?
¿No trabaja Juan?	Doesn't John work? Isn't John working?
Ud. no le conoce, ¿verdad?[1]	You don't know him, do you?

B. The present tense is also used in Spanish for an action that *has been going on since* a certain date or time (and is still going on).

Está en el ejército desde junio.	He has been in the army since June (and he still is).
Le espero desde la una.	I have been waiting for him since one o'clock.

EJERCICIOS

A. Cambie las frases siguientes según los sujetos indicados:

1. Llevo ropa muy ligera hoy.
   (El niño, Uds., las muchachas, tú, Pablo y yo)
2. Mete las camisas en el cajón.
   (Su madre, mis hermanas, yo, mi hermano y yo, tú)
3. La criada sacude los muebles.
   (Las criadas, la niña, yo, tú y María, Uds.)
4. ¿A qué hora abren la tienda?
   (Ud., nosotros, tú, tu padre, vosotros, Uds.)
5. ¿No trabajas hoy?
   (Juan, los carpinteros, Ud., Pepe y yo)

B. Conteste en español:

1. ¿A qué hora se levanta Ud. los días de entresemana? ¿Y los domingos?
2. ¿Desde cuándo vive Ud. en la casa (o piso) que tiene ahora?
3. ¿Cuántas materias estudia Ud. este semestre? ¿Cuáles son?

[1] The corroborating question *don't you?*, *doesn't he?*, *haven't they?*, etc., is usually translated by **¿no?**; and *do you?*, *does he?*, *have they?*, etc., by **¿verdad?**

4. ¿Trabaja Ud. fuera de la universidad?
5. ¿Conoce Ud. a muchas personas de otros países? ¿De dónde son?

C. Traduzca al español:

1. Do you want to go? —Only if they are going too. 2. Is Mary waiting for us? 3. You know how to dance, don't you? 4. Since when have they been living with you? 5. We don't work hard in the summer. 6. He says that he is not going to buy it. 7. The Molinas don't come here, do they? 8. I have been married since March.

2. The Imperfect and the Preterite Tenses

A. General view

Spanish has two simple past tenses: the imperfect and the preterite. Their usage depends on the *concept* which the speaker is trying to communicate, and they are never interchangeable without a change in the meaning of the sentence. The difference between the imperfect and the preterite can be visualized in the accompanying diagram.

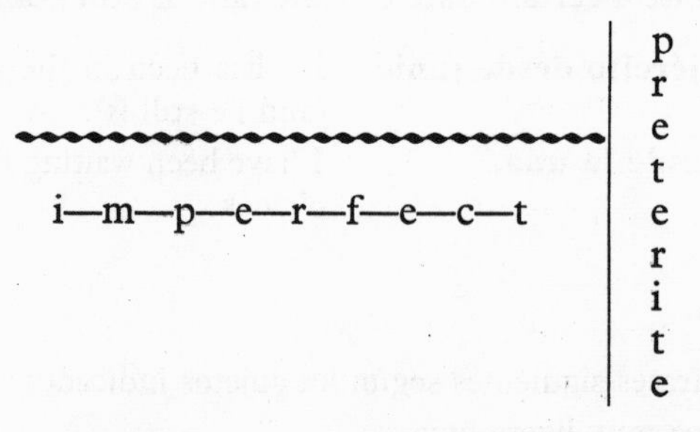

The continuous moving line of the imperfect relives an action or state as it was taking place in the past. It describes a past action in its process or paints the background of an event. The abrupt, incisive stroke of the preterite cuts into the past, recording its events as completed units in time, reporting merely the fact that they took place.

THE IMPERFECT IS THE PICTORIAL PAST.
THE PRETERITE IS THE RECORDING PAST.

B. Uses of the imperfect

1. It tells what *was happening* at a certain time.

Se inclinaba sobre el precipicio, cuando...	He was leaning over the precipice, when . . .
¿Qué hacían?	What were they doing?
—Hablaban de ti y se reían.	—They were talking about you and laughing.

2. It recalls what *used to happen*[2] over a period of time.

Cuando vivíamos en Madrid, íbamos a menudo al Prado.	When we lived in Madrid, we used to go (would go, or went) to the Prado often.
Mi tía escuchaba la radio todo el día.	My aunt used to listen (would listen) to the radio all day.

3. It describes a physical, mental, or emotional state in the past.

Nuestra casa era roja.	Our house was red.
Todos le querían.	Everybody liked him.
No sabía la respuesta.	He didn't know the answer.

4. It tells the time in the past; it sets the stage upon which another action was played.

Eran las nueve.	It was nine o'clock.
Era la Nochebuena...	'Twas the night before Christmas . . .
No había nadie en el cuarto.	There was nobody in the room.

C. Uses of the preterite

1. It records, reports, narrates. It views an event or a series of events as a single completed unit in the past, no matter how long it lasted nor how many times it was repeated.

Anoche fuimos al cine.	Last night we went to the movies.
¿A qué universidad asistió Ud.?	What university did you attend?
En 1964 nuestro equipo ganó cien partidos.	In 1964 our team won a hundred games.
Pasó toda su vida en el Japón.	He spent his whole life in Japan.

Notice that the imperfect and the preterite may, and often do, appear in the same sentence. Only the meaning of each clause will determine which tense is to be used.

El campeón caía cuando sonó la campanilla.	The champion was falling when the bell rang.

[2] *Used to* is often replaced by *would* in English. Be careful to distinguish between *would* meaning an habitual or recurrent action, and *would* as a conditional.

2. With certain verbs, the preterite produces an essential difference in translation, as well as in meaning.

Sabíamos que estaba de vacaciones.	We *knew* that he was on vacation. (Mental state.)
Supimos que estaba de vacaciones.	We *found out* (*learned*) that he was on vacation. (Mental action indicating beginning of knowledge.)
Quería llamarnos.	He *wanted* to call us. (Mental state.)
Quiso llamarnos.	He *tried* to call us. (The act of putting his will into effect.)
No quería pelear.	He *didn't want* to fight.
No quiso pelear.	He *refused* to fight.
¿Le conocía Ud.?	Did you *know* him?
Le conocí hace años.	I *met* him (made his acquaintance) years ago.
Podía hacerlo.	He *was able* to do it. (He was capable of doing it.)
Pudo hacerlo.	He *succeeded* in doing it. (He was able and did.)

EJERCICIOS

A. Repase las formas regulares del imperfecto y del pretérito.

B. Cambie al imperfecto:

1. Tomo este camino. 2. No leen el libro. 3. Levanta la mano. 4. Miran el cuadro. 5. Lavamos el piso. 6. ¿Enseñáis español? 7. No trabajo en la tienda. 8. ¿Cambias el dibujo? 9. ¿No aprendes francés? 10. Pierden tiempo.

C. Cambie al pretérito:

1. No me gusta. 2. Nos lo manda. 3. No se lo compramos. 4. Llamaban a la puerta. 5. Escribían la carta. 6. Rompes la caja. 7. ¿Abrís la ventana? 8. El pobre comía el pan. 9. No cojo la pelota. 10. Hablo con Juan.

D. Conteste en español:

1. ¿En qué asignatura salió Ud. mejor el semestre pasado?
2. ¿Conoció Ud. a mucha gente nueva el verano pasado?
3. De niño, ¿dónde pasaba Ud. sus vacaciones de verano? ¿Viajaba mucho?
4. ¿Prefería entonces el mar o las montañas? ¿Cuál le gusta más ahora?
5. ¿A qué hora se acostaba cuando tenía diez años? ¿Y ahora?

E. Traduzca al español:

1. I came, I saw, I conquered. 2. It was midnight. The house was dark and seemed empty. We opened the door and, suddenly, we heard a scream. 3. Jim never used to send me pretty flowers. Jim never used to fill my lonely hours. Now do you understand why I didn't like him? 4. Why did your father refuse to go? —Because it was raining. 5. Did you know that our school won the championship in 1872?

3. **Hacer** in Time Expressions

A. When a situation *has been going on* for a certain period of time (*and still is*), the impersonal **hace... que** (*now it makes*) states the length of time, and the following verb is also in the present.

Hace dos años que vive en España.	He has been living in Spain for two years.
Hace seis meses que la conoce.	He has known her for six months.

B. When a situation *had been going on* for a certain period of time (*and still was going on, until . . .*), **hacía... que** states the length of time, and the following verb is also in the imperfect.

Hacía dos años que vivía en España.	He had been living in Spain for two years.
Hacía seis meses que la conocía cuando se casaron.	He had known her for six months when they got married.

C. After a verb in the preterite or imperfect, **hace** + period of time means *ago*. When **hace...** begins the sentence, it is generally followed by **que.**

Murió hace tres días. **Hace tres días que murió.**	He died three days ago.
La vi hace media hora. **Hace media hora que la vi.**	I saw her half an hour ago.
Tocaba muy bien hace cinco años.	He used to play very well five years ago.

EJERCICIOS

A. Cambie según los sujetos, verbos y tiempos indicados:

1. Hace dos horas que **el niño** duerme. (los niños) 2. Hace siete meses que **estoy casada.** (Pablo y yo) 3. ¿Cuánto tiempo hace que **trabajas** aquí? (tú y Pepe) 4. Hace años que los **conocemos.** (tratar) 5. **Hace** horas que están esperando. (Hacía) 6. ¿Hace mucho tiempo que **estudias** ciencias? (enseñar) 7. Hace diez años que le **sirve.** (ayudar) 8. **Hace** tres días que llueve. (Hacía) 9. **Hace** una hora que nieva. (Hacía) 10. Le

vi hace poco. (hablar) 11. **Vino** hace una hora. (Llamar) 12. **Volvió** hace un mes. (Sus padres) 13. **Cantaba** bien hace unos años. (tocar) 14. Hace tres semanas que **murió.** (nacer)

B. Conteste en español:

1. ¿Cuánto tiempo hace que estudia Ud. el español?
2. ¿Dónde estaba Ud. hace media hora? ¿Y hace dos horas?
3. ¿Llegó su familia hace poco a esta ciudad?
4. ¿Quién es su mejor amigo? ¿Hace mucho tiempo que le conoce?
5. ¿Cuánto tiempo hacía que se conocían sus padres antes de casarse?

4. **Acabar de** to have just

The idiom **acabar de,** followed by an infinitive, is used only in the present and imperfect. In the present, it is translated as (*I, you, etc.*) *have just* . . ., and in the imperfect as *had just* . . .

Acaban de llegar.	They have just arrived.
Acabábamos de comer.	We had just eaten.

EJERCICIO

Diga en español:

1. My wife has just arrived. 2. No, thanks. We have just eaten. 3. They have just announced it. 4. I have just read it. 5. Had you just come (tú)? 6. He had just spoken to her. 7. She has just died. 8. They had just graduated.

EJERCICIO DE REPASO

1. While he wrote, the student was talking to himself in a low voice.
2. Suddenly, a man came in from the street and said that he wanted to speak to the principal.
3. They were taking the exam in a building that was ten minutes away from their house.
4. The principal wouldn't believe it until he saw the portable receiver.
5. The student said that he was wearing the bandage because his ear hurt.
6. In his wrist watch they found a transmitter which worked perfectly.
7. Thanks to this device, his older brothers could help him when he didn't know the answers.
8. The three brothers were suspended five days ago. I understand that their family has been living in this town since 1910.
9. Public opinion has been discussing (**comentar**) the matter for two weeks.
10. The majority seemed to think that the suspended students deserved a prize for their ingenuity.

PART B

5. The Present Tense

A. The present tense is often used instead of the future to give the action a more immediate and graphic character.

Te veo mañana.	I'll see you tomorrow.
Me llama esta noche.	He will call me tonight.
Se lo doy a las seis.	I shall give it to you at six.

B. The present also appears frequently in place of the preterite to render the past more vivid.

Se dio la orden de tomar el pueblo, y nuestras tropas se lanzaron al ataque. Salvan los parapetos, se apoderan de la primera línea de trincheras, y a los veinte minutos, el enemigo inicia una retirada precipitada.	The order was given to take the town, and our troops rushed to the attack. They cleared the parapets, gained possession of the first line of trenches, and twenty minutes later, the enemy began a hasty retreat.

C. The present is used occasionally instead of both the pluperfect subjunctive and the conditional perfect in contrary-to-fact sentences, again for the sake of vividness.

Si me ve, me mata.	If he had seen me, he would have killed me.

6. The Imperfect and the Preterite Tenses

A. Further analysis of their psychology

In many instances, English does not reveal, or at best, intimates only by context whether the past action to which it refers is viewed as a completed unit in time, or whether it is being described in its process. Spanish, however, maintains the clear distinction between these viewpoints by the use of the preterite and imperfect. Consider the following:

(1) My brother was sick last week.	a. **Mi hermano estuvo enfermo la semana pasada.** (The speaker is recording the fact of his brother's illness. His brother took sick last week and then recovered.)

b. **Mi hermano estaba enfermo...** (Here the speaker is describing his brother's condition at that time. He makes no reference to the beginning or conclusion of the illness.)

(2) Her husband was a professor.

a. **Su marido fue profesor.** (His career as a professor is viewed as a completed whole.)

b. **Su marido era profesor.** (This statement describes his activity at that time or over a period of time.)

(3) I had to study.

a. **Tuve que estudiar.** (I was compelled to and did.)

b. **Tenía que estudiar.** (At a certain time or as a general rule, I was in the position of having to study. Whether or not I actually did study is unresolved.)

(4) Last Sunday, the family gathered. First, the father spoke, and then they all discussed the events of the week.

El domingo pasado, se reunió la familia. Primero habló el padre y después, todos comentaron los sucesos de la semana.

In this case, the phrase *Last Sunday* indicates the narration of acts that are being reported as completed units in time. Thus: preterite. If the imperfect were used here, the necessary implication would be *The family was gathering* . . .

Every Sunday, the family gathered. First, the father spoke, and then they all discussed the events of the week.

Todos los domingos, se reunía la familia. Primero hablaba el padre, y después todos comentaban los sucesos de la semana.

In this paragraph, the phrase *Every Sunday* implies the description of an habitual action. Thus: imperfect.

B. Indirect discourse

When a direct statement is not given as a quotation, but is included within another statement, the construction is known grammatically as indirect discourse. (*He says that . . ., They explained that . . .*) The imperfect is used for an indirect quotation in the past, unless the subordinate clause actually implies a prior past (pluperfect) action.

Dijo que ganaba mucho dinero.	He said that he earned a lot of money. (He said: I earn a lot of money.)
Dijo que ganó mucho dinero.	He said that he (had) earned a lot of money. (He said: I earned a lot of money.)

C. The imperfect in result clauses

In everyday speech, the imperfect is very commonly used in the result clause of a condition contrary to fact.

Si *yo* **lo tuviese, se lo daba.**	If *I* had it, I would give it to him.
Si lo supieran, nos echaban de casa.	If they knew, they would throw us out.

7. **Soler** to be accustomed to, to (do) generally

Soler + infinitive is used very often in the present and imperfect to portray a habitual action.

Suele pasar por aquí a estas horas.	He usually comes by here at this time.
Solían desayunar a las seis.	They used to breakfast at six.

8. **Hacer** in Time Expressions

A. **Hacía... (que)** followed by a verb in the pluperfect, means *previously* or *before*. Of course, **hacía...** may follow the main clause in this usage.

Hacía cinco años que había renunciado su puesto.	He had given up his job five years before.
Había renunciado su puesto hacía cinco años.	

B. The main verb may precede the **hace** construction in sentences that describe a situation that *has been* or *had been going on* for a period of time. In such cases, **hace** or **hacía** is generally preceded by **desde**.

LECCIÓN SEGUNDA

THE FUTURE AND CONDITIONAL TENSES

Adaptado de

ESPAÑA SEMANAL

Madrid, 4 de agosto de 1963

Submarino Turístico Se Está Construyendo en Suiza

Hasta ahora los "submarinos de bolsillo" sólo se construían con fines de investigación científica o con fines militares. Ayer por primera vez se anunció que una empresa suiza aplicaría al turismo los conocimientos en la materia. Un mesoscafo, el primer sumergible turístico, se está construyendo ya en la pequeña ciudad de Monthey y será botado a principios del año próximo. El mesoscafo se distingue de otros sumergibles experimentales en que no puede detenerse para investigar en las profundidades y luego reanudar su movimiento, sino que debe estar continuamente en movimiento.

Aunque parezca increíble, unas dos mil personas ya han reservado pasaje en el primer submarino de paz. Se cree que habrá otras cien mil personas que acudirán a reservar plazas de aquí hasta fines de año. El sumergible no navegará por el momento más que en el lago Leman. Esto permitiría reducir al mínimo los riesgos de accidente. Como va destinado a fines turísticos, el submarino dará a los pasajeros las más amplias posibilidades de visión compatibles con la seguridad.

Los primeros viajes consistirán en una vuelta por el centro del lago Leman o de Ginebra donde la profundidad es mayor. El recorrido durará aproximadamente media hora y los viajeros podrán contemplar por veinte francos suizos la flora y fauna de las profundidades. El submarino estará provisto de potentes reflectores que convertirán los misterios de los abismos en un espectáculo asequible a los viajeros.

Si el submarino experimental confirma su interés para los turistas y ofrece las esperadas condiciones de seguridad, la misma empresa se aventurará a proyectos mucho más ambiciosos: la construcción de grandes submarinos no sólo para la exploración submarina sino para verdaderos viajes. Como se sabe, aun en las peores condiciones de tiempo, a determinada profundidad se puede navegar con la más absoluta estabilidad. Los submarinos de transporte podrían emplearse para recorridos relativamente cortos en los que el mar suele estar siempre agitado.

PREGUNTAS

1. ¿Con qué fines se construían hasta ahora los "submarinos de bolsillo"?
2. ¿Qué se anunció ayer por primera vez?
3. ¿Cuándo será botado el primer sumergible turístico?
4. ¿Cuántas personas han reservado pasaje ya?
5. ¿Cuántas personas acudirán a reservar pasaje para fines de año?
6. ¿Por qué navegará el submarino sólo en el lago Leman por el momento?
7. ¿Qué podrán contemplar los viajeros?
8. ¿De qué estará provisto el submarino?
9. ¿A qué proyectos se aventurará la compañía suiza si éste resulta bien?
10. ¿Sabe Ud. para qué recorridos podrían emplearse los submarinos de transporte?

CONVERSACIÓN

1. ¿Le interesaría a Ud. un viaje turístico en submarino? ¿Por qué? ¿Ha estado Ud. alguna vez en un submarino?
2. ¿Qué viajes ha hecho Ud. hasta ahora? ¿Cómo los realizó? ¿Prefiere Ud. viajar solo o acompañado?
3. Si Ud. pudiera hacer un viaje a cualquier parte del mundo, ¿adónde iría? ¿Por qué?
4. ¿Le gusta más viajar en avión, en tren, en barco o en coche?

PART A

10. The Future Tense

A. General meaning and function

Exactly as in English, the future tense in Spanish refers to an action that *is going to* take place. It is translated in English as *will* or *shall* (*go*, *do*, etc.)

Su tren llegará a las once.	His train will arrive at eleven.
Nos veremos en la biblioteca.	We shall meet at the library.

B. The future of probability

In Spanish, the future is used also to convey the idea of conjecture or probability with regard to an action in the present.

Ya estará aquí.	It probably is here already. It must be here already. (*Must* in this case indicates likelihood not necessity.)
¿Quién será?	I wonder who he is. Who can he be?

EJERCICIOS

A. Repase las formas regulares del futuro (p. 315).

B. Cambie según los sujetos indicados:
1. Juan firmará el recibo.
(Tú, mis hermanos, yo, mis padres y yo)
2. Le escribiré mañana, ¿está bien?
(Su novia, los niños, tú, vosotras)
3. Volverán pronto, ¿no?
(Los vecinos, Ud., nosotros, Ana)
4. Iré con mi amigo esta noche.
(Uds., Jaime, tú, vosotros, tú y yo)

C. Conteste en español:

1. ¿Qué hora será cuando termine esta clase? 2. ¿A qué hora se levantará Ud. mañana? 3. ¿A qué hora volverá a casa hoy? 4. ¿Cuántos años tendrá Ud. en 1999? 5. ¿Qué hará Ud. el verano que viene? 6. ¿Cuándo se graduará Ud. de la universidad?

D. Diga en español:

1. I shall put it on the table. 2. Where can they be? 3. Will you have time? 4. We shall not be able to go with you. 5. I wonder what time it is. 6. He says that he will write to me every day.

11. Other Meanings of the English *will*

In English, *will* is often used in the sense of *to will*, *to be willing*, or *please*. In such cases, *will* is rendered in Spanish by the verb **querer**, and not by the future.

¿Quiere Ud. cerrar la puerta?	Will you (please) close the door?
¿Quieren Uds. sentarse un momentito?	Will you be seated for a moment?
No quiere escucharnos.	He won't (will not, doesn't want to) listen to us.

EJERCICIO

1. Will you (please) turn on the radio? 2. I think they'll come. 3. Some people won't spend money for education. 4. What God wills will be. 5. Can it be worth so much? 6. Will you repeat that? You must be mistaken.

12. The Conditional Tense

A. Meaning and function

1. The conditional is generally translated in English as *would* (*go*, *do*, etc.) and occasionally, in the first person, as *should.*
2. Primarily, the conditional is the future of a past action. As such, it has all the uses of the future tense, but with regard to the past. In the language of a mathematical ratio it can be expressed as follows:

CONDITIONAL : PAST = FUTURE : PRESENT
(Conditional is to Past as Future is to Present)

B. Uses

1. The conditional tells what *was going to* take place.

Dijo que vendría.	He said that he would come.
Nos aseguraron que seríamos los primeros.	They assured us that we would be the first.

2. It conveys the idea of conjecture or probability with respect to a past action.

Serían las tres.	It was probably three o'clock. It was around three o'clock. It must have been three o'clock.
¿Quién sería?	I wonder who it was. Who could it be?

3. It is also used to state the result of a contrary-to-fact clause beginning with *if*. (It tells what would happen *if* something were so.)

Si tuviera tiempo, te diría más.	If I had time, I would tell you more.
Si Paco estuviera aquí, él sabría hacerlo.	If Frank were here, he'd know how to do it.

At times, the *if* clause is not stated, but implied.

¿Haría Ud. tal cosa?	Would you do a thing like that? (If you were in that situation.)
¿Quién lo creería?	Who would believe it? (If he were told so.)

4. It may be used as a polite or softened version of the future.

Tendría mucho gusto en invitarlos.	I should be happy to invite them.
¿Sería Ud. tan amable?	Would you be so kind?

EJERCICIOS

A. Repase las formas regulares del condicional (p. 315).

B. Cambie los verbos en el condicional según los sujetos indicados:

1. Dijo que ganaría María.
(tú, vosotros, María y Consuelo)
2. Me escribió que no podría hacerlo.
(los alumnos, mi primo y yo, Uds.)
3. De todas maneras yo no sabría contestarle.
(el otro, nosotras, tú)
4. ¿Me darías este juguete?
(Gil, los niños, vosotras)

C. Conteste, empleando los verbos indicados; tenga cuidado de distinguir entre el condicional y el imperfecto:

1. ¿Qué haría Ud. si lloviese mañana? —(**Quedarse**) en casa.
2. ¿Qué pasaría si él estuviera aquí? —Nos (**dar**) el dinero.
3. ¿Qué les dijo Ud.? —Que (**tener**) mucho gusto en invitarlos.
4. ¿Adónde iba Ud. siempre que llovía? —(**Ir**) al cine.
5. ¿Qué hora sería cuando volviste a casa? —(**Ser**) la una.
6. ¿Qué escribieron en la carta? —Que (**venir**) pronto él y su hermana.
7. ¿Qué ocurriría si faltase a diez clases? —(**Perder**) la asignatura.
8. ¿Qué anunció? —Que las tropas (**llegar**) al día siguiente.
9. ¿Qué prometió? —Que no (**volver**) a hacerlo.
10. ¿Qué hacían Uds. por la tarde? —(**Ir**) al casino.

D. Traduzca al español:

1. Would you do me a favor? 2. He said that he would buy it. 3. They announced on the radio that it would rain. 4. I wonder why they came. 5. Wouldn't you go for (**por**) a friend? 6. It must have been 9:30 when they returned.

13. Other Meanings of *would* and *should*

Aside from the conditional usages discussed above, *would* and *should* have several other meanings in English. Spanish translates each of these in its most literal and accurate sense.

A. *Would*

1. When *would* means *used to*, it is translated by the imperfect.

Siempre que llovía, íbamos al cine.	Whenever it would rain, we would go to the movies.

2. When *would* means *willed*, it is translated by *querer*, usually in the preterite. This sense of *would* appears most frequently in the negative.

No quiso admitir que estaba equivocado.	He would not admit that he was wrong.
Se lo rogamos, pero no quisieron perdonarle.	We begged them, but they wouldn't pardon him.

3. When *would* means *please*, or merely conveys a softened request, it may be translated, like *will*, by the present of **querer.**

¿Quiere Ud. traerme un pañuelo?	Would you bring me a handkerchief?

B. *Should*

Aside from the occasional, and increasingly rare use of *should* for the first person of the conditional (I should, you, he would, etc), there are three other important meanings and translations of *should.*

1. When *should* means *ought to*, it is translated by **deber.**

Debe estudiar, pero no quiere.	He should study, but he doesn't want to.
Todo el mundo debe votar.	Everyone should vote.

2. When *should* follows *if*, it denotes a condition that is probably contrary to fact. It is then translated by the imperfect subjunctive.

Si lloviera, tendríamos que suspender el partido.	If it should rain, we would have to cancel the game.
Si vinieran esta noche, no sabría qué darles de comer.	If they should come tonight, I wouldn't know what to feed them.

3. When *should* indicates probability, it is translated either by **deber** (**de**) or by the future of probability.

¿Qué hora es? —Serán las ocho.	What time is it? —It should be eight o'clock.
Ya estará aquí. **Ya debe** (**de**) **estar aquí.**	He should be (he probably is) here already.

EJERCICIO

Conteste en español:

1. ¿Qué debe hacer un estudiante para sacar buenas notas?
2. ¿Qué deben hacer los automovilistas para evitar accidentes?
3. ¿Qué compraría Ud. si alguien le diera cien dólares? ¿Y mil dólares?
4. ¿Qué haría Ud. si no pudiera asistir a la universidad?
5. ¿Debe abrirse a las mujeres la presidencia de los Estados Unidos?

EJERCICIO DE REPASO

1. The new pocket submarine will be launched early next year.
2. This submarine will be able to stop in order to explore the undersea depths.
3. There must be a hundred thousand people who will want to reserve space between now and the end of the year.
4. The Swiss company announced yesterday that the craft would sail only on Lake Geneva.
5. The submarine would be built with the greatest possible precautions for the safety of the passengers.
6. The first trip would consist of a tour through the middle of the lake.
7. I wonder how long the trip will take. —You should ask the company. They must know (**lo**).
8. They will be able to look at the flora and fauna through some special portholes.
9. The submarine will also have powerful searchlights which will allow the passengers to see some marvelous things.
10. The sea must have been very rough because they all became seasick. But in a submarine one can always navigate with absolute stability.

PART B

14. Expressions of Obligation

A. **Tener que** to have to

This is a term of compulsion. Since it is used in every person, it applies directly to the person involved.

Tengo que estudiar.	I have to (must) study.
Uds. tendrán que verle.	You will have to see him.
Tuvieron que ir.	They had to go (and did).

B. **Hay que** one must

1. This impersonal expression is also a strong indication of obligation, but to the extent that it does not pertain to the individual directly, it is often somewhat weaker in effect than **tener que.**

Hay que trabajar.	One must work. It is necessary to work.

Es necesario is a synonym for **hay que.**

2. Sometimes the implication of **hay que** is actually personal but even then it is closer to **deber** than to **tener que** in concept.

No hay que olvidar que todavía son aliados nuestros.	We (one) mustn't forget that they are still our allies.

C. **Deber** to be obligated to (ought to, should)

Deber generally conveys a concept of moral obligation. (Recall that the noun **el deber** means *duty.*) However, within the usage of **deber,** there is a perceptible gradation of the degree of obligation implied.

1. Obligation in the present

a. The present indicative of **deber** conveys a fairly strong attitude of obligation.

Ud. debe aprender a bailar.	You ought to (should) learn to dance.

b. The **-ra** form of the imperfect subjunctive or the conditional lends a milder tone to the expression of obligation.

Ud. debiera aprender a bailar. **Ud. debería aprender a bailar.**	You really should learn to dance. (It would be nice if you did.)

2. Obligation in the past

a. The imperfect of **deber** expresses obligation that was contemporary or future to another past action.

Sabía que debía hacerlo.	I knew that I ought to do it.
Dijo que debíamos invitarlos.	He said that we should (ought to) invite them.

b. The preterite of **deber** expresses obligation at a prior moment.

Ud. debió ofrecérselo.	You ought to have (should have) offered it to him (at that time).
Debieron aceptarlo.	They ought to have (should have) accepted it (at that moment).

c. The imperfect of **deber,** followed by **haber** and a past participle places more emphasis upon the prior nature of the action to which it refers.

Sabía que no debía haberlo dicho.	I knew that I ought not to have said it (before).
Dijo que debíamos haberlos invitado.	He said that we should have (already) invited them.

d. The **-ra** form of the imperfect subjunctive of **deber,** followed by **haber,** again imparts a softer tone to obligation in the past.

Debiéramos haberlos invitado.	We should have invited them.

D. **Haber de** to be (supposed or expected) to

1. **Haber de** usually implies little more than futurity, with the mildest added sense of obligation.

Ha de cantar en el Palacio.	He is to sing at the Palace.
Habíamos de cenar con ellos.	We were (supposed) to have dinner with them.
¿Cómo había de saberlo ella?	How should she have known (was she to know)?

2. On occasion, it acquires the more forceful connotations of **deber** or **tener que.**

¿Por qué no he de decirlo ahora mismo?	Why shouldn't I say it right now?
Uds. han de aprenderlo todo de memoria.	You are to (should, must) learn it all by heart.

3. In literary usage, the preterite of **haber de** conveys merely the fact of a completed action, without obligation or necessity.

Hubieron de verle al día siguiente.	They saw him on the following day.

15. Other Uses of **deber**

A. Probability

Deber, sometimes followed by **de,** is used as an exact equivalent of the future (or conditional) of probability.

Debe (**de**) **tener por lo menos cincuenta años.** **Tendrá por lo menos cincuenta años.**	He must be (probably is) fifty years old.
Debían (**de**) **ser las once cuando volvieron.** **Serían las once cuando volvieron.**	It must have been (probably was) eleven o'clock when they returned.
Debe (**de**) **habérnoslo mandado.** **Nos lo habrá mandado.**	He probably has (must have) sent it to us.
Debía (**de**) **haberla visto antes.**[1] **La habría visto antes.**	He probably had seen her before.

B. Expectation or supposition

In this sense, **deber,** generally used in the present and imperfect indicative, corresponds to **haber de.**

El vapor debe (**ha de**) **entrar en muelle a las nueve.**	The ship is supposed to dock at nine o'clock.
Me dijeron que debían (**habían de**) **marcharse al día siguiente.**	They told me that they were to leave on the next day.

C. Necessity

Occasionally, **deber** is used with approximately the meaning of **tener que.** However, **deber** always retains its implication of obligation or duty, rather than the compulsion or necessity implied by **tener que.**

Antes de poder ingresar en la Universidad, debo aprobar un examen especial.	Before being able to enter the University, I must (am obliged to) pass a special examination.

[1] This construction is less frequent than the conditional perfect.

EJERCICIOS

I. Tradúzcase al español.

JOE: Listen, Frank. There is going to be (**Va a haber**) a party tomorrow at the club and I want you to take my sister-in-law. She was supposed to go with a fellow that she met last week, but he had to go to Washington on (**por**) business.

FRANK: I'm sorry, Joe. I would have liked very much to go, but I have something very important to (**que**) do.

JOE: Nonsense! You know, Frank, you work too hard. You don't know how to live. I think you should get married.

FRANK: The same old story (**Lo de siempre**)! How many times do I have to tell you that I am still too young (**muy joven para**) to marry, and that a man should not marry before he is thirty years old.

JOE: Too young! Man, you are twenty-eight years old! That business of (**eso de**) waiting so long before marrying seems rather ridiculous to me. You should have taken the step a long time ago. You would have been happier.

FRANK: Don't worry. I am perfectly happy. I am sure I would be very unhappy if I had married early. A man should have enough experience in life before facing such a complicated matter.

JOE: You are speaking of marriage as if it were a serious problem. . . .

FRANK: And it is! Look what happened to your friend Dick. He married when he was twenty-one, and after his experiences of the past two years, he must be the most unhappy fellow in the world. By the way, you too married when you were twenty-one. Tell me the truth. Are you very happy?

JOE: You shouldn't ask even your best friends indiscreet questions. Besides, why should you be luckier than I?

II. Composición.

1. Por qué quiero casarme
2. Por qué no pienso casarme
3. Lo que haría si fuera millonario
4. Lo que haré cuando me gradúe
5. El deber más importante del hombre

LECCIÓN TERCERA

COMPOUND TENSES — HABER AND TENER — DIRECT COMMANDS

Adaptado de

PUEBLO

Madrid, 15 de agosto de 1963

Horóscopo

[¿Se ha preguntado Ud. alguna vez: "¿Qué me traerá la suerte? ¿Habré triunfado o fracasado en la vida?" El hombre siempre ha tenido mucho interés en conocer el futuro. En tiempos antiguos, había más astrólogos que médicos. En efecto, todavía hay muchas personas que creen en la astrología. Estudiemos por un momento el horóscopo siguiente y veamos lo que nos tiene reservado el destino.]

21 de marzo a 20 de abril. *Amor:* Recibirá cartas agradables. *Trabajo:* Obtendrá una ventaja profesional. *Salud:* Sufrirá trastornos nerviosos. ... Trate de poner en práctica todos sus proyectos profesionales, que hasta ahora no ha podido realizar.

21 de abril a 21 de mayo. *Amor:* Revele sus sentimientos verdaderos. *Trabajo:* Termine los asuntos que trae entre manos. *Salud:* Aumentará su capacidad de resistencia. ... Se ganará el afecto de una persona con quien llegará fácilmente a entablar relaciones amorosas.

22 de mayo a 21 de junio. *Amor:* Magníficas perspectivas sentimentales. *Trabajo:* Firmará un acuerdo interesante. *Salud:* Domine sus impulsos nerviosos. ... Algunos disgustos con sus familiares o personas de su círculo le obligarán a buscar un cambio de ambiente y a distraerse más a menudo.

22 de junio a 22 de julio. *Amor:* Habrá una agradable velada en su hogar. *Trabajo:* Olvide sus proyectos viejos. *Salud:* Sufrirá molestias intestinales. ... Su vida íntima podrá ser muy agradable, pero discipline sus nervios y domine todos sus impulsos. No establezca nuevas amistades.

23 de julio a 22 de agosto. *Amor:* Declare sinceramente sus sentimientos. *Trabajo:* Se le presentarán buenas oportunidades. *Salud:* No se exponga demasiado al sol. ... Le amenazará una grave depresión sentimental, de la que Ud. será únicamente responsable. La ruptura amorosa no se solucionará en mucho tiempo.

23 de agosto a 23 de septiembre. *Amor:* Limite sus ambiciones afectivas. *Trabajo:* Fíjese una meta específica. *Salud:* Vigile su dieta. ... Ciertas satisfacciones de carácter sentimental le compensarán de otras contrariedades materiales. Aproveche sus oportunidades.

24 de septiembre a 23 de octubre. *Amor:* Cuide sus relaciones amorosas. *Trabajo:* No repita los viejos errores. *Salud:* Preste atención a los dientes. ... Tenga cuidado con sus palabras, ya que pueden ser mal interpretadas por otros. Pero acepte las cosas como se presenten.

24 de octubre a 22 de noviembre. *Amor:* Toda prudencia es poca. *Trabajo:* Cumpla con sus obligaciones. *Salud:* Magnífica vitalidad. ... Tendrá con la persona amada una disputa de graves consecuencias. No intenten después reconciliarse.

23 de noviembre a 21 de diciembre. *Amor:* Numerosos contratiempos. *Trabajo:* Muchos proyectos nuevos. Póngalos en práctica. *Salud:* Recuperación lenta. ... Conocerá a una persona que en poco tiempo llegará a representar un capítulo muy importante en su vida. Muéstrese siempre amable.

22 de diciembre a 20 de enero. *Amor:* Resolverá un problema afectivo. *Trabajo:* Limite sus gastos. *Salud:* Desaparecerá la depresión nerviosa. ... La nobleza o generosidad de alguien que antes no había mantenido con Ud. estrechas relaciones hará cambiar en parte el curso de sus sentimientos actuales.

21 de enero a 18 de febrero. *Amor:* Compórtese con prudencia. *Trabajo:* Dedíquele todo su tiempo. *Salud:* Sus reflejos serán buenos. ... Aplace para mejor ocasión todas sus entrevistas profesionales y afectivas.

19 de febrero a 20 de marzo. *Amor:* Actúe con tacto. *Trabajo:* Cuídese de no recibir sorpresas. *Salud:* No se canse demasiado. ... Recibirá una invitación que le llenará de turbación. Domine sus sentimientos y todo se desarrollará perfectamente.

PREGUNTAS

1. ¿Qué preguntas nos hacemos todos de vez en cuando?
2. ¿Qué había en tiempos antiguos?
3. Según el horóscopo, ¿qué debe hacer una persona nacida el 1° de abril?
4. ¿Qué recomienda para una persona nacida el 5 de mayo?
5. ¿Qué le pasará a la persona nacida a principios de junio?
6. ¿Qué dice el horóscopo sobre las personas nacidas hacia fines de julio?
7. ¿Qué perspectivas sentimentales tiene la persona nacida entre el 24 de octubre y el 22 de noviembre?
8. ¿Cuál de las predicciones le parece más favorable?
9. ¿Cuál le parece menos favorable?
10. ¿Qué dice el horóscopo de Ud.?

CONVERSACIÓN

1. ¿Cree Ud. en la astrología? ¿Por qué?
2. ¿Conoce Ud. personalmente a alguien que crea en los horóscopos? ¿Quién es? ¿Han resultado verdaderas o falsas la mayor parte de sus predicciones?
3. En su opinión, ¿quién domina: el hombre o el destino?
4. ¿Ha consultado Ud. alguna vez a un adivino? ¿Qué le gustaría saber del futuro? ¿Qué cosas no le gustaría saber?

PART A

16. The Compound Tenses of the Indicative

The compound (or perfect[1]) tenses in Spanish correspond closely in formation and meaning to the compound tenses in English. They all consist of the auxiliary verb **haber** followed by a past participle. Note that the past participle does not change its ending.

A. The present perfect is formed by the present indicative of **haber,** plus the past participle of the main verb. It is translated in English as *has* (*been*), *have* (*gone*), etc.

[1] *Perfect* (from the Latin *perfectum*) means *completed.* The function of the auxiliary verb **haber** is to state when.

¿Ha salido ya?	Has he gone out yet?
Lo he oído muchas veces.	I have heard it many times.

B. The pluperfect consists of the imperfect of **haber** and a past participle and corresponds to the English prior past—*had* (*been*), *had* (*gone*), etc.

La habían descubierto en una cueva.	They had discovered it in a cave.
Ya habíamos gastado todo el dinero.	We had already spent all the money.

C. The preterite perfect (the preterite of **haber** plus a past participle) also indicates a prior past and is translated in English like the pluperfect. However, it is used only rarely, primarily after conjunctions of time.

Así que hubieron terminado la comida...	As soon as they had finished the meal . . .

D. The future perfect (the future of **haber** plus a past participle) has the usual meaning *will* (*shall*) *have* (*arrived*, *told*, etc.).

¿Se habrán ido para el quince?	Will they have left by the fifteenth?

It also expresses probability with respect to a recently past action.

Ya la habrá echado al correo.	He has probably mailed it already.

E. The conditional perfect (the conditional of **haber** plus a past participle) means *would have* (*arrived*, *told*, etc.).

Yo lo habría guardado.	*I* would have kept it.

It may also indicate probability or conjecture with respect to a pluperfect (past perfect) action.

La habrían perdido antes.	They had probably lost it earlier.

EJERCICIOS

A. Repase las formas de los tiempos compuestos (pp. 316–317).

B. Cambie al pluscuamperfecto (pluperfect):

1. Me he levantado. 2. No se ha lavado las manos. 3. Ya hemos almorzado. 4. ¿Te has cepillado los dientes? 5. ¿Han salido ya los niños? 6. ¿Habéis llamado al almacén? 7. Lo ha hecho Ud. muy bien. 8. Los han roto. 9. No la he escrito todavía. 10. ¿Han venido todos?

C. Cambie para expresar probabilidad:

1. Han llegado ya. 2. Nos ha visto. 3. No lo han dicho. 4. Había mentido. 5. No habéis entendido. 6. Ha estado trabajando. 7. Los habían comprado nuevos. 8. ¿Has perdido tu cuaderno? 9. Me he equivocado. 10. Nos habíamos dormido.

D. Diga en español:

1. Has Anita written the letters? 2. We have bought new furniture. 3. Have you been able to find their address? 4. John would have done it easily. 5. He probably has told the truth. 6. They must have left already. 7. Had you finished the homework, boys?

17. Other Uses of **haber**

Haber may be used as a principal verb in the following three expressions. (Notice that in none of these does **haber** ever mean *to have.*)

A. The impersonal **hay** there is, there are

Hay veinte estudiantes en nuestra clase.	There are twenty students in our class.
Pero hay sólo uno bueno.	But there is only one good one.

In all other tenses, the normal third person singular form of **haber** is used.

Había mucha gente (muchas personas) en la calle.	There were many people in the street.
Hubo un accidente.	There was an accident.

B. The impersonal **hay que** one must, it is necessary

In this construction, too, the third person singular form of **haber** is used in all tenses other than the present.

Hay que tener fe.	One must have faith.
Habrá que investigarlo.	It will be necessary to investigate it.

C. **Haber de** to be (supposed) to, to be expected to

This is the only case in which **haber,** as an independent verb, may be conjugated in every person.

El avión ha de aterrizar a las seis.	The plane is to land at six.
Nuestros amigos habían de estar en él.	Our friends were to be on it.

EJERCICIOS

A. Conteste en español:

1. ¿Cuántos días hay en un año? ¿Cuántos meses hay? 2. ¿Cuántos estudiantes hay en su clase de español? ¿Cuántos había el semestre pasado? ¿Hay más muchachos o muchachas ahora? 3. ¿A qué hora ha de volver Ud. a casa hoy? 4. ¿Qué días feriados habrá este semestre? 5. ¿Hay que tener dinero para vivir feliz? ¿Por qué?

B. Traduzca al español:

1. There is a tavern in our town. 2. And there I have often sat me down. 3. One night we were to have a party there. 4. Our friend Charlie had come back from the army. 5. As you know, one must spend a lot of money on such occasions. 6. Fare thee well, for I must leave thee.

18. Uses of **tener**

A. **Tener,** unlike **haber,** is never an auxiliary verb. Its basic meaning is *to have* (and *to hold, to possess*).

Tengo veinte y un primos.	I have twenty-one cousins.
No ha tenido tiempo.	He hasn't had time.

B. Important idioms using **tener**

tener calor to be (feel) warm
tener hambre to be hungry
tener miedo to be afraid
tener razón to be right
tener cuidado to be careful
tener frío to be (feel) cold
tener sed to be thirsty
tener sueño to be sleepy
no tener razón to be wrong
tener gana(s) **de** to feel like, to be in the mood to

tener que + infinitive to have to
tener... años de edad to be . . . years old

With these idioms, *very* is translated by the adjective **mucho.**

EJERCICIO

Conteste en español:

1. ¿Cuántos años tiene Ud.? ¿Cuántos tienen sus padres?
2. ¿Qué tiene Ud. ganas de hacer este fin de semana?
3. ¿A qué hora empieza Ud. a tener hambre por la tarde?
4. ¿Qué bebida le refresca más cuando tiene sed?
5. ¿Qué tiene Ud. que hacer esta noche? ¿Qué tuvo que hacer anoche? ¿Qué tendrá que hacer mañana?
6. ¿Le molesta más tener frío o calor?
7. ¿Tiene Ud. miedo de los perros? ¿Tiene miedo de otros animales?
8. ¿Cuándo tendremos que terminar esta lección?

Chart of Direct Command Formation

	Affirmative	Negative
tú	3rd person singular present indicative (except **ten, ven, pon, haz, sal, sé, di, ve**)	Present Subjunctive
vosotros	infinitive: final **r** > **d**	Present Subjunctive
Ud. **Uds.**	Present Subjunctive	Present Subjunctive
nosotros	Present Subjunctive or **Vamos a** + infinitive	Present Subjunctive

19. The Familiar Commands

The affirmative command forms of **tú** and **vosotros** are called the imperative.

A. The affirmative command form of **tú** is the same as the third person singular of the present indicative, except for the following eight verbs:

tener, ten	have	**hacer, haz**	do, make
poner, pon	put	**ser, sé**	be
venir, ven	come	**decir, di**	say, tell
salir, sal	go out	**ir, ve**	go

Cómprame un abrigo de visón, amorcito.	Buy me a mink coat, darling.
¡Ten paciencia!	Be patient!

B. The affirmative command of **vosotros** is formed by changing the final **r** of the infinitive to **d.**

amar > **amad** **poner** > **poned** **decir** > **decid**

1. If the reflexive pronoun **-os** is attached, the **-d** disappears. Note that verbs ending in **-ir** then require a written accent on the last **i.**

¡Amaos!	Love each other!
¡Vestíos!	Get dressed!
Poneos los guantes, niños.	Put on your gloves, children.

2. **Irse** is the only verb in the language that does not drop the final **-d** in the **vosotros** affirmative command.

Idos en seguida.	Go away at once.

C. The negative familiar commands take the corresponding form of the present subjunctive.

No lo hagas, Diego.	Don't do it, Jim.
No le escuchéis, amigos.	Don't listen to him, friends.

EJERCICIO

Cambie al imperativo:

1. Comes mucho. Hablas bien. Trabajas fuerte. ¿Abres la puerta? Haces mejor. Vienes temprano. ¿Sales ahora? Tienes paciencia.
2. No compras nada. No lo rompes. No le escribes nunca. No le llamas a menudo. No la pones ahí. No me dices nada. No lo haces así. No les escuchas.
3. Habláis con el jefe. Tomáis mucho. Bebéis de lo mejor. ¿Abrís todas las cajas? ¿Ponéis la radio? ¿Venís en seguida?
4. No lo creéis. ¿No la vendéis? ¿No las compráis? No cocináis tanto. No barréis hoy. No lo escribís ahora.

20. The Polite Commands—**Ud.** and **Uds.**

All polite commands, both affirmative and negative, use the corresponding form of the present subjunctive.

El mejor régimen: coma bien, pero no trague nada.	The best diet: Eat well, but don't swallow anything.
No toquen nuestra bandera.	Don't touch our flag.

21. The First Person Plural Command Forms

Let us or *Let's* is actually a direct command that involves *you* and *me*. Spanish expresses this concept in two ways.

A. The first person plural of the present subjunctive

Comamos ahora.	Let's eat now.
Mostrémosle quién manda aquí.	Let's show him who's boss here.
No vayamos con ellos.	Let's not go with them.

1. **Vamos** is used for *let's go*.

Vamos al parque.	Let's go to the park.

2. When the reflexive pronoun **nos** is attached to the affirmative command, the **-s** of the verb ending disappears, and the

normally stressed syllable requires a written accent. The **-s** also disappears before **se.**

Démonos prisa.	Let's hurry.
Digámoselo.	Let's tell it to him.

B. **Vamos a** + infinitive (only in affirmative commands)

Vamos a cantar.	Let's sing.
Vamos a visitar a mi tío.	Let's visit my uncle.

22. The Position of Object Pronouns with Direct Commands

A. Affirmative commands

Object and reflexive pronouns must be attached to the end of a direct affirmative command.

Póntelos, niño.	Put them on, child.
Digámosle la verdad.	Let's tell him the truth.

B. Negative commands

Object and reflexive pronouns must be placed in their normal position before a negative command.

No lo devolvamos todavía.	Let's not return it yet.
No los pongas (pongáis, ponga, pongan) allí.	Don't put them there.

EJERCICIO

A. Repita, y después haga negativas las frases siguientes:
1. Hábleme. Abralas. Ciérrelo. Cómprelos. Dénosla. Dígaselo.
2. Pónganlo ahí. Déjenle en paz. Pónganse los guantes. Pregúntenselo. Háganme un favor. Vístanse ahora. Sírvanse. Guárdenmela.
3. Sentémonos aquí. Traigámoselo. Vamos con ellos. Vamos a llamarla. Leámoslo. Vamos a acostarnos. Vamos a salir. Mandémoselos. Vamos a pedírselo.

B. Haga afirmativas las siguientes:
1. No lo haga. No se lo digan. No le escuchen. No la olvide. No nos llame. No se lo quiten. No se siente.
2. No vengas hoy. No lo rompas. No te sientes. No me lo digas. No te pongas de pie. No se lo quites.

EJERCICIO DE REPASO

1. There are many people who have devoted their lives to the study of astrology.
2. Let's see whether we can take advantage of it.

3. I would have told them: Enjoy yourselves more and you will have fewer problems.
4. Do not phone them, but write to them every week.
5. Watch your diet, but don't lose too much.
6. Your words will be wrongly interpreted and you will have lost a great opportunity. —For Heaven's sake!
7. Fulfill your obligations and do not repeat the old mistakes.
8. He had always acted prudently until he met her. —Well, that's life.
9. Do not postpone this matter or there will be serious problems.
10. He probably still hasn't received the invitation they sent him.

PART B

23. Compound Tenses

A. Present perfect and pluperfect after **hacer**

In expressions of time, **hacer... que** may be followed by the present perfect or pluperfect if the sentence is negative.

Hace mucho tiempo que no le he escrito.	I haven't written to him for a long time.
Hacía mucho tiempo que no le había escrito.	I hadn't written to him for a long time.

But:

Hace mucho tiempo que le escribo.	I have been writing to him for a long time.

B. Preterite perfect

The preterite perfect is used only after conjunctions of time.

Así que hubo terminado su trabajo, se dirigió a los huéspedes.	As soon as he had finished his work, he turned to the guests.

However, this construction is usually avoided in one of three ways:

1. Simple preterite

   Así que terminó su trabajo...

2. Past participle (sometimes preceded by **habiendo**)

   Terminado su trabajo... (Habiendo terminado...)

3. Infinitive (in the case of those conjunctions which also have prepositional forms)

   Después de haber terminado su trabajo...
   Después de terminar su trabajo...

C. Increased use of the present perfect

In Madrid today, the present perfect is very often heard in place of a preterite.

Hoy me he levantado tarde.	Today I got up late.
He cogido el Metro en la Gran Vía.	I took the subway on the Gran Vía.

24. Haber as an Independent Verb

A. **Hay** there is, there are

1. This construction may be used in all the compound tenses. **Haber** then serves as both the auxiliary and the main verb.

Ha habido una equivocación.	There has been a mistake.
¿Habrá habido jamás un estudiante como éste?	Can there ever have been a student like this?

2. The infinitive **haber,** used after another verb, still retains the impersonal sense of *there is, there are* (*there . . . be*)

Va a haber una fiesta.	There is going to be a celebration.
Tiene que haber un enchufe en cada cuarto.	There has to be an outlet in each room.
Debe (**de**) **haber uranio aquí cerca.**	There probably is (must be) uranium near here.
Puede haber soldados enemigos en el bosque.	There may be enemy soldiers in the woods.

Note that the main verb is always singular, since the whole expression is impersonal.

3. **Hay** is used very frequently to express distance.

¿Cuánto hay de aquí a Caracas?	How far is it from here to Caracas?
Hay veinte millas de allí a Santiago.	Santiago is twenty miles from there.

4. **Hay** is often separated from **que** by one or several words. **Que** then gives the following infinitive a passive implication that corresponds to the English *to be seen, done,* etc.

Aquí hay muchos grandes edificios que ver.	There are many large buildings to see (to be seen) here.
Siempre había mucho que hacer.	There was always a great deal to do (to be done).

This construction does not convey the idea of necessity that is implicit in **hay que.**

Hay muchas cosas que estudiar.	There are many things to study.
Hay que estudiar muchas cosas.	One must study many things.

B. **He aquí** here is, this is, here are, these are

He aquí is used mainly in literary Spanish. It appears frequently in newspaper captions explaining news pictures, and in radio announcements.

He aquí los premios que se concedieron ayer.	These are the prizes that were given out yesterday.
He aquí la dirección de nuestra tienda en su vecindad.	Here is the address of our store in your neighborhood.

25. Tener

A. **Tener... que**

When **tener** is separated from **que** by one or more words, it loses its connotation of compulsion. Here again, the passive implication of **que** is apparent.

Tengo algo que contarte.	I have something to tell you.
Tendrá algunos libros raros que vender.	He probably has some rare books to sell.

But:

Tengo que contarte algo.	I have to (must) tell you something.

B. **Tener** + past participle

Tener, followed by a past participle, describes the resultant state of a completed action. It is close in meaning to **estar** + past participle, but adds the identity of the possessor.

Tengo preparada la lista.	I have the list (already) prepared.
¿Ya tienes escritas las cartas?	Do you have the letters written already?

Note especially that this construction does not form a compound tense. **Tener** is a main verb, not an auxiliary, and the past participle functions merely as an adjective.

C. **Tener,** followed by the personal **a,** means *to have (someone) in a certain place.*

Tengo a mi mujer en la Florida.	I have my wife in Florida. (My wife is in . . .)

D. The preterite of **tener** may mean *received.*

Ayer tuve (**una**) **carta de mi novio.**	Yesterday I received a letter from my boyfriend.
Hace dos días tuvimos noticias suyas.	Two days ago we received word from them.

26. Direct Commands

A. Impersonal commands

In Spanish, the direct command form, used with the reflexive **se,** may express an action that the speaker wills to be done. This construction is found most frequently in written instructions, in textbooks, and in biblical references.

Hágase la voluntad de Dios.	God's will be done.
Véase el capítulo cuarto.	See the fourth chapter.
Tradúzcanse al español las oraciones siguientes.	Translate the following sentences into Spanish.
Escríbase una composición sobre el tema siguiente.	Write a composition on the following subject.

B. The infinitive as a command

The infinitive is occasionally used with the force of a command, especially in written orders, signposts, etc.

No Fumar.	No smoking. Do not smoke.
No Estacionar de Aquí a la Esquina.	No parking from here to the corner.
Traducir al español las frases siguientes...	Translate into Spanish the following sentences . . .

EJERCICIOS

I. Traducir al español.

Here is a story that I remember from my childhood. One day, when I was eight years old, my friends and I were playing (**a**) settlers and Indians. I was supposed to help my friend Riqui make a bow. We had everything ready, but we had to find something sharp to cut a branch in two. Suddenly I thought of my grandfather's sword, which was hanging (**estaba colgada**) on the wall in the dining room. I got it and took it with me to my friend's house.

That same evening, my grandfather called me to his room. As soon as I had closed the door, he said: "Paco, what have you done with my sword?"

"But grandfather," I answered, "nothing."

"Don't lie to me, boy. I know that you took it. So tell me the truth. Where is it?"

I realized that it was useless to keep on lying.

"Well, grandfather," I said, "Riqui needed a bow to defend his family against the Indians, so . . ."

"All right, all right, continue." My grandfather was losing patience.

"Well, I thought that I could borrow your sword to cut a branch . . ."

My grandfather's face was becoming redder and redder (**cada vez más colorada**).

"And so you have taken my beautiful sword? All right, where do you have it hidden now?"

"Unfortunately, grandfather, it was very old . . . and it broke . . ."

I thought that my grandfather was going to spank me right there and then (**en el acto**) but suddenly, a smile covered his face.

"Listen, man," he said. "Why waste time talking? We have to hurry, or the Indians will have won the battle before Riqui gets (*present subjunctive*) his bow. Would you like to help me make him a real bow?"

I would have cried with joy, but soldiers don't cry. Besides, we were so busy. The Indians were coming . . .

II. Composición.

1. Recuerdos de familia
2. La persona que ha tenido más influencia en mi vida
3. La persona que admiro más

Chart of Personal Pronouns

Person	Subject		Object of Preposition		Reflexive Object of Preposition	
Singular						
1	**yo**	I	(**para**) **mí**[a]	(for) me	(**para**) **mí**[a]	(for) myself
2	**tú**	you	(**para**) **ti**[a]	(for) you	(**para**) **ti**[a]	(for) yourself
3	**él**	he	**él**	him		
	ella	she	**ella**	her	**sí**[a]	himself, herself, yourself, itself
	usted (**Ud.**)	you	**usted** (**Ud.**)	you		
Plural						
1	**nosotros**	we	**nosotros**	us	**nosotros**	ourselves
2	**vosotros**	you	**vosotros**	you	**vosotros**	yourselves
3	**ellos**	they	**ellos**	them		
	ellas	they (*f.*)	**ellas**	them	**sí**	themselves, yourselves
	ustedes (**Uds.**)	you	**ustedes** (**Uds.**)	you		

[a] After the preposition **con**, **mí**, **ti**, and **sí** become **-migo**, **-tigo**, **-sigo**.

Person	Direct Object of Verb		Indirect Object of Verb		Reflexive	
Singular						
1	**me**	me	**me**	to me	**me**	(to) myself
2	**te**	you	**te**	to you	**te**	(to) yourself
3	**le, lo**	him, it				
	la	her, it	**le**	to him, to her, to you, to it	**se**	(to) himself, herself, yourself, itself
	le, lo, la	you (**Ud.**)				
Plural						
1	**nos**	us	**nos**	to us	**nos**	(to) ourselves
2	**os**	you	**os**	to you	**os**	(to) yourselves
3	**los, les**	them				
	las	them (*f.*)	**les**	to them, to you	**se**	(to) themselves, yourselves
	los, les, las	you (**Uds.**)				

LECCIÓN CUARTA

PERSONAL PRONOUNS

Adaptado de

DOMINGO

Madrid, 18 de agosto de 1963

Cirugía Estética

No sabemos si las leyes de la cirugía estética han cambiado o no. Pero lo que sí podemos asegurar es que ha cambiado la ley referente a las actividades de la cirugía estética.

Hace años, en 1928, una dama de París, propietaria de una casa de modas, fue a visitar a un cirujano.

—Doctor, soy muy desgraciada.

—¿Qué le sucede?

La dama le mostró las piernas, que eran enormemente gruesas, y le dijo que esta mala conformación era la causa de su desgracia.

—No es fácil arreglar esto. A los médicos no nos gusta rebajar piernas.

—Doctor, estoy decidida a todo, incluso a suicidarme si Ud. no me opera. No me queda más remedio.

—Está bien. Si Ud. insiste, la operaré.

Unos días más tarde, la dama fue a la clínica del doctor y poco después pasaba al quirófano. Todas las operaciones pueden fracasar, y aquélla fue una de ellas. Fue necesario amputar una pierna a la paciente, y ésta, una vez que abandonó el hospital, llamó a un abogado y presentó una demanda contra el cirujano reclamándole daños y perjuicios, valorándolos en medio millón de francos. La causa despertó vivo interés y la sentencia fue objeto de calurosos y apasionados comentarios.

El juez condenó al médico al pago de 200,000 francos, declarando que el cirujano había cometido una falta por el solo hecho de haber realizado una operación sobre un miembro sano. Consagraba con su sentencia una vieja tesis, según la cual la cirugía debe tener por objeto salvar la vida humana o restablecer la salud. Desde aquella época la ley ha evolucionado y, naturalmente, la cirugía estética también. Hoy la cirugía estética, con sus tres aspectos de reparadora, correctora y estética pura, es una rama muy extendida de la medicina.

PREGUNTAS

1. ¿Cuándo ocurrió el caso que se refiere en este artículo? ¿Dónde fue?
2. ¿Por qué fue la dama al cirujano?
3. ¿Qué dijo el médico al principio cuando la señora le explicó su problema?
4. ¿Cómo le convenció la señora a operarla?
5. ¿Cómo resultó la operación?
6. ¿A quién llamó entonces la señora?
7. ¿Cuánto dinero le reclamó al cirujano?
8. ¿Cuál fue la decisión del juez?
9. ¿Sobre qué tesis basaba su decisión?
10. ¿Cómo es la cirugía estética hoy?

CONVERSACIÓN

1. ¿Qué piensa Ud. del caso de la señora parisiense y el cirujano? ¿Qué habría hecho Ud. si fuera el médico? ¿Cómo lo habría decidido Ud. si fuera el juez?
2. ¿Conoce Ud. a alguien que haya tenido una operación de cirugía estética? ¿Quién fue? ¿Cómo resultó?
3. ¿Cree Ud. que el hombre tiene el derecho de cambiar radicalmente la cara que Dios le ha dado? ¿En qué circunstancias no la tiene?
4. ¿Le gustaría a Ud. cambiar su fisonomía en algún respecto? ¿Piensa Ud. hacerlo algún día?

PART A

27. Subject Pronouns

A. Forms and meaning

Person	*Singular*		*Plural*	
1	**yo**	I	**nosotros(as)**	we
2	**tú**[1]	you	**vosotros(as)**[1]	you
3	**él**	he	**ellos**	they
	ella	she	**ellas**	they (*f.*)
	usted (Ud.)[2]	you	**ustedes (Uds.)**[2]	you

B. Omission of the subject pronoun

These pronouns are usually omitted when the verb is expressed, and their needless insertion or repetition is entirely incorrect.

Salimos para el campo dentro de una semana.	We are leaving for the country within a week.
Si quieres, iré contigo.	If you wish, I'll go with you.

Ud. and **Uds.** may be used or omitted at the discretion of the speaker, but even with these it is best to avoid excessive repetition.

C. Uses of the subject pronoun

1. It is used for emphasis or for clarification.

Emphasis:

Tú puedes quedarte.	*You* can stay.
Yo me voy.	*I'm* going.

Remember: When you would raise your voice to stress the subject pronoun in English, insert the pronoun in Spanish.

Clarification:

Siempre que él decía que sí, ella decía que no.	Whenever he said yes, she said no.
¿No me dijo Ud. que ella no venía?	Didn't you tell me that she wasn't coming?

[1] The familiar **tú** and **vosotros** forms are used only when the speaker is addressing a child, a relative, or anyone with whom he is on intimate terms. In Latin America, **vosotros** is generally not used. **Uds.** covers both the polite and familiar plural.

[2] The polite forms, **Ud.** and **Uds.** (also abbreviated **V.**, **Vd.**, and **Vds.**) are used in any relationship of respect or lack of familiarity. In dealing with strangers, it is advisable to maintain the polite form, unless specifically requested to use the familiar.

2. It is used after the verb **ser,** or may stand alone.

¿Es Ud. el gerente?	Are you the manager?
—Sí, soy yo.	—Yes, I am (it's me).
¿Quién ganó? —El.	Who won? —He (did).

EJERCICIO

1. I know that you'll win, Russell. 2. Who came in? —We did. 3. I don't doubt that you're tired. 4. Now do you see? He was right and you (*pl.*) were wrong. 5. Do they know that we have already sent it? 6. *She* isn't here, but *he* can give you the information.

28. The Position of Object Pronouns

A. With relation to the verb

1. Object pronouns must be attached to the end of a direct affirmative command.

Tómelo.[3]	Take it.
Dámelos.	Give them to me.

They usually are attached to the end of an infinitive or present participle.

Al leerlo, se puso pálido.	Upon reading it, he turned pale.
Va a verlos mañana.[4]	He is going to see them tomorrow.
Estamos preparándolo[5] **ahora mismo.**	We are preparing it right now.

2. In all other cases, object pronouns are placed immediately before the entire verb form (e.g., before **haber** in a compound tense).

¿Me perdonarás?	Will you forgive me?
Ya lo han visto.	They have already seen it.

[3] Note that the addition of an extra syllable onto a command form of more than one syllable makes a written accent on the stem vowel necessary.

[4] Object pronouns may stand before conjugated forms of **ir**, **querer**, **poder**, and **saber** when these verbs precede an infinitive.

[5] With a progressive tense, the object pronoun may stand before **estar: Lo estamos preparando.**

B. With relation to each other

The rule for the placement of two object pronouns with respect to each other has no exceptions:

INDIRECT BEFORE DIRECT, REFLEXIVE FIRST OF ALL

Devuélvamelo.	Give it back to me.
El niño se lo comió todo.	The child ate it all up.
Se nos murió el gato.	Our cat died on us.

29. Direct Object Pronouns

A. Forms and meaning of direct object pronouns

Person		*Singular*		*Plural*
1	**me**	me	**nos**	us
2	**te**	you	**os**	you
3	**lo**	him, it (*m.*)[6]	**los**	them, you
	la	her, it, you (*f.*)	**las**	them, you (*f.*)
	le	him, you (*m.*)	**(les)**[7]	(them, you)

Note that **lo** may refer to a masculine person or thing, but that the direct object **le** refers only to a person.

Mi madre la conoce, pero yo no.	My mother knows her, but I don't.
Te vimos allí la semana pasada.	We saw you there last week.
Le (lo) han escogido para encabezarla.	They have chosen him to head it.

B. Special use of **lo**

Lo supplies the missing object for verbs that usually require an object in Spanish. Such verbs include **saber, decir, preguntar,** and **pedir.**

Amor mío, eres adorable, encantadora, hermosísima. —Sí, lo sé.	Darling, you are lovely, charming, beautiful. —Yes, I know.
Pregúnteselo.	Ask him.
No se lo diga a ellos.	Don't tell them.

[6] **Lo**, rather than **le**, is much more frequent in Spanish America for *him*.

[7] **Les**, which is used very frequently in Spain for **los** as a direct object pronoun, refers only to persons.

EJERCICIOS

A. Substituya los objetos directos por el pronombre apropiado:

1. Di **un libro** a Luis. 2. Vendieron **la casa** hace tres días. 3. Ofrecimos **unos juguetes** a los niños. 4. Escribiré **una carta** a Elisa. 5. Me pidió prestada **la pluma.** 6. No había visto **el nuevo coche.** 7. Habrían robado **la caja.** 8. Regaló **las flores** a su novia.

B. Conteste afirmativamente, substituyendo el objeto por un pronombre:

1. ¿Has escrito **las cartas?** 2. ¿Recibió Ud. **los libros?** 3. ¿Han encontrado **las zapatillas?** 4. ¿Conoce Ud. **a mis amigos?** 5. ¿Firmarán Uds. **los contratos?** 6. ¿Habéis visto **la casa?**

C. Conteste negativamente:

1. ¿Ha arreglado Ud. **el motor?** 2. ¿Veía Ud. mucho **a Ana?** 3. ¿Habrán encontrado los niños **al perro?** 4. ¿Habría creído Ud. **eso?** 5. ¿Quieres contarme **una historia?**

30. Indirect Object Pronouns

A. Forms and meaning of indirect object pronouns

The indirect object pronouns are the same as the direct object pronouns, except in the third person:

me to me	**nos** to us
te to you	**os** to you
LE to him, to her, to you.	**LES** to them, to you.

Escribámosle en seguida.	Let's write to him immediately.
No. Ya nos telefoneó esta mañana.	No, he already phoned us this morning.
Haga el favor de mandármelo.	Please send it to me.

B. Special use of se

When the indirect and direct object pronouns are both in the third person, the indirect becomes **se.** Thus:

Indirect		*Direct*		
le	+	**lo**	=	**SE lo**
les		**la**		**la**
		los		**los**
		las		**las**

Le dimos el disco.	We gave the record to him.
Se lo dimos.	We gave it to him.
¿Les mostrarás tu nueva casa?	Will you show them your new house?
¿Se la mostrarás?	Will you show it to them?

C. The indirect object with **pedir** and **preguntar**

Pedir (to ask for, to request) and **preguntar** (to ask a question, to inquire) logically take the indirect object, since the speaker makes a request or addresses a question *to* somebody.

Se lo pediré a Juan.[8]	I will ask John for it.
No le preguntes eso.	Don't ask her that (question).

EJERCICIOS

A. Substituya las palabras indicadas por los pronombres apropiados:

1. Ya he mandado **el libro a Luis.** 2. Di **las plumas a Juan.** 3. Vendieron **dos pares de zapatos a mis amigos.** 4. Hemos escrito **la carta a Diego.** 5. Pediremos **dinero al Sr. Moreno.** 6. No quieren enviar **las cosas a Rosario.** 7. ¿Piensa Ud. comprar **el regalo a López?** 8. ¿Contará Ud. **la historia a sus nietos?** 9. ¿Piensa Ud. pedir prestado **el disco a Luisa?** 10. No quiero enseñar **el cuadro a tus hermanos.**

B. Conteste afirmativamente siguiendo el modelo:

¿Se lo di a Ud.? **Sí, me lo dio.**

1. ¿Me lo pidió Ud.? 2. ¿Nos lo dijeron Uds.? 3. ¿Se lo hemos explicado ya a Uds.? 4. ¿Me lo preguntó Ud.? 5. ¿Nos lo comprarás? 6. ¿No se lo he dado a Uds.? 7. ¿Nos la han enviado tus padres? 8. ¿Se lo traigo a Ud.? 9. ¿Nos lo dirán Uds.? 10. ¿Os lo habíamos recomendado?

C. Traduzca al español:

1. If I find it, I'll give it to you. 2. Don't ask John for anything. 3. Will you read them to us? 4. They have just sold it (*f.*) to them. 5. Don't look at me like that (**así**). 6. I don't know the answer; ask someone else. 7. Who put it there? Take it away immediately.

31. The **gustar** Construction

GUSTAR MEANS **TO BE PLEASING**. IT DOES NOT MEAN **TO LIKE**

The English *to like* is translated by a special construction using the verb **gustar.** The English subject (*I*, *you*, *they* like, etc.) becomes the indirect object in Spanish—*the one(s) to whom something is pleasing*.

[8] Notice that with **pedir**, **preguntar**, and **gustar**, the indirect object pronoun must be used, even though the noun to which it refers is stated.

Me gusta estudiar.	I like to study. (Studying is pleasing to me.)
¿De veras? Pues, a mí me gustan las mujeres.	Really? Well, I like women. (To me, women are pleasing.)
¿Les gustó a sus padres el viaje?	Did your parents like the trip? (Was the trip pleasing to them?)
Nos gustaría conocerle.	We would like to know him.

The English *to have . . . left* (*remaining*) and *to lack* or *need* use a similar construction with the verbs **quedar** and **faltar.**

¡Pobre señor Vanderféler!	Poor Mr. Vanderfeller!
Le quedan sólo diez millones de dólares.	He has only ten million dollars left. (Only ten million dollars are remaining to him.)
Nos falta dinero para terminarlo.	We lack money to finish it. (Money is lacking to us.)

EJERCICIOS

A. Cambie según las personas, verbos, o sujetos indicados:

1. Me gusta mi profesor de español.
(Nos, te, a Juan, les, os)
2. No nos gustó el caballo.
(los caballos, la película, esos fulanos)
3. Le gustará su apoyo.
(faltará, faltaría, quedará, quedaría)
4. ¿Les gusta bailar?
(a María, a ti, a ti y a Pepe, a Ud., a esos jóvenes)

B. Conteste en español:

1. ¿Qué estación del año le gusta más? ¿Por qué? 2. ¿Le gustan más los coches americanos o los europeos? 3. ¿Cómo le gusta pasar los fines de semana? 4. ¿Le gustaría no tener que trabajar nunca? ¿Por qué? ¿Qué haría? 5. ¿Qué colores le gustan más? ¿Cuáles le gustan menos? 6. ¿Qué película reciente le gustó más? ¿Por qué? 7. ¿Cuántos créditos le faltan para terminar su bachillerato? 8. ¿Cuánto dinero le queda para el resto de la semana? 9. ¿Cuántos amigos le quedan de su niñez? 10. ¿Cuánto tiempo falta para las seis?

32. Pronoun Objects of a Preposition

A. Forms and meaning

1. These pronouns have the same form as the subject pronouns, except in the first and second person singular.

Person	*Singular*		*Plural*	
1	**(para) mí**	(for) me	**(para) nosotros(as)**	us
2	**ti**	you	**vosotros(as)**	you
3	**él**	him	**ellos**	them
	ella	her	**ellas**	them (*f.*)
	Ud.	you	**Uds.**	you

2. **Conmigo** and **contigo**

After the preposition **con** (with), the first and second person singular forms become **conmigo, contigo.** All the other forms remain unaltered: **con él, con ella, con Uds.,** etc.

B. After verbs of motion

Verbs of motion are followed by the preposition **a** plus a prepositional object pronoun (not an indirect object pronoun).

Corrió a ella.	He ran to her.
Ven a mí, Paquito.	Come to me, Frankie.

C. For emphasis or clarification

Spanish makes use of the prepositional phrases **a mí, a ti, a él,** etc., IN ADDITION TO the direct or indirect object pronoun for purposes of emphasis or clarification. Clarification is often necessary when the indirect object is in the third person (**le, les**), and particularly when it becomes **se,** unless the person referred to is perfectly obvious.

Le vi a él, no a ella.	I saw *him*, not *her*.
Me lo dio a mí; no se lo dio a Ud.	He gave it to *me*; he did not give it to *you*.

EJERCICIO

Substitúyanse las palabras indicadas por el pronombre apropiado:

1. Se lo preguntaré **a mis hermanas.** 2. Este aparato no es para **los técnicos nuevos.** 3. El dinero es para **mí y para Alonso.** 4. No me habló de **sus dificultades.** 5. No iré con **los otros.** 6. No se marcharía sin **ti y sin Carlos.** 7. Hazlo por **tu madre y por mí.** 8. Déselo **al viejo.** 9. No se lo diga **a esos murmuradores.** 10. Se reía **de Elsa.**

EJERCICIO DE REPASO

1. Come with me. I have an interesting case to (**que**) tell you.
2. Some years ago the owner of a fashion house came to see me about a case of plastic surgery.

3. I did not like her idea and I told her that it didn't interest me.
4. She went to another surgeon and told him: "I'll commit suicide if you don't operate on me." Well, he accepted her.
5. She was in the operating room for six hours, and finally, the surgeon succeeded in (**logró**) saving her.
6. The patient sued the doctor for damages, but the jury refused to convict him.
7. The judge, however, made him pay her 200,000 francs.
8. According to him, the doctor had made a serious mistake in (**al**) acceding to the wishes of the patient.
9. Plastic surgery has changed greatly since then and such cases don't happen often today.
10. To tell the truth, we like to operate only if we are sure (**de**) that it is absolutely necessary.

REPASO DE VERBOS

Estudie los tiempos del indicativo de los verbos siguientes: pensar, cerrar, contar, mover, perder (pp. 318–319).

Háganse mandatos:

pensar (Ud., tú); entender (Uds., vosotros); almorzar (Ud., tú); no perder (tú, vosotros); recordar (Ud., Uds.); mover (tú, Ud.); no merendar (Uds., vosotros)

PART B

33. The Neuter Pronoun **ello**

Ello, which refers to a whole idea, situation, or statement, is used as subject of the verb or as object of a preposition.

A. As subject, **ello** appears frequently in the expression **ello es que...** the fact is that . . .

Ello es que nunca mató a nadie.	The fact is that he never killed anyone.

B. **Ello** is used more often as object of a preposition.

En ello me va la vida.	My life is at stake in it (in this).
De ello depende todo el asunto.	The whole affair depends on it.

34. Special Situations with the Subject *you*

A. When *you* refers to two persons with whom the speaker has a different relationship, the verb form is determined by the degree of intimacy with the one addressed first.

Ya veo que tú y este señor no estáis de acuerdo.	I see that you and this gentleman don't agree.
Por lo visto Ud. y mi hijo se han hecho amigos.	Apparently you and my son have become friends.

B. The Argentinian **vos**

In Argentina, particularly in and around Buenos Aires, **tú** is popularly replaced by **vos,** and the verb form is a combination of the normal Spanish **tú** and **vosotros** forms.

¿Lo tenés vos?	Do you have it?
Sentate.	Sit down.

As in the rest of Latin America, **vosotros** is regularly replaced by **Uds.**

35. Subject Pronouns after Certain Prepositions

After **entre** (between, among), **incluso** (including), and **según** (according to) the subject pronouns are required.

Decidámoslo entre tú y yo.	Let's decide it between you and me.
Iremos todos, incluso tú.	We'll all go, including you.

With the reflexive, however, **sí** or **ellos** may be used after **entre.**

Lo arreglaron entre sí. **Lo arreglaron entre ellos.**	They settled it among themselves.

36. The Indirect Object to Express Possession

The indirect object pronoun is used to express possession with actions involving parts of the body, articles of clothing, or personal effects.

La madre les lavó las manos.	The mother washed their hands.
Le puso el sombrero y le despidió.	She put his hat on him and sent him off.
Me han robado la cartera.	They have stolen my wallet.

Notice that the definite article is used instead of the possessive adjectives.

37. Further Uses of the Indirect Object Pronoun

A. To express separation

Les quitará la finca.	He will take the property away from them.
Nos robó todo lo que teníamos.	He stole everything we had.
No le compre nada a Pérez.	Don't buy anything from Perez.

B. To indicate the person in whose interest or with respect to whom an action takes place

¿Me arreglará Ud. la televisión?	Will you fix my television set (for me)?
Te he comprado una bata.	I have bought you a robe.
Se nos murió el caballo.	The horse died on us.
Se me fue la criada.	My maid left me (went away from me).

C. With impersonal expressions

The indirect object pronoun may be used with many impersonal expressions, and corresponds to the English *for me*, *for him*, etc. The infinitive then replaces a dependent clause and no subjunctive is necessary.

Me es imposible verte hoy.	It is impossible for me to see you today.
No le basta gastar su propio dinero.	It isn't enough for him to spend his own money.
Les fue necesario abandonar el coche.	It was necessary for them to abandon the car.

D. With **agradecer** and **pagar**

Agradecer (to thank someone for) and **pagar** (to pay for) both employ the indirect object to state the person to whom the thanks are given, or to whom the sum is paid. Remember that *for* is included within the verb.

Se lo agradezco.	I thank you for it.
¿Cuándo me lo pagarás?	When will you pay me for it?

38. Replacement of the Indirect Object Pronoun by a Phrase

If the direct object pronoun in Spanish is in the first or second person (**me, te, nos, os**) a prepositional phrase is used instead of the indirect object pronoun.

Me presentaron a él.	They introduced me to him.
Te mandará a ella.	He will send you to her.

But:

Me lo presentaron.	They introduced him to me.
Se la presentaron.	They introduced her to him (to her, to you, to them).
Te la mandará.	He will send her to you.

39. Redundant (Repetitive) Object Pronouns

A. When **todo**—everything—or **todos(as)**—all (of them)—is direct object of a verb, the direct object pronoun (**lo, la, los, las**) is also used.

Lo sabe todo.	He knows everything.
Ya los conocía a todos.	I already knew them all.

B. For anticipation

When the indirect object noun is a person, the indirect object pronoun is often used in addition to the noun. This anticipating pronoun is especially frequent with **decir, pedir, preguntar,** and **gustar,** or when the direct object is a pronoun not referring to a person.[9]

Se lo diremos a Raúl.	We'll tell Ralph.
No se lo muestre a mi padre.	Don't show it to my father.

C. When a noun or a prepositional object pronoun precedes the verb, the redundant direct or indirect object pronoun is generally used also.

Este reloj lo compré en Venecia.	This clock I bought in Venice.
A él no le digo nunca nada.	To him I never say anything.

40. Special Uses of the Direct Object Pronouns

A. With **ser** or **estar, lo** is used to refer back to an adjective, a noun, or a whole idea. Note that **ser** can never stand alone.

[9] When the direct object refers to a person, the redundant indirect object pronoun is not used: **No lo entregarán a la policía.** They will not hand him over to the police.

Esta lección parece fácil. —Lo es.	This lesson seems easy. —It is.
¿Están cansados? —Sí que lo están.	Are they tired? —Indeed they are.
¿Son amigos suyos? —No, no lo son.	Are they friends of yours? —No, they are not.

B. The direct object pronouns **lo, la, los, las** correspond at times to the English *any* in negative sentences. With the impersonal **hay** (there is, there are) they are usually the equivalent of the English *some.*

¿Hay agua aquí? —No la hay.	Is there water here? —There isn't any.
Enemigos, no los tenía.	As for enemies, he didn't have any.
¿Hay osos allí? —Sí, los hay.	Are there bears there? —Yes, there are.
Los hay que creen en las hadas.	There are some who believe in fairies.

C. In highly idiomatic constructions, **la** and **las** are perhaps convenient substitutes for the word **cosa**(**s**).

No sé cómo se las arregla.	I don't know how he manages (things).
Se las echa de Don Juan.	He pretends to be a Don Juan.
¡Ud. no me la pega a mí!	You aren't fooling me! (You are not sticking it on to me.)
¡Me las pagarás!	I shall get even with you. (You will pay me for the things that you have done.)

D. **La** and **las** may also be found in place of the indirect object pronouns **le** and **les** with the meaning *to her*, *to them* (*f.*). The usage, however, is not generally accepted.

41. Placement of Object Pronouns

A. When a conjugated verb form is followed by an infinitive and each has a direct (not reflexive) object pronoun, the two pronouns are normally placed before the main verb.

Se lo oí decir.	I heard him say it.
Te lo hará saber.	He will have you know it (let you know).

Note that the pronoun referring to a person is converted into an indirect object pronoun, since one verb cannot have two direct objects.

B. In literary usage, the object pronoun is often attached to a conjugated verb form that begins a sentence or an independent clause.

Hallábanse entonces en Granada.	They were in Granada at that time.
Érase que se era...	Once upon a time . . .

EJERCICIOS

I. Traducir al español.

A. A few weeks ago, Joe phoned me long distance. He asked me whether I could buy certain rare books for him. The next day, I went to many bookstores, but I was unable to find them anywhere. The fact was that they were almost impossible to (**de**) obtain. I called to tell him that I would try to send them to him as soon as possible. Then I wrote to all the book dealers in town. It seemed that those books were very important to him. Finally I found them, paid for them, and mailed them to him. A few days later, I received his answer. He thanked me for everything, but said that he no longer needed them. He had already read them in the library. Now what do you think of that?

B. When the Captain introduced me to him, I had the impression that I had seen him somewhere, but I could not remember where. This impression changed into (**se volvió**) certainty when he used several times in his conversation the expression: **Se cae de su peso.** Now I was sure that I had heard him say it on some occasion. I couldn't help thinking about it all evening. Finally, I decided to ask him. At first, he didn't recognize me, but after looking at me for a long time, he exclaimed: "Of course! It was on the boat, five years ago. Don't you remember what happened that night?"

II. Composición.

Lo que pasó aquella noche en el barco

LECCIÓN QUINTA

Personal Pronouns (CONTINUED): THE REFLEXIVES

Adaptado de

DOMINGO

Madrid, 18 de agosto de 1963

Noticias Cortas

Buenos Aires. Se ha comprobado que las jóvenes deben esperar cada vez más tiempo para casarse. He aquí, por ejemplo, la estadística sacada de una sección del Registro Civil de un barrio donde casi todas las clases sociales están representadas. Esta estadística demuestra que la mayor parte de las mujeres casadas en el curso del año pasado tenían de treinta a cuarenta años.

¿Acaso la jovencita de nuestros días tendrá menos atractivos a los ojos de los hombres que antes? En realidad, la mujer que ha dejado atrás sus pequeñas fantasías de niña tiene mucho encanto. Ella se da cuenta exactamente de la significación del matrimonio y los hombres opinan que será mejor compañera que la jovencita, la cual no piensa más que en divertirse.

Patti. Un viejecito enérgico de setenta y ocho años raptó ayer a una señorita de setenta y tres años, alegando que los parientes de su amada se oponían al casamiento. Los enamorados se conocían desde hacía cincuenta años, y su siempre proyectado matrimonio, contra el cual era unánime la oposición de los familiares de ella, se cristalizó finalmente por medio del sistema clásico: escalerilla, fuga, y casamiento.

Nueva York. Los altos precios que se fijan a las obras de arte, sobre todo pinturas, suelen parecer excesivos hasta a los millonarios. Cierto coleccionista se creyó estafado cuando pagó la suma de cuatrocientos mil dólares por un retrato del Rey Felipe IV de España. El banquero que compró el cuadro supo por un amigo que el propio Monarca sólo había pagado por su retrato 7,600 reales. Pero entonces el millonario hizo números, y descubrió que esa cantidad, al seis por ciento de interés compuesto, si hubiera estado depositada en un banco en 1645, representaría ahora mayor suma que el precio fijado a la pintura. El coleccionista confesó entonces: "Me doy cuenta de que me he comprado una verdadera ganga pictórica."

Roma. Junto a la sala de guardia de la villa del Emperador Adriano, cerca de Roma, colocaron un letrero que decía: "Arqueólogos en servicio. Mantenerse a distancia." No obstante, la policía resolvió acercarse para ver qué arqueólogos eran aquéllos. Sobre el húmedo pavimento romano, fue descubierta una huerta ilícita de hongos. La policía está en busca de los "nuevos arqueólogos".

PREGUNTAS

1. ¿Qué se ha comprobado recientemente en Buenos Aires?
2. Según la estadística, ¿a qué edad se casan la mayor parte de las mujeres allí?
3. ¿De qué se da cuenta la mujer más madura?
4. ¿En qué piensa la jovencita, según el periodista?
5. ¿Por qué raptó el viejo a su novia?
6. ¿Desde cuándo se conocían?
7. ¿Por qué se creyó estafado el millonario coleccionista?
8. ¿De qué se dio cuenta al hacer números?
9. ¿Qué se leía en el letrero que colocaron en la villa de Adriano?
10. ¿Qué hacían en realidad los "arqueólogos"?

CONVERSACIÓN

1. ¿Qué edad considera Ud. mejor para casarse una mujer? ¿Y para casarse un hombre? ¿Es importante esperar hasta que los novios tengan cierta seguridad económica?
2. ¿Qué piensa Ud. del caso de los viejos enamorados? ¿Cree Ud. que los jóvenes deben hacer mucho caso de los consejos de sus familiares respecto a su casamiento? Si no les gusta a los padres el novio de su hija (o la novia de su hijo), ¿tienen el derecho de decírselo?
3. ¿Le interesa a Ud. el arte? ¿Qué periodo le gusta más? ¿Quiénes son sus artistas predilectos? ¿Tiene Ud. en casa una obra de arte original? ¿Sabe Ud. pintar o dibujar?

PART A

42. Forms of the Reflexive Pronouns

A. Object of a verb

me (to) myself
te (to) yourself
SE (to) himself, herself, yourself (**Ud.**), itself, themselves, yourselves (**Uds.**)
nos (to) ourselves
os (to) yourselves

Notice that the reflexive pronoun may serve as either the direct or the indirect object of the verb.

B. Object of a preposition

(**por**) **mí** (for) myself
(**por**) **ti** (for) yourself
(**por**) **SÍ** (for) himself, herself, yourself (**Ud.**), itself, themselves, yourselves (**Uds.**)
(**por**) **nosotros, as** (for) ourselves
(**por**) **vosotros, as** (for) yourselves

After the preposition **con,** the reflexive **mí, ti,** and **sí** become **–migo, –tigo, –sigo.**

Lo hizo para sí (misma). She made it for herself.
Se lo llevó consigo. He took it away with him.

43. General Function

A. A reflexive pronoun is used when the object of a verb (or preposition) refers to the subject of the sentence.

¿Te diviertes? Are you enjoying yourself?
Se compró un coche. He bought himself a car.
Piensa sólo en sí misma. She thinks only of herself.

B. Any verb can be used with the reflexive if the subject does the action to itself.

Me dije: Sé firme. I told myself: Be firm.
Siempre te cortas. You always cut yourself.
No se quemen. Don't burn yourselves.

EJERCICIO

Cambie según los sujetos indicados:

1. Fernando se cortó la mano. (yo, los niños, Pepe y yo)
2. Cúidese un poco más. (Uds., nosotros, tú, vosotros)
3. Van a divertirse mucho. (Elena, mi primo y yo, los alumnos, tú, tú y Miguel)
4. No te hagas daño. (Ud., Uds., vosotros, nosotros)
5. Lo hace para sí. (yo, Pepe, Jorge y yo, tú, ellos)
6. Nos hallábamos en peligro. (nuestras tropas, el espía, yo)
7. Siempre habla de sí mismo. (tú, vosotros, ese muchacho, esas mujeres)

44. Other Uses of the Reflexives

A. Many intransitive verbs in English (verbs that cannot take a direct object) are expressed in Spanish by making a transitive verb reflexive.

alegrar	to make happy	**alegrarse**	to be glad
sentar	to seat	**sentarse**	to sit down
acostar	to put to bed	**acostarse**	to go to bed
despertar	to awaken (somebody)	**despertarse**	to wake up (oneself)
levantar	to raise	**levantarse**	to rise, get up

Ahora me acuesto.	Now I lay me down to sleep.
Se sentaron en el sofá.	They sat down on the sofa.
¡Levántense todos!	Get up, everybody!

B. It translates *to get* or *become* + adjective

vestir	to dress (somebody)	**vestirse**	to get dressed, dress (oneself)
lavar	to wash (something or someone)	**lavarse**	to get washed, wash (oneself)
casar	to marry (off), join in marriage	**casarse**	to get married, marry
enfadar	to anger	**enfadarse**	to get angry
sorprender	to surprise	**sorprenderse**	to be(come) surprised

Lávate la cara, chico	Wash your face, boy
No se enfaden, por favor.	Don't get angry, please

C. Some verbs change their meaning when the reflexive is added.

ir to go	**irse** to go away
llevar to take, bring	**llevarse** to take away, carry off
dormir to sleep	**dormirse** to fall asleep
probar to try; to taste	**probarse** to try on
reír to laugh	**reírse** (**de**) to laugh (at)
hacer to make; to do	**hacerse** to become
quitar to take off or away (from someone)	**quitarse** to take off (one's own clothing, etc.)
poner to put; to put on (someone)	**ponerse** to put on (oneself); to become (+ adjective)

Duérmete, mi nene.	Go to sleep, my baby.
¿Puedo quitármelo ahora?	May I take if off now?
No quiere probárselo.	He doesn't want to try it on.
¡Vete!	Go away! (Get thee hence—reflexive in Old English)

D. A few verbs and many idiomatic expressions are normally reflexive in Spanish. These are some of the most common:

atreverse (**a**) to dare	**arrepentirse** (**de**) to repent
quejarse (**de**) to complain	**burlarse** (**de**) to make fun of
acordarse (**de**) to remember (about)	**olvidarse** (**de**) to forget (about)
darse cuenta (**de**) to realize	**fijarse** (**en**) to notice

EJERCICIOS

A. Conteste en español:

1. ¿A qué hora se durmió Ud. anoche? 2. ¿A qué hora se levantó esta mañana? 3. ¿Se vistió en seguida? 4. ¿Qué se llevó consigo al salir de casa? 5. ¿Se enfada Ud. frecuentemente? ¿Qué le enfada más? 6. ¿Qué piensa Ud. hacerse algún día? 7. ¿Se olvidó de algo importante recientemente? ¿Qué fue? 8. ¿Cuándo espera Ud. graduarse de esta escuela? 9. ¿Conoce Ud. a alguien que se queje siempre? ¿Se queja Ud. mucho? 10. ¿Se ha reído mucho de algo últimamente? ¿De qué?

B. Traduzca al español:

1. Wake up. It's eight o'clock. And wake up your brother too. 2. I have just bought myself a new hat. Do you like it? 3. We're very happy to be here with you today. 4. Go away. I don't want to talk to you. You always

make fun of me. 5. First they put the children to bed. Then they ate and went to bed. 6. He wouldn't dare to stand up now, would he? 7. Johnny, darling, do you remember the little cafe where we used to meet? —No. Besides, my name isn't Johnny. I'm Ralph.

45. The Reciprocal Reflexive

The reflexive is used to indicate that two or more persons are doing the action to each other.

Se quieren mucho.	They love each other.
Nos escribíamos a menudo.	We used to write to each other often.
Ayudaos, amigos.	Help each other, friends.

Uno a otro (**una a otra,**[1] **unos a otros, unas a otras**[1]) may be added if clarification is needed.

Se miman demasiado uno a otro.	They pamper each other too much.
Se hacen mucho daño unos a otros.	They hurt each other very much.

Without the additional phrase, the implication might be: they pamper (or hurt) *themselves*.

EJERCICIOS

A. Conteste afirmativamente:

1. ¿Se quieren Uds. mucho? 2. ¿Os escribís a menudo? 3. ¿Debemos ayudarnos uno a otro? (Sí, vosotros...) 4. ¿Se verán Uds. mañana? 5. ¿Podemos hablarnos ahora? (Sí, Uds....) 6. ¿Hace mucho tiempo que se conocen los novios?

B. Conteste negativamente:

1. ¿Se vieron Uds. anoche? 2. ¿Os conocisteis en aquella fiesta? 3. ¿Se miran con rencor? 4. ¿Nos encontraremos en el cine? 5. ¿Se escribirán todos los días? 6. ¿Se han casado Uds. ya?

46. The Impersonal Reflexive

Se + the third person singular of a verb often corresponds to the English impersonal *one* (or the colloquial *you*).

[1] The feminine is used only when both or all parties are women.

Se come bien allí.	One eats well there. (You get good food there.)
¿Por dónde se va al centro?	How does one (how do you) get downtown?
Se sale por esta puerta.	One leaves (you leave) through this door.
Leyendo, se aprende mucho.	By reading, one learns a great deal.

EJERCICIO

Diga en español:

1. One doesn't say such a thing. 2. How does one get out of here? 3. That isn't known yet. 4. How can one study in this house? 5. One shouldn't work too hard. 6. The food is good here (One eats . . .). 7. By listening, one learns to speak.

47. The Reflexive to Express the Passive Voice

The reflexive is frequently used in Spanish to translate the passive voice in English, when the doer of the action is not mentioned (cf. **140**B).

Aquí se habla español.	Spanish is spoken here.
Se abren las puertas a las ocho y cuarto.	The doors are opened at 8:15.

48. The Meaning and Uses of **mismo**

A. The adjective **mismo**, when used before a noun, normally means (*the*) *same* and, on occasion, corresponds to the emphatic adjective *very*.

Tuvimos el mismo profesor, pero no las mismas notas.	We had the same teacher, but not the same grades.
La misma idea me choca.	The very idea upsets me.

B. **Mismo,** used after a noun, a subject pronoun, or a prepositional phrase, is often translated as *myself*, *yourself*, *itself*, etc. However, **mismo** is NOT a reflexive. It is merely an adjective that serves to intensify or emphasize a reflexive phrase or whatever other word it modifies.

Voy a hablar con el patrón mismo.	I'm going to talk to the boss himself.
Ella misma se lo dijo, ¿no?	She herself told you, didn't she?
Habla por ti mismo, Juan.	Speak for yourself, John.

C. **Mismo** may also be an adverb, and as such, retains its intensifying meaning *very*, *right* (*away*), etc.

Hoy mismo.	This very day.
Ahora mismo.	Right now.
Aquí mismo.	Right here.

D. **Lo mismo que** the same as

El dijo lo mismo que yo.	He said the same (thing) as I (did).

EJERCICIO

Exprese más enfáticamente, usando **mismo**:

1. Yo lo quiero hacer. 2. Vamos a hablar con el patrón. 3. Se habla siempre. 4. Iremos mañana. 5. Lo haré ahora. 6. Lo encontró aquí. 7. Piensa sólo en sí. 8. ¿Lo dijo ella? 9. ¿Las aceptaron los jefes? 10. Te contesto hoy.

EJERCICIO DE REPASO

1. Before marrying her, I told her I didn't like studious women.
2. Almost all classes of society were represented on the list of the hall of records (**en el Registro Civil**).
3. I wonder whether she realizes the importance of this event.
4. Men do not like girls who think only about having a good time.
5. He warned them that he would abduct her if they opposed the marriage.
6. How long had they known each other when they got married? Fifty years!
7. He believed himself cheated after paying a million dollars for the painting and he got angry.
8. Afterwards he realized that he had gotten himself a bargain.
9. On the sign that they placed near the villa, one could read: "Keep away."
10. When they heard the shots, they approached the house and broke down the door.

REPASO DE VERBOS

Estudie los verbos **sentir, pedir, morir, dormir, vestir** (pp. 319–320).

1. Cambie al pretérito:
   Lo siento. Se duerme. Me lo pide. Nos siguen. Los niños duermen. Su tía muere. Me visto. Elda lo repite. Se lo advertimos. ¿No te sirves? ¿Seguís así?
2. Cambie al imperativo:
   Ud. duerme mucho. ¿Te vistes ahora? Lo seguimos. Se lo advierte. ¿Lo repiten? Me la piden. No seguís. No lo consentís. No os vestís tan pronto.

PART B

49. Subtle Changes of Meaning Through the Reflexive

A. The reflexive may serve to intensify an action. English usually conveys this idea by adding an adverb, which often is absolutely meaningless.

Se lo comió todo.	He ate it all up.
Entró tambaleándose.	He entered reeling about (or around).
Se ha muerto su abuelo.	His grandfather has passed away.
Me caí al entrar.	I fell down as I came in.

B. Other times, the reflexive gives a more subjective or intimate feeling with respect to the person who is performing the action. It places a little more emphasis on him, shows a little more of his will in doing the action.

Sé lo que me hago.	I know what I'm doing.
Me quedo, venga lo que venga.	I'm staying, come what may.
Se reía siempre que le hablaban de eso.	He laughed whenever they spoke to him about that.
Me temo que será él.	I suspect it will be he.

C. Very frequently, a reflexive passive construction is used instead of an active verb to imply that the action is accidental or unexpected.

¡Dios mío! Se me olvidaron los billetes.	Oh, my! I forgot the tickets. (They slipped my mind.)
Se le ha perdido la carta.	He has lost the letter. (It has disappeared on him.)
Se nos ocurre una idea.	We have an idea. (An idea occurs to us.)
Dejó caer la caja y se le rompieron todas las tazas.	He dropped the box and broke all the cups. (They got broken on him.)

50. Impersonal Constructions

A. The reflexive **se** is often used as the equivalent of the English *one*, *you*, *they* (cf. **46**).

Se dice que va a llover.	They say (one says) that it is going to rain.
No se fumaba en público en aquellos tiempos.	One didn't smoke in public in those times.

B. However, if this type of impersonal construction is formed with a verb which is already reflexive, the impersonal **uno** or the third person plural is required.

Cuando uno se acuesta tarde, se levanta tarde.	When one goes (you go) to bed late, one gets up (you get up) late.
En el ejército se levantan muy temprano.	In the army one gets up (you, they get up) very early.

C. After **hay que** or an impersonal expression with **ser,** the normal reflexive remains.

Hay que sentarse muy cerca para oír bien en ese teatro.	One (you) must sit very close in order to hear well in that theater.
Es necesario (importante, imposible) prepararse para el porvenir.	It is necessary (important, impossible) to prepare one's self for the future.

D. The impersonal **uno**

Uno has a more intimate or personal connotation than **se.** Very often, it is used when the speaker is actually referring to himself or to the person addressed.

A veces, uno quiere hacer bien, y hace mal.	At times, a person (one, you, I) means to do good, and does harm.
Una no puede decidirse tan aprisa.	One (a girl, I, she, etc.) can't decide in such a hurry.
Lo que uno no sabe, no le hace daño.	What one doesn't know doesn't hurt him.

Lo que no se sabe would mean *What isn't known.*

51. *Each other* after Prepositions

When the reciprocal *each other* follows a preposition other than *to,* the reflexive pronoun is not used. Instead, the verb is followed by **(el) uno** + preposition + **(el) otro,** etc.

Siempre hablan mal el uno del otro.	They always speak ill of each other.
Los vi luchando (los) unos contra (los) otros.	I saw them fighting one against the other.
Esas hermanas se sacrificarían una por otra.	Those sisters would sacrifice themselves for one another.

52. Pronoun Objects of Reflexive Verbs of Motion

Like all verbs of motion, reflexive verbs of motion usually require **a,** followed by the prepositional object pronoun.

Está acercándose a ella ahora.	It is approaching her now.
Me dirigí a él.	I turned to him.

However, when the reflexive pronoun is in the third person—**se**—it is sometimes possible to use the unstressed indirect object pronoun forms **me, te, le, nos,** etc., instead of the prepositional object. This is especially frequent with the verb **acercarse** to approach.

Se nos acercó.	He approached us.
Se acercó a nosotros.	

But:

Me acerqué a él.	I approached him.

53. Reflexive vs. Nonreflexive Pronouns

A. With **llevarse**

In Spain, the reflexive prepositional pronoun is generally used with the idiom **llevarse con** to carry off, to take away with one.

Me lo llevé conmigo.	I took it away with me.
Se lo llevó consigo.	He took it away with him.

In Spanish America, the nonreflexive prepositional pronoun is more frequent with this construction. Of course, the difference is notable only in the third person.

Se lo llevó con él.	He took it away with him.

B. With **traer**

Traer, followed by **conmigo, contigo,** etc., acquires the meaning *to have with* (*one*).

¿Trae consigo el dinero?	Does he have the money with him?

In Spanish America, the nonreflexive pronoun is again more common.

¿Trae con él el dinero?	Does he have the money with him?

EJERCICIOS

I. Tradúzcase al español.

Tell me, have you ever gone to bed and found that you couldn't fall asleep, that the thoughts kept (**iban**) crossing each other in your mind and that they simply couldn't stop? Well, that happened to me a few nights ago, and I still remember it all to (**hasta**) the last detail.

It was late and I had had a very good time that evening at a friend's house. When I got home, I undressed immediately, bathed and prepared for bed. I felt like having (**tomar**) a cup of coffee, but I didn't dare because I needed the sleep. The bed was comfortable. There wasn't any noise. I was tired and I knew that I had to get up early the (**al**) next day. And yet, I couldn't close my eyes. I began to think of many things—big things, little things, important things, nonsense. I thought about the letter that I had forgotten to mail, about the eyeglasses I broke. I thought about you and about myself and about all the people I know. And I asked myself: "What would I do if I found (*imperfect subjunctive*) myself in their place? What would my neighbor do if he found himself in mine? What (**Cuáles**) are the infinite possibilities of human behavior? Is man born pure, or does he purify himself by contact with civilization? What . . . ? And then a little anecdote occurred to me. I'm going to tell it to you, and I shall give it two endings. You can decide which you like better.

A bee had fallen into a glass of water. Its wings were soaked and it was trying desperately to get to the edge of the glass. In front of it, very near, was salvation, but its efforts seemed useless. The water that filled the glass was like a sea that had no end. A little boy approached. He looked for a moment with rapt attention, and realized that the bee was dying. Suddenly he took a straw and put it in the glass. The bee seized the straw and with its last strength (**fuerzas**) reached the edge and was saved.

1st ending: —See, little bee —said the boy—. One must never give up. There is hope even for the weakest.

2nd ending: —Come here, little bee —said the boy, as (**mientras**) he took it in his hands, threw it to the floor, and crushed it with his foot.

II. Composición.

Escriba Ud. una composición discutiendo las preguntas siguientes: ¿Cuál de las dos conclusiones prefiere Ud.? ¿Cuál considera Ud. más fiel a la realidad? ¿Cree Ud. que el hombre nace puro y que es educado a la crueldad, o que la educación es el proceso de limitar sus instintos egoístas o crueles?

LECCIÓN SEXTA

DEMONSTRATIVES AND POSSESSIVES

Adaptado de

EL ESPECTADOR

Bogotá, 27 de julio de 1963

40 Horas Permaneció Libre el Jaguar

La noticia de que un tigre había escapado produjo una verdadera histeria colectiva durante cuarenta horas en la vecindad del criadero de perros finos "La Perla". Las gentes empezaron a armarse, a cerrar con mucho cuidado sus puertas, a vivir en estado de alerta. Empezaron a circular las más increíbles versiones. Alguien dijo, "Se escapó un león de un circo y anda por estas carreteras." La tensión aumentó, y pronto se convirtió en cosa de vida o muerte. La policía mandó varias unidades. "Jacqueline" entre tanto se escondió. Cuando tuvo hambre la noche del jueves, burló el cerco de perros y cazadores e hizo su última treta: se comió la carne que le habían colocado en la jaula. No cayó en la trampa. Ese fue su máximo error. Si hubiera quedado allí, no la habrían matado ayer por la tarde.

Un oficial localizó al animal en un juncal. Le hizo un disparo pero no le dio. A las cinco de la tarde los hermanos Gamboa, cazadores profesionales, entraron al juncal. Hubo unos minutos de angustia expectativa. Silencio absoluto. De pronto sonó un ruido seco, luego otro, luego un tercero. Fueron tres disparos. "Jacqueline" no hizo resistencia. Cayó muerta.

El dueño del jaguar no pudo ocultar su pesar por la muerte trágica de uno de sus protegidos favoritos. "Le confieso", dijo, "que tanto yo como mi esposa y nuestros hijos sentimos mucho su muerte. Pero mejor así. Si se la hubiera capturado viva, el porvenir que le esperaba era un verdadero infierno por toda la vida en aquel cautiverio que era la jaula. Ante eso, era mejor la muerte."

"Don Juan, ¿fue necesario matar a Jacqueline?"

"No. Era posible capturarla viva, pero esto se habría demorado. Había una tremenda psicosis y había que poner fin a esa situación."

"Entonces, ¿usted estaba dispuesto a darle muerte?"

"Es verdad. Yo estaba dispuesto a aceptar esa posibilidad, pero sólo como último recurso."

"¿Pero no cree Ud. que el animal cayó en franca lid, esto es, en una cacería?"

"Aquello no fue una cacería. Fue un asesinato. Además, no me gusta la cacería, porque considero que tenía su razón sólo en aquellas épocas cuando ayudaba a proveer carne. Hoy en día eso es injustificable."

En la cara del dueño hay fatiga, cierto sentimimento de dolor, se podría decir que de culpa, mientras se aleja pensativo.

PREGUNTAS

1. ¿Cuánto tiempo estuvo libre el jaguar?
2. ¿Qué empezaron a hacer las gentes de la vecindad?
3. ¿Qué rumores empezaron a circular?
4. ¿Qué hizo la policía?
5. ¿Cuál fue la última treta que hizo el animal?
6. ¿Dónde localizaron a Jacqueline?
7. ¿Cómo la mataron?
8. ¿Por qué dijo su dueño que era mejor así?
9. ¿Por qué fue necesario poner fin a esa situación?
10. ¿Qué opina Don Juan sobre la cacería?

CONVERSACIÓN

1. ¿Le gusta a Ud. la cacería? ¿Por qué? ¿Qué animales ha cazado Ud.? ¿Cree Ud. que se puede justificar la cacería si no se necesita para proveer carne?
2. ¿Ha tenido Ud. alguna vez un protegido? ¿Qué fue? ¿Cómo lo obtuvo? ¿Lo tiene todavía? ¿Le ha enseñado a hacer una treta especial? ¿Cree Ud. que es justificable gastar dinero en los protegidos cuando hay mucha gente pobre en todas partes del mundo?
3. ¿Cree Ud. que la ley debe permitir al individuo tener en su casa cualquier animal que le guste? ¿Qué animales permitiría Ud.? ¿Cuáles prohibiría?

PART A

54. The Meaning and Function of Demonstratives

The demonstratives (*this*, *these*, *that*, *those*) are so called because they point out (they demonstrate) which one(s) of a group the speaker wishes to indicate. Since a demonstrative is either an adjective or a pronoun, its form in Spanish must agree with the noun it modifies or to which it refers.

55. Demonstrative Adjectives

A. Forms and meaning

Singular			*Plural*		
M.	F.		M.	F.	
este	**esta**	this (near me)	**estos**	**estas**	these
ese	**esa**	that (near you)	**esos**	**esas**	those
aquel	**aquella**	that (over there)	**aquellos**	**aquellas**	those

To keep in mind the difference between **este** (this) and **ese** (that), remember: In Spanish, *this* and *these* both have *t's*.

B. Uses of demonstrative adjectives

1. **Este** points out something or someone that is near the speaker in space, time, or thought.

Este impermeable es maravilloso.	This raincoat is marvelous.
Estos niños parecen tener hambre.	These boys seem to be hungry.

2. **Ese** points out something that is near the person addressed, or that is not too far removed from the speaker in space, time, or thought.

Haga Ud. el favor de darme ese cuaderno.	Please hand me that notebook.
¡Esa idea tuya es estupenda!	That idea of yours is wonderful!

3. **Aquel** points out something that is far removed from the speaker in space, time, or thought.

Aquellos edificios al otro lado de la plaza...	Those buildings across the square . . .
En aquella época, no tenían electricidad.	In that era, they didn't have electricity.

4. Demonstrative adjectives are generally repeated before each noun they modify, especially if the nouns are of different genders.

Este hombre y esta mujer fueron los primeros en llegar.	This man and woman were the first to arrive.

EJERCICIOS

A. Cambie según los sujetos indicados:

1. Este sombrero es nuevo.
   (casa, lápices, plumas, profesor, alfombra)
2. Ese perro es más grande.
   (mesa, vasos, lámparas, salón, bombillas)
3. Aquel cerro está muy lejos.
   (árboles, escuelas, jardines, edificio)

B. Diga en español:

1. These brushes; those dresses; those mountains in the distance.
2. This spring we shall not go to that hotel.
3. That restaurant that you mentioned turned out excellent.
4. Give me this pitcher and those glasses. No, not those over there.

56. Demonstrative Pronouns

A. Formation and function

Demonstrative pronouns are formed by placing a written accent on the stressed vowel of the demonstrative adjective. Thus: **éste, ése, aquél,** etc.

They may be used as subject or object of a verb, or may stand alone. They will never appear immediately before a noun.

Aquéllos sí fueron buenos tiempos.	Those were the good old days.
¿Cuáles prefiere Ud.? —Éste, ése y aquéllos.	Which ones do you prefer? —This one, that one, and those (over there).

B. The latter and the former: **éste** and **aquél**

Éste (the one most recently mentioned) is used to indicate *the latter*, and **aquél,** *the former*. In Spanish, when both are mentioned, *the latter* always comes first.

¿Conoce Ud. las revistas *Epoca* y *Hoy*? Pues ésta es semanal y aquélla es mensual.	Do you know the magazines *Epoch* and *Today*? Well, the former is monthly and the latter is weekly.
Allí están los doctores Campo y Montes. Este es bioquímico y aquél es cirujano.	There are Drs. Campo and Montes. The former is a surgeon and the latter is a biochemist.

C. The neuter demonstratives: **esto, eso, aquello**

These forms are invariable, since they refer to a whole idea rather than to a specific noun. Note that they never have a written accent.

Esto es lo que quiero.	This (in general) is what I want.
¡Eso es!	That's it!

EJERCICIOS

A. Complete las frases siguientes, empleando los demostrativos apropiados:

1. ______ libros aquí no me parecen muy interesantes. 2. Acabo de comprar ______ camisas ahí. 3. ______ montañas que se ven a lo lejos están cubiertas de nieve. 4. ______ flor que lleva Ud. en el ojal le da un aire muy festivo. 5. Me gusta mucho ______ sombrero tuyo. 6. De todas las casas, ______ en la colina me parece la mejor. 7. Acaban de llegar Carlos y Alfredo. ______ es un alumno sobresaliente, y ______ es muy vago. 8. ¿Conoce Ud. a Marcela y Leonor? ______ es la viuda del magistrado y ______ es la alcaldesa.

B. Traduzca al español:

1. This typewriter doesn't work. May I (**Puedo**) use that one? 2. You shouldn't wear that orange tie with this shirt. 3. Now this is what we're going to do. 4. That's not fair. He chose this card and you gave him that one. 5. I'm going with Steven Balón and Louis Romero. You know them. The former is my old roommate and the latter is my brother-in-law. 6. That's it, Gary. Wonderful! Please play (**tocar**) those pieces again.

57. Pseudo-Demonstratives

English frequently uses *that* and *those* not to point out something, but merely as a substitute for a noun. Since this is not a true demonstrative, Spanish uses the definite article instead of the demonstrative pronoun.

La Facultad de Educación y la de Humanidades...	The School of Education and that of Liberal Arts . . .
Nuestra casa y las del otro lado de la calle son de ladrillos.	Our house and those (the ones) across the street are of brick.[1]
Los que vinieron se divirtieron mucho.	Those (the ones) who came had a very good time.
Lo de Gómez...	That matter of (concerning) Gomez . . .

[1] If the speaker were pointing out *those* houses **aquéllas al otro lado** would be entirely correct in this sentence.

EJERCICIO

Substituya las palabras indicadas por el artículo apropiado:

1. Quiero comparar este abrigo con **el abrigo** de mi hermano. 2. El Ministerio de Hacienda y **los Ministerios** de Defensa y de Educación... 3. Los diputados conservadores se han unido ahora con **los diputados** liberales. 4. El Museo de Bellas Artes y **el Museo** de Historia Natural estarán por aquí. 5. Nuestra clase y **las clases** del Sr. Otero... 6. Nuestra casa y **la casa** de mis padres son de madera. 7. Este coche y **el coche** de Juan son azules. 8. Estos sonetos y **los sonetos** de Quevedo se parecen mucho.

58. Possessive Adjectives

A. Their function

1. Possession is expressed in Spanish by **de.**

La hija del presidente...	The President's daughter . . .
Esta bolsa es de Clara.	This purse is Claire's.

2. Possessive adjectives (and pronouns) replace possessive nouns.

Su hija...	His daughter . . .
Esta bolsa es (la) suya.	This purse is hers.

B. Unstressed forms (which always precede the noun)

mi(s) my	**nuestro** (**a, os, as**) our
tu(s) your	**vuestro** (**a, os, as**) your
su(s) his, her, your (**de Ud.** or **de Uds.**), their	

Like all adjectives, a possessive must agree with the noun it modifies. Notice that only the first and second person plural forms have feminine endings.

mis padres my parents **su tienda** their store
nuestra tía our aunt

C. Stressed forms (which always follow the noun)

mío (**a, os, as**) (of) mine	**nuestro** (**a, os, as**) (of) ours
tuyo (**a, os, as**) (of) yours	**vuestro** (**a, os, as**) (of) yours
suyo (**a, os, as**) (of) his, (of) hers, (of) yours (**de Ud.** or **Uds.**), (of) theirs	

These forms will either follow the noun or stand alone after the verb **ser.** They are frequently used also in exclamations. For clarification or emphasis, **suyo** may be replaced by **de él, de ella, de Ud., de ellos,** etc.

Es un pariente nuestro.	He is a relative of ours.
La idea fue suya (or **de él**), **la ejecución mía.**	The idea was his, its execution, mine.
El problema es suyo (or **de ellos**).	The problem is theirs.
¡Hijo mío!	My son!

EJERCICIOS

A. Conteste afirmativamente las preguntas siguientes, empleando el posesivo apropiado:

1. ¿Es de los Ramírez la casa? 2. ¿Es mío este plato? 3. ¿Son de Ud. esas fincas? 4. ¿Son nuestras estas camas? (2*a persona plural*) 5. ¿Serán mías aquellas tazas? (2*a persona singular*) 6. ¿Es tuyo ese botijo? 7. El bolso no es de María, ¿verdad? 8. La cartera no es tuya, ¿eh? 9. ¿Son de su hermana esos abrigos de pieles? 10. ¿Son de Uds. aquellas maletas?

B. Diga en español:

1. The farm is ours, but the house is Mr. Pardo's. 2. My friends, this is a great opportunity. 3. Our securities have gone down this month. 4. His prices are always very high. 5. Their company has just received an important contract. 6. This is mine, but I'll share it with you. 7. Her father took ill last night.

59. Replacement of the Possessive Adjective by the Definite Article

A. If clarification is needed in the third person, **su** may be replaced by **el... de, la... de,** etc.

Han llegado todas las maletas de Uds., pero no las de ellos.	All your suitcases have arrived, but not theirs.
¿Quiere Ud. darme la dirección de ella?	Will you give me her address?

B. With parts of the body, articles of clothing, and personal effects, the definite article generally replaces the possessive adjective. The possessor is indicated by an indirect object pronoun (if the subject does the action to someone else) or by a reflexive (if the subject does the action to himself).

Les puse la chaqueta.[2]	I put their jackets on them.

[2] Notice that since each person is putting on *one* jacket, Spanish uses the singular noun. Witness: **Quítense el sombrero.** *Take off your hats.* **Cuando terminen, levanten la mano.** *When you finish, raise your hands (one hand).* But: **cuando terminen, levanten las manos.** *When you finish, raise your hands (both hands).*

Se puso la chaqueta.	He put on his (own) jacket.
Lávate las manos y la cara antes de comer.	Wash your hands and face before eating.
Me quitó el aliento.	It took my breath away.

Of course, if the possessor is not otherwise revealed, the possessive adjective is used.

Se puso mi chaqueta.	He put on my jacket.
Quise abrir tu paraguas, pero estaba roto.	I tried to open your umbrella, but it was broken.

EJERCICIO

Substituya los sustantivos siguientes por pronombres (**Mi casa:** la mía). En el caso de una frase en tercera persona, indique las dos construcciones posibles (**Las casas de Raúl:** las suyas, las de él):

1. Nuestro tío. 2. El abuelo de Paquita. 3. Mis manzanas. 4. Tus maletas. 5. Los ojos de mi novia. 6. Los peines de esas muchachas. 7. El contrato del Sr. Palos. 8. Mi padre. 9. Las sillas de los niños. 10. Vuestro cenicero.

60. Possessive Pronouns

A. Formation

Possessive pronouns consist of the definite article plus the stressed form of the possessive adjective: **el mío, los tuyos, la suya,** etc.

B. Use

They may serve as subject or object of a verb, may follow **ser,** or may stand alone.

¿En qué coche vamos? **—El tuyo es el mejor.**	In which car shall we go? —Yours is the best.
No tengo pluma. ¿Puedo pedirle prestada la suya (or **la de Ud.**)**?**	I don't have a pen. May I borrow yours?
¿Cuáles son los nuestros?	Which are ours?

EJERCICIO

1. Don't give me *your* pen; give me *his*. 2. I have to wash my hair tonight. 3. Her parents live in the city, but his live in the country. 4. My car and hers are blue. 5. Close your eyes and put out your hands. 6. Let's take off our ties. 7. They have put on their white shirts.

EJERCICIO DE REPASO

1. They say that a lion has escaped from the circus and is walking along this road. —Good. I like animals.
2. Several persons called a friend of mine, inquiring about the lion hunt.
3. That incident soon turned into a matter of life or death and our relatives began to arm.
4. Two animals fell into his trap. None fell into mine.
5. One of these hunters fired three times at the tiger but he missed.
6. A newspaperman asked him if he thought that the animal's death was necessary.
7. The owner declared: "That wasn't a hunt; that was murder."
8. My children, my wife and I are very sorry about the loss of our pet.
9. We don't like hunting. In those days it was necessary, but not now.
10. The jaguar was his and he loved it. Therefore he was unwilling to kill it, except as a last resort.

REPASO DE VERBOS

Estudie los verbos de cambios ortográficos (pp. 320–324).

1. Escriba en el presente del indicativo:
   yo: vencer, coger, dirigir, distinguir, enviar, continuar, seguir
2. Escriba en el pretérito:
   yo: sacar, pagar, empezar, buscar, gozar, averiguar
   Paco: reír, leer, creer, construir, destruir
   todos: reír, leer, creer, construir, destruir

PART B

61. Further Uses of the Demonstratives

A. In business letters

1. **Ésta** and **ésa** are frequently used in commercial Spanish to mean *this city* (the one in which the letter is written) and *your city* (the one to which the letter is sent). **Esta plaza** and **esa plaza** are also used in that sense.

Estoy seguro de que los artículos tendrán muy buena acogida en ésta (en esta plaza).	I am sure that the goods will have an excellent sale in this city.
Espero que Uds. puedan colocar mis telas en ésa (en esa plaza).	I hope that you will be able to market my fabrics in your city.

2. **Ésta** may refer also to the letter being written.

Le mando ésta para participarle que...	I am sending you this letter to inform you that . . .

B. The derogatory demonstrative

Placed after the noun, the demonstrative adjective **ese** expresses contempt. At times, the pronoun **ése** also acquires this connotation.

El tío ese empieza a molestarme.	That (unpleasant, nasty) guy is beginning to annoy me.
La mujerona esa tendrá que habérselas conmigo.	That (miserable) mass of woman will have to reckon with me.
Ése viene a matarte, según dice.	That fellow is coming to kill you, so he says.

C. The neuter demonstratives followed by **de**

Esto de, eso de, and **aquello de** have varied translations in English. Most frequently, they correspond to the English *this* or *that matter of*, *business of*, *idea of*, *question of*, and at times they are preferably not translated at all.

Esto de acostarse temprano es sólo para los viejos.	This business of going to sleep early is only for old people.
Eso de aprender idiomas no es tan fácil como me imaginaba.	(That matter of) learning languages is not as easy as I imagined.

D. **Aquel** as part of a compound relative, *the one . . . whom*

When *whom* is object of a preposition, **aquel(los)** translates the subject pronoun *the one*(*s*).

Aquellos de quienes habla Ud. son amigos míos.	The ones (those) of whom you are speaking are friends of mine.

62. Possessives

A. Stressed adjective vs. pronoun

After the verb **ser,** both the stressed adjective (**mío,** etc.) and the pronoun (**el mío**) are correct. However, there is a difference in meaning between the two constructions. The adjective merely indicates possession, whereas the pronoun stresses the selection of one or more objects from among a group.

Todas esas casas son mías.	All those houses are mine.
¿Cuál de esas casas es la de Ud.? —Ésta es la mía.	Which of those houses is yours? — This one is mine (the one that I live in).
Esa pluma es tuya, ¿no?	That pen is yours, isn't it? (You are its owner.)
¿Esa pluma es la tuya, no?	That pen is yours, isn't it? (The one that belongs to you.)

B. Special use of the masculine plural pronouns

Los míos, los tuyos, etc., are used to refer to relatives, intimate friends, subordinates, etc.

Recuerdos a los tuyos.	Regards to your family.
Los nuestros ocuparon el pueblo.	Our men (troops) occupied the town.

C. The neuter forms

With the neuter article **lo,** the possessive pronoun acquires an abstract sense: **lo mío** what is mine, etc.

No codiciamos lo suyo.	We don't covet what is his.
No tienes ningún derecho a lo mío.	You have no right to what is mine.
Quédate con lo tuyo.	Keep what you have.

D. The possessive adjective with parts of the body and personal effects

When there is no doubt as to the identity of the possessor, the definite article is used with parts of the body, articles of clothing, etc. (see **59**B). But in cases in which the possessor could not be identified by the use of the definite article, the possessive adjective is required. This occurs especially when the part of the body or personal effect is the subject of the verb.

Sus pies se negaron a caminar.	His feet refused to walk.
Mis ojos ya no veían.	My eyes could see no more.
Te daré mi corbata para que te la pruebes.	I shall give you my necktie, so that you may try it on.

EJERCICIOS

I. Traducir al español.

My little boy, like all children, was very possessive. Everything he saw had to be his. When we took him to a store, his eyes would open wide with joy, and he would say to us: I need this truck and that one and that one over there, and these little cars and that big ball, and that red airplane and those with the silver wings. He needed them all desperately, it seems, but when he had them home, he would forget about them. Still, he would not let his little brother even touch his possessions. "This will not do (**servir**)." we decided. "We'll have to show him that that kind of conduct deserves no rewards."

That afternoon, we went to the new department store in our town. As usual, the little toy collector put his hands on everything, and asked us for everything he saw, but we closed our ears to his pleas. Finally, he realized what was happening. He looked at us, his big blue eyes filled with tears, and said: "I know that I have been very selfish. Won't you buy something at least for my little brother? I don't want anything for myself."

"Well," we thought, "this is a real change." And we bought the baby a large number of new toys. "Now you see, darling," we warned him, "you must learn to share things with others." "That's right," he replied.

Satisfied, we returned home. As soon as we entered the house he showed his brother all the presents we had just bought.

"See, baby," he said. "All these are yours. But remember, what's yours is ours. I have learned to share things."

II. Composición.

1. La educación de un niño
2. Lo que haría yo si fuera madre (padre) de familia
3. La educación de un adolescente
4. ¿Hasta dónde llega la disciplina familiar?

LECCIÓN SÉPTIMA

THE SUBJUNCTIVE

Adaptado de

AMÉRICAS

Unión Panamericana, diciembre de 1962

La OEA en Acción

En la reunión celebrada en Washington el 2 y 3 de octubre de 1962, los Ministros de Relaciones Exteriores de las Repúblicas Americanas y sus representantes especiales discutieron el problema de Cuba. En el comunicado emitido al concluir las conversaciones, calificaron unánimemente a la intervención chino-soviética en Cuba "como ensayo de convertir a dicha isla en base armada para la penetración del comunismo en América y de acción subversiva contra las instituciones democráticas del continente". Reiterando su adhesión a los principios de autodeterminación y no intervención, recomendaron que los miembros de la OEA dieran una respuesta colectiva a la amenaza presente y que consideraran futuras limitaciones al comercio con Cuba, especialmente el de artículos de importancia estratégica. Los Ministros se han manifestado de acuerdo también en la necesidad de que los países intensifiquen las medidas para "impedir que agentes y grupos del comunismo internacional desarrollen actividades de carácter subversivo". Finalmente, los Ministros expresaron "el tradicional afecto de todos los pueblos de América hacia el hermano pueblo de Cuba y su profundo sentimiento por las víctimas del régimen actual". Y añadieron: "Esperemos que el pueblo cubano pueda reintegrarse plenamente algún día a la familia americana con un gobierno compatible con los principios y própositos del sistema americano."

Antes de la reunión, el Dr. José A. Mora, Secretario General de la OEA, declaró en una conferencia de prensa que él consideraba la reunión extraoficial como "un método flexible y útil para intercambiar ideas". Afirmó que: "En defensa del principio de la no intervención debe condenarse la acción intervencionista de potencias extranjeras en nuestro hemisferio. Es necesario que la comunidad americana avance en el camino de contribuir a la preservación de las libertades amenazadas y que se esfuerce por ayudar a que los pueblos que padecen bajo los sistemas totalitarios puedan expresar libremente su voluntad. Ahora más que nunca urge que los países americanos fortalezcan el sistema de la democracia representativa y redoblen sus esfuerzos por alcanzar el progreso de los pueblos."

PREGUNTAS

1. ¿Qué reunión se celebró en Washington el 2 y 3 de octubre de 1962?
2. ¿Qué problema discutieron?
3. ¿Cómo calificaron a la intervención chino-soviética en Cuba?
4. ¿A qué principios reiteraron su adhesión?
5. ¿Qué recomendaron que hicieran los miembros de la OEA?
6. ¿Sobre qué artículos considerarían imponer limitaciones comerciales?
7. ¿Qué otras medidas serían necesarias?
8. ¿Qué actitud expresaron los ministros respecto al pueblo de Cuba?
9. ¿Qué esperanza añadieron?
10. ¿Qué urge ahora más que nunca?

CONVERSACIÓN

1. ¿Recuerda Ud. la crisis nuclear sobre Cuba? ¿Cuántos años tenía Ud. entonces? ¿Cómo reaccionó su familia? ¿Está Ud. de acuerdo con la actuación de los Estados Unidos respecto a Cuba durante aquella crisis?
2. ¿Qué problema internacional considera Ud. más urgente o peligroso ahora? ¿Qué problemas domésticos son de más importancia?
3. ¿Cree Ud. que es posible evitar para siempre las guerras? ¿Por qué?
4. ¿Qué sabe Ud. de la OEA? ¿Qué países la integran? ¿Cree Ud. que tenemos el derecho de impedir que se establezca un gobierno comunista en Hispanoamérica? ¿Cuál debe ser nuestra posición respecto a cualquier gobierno totalitario en Hispanoamérica?

63. General View of the Subjunctive

A. The subjunctive in English

The subjunctive is more widely used in English than many people realize. Often it escapes notice because its forms differ from the indicative only in the third person singular and in certain irregular verbs. In other cases, it makes use of the auxiliaries *may*, *might*, or *should*. These are its most common uses:

1. It appears regularly after certain verbs of suggesting, requesting, and ordering.

   It is urgent that she *leave* at once.

   The President insisted that we *be* there on time.

   They should demand that he *sign* it.

2. It follows many expressions of emotion, particularly of hope.

   I wish I *were* in Dixie.

   May the coming year bring peace to all. (I hope that . . .)

   God *be* praised. (I pray that . . .)

3. It expresses unreality:

   Doubt, uncertainty

   It is incredible that he *should* volunteer for that mission.
   It is possible that he *may* come.

   Indefiniteness

   Come what *may*.
   Wherever you *may* go. (No definite place.)

   Purpose

   I tell you this so that you *may* be prepared.

   And conditions that are contrary to fact.

   If I *were* you (but I am not), I would read this carefully.

THESE ARE PRECISELY THE CONCEPTS OF THE SUBJUNCTIVE IN SPANISH AS WELL.

B. The subjunctive in Spanish

In Spanish, the indicative is the mood of black and white, of bald fact, of assertion, of certainty. The subjunctive is tinged with the hues of subjectivity, the nebulousness of unreality. It appears in the subordinate clause whenever the subordinate statement bears the implication of command or reflects the color of an emotion, whenever its positive existence is clouded by uncertainty, indefiniteness, or an assumption contrary to fact. Its usage can be reduced to three essential concepts, to which it adheres consistently and logically. These concepts, and not any particular verb, phrase, conjunction, or type of clause, will produce a subjunctive in Spanish.

64. The First Concept of the Subjunctive: Indirect or Implied Command

A. When one person, speaking directly to another, gives him an order, that is a direct command.

Ten cuidado, Pepe.	Be careful, Joe.
Siéntese, por favor.	Sit down, please.

B. When the order is not given directly, but is incorporated into a request or an expression of one person's will that someone else do something, that is an indirect or implied command. The force of that command, no matter how weak or how strong, will produce the subjunctive in the subordinate clause.

Te ruego que tengas cuidado, Pepe.	I beg you to be careful, Joe. ("Joe, I beg you—be careful!")
Les dijo que se sentaran.	He told them to sit down. ("Sit down," he told them.)
Quiero que todo el mundo vea esto.	I want everyone to see this. ("See this, everyone!")
Insistimos en que vaya.	We insist upon his going (or that he go). (We insist: "Go!")
¿Les escribió Ud. que viniesen?	Did you write them to come? (Did you write to them "Come!"?)
Pídale que vuelva.	Ask him to come back. (Say to him: "Please come back".)
El capitán mandó que lo soltasen.	The captain ordered[1] them to release him.
No permitas que te engañen.	Don't allow[1] them to fool you.

Sometimes the main clause is omitted, but the indirect command is still apparent. In such cases, the English *let* is not a request for permission, but an expression of the speaker's will.

¡Que cante Juanito!	(Let) Johnny sing![2] (I want Johnny to sing.)
Que bailen todos ahora.	(Let) everyone dance now. (I want everyone to dance now.)

[1] Verbs of ordering or forcing, permitting, or forbidding may also take the infinitive.

Les mandó soltar a los prisioneros.

No les permitas engañarte.

After **hacer**, **dejar**, **permitir**, and **mandar**, the infinitive is more common.

[2] There is an important difference in Spanish between **Que cante Juanito** and **Deje Ud. que cante Juanito** (or **Déjele cantar**), although they are both translated in English as: *Let Johnny sing*. The first sentence involves only the speaker and is merely the expression of his will that Johnny sing. The second involves another person, of whom the speaker is requesting permission for Johnny to sing.

C. Note that it is not the verb itself, but the implication of command that calls for a subjunctive in the subordinate clause. If there is no change of subject, there can be no implication of command and, therefore, no subjunctive.

Quiero irme.	I want to go away.
Quiero que te vayas.	I want you to go away.

EJERCICIOS

A. Estudie el subjuntivo de los verbos que hemos repasado hasta ahora.

B. Cambie las frases siguientes según las indicaciones:

1. **Quiero que** lo haga Jorge.
   (Insistiré en que, Aconsejan que, ¿Pides que... ?, Dirán que)
2. **Insisten en que** ella venga también.
   (Prefiero que, ¿Decís que... ?, Sugerimos que, No quiero que)
3. **Les** dirá que **se vayan.**
   (Me, Te, a Juan, a Ud., Nos, Os)
4. **¿Nos** aconsejan que lo **compremos?**
   (Te, Os, Me, a mi padre, a sus vecinos)
5. Mándemelo en seguida.
   (Quiero que, Le ruego que, Insisto en que, Les pido que, Te pido que)
6. **¿No le escribiste** que viniera lo antes posible?
   (¿No le pediste, ¿No me pediste, ¿No les dijiste, ¿No nos dijiste . . . ?)

C. Diga en español:

1. Let's write him that we are coming. 2. Let's write him to come. 3. They want to see the play. 4. They want us to see the play. 5. He prefers to tell it now. 6. He prefers that you tell it now. 7. Tell him to hurry. 8. Tell him that I'll hurry. 9. I insist on going with you. 10. But I don't want you to go with me. 11. Allow me to help you. 12. Our lawyer recommends that we don't sign it. 13. Ask him (**pedir**) to give us the money. 14. Ask him (**preguntar**) whether he is coming.

65. The Second Concept of the Subjunctive: Emotion

A. When the main clause expresses pleasure, regret, surprise, pity, fear, anger, hope, or any other emotion concerning the action of the subordinate clause, the impact of that emotion will bring forth a subjunctive in the subordinate clause.

Teme que le reconozcan.	He is afraid that they will recognize him.
Me alegro de que haya ganado Ud.	I am happy that you have won.
Espero que estés contento ahora.	I hope you are satisfied now.
Sentimos que no pudieran venir.	We were sorry they couldn't come.
Es lástima que esté enferma.	It's too bad that she is ill.
Ojalá que estuviera con él.	If only (how I wish) I were with him.

B. If there is no change of subject, the infinitive should normally be used.

Siente estar tan lejos.	He is sorry that he (himself) is so far away.

But:

Siente que ella esté tan lejos.	He is sorry that she is so far away.

EJERCICIOS

A. Cambie las frases siguientes según las indicaciones:

1. **Siento** que Miguel esté ausente.
(Temo, Me sorprende, No me gusta, Sentía, Lamentaba, Esperaba, Es lástima, Ojalá, Me molesta, Me molestaba)
2. Se alegran **de que te hayas** quedado.
(de que Juan, de que Uds., de que Raúl y yo, de que tú y Ana)
3. Esperamos que **llame** pronto.
(decidir, salir, empezar, decírnoslo, traerlas)

B. Conteste las preguntas siguientes ateniéndose al modelo:

¿Quiere Ud. verlo? **No, quiero que lo vea Juan.**

1. ¿Espera Ud. acabarlo? No, ______________ mi hijo.
2. ¿Siente Ud. tener que marcharse? No, ______________ ellos.
3. ¿Le sorprende sacar esa nota? No, ______________ María.
4. ¿Insiste Ud. en dársela? No, ______________ tú.
5. ¿Teme Ud. perder el puesto? No, ______________ el pobre.

Ahora conteste según este modelo:

¿Sentía Ud. perderlo? **No, sentía que lo perdiera Pablo.**

6. ¿No querían Uds. vendérsela? No, ______________ su vecino.
7. ¿Le gustaría asistir? No, ______________ mi esposa.
8. ¿Deseaba Ud. comérselo? No, ______________ tú.
9. ¿Esperabas ir con él? No, ______________ vosotros.
10. ¿Le molestaba oírlo? No, ______________ Uds.

66. The Sequence of Tenses

Main Clause	*Subordinate (Subjunctive) Clause*
Present Future Present perfect	Same tense as in English
Past Conditional	Imperfect subjunctive or Pluperfect subjunctive

A. If the main clause is in the present, future, or present perfect, the subordinate clause subjunctive is in the same tense as the English. Remember, of course, that the present subjunctive refers also to future action.

Es lástima que no vengan.	It's a pity that they aren't coming (or won't come).
Es lástima que no hayan venido.	It's a pity that they haven't come.
Es lástima que no vinieran.[3]	It's a pity that they didn't come.

B. If the main clause is in the past or conditional, use only a past subjunctive: imperfect subjunctive for a simple tense; pluperfect subjunctive for a compound tense.

Sentían que él no estuviese allí.	They regretted that he was not there.
Sentían que él no hubiese estado allí.	They regretted that he had not been there.

EJERCICIOS

A. Cambie para indicar que la acción está recién concluida:

Espero que venga. **Espero que haya venido.**

1. Temo que muera. 2. Se alegra de que vuelvan. 3. Ojalá que no sea Carmen. 4. Sentimos que estés tan cansado. 5. Me molesta que no quiera verme. 6. Nos gusta que toquen el piano. 7. ¿Le sorprende que diga eso? 8. Espero que lo termine.

B. Cambie las frases siguientes al pasado:

Quiero que lo haga. **Quería que lo hiciera.**

1. Quiero verte en seguida. 2. Quiero que lo veas en seguida. 3. Ojalá que no haya más dificultades. 4. Temen que lo perdamos. 5. Me alegro

[3] When the main clause is in the present, the imperfect subjunctive is used primarily for a past action that is prior to another or that is considered definitely over. **Es lástima que no llamaran antes de que Luis se fuera.** *It's a shame they didn't call before Louis left.* **Es posible que muriera cerca de 1930.** *It is possible he died around* 1930. Otherwise, the present perfect subjunctive is more frequent after a present tense.

de que ganes. 6. No me gusta que se vaya tan temprano. 7. Sienten tener que dejarlo. 8. Sentimos que tengan que dejarlo. 9. Os ruego que volváis pronto. 10. No le dejará comprarlo. 11. No permiten que la vea todos los días. 12. Le digo que me pague en seguida.

EJERCICIO DE REPASO

1. The representatives of three nations have written the secretary of the United Nations to include this matter in the agenda.
2. They will ask all the countries to reiterate their adherence to the principles of self-determination and non-intervention.
3. The members insist that the other governments give a collective answer to the threat.
4. I hope that they will also consider future limitations to trade with that country.
5. They agreed to prevent these groups from carrying out subversive activities in our country.
6. We regret that our nation has not been able to rejoin completely the family of democratic countries.
7. Let them go to the meeting, discuss this problem, and exchange ideas with the others.
8. They feared that the new technique of aggression would be successful in other parts of Latin America.
9. You must tell them to continue contributing to the preservation of our liberties.
10. We wanted them to help the other peoples to express their will freely.

LECCIÓN OCTAVA

THE SUBJUNCTIVE

(CONTINUED)

Adaptado de un artículo por "Adlih"

NOVEDADES

México, D.F., 8 de septiembre de 1963

La Relatividad

Pensarán Uds. que vamos a convertirnos en Einstein, pero no, no es esa clase de relatividad sobre la que nosotros vamos a hablar. Es sencillamente que a través de nuestra vida las cosas que en un momento parecen tener una importancia vital, más tarde se convierten en... sólo una cosa más. En realidad, todo es relativo. Por ejemplo, cuando éramos pequeños y veíamos a muchachos mayores que nosotros, ¡cómo deseábamos estar como ellos! Pero ahora cuando vemos a personas de edad más avanzada y nos parecen muy viejas, ya nos damos cuenta de que no nos parecerán tan ancianas cuando nosotros lleguemos a tener esa misma edad.

Igualmente les pasará a todos los jóvenes con su profesión. Cuando inicien su carrera, querrán que todo el mundo sepa que van a ser médicos, o abogados, o arquitectos. Veinte años después no querrán ni hablar de ella. Y cuando tengan la primera novia, pensarán que en el mundo no hay otra mujer, no digamos que la supere, no, ni siquiera que se le compare. Odiarán a todas aquellas personas que les aconsejen bien, aunque sean sus padres, a quienes convertirán casi en sus enemigos. Conozco a unos jóvenes que se consideran verdaderos don Juanes, y no hay quien los haga caer en una trampa. Y aun ahora, les recomiendo prudencia y cautela, no se vayan a pasar de listos y después se arrepientan por todo el resto de su vida.

En fin, amigos míos, deseo que todas sus experiencias, buenas o malas, les sirvan para el futuro, para cuando tengan que enseñar todo lo que Uds. aprendieron a las generaciones venideras. Y que cuando sus hijos deseen fervientemente algo y luchen por alcanzarlo, ojalá que Uds. puedan comprenderlos y estimularlos con sus consejos y ejemplos, bajando a su edad y a su mentalidad.

¿Ven Uds. la relatividad en la vida? Todo es relativo a la edad, a la experiencia, a los deseos, a los negocios, a la posición, y después, todo deja de tener importancia. Pero lo que yo les sugiero es que en todo tiempo gocen y vivan sus momentos de triunfo y de derrota, y hagan que sean lo más fructíferos posible. Cuando sean viejos, éstos serán sus mejores recuerdos cada vez que evoquen el pasado.

PREGUNTAS

1. Cuando éramos pequeños, ¿qué pensábamos cuando veíamos a muchachos mayores?
2. ¿De qué nos damos cuenta ahora cuando vemos a personas de edad más avanzada?
3. ¿Qué querrán los jóvenes cuando inicien sus carreras?
4. ¿Qué pensarán cuando tengan la primera novia?
5. ¿Cómo considerarán a sus padres?
6. ¿Qué recomienda el autor del artículo a los jóvenes don Juanes?
7. ¿Para cuándo deben servirnos todas nuestras experiencias?
8. ¿Qué debemos hacer cuando nuestros hijos deseen algo fervientemente?
9. ¿Por qué podemos decir que todo es relativo?
10. ¿Qué sugiere el autor que hagamos en todo tiempo?

CONVERSACIÓN

1. ¿Cuáles son los primeros recuerdos de su niñez? ¿Quiénes fueron sus primeros amigos? ¿Los ve todavía? ¿Recuerda Ud. algo que una vez le pareciera importantísimo y que ahora no le interesa nada?
2. ¿Está Ud. de acuerdo con el autor de este artículo sobre la actitud de los jóvenes respecto al amor? ¿Y respecto a sus padres? ¿Ha pensado Ud. alguna vez que sus padres no le entendían, o que eran sus enemigos?
3. Cuando Ud. era niño, ¿a quién admiraba más? ¿A quién admira más ahora?
4. ¿Cuáles eran sus pasatiempos favoritos hace cinco años? ¿Y ahora? ¿Cree Ud. que cambiarán mucho sus gustos en el futuro?

67. The Third Concept of the Subjunctive: Unreality

The subjunctive wears the cloak of unreality. It reflects the doubtful, uncertain, indefinite, the unfulfilled, the impositive. It appears in the subordinate clause whenever the idea upon which that clause depends places it within the realm of the unreal. In this paragraph and in **68–70**, we shall analyze the varied situations in which the concept of unreality produces the subjunctive.

A. The shadow of a doubt

When the idea of the main clause places the subordinate clause action in the shadow of doubt, the uncertain reality of that action is expressed by the subjunctive.

Dudo que nos haya visto.	I doubt that he has seen us.
No están seguros de que sea ella.	They aren't sure that it is she.

If doubt is not cast on the subordinate clause action, there is no subjunctive.

Estoy seguro de que es él.	I am sure that it is he.

B. Denial

When the idea of the main clause denies the existence of the subordinate clause action, the unreality of that action is also expressed by the subjunctive.

Negó que lo hicieran.	He denied that they did it.
No es verdad que lo dijera.	It isn't true that he said it.

But:

No negó que lo hicieron.	He didn't deny that they did it.

C. Subjunctive and indicative with **creer**

The verb **creer** (to think, to believe) illustrates how the speaker's expression of doubt, and not the verb itself, determines whether the subjunctive or the indicative will be used.

1. **Creer,** used in an affirmative statement, is regularly followed by the indicative, because the speaker, in saying, "I believe," does not normally want to imply, "I doubt."[1]

[1] When the speaker wishes to express serious doubt, the subjunctive is possible. **Creo que venga.** I think he may possibly come.

Creo que vendrá.	I think that he will come.
Creían que habíamos fracasado.	They thought that we had failed.

2. In questions or negative statements, **creer** will produce a subjunctive if the speaker wishes to cast doubt on the subordinate clause action, and the indicative if he makes no implication of doubt.

¿Cree Ud. que se atreva?	Do you think he will dare? (I doubt it.)
¿Cree Ud. que se atreverá?	Do you think he will dare? (I think so, or I have no opinion.)
No creo que le castiguen.	I don't think (I doubt) that they will punish him.
No creo que le castigarán.	I don't believe that they will punish him. (I fully believe that they will *not* punish him.)
¿No cree Ud. que ella es bonita?	Don't you think she's pretty? (I do.)

D. The subjunctive after conjunctions indicating uncertainty or unreality:

1. Some conjunctions, by their very meaning, always concede that the subordinate clause action is not a certainty. Such conjunctions include **a menos que** (unless), **en caso de que** (in case), **con tal que** (provided that). These are always followed by the subjunctive.

En caso de que venga, dígale que he salido.	In case he comes, tell him that I have gone out.
A menos que ella insista, no se lo mostraremos.	Unless she insists, we will not show it to her.

2. Other conjunctions such as **aunque** (although, even though, even if), **dado que** (granted that), **a pesar de que** (in spite of the fact that) will be followed by the subjunctive if the speaker implies an uncertain assumption, and by the indicative if he implies a certainty or a belief. In many cases, English will indicate uncertainty by using the auxiliary *may*.[2]

[2] In a main clause, *may* has two possible meanings: permission and uncertainty. Spanish uses the indicative of **poder** for both.

¿Puedo salir? May I go out? **Puede ser él.** It may be he.

Aunque sea listo, no lo sabe todo.	Although he may be smart, he doesn't know everything.
Aunque es listo, no lo sabe todo.	Although he is smart, he doesn't know everything.
Dado que tenga Ud. razón, ¿qué vamos a hacer?	Granted that you may be right (but I have my doubts), what shall we do?
Dado que tiene Ud. razón...	Granted that you are right (and I think you are) . . .

3. The conjunction **sin que** (without) is always followed by the subjunctive because, by its very meaning, it negates the reality of the subordinate clause action.

Salieron sin que los viéramos.	They left without our seeing them.

Obviously, since the subordinate clause action did not take place, it is unreal or nonexistent.

Note that if there is no change of subject, the preposition **sin,** followed by the infinitive, must be used.

Se lo llevó sin pedirnos permiso.	He took it without asking us for permission.

EJERCICIOS

A. Cambie:

1. **Niega** que su hijo lo haya hecho.
   (Negó, Duda, No cree, No creía, No niegan, No dudaban)
2. **Dudábamos** que él viniera al día siguiente.
   (Creíamos, No creíamos, ¿Era posible...?, ¿Cree Ud....?)
3. **En caso de que** llame, no le diga nada.
   (A menos que, Aunque, Dado que, A pesar de que)
4. No **os** dará nada a menos que se lo **pidáis.**
   (te, le, les, nos)
5. **Salió** sin que yo me enterara.
   (No podrá salir, Nunca sale, Volvió, Siempre vuelve)

B. Conteste en español:

1. ¿Cree Ud. que lloverá mucho este mes? 2. En caso de que llueva el sábado, ¿qué hará Ud.? ¿Y si hace calor? 3. ¿No cree Ud. que sus profesores son unos verdaderos genios? 4. ¿Debo creer que Ud. siempre dice la verdad? 5. ¿Puede uno sacar buenas notas a menos que estudie? 6. ¿Cree Ud. que la mayor parte de los estudiantes de esta clase sepan

más que Ud.? 7. ¿Es posible que nuestro equipo de fútbol gane todos los partidos este año? 8. Aunque no lo hable bien todavía, ¿le gusta hablar español?

C. Traduzca al español:

1. I'm not sure that you have told us everything. 2. Do you think he'll return to his family some day? 3. Ricardo wouldn't do anything without our knowing about it. 4. Of course, we don't doubt that you are capable of filling the position. 5. The thief denied that they were with him. 6. In case a woman answers, tell her that you were calling another number. 7. Even though he may get here in (**con**) time, I doubt that he'll go with us. 8. You know, I just got a wonderful grade, and without studying! Now don't you think I'm brilliant?

68. Unreality (*continued*): Indefiniteness

Indefiniteness is an integral part of the concept of unreality. These are the circumstances in which it generally appears.

A. Indefinite antecedent

1. When the subordinate clause refers back to someone or something that is uncertain, indefinite, hypothetical, or nonexistent, the subjunctive must be used.

¿Hay alguien que comprenda esto?	Is there anyone who understands this? (There may not be such a person.)
Busca un marido que sea guapo, inteligente y rico.	She is looking for a (hypothetical) husband who is handsome, intelligent, and rich.
No hay nadie que tenga todas esas cualidades.	There is nobody who has all those qualities. (The person is nonexistent.)
Lo que tú digas de aquí en adelante no me interesa nada.	What you may say from now on doesn't interest me at all. (It has not been said yet, therefore indefinite.)
Haré lo que pueda.	I shall do what I can. (Future, thus indefinite.)
El estudiante que saque la mejor nota recibirá una medalla.	The student who (whichever student) gets the best grade will receive a medal.

2. But, if the subordinate clause refers back to someone or something that is specific, definite, or existent, the indicative is used.

Hay muchas personas que comprenden esto.	There are (there do exist) many people who understand this.
Tiene un marido que es guapo, inteligente y rico.	She has a husband who is handsome, intelligent, and rich.
Lo que tú dices no me interesa nada.	What you are saying doesn't interest me at all.
Hice lo que pude.	I did what I could.

3. If the subordinate clause describes an action that occurs as a general rule, the indicative must again be used. Obviously, there is nothing indefinite about such a circumstance or object of reference.

Hago lo que puedo.	I do what I can.
Cada año el estudiante que saca la mejor nota recibe una medalla.	Each year, the student who gets the best grade receives a medal.

EJERCICIOS

A. Cambie las frases siguientes según las indicaciones:

1. No hay nadie que lo **sepa** todavía.
   (tener, decir, creer, seguir, negar)
2. Buscaba una mujer que **supiera guisar.**
   (ser rica, cantar bien, poder ayudarle, haber vivido en Lima)
3. **Hará** lo que pueda.
   (Siempre hace, Hizo, Dijo que haría)
4. **Hay** un almacén donde lo venden barato.
   (Conozco, ¿Hay...?, ¿Habrá...?, Había)

B. Conteste en español:

1. ¿Hay una materia que le interese más que las otras? ¿Cuál es? 2. ¿Tiene Ud. un amigo que haya vivido en el extranjero? 3. ¿Se casaría Ud. con una persona que no tuviera mucha educación? 4. ¿Hay un almacén por aquí donde vendan máquinas de escribir? 5. ¿Ha visto Ud. alguna vez una obra de arte que considere perfecta?

C. Traduzca al español:

1. Can you find me a book that has all the answers to his questions? 2. Look, Pete. I have just found a book that has what you wanted. 3. Do you know a store where I can buy rare stamps? 4. Give me ten men who are stout-hearted men. 5. There is nobody, but nobody who sells more cheap(ly) than we. And in case there is somebody, he will be bankrupt soon. I even doubt that *we* are solvent! 6. Would you like to talk to someone who has already taken that trip?

B. Indefinite or incompleted future action

1. The subjunctive is used after conjunctions of time if the action has not yet been completed at the time of the main clause action. Conjunctions of time include **cuando** (when), **así que, tan pronto como, en cuanto** (as soon as), **hasta que** (until), **después de que** (after), etc. Clearly, an action that still has not (or had not) transpired must as yet be nonexistent, and therefore, indefinite or uncertain of conclusion.

Juanito saldrá para Europa así que reciba el dinero.	Johnny will leave for Europe as soon as he receives the money.
Esperemos hasta que vengan.	Let's wait until they come.
Su madre prometió ayudarle hasta que consiguiera un empleo.	His mother promised to help him until he got a job. (At that time, he had not yet gotten a job.)

2. If there is no suggestion of an uncompleted future action, the conjunction of time will be followed by the indicative.

Esperamos hasta que vinieron.	We waited until they came.
Así que vio al policía echó a correr.	As soon as he saw the policeman, he began to run.
Siempre que lo veo, me enamoro de nuevo.	Whenever I see him, I fall in love again.

3. **Antes de que** (before) by its very meaning always indicates that the subordinate clause action had not yet happened at the time of the main clause. Therefore, **antes de que** will always be followed by the subjunctive.

Vámonos antes de que nos vean.	Let's leave before they see us.
Se acercó al rey antes de que pudieran detenerle.	He approached the king before they could stop him.

EJERCICIOS

A. Substituya el infinitivo por la forma apropiada:

1. Cuando (**sentirse**) mejor ella, nos hará una visita. 2. Me dijo que esperaría hasta que yo (**volver**). 3. Antes de que (**empezar**) la función, tomaremos una copa. 4. En cuanto (**venir**) ellos, les pediré el dinero. 5. Así que (**verme**) Juan, salío de la habitación. 6. En cuanto (**llamar**) los demás, les diré que te (**ayudar**).

B. Conteste en español:

1. ¿Qué piensa Ud. hacer cuando se gradúe de la universidad? 2. ¿Qué tiene Ud. que hacer cuando vuelva a casa hoy? 3. ¿Qué hace Ud. primero cuando se levanta por la mañana? 4. ¿Piensa Ud. irse de vacaciones así que termine el semestre? 5. ¿Qué hará Ud. antes de que empiecen los exámenes finales? 6. ¿Qué ropa usamos cuando llueve? ¿Y cuando nieva?

EJERCICIO DE REPASO

1. The people who seem old to you now will not seem so old to you when you reach their age.
2. He didn't think there was a woman who could surpass her.
3. Even if his parents give him good advice, the young lover (**enamorado**) will hate them.
4. Before he finishes, you'll realize that he was right.
5. I hope they won't outsmart themselves and be sorry for the rest of their lives.
6. I didn't want him to do it because I doubted that the experience would help him.
7. They will never achieve it unless you understand them and stimulate them with your advice.
8. He was laughing at them all without anybody's being aware of it (**enterarse**).
9. If only their experiences serve them for the future, when they have to teach the younger generations!
10. She'll keep evoking the past until she learns how to live in the present.

REPASO DE VERBOS

Estudie los verbos **ir** y **venir** y después diga en español:

I'm coming. He came. She went. I hope they come. Go! (**Uds.**) They won't come. He told us to go. Aren't you coming? (**tú, vosotros**)

LECCIÓN NOVENA

THE SUBJUNCTIVE (CONTINUED)

Adaptado de

EL TIEMPO

Bogotá, 6 de septiembre de 1963

¿Por Qué Está Usted Soltero?

[Tomamos de la revista *Mujer* la siguiente encuesta "apta para solteros únicamente". He aquí algunas de las respuestas.]

Un hombre de negocios nos contestó: "Estoy soltero porque he tenido muchas decepciones amorosas y siempre dudo de las mujeres por esa razón. Es muy posible que el matrimonio sea esencial en la vida, porque uno se va sintiendo solo; pero es difícil dar el paso, y más para los que pasamos de los treinta años. Lógicamente, si fuera el matrimonio el estado ideal, habría más personas que lo dijesen".

Un ingeniero nos respondió lacónicamente: "Señorita, si la hubiera visto a Ud. antes, lo habría pensado".

Una representante por el departamento de Antioquia dijo: "Si hubiese encontrado el hombre a quien le faltase la costilla de la cual estoy hecha, me habría casado. En mi concepto, el estado ideal es el opuesto al que uno esté viviendo actualmente. Así, si yo estuviese casada, sería la soltería, y estando soltera es el matrimonio".

Otra señorita nos respondió así: "No me casé por dos razones: la primera porque ambicioné hacerlo con un hombre superior y a ninguno de ellos le interesó hacerme su esposa; la segunda porque no tuve tiempo. Tal vez si no hubiera tenido que cuidar de mis hermanos menores después de la muerte de mi padre, ya me habría casado. En mi opinión, el estado ideal es el de viuda rica. Una tendrá la alegría de los hijos y el recuerdo de un marido que si fue bueno, se bendecirá. Si fue malo, tendrá la satisfacción de haberlo perdido. En efecto, la soltería tiene la grandísima ventaja de que nadie depende de uno, ni uno de nadie".

Una doctora, magistrada del Tribunal Superior, dijo: "Para una mujer que escoge una carrera liberal como es el derecho, es difícil conseguir el hombre que llene todos los requisitos que una quisiera. Porque si hay un hombre que haya desempeñado puestos importantes, no le gusta que su prometida sea tan ilustrada e importante como él. Parece que los hombres piensan que no es fácil que una intelectual sea una buena esposa. Sin embargo, para que un matrimonio sea feliz, conviene que la mujer haya alcanzado cierto nivel de educación. En síntesis, yo creo que he sido muy exigente y no he conseguido el hombre que reúna todas las condiciones intelectuales, económicas y morales que deseo".

PREGUNTAS

1. ¿Qué razón ofrece el hombre de negocios por no haberse casado?
2. ¿Por qué no cree que el matrimonio sea el estado ideal?
3. ¿Qué contestó el ingeniero?
4. ¿En qué circunstancias se habría casado la representante de Antioquia?
5. ¿Por qué razones no se casó la otra señorita?
6. Según el concepto de ella, ¿cuál es el estado ideal? ¿Por qué?
7. ¿Qué ventaja encuentra ella a la soltería?
8. ¿Qué es difícil para la mujer que escoge una carrera liberal?
9. ¿Qué no le gusta al hombre que haya desempeñado puestos importantes?
10. ¿Qué piensan los hombres sobre las mujeres intelectuales?

CONVERSACIÓN

1. ¿Piensa Ud. casarse algún día? ¿Ha pensado Ud. alguna vez en la posibilidad de quedarse soltero (o soltera)? ¿Le da miedo? ¿Por qué? En su opinión, ¿cuál es el estado ideal?
2. De todas las personas entrevistadas arriba, ¿quién le gusta más? ¿Quién le gusta menos? ¿Quién le parece más interesante? ¿Y menos interesante?
3. ¿Es verdad que a los hombres no les gusten las mujeres intelectuales? ¿Se casaría Ud. con una mujer (u hombre) que tuviera menos educación que Ud.? ¿Se casaría con una mujer (u hombre) que tuviera mucha más educación que Ud.? ¿Puede durar el amor si la pareja no tiene muchos intereses comunes?

PART A

69. Unreality (*continued*): Condition Contrary to Fact

A condition contrary to fact is a most obvious case of unreality.

A. Exactly as in English, when a clause introduced by *if* makes a supposition that is contrary to fact (*if I had known*, but I didn't, etc.), a past subjunctive must be employed. The imperfect subjunctive is used for a simple tense; the pluperfect subjunctive, for a compound tense.

Si estuviera[1] **aquí mi hermano, nos dejarían entrar.**	If my brother were here (but he isn't), they would let us in.
Si yo hubiera[1] **sabido que venía Ud., habría hecho una torta.**	If I had known (but I didn't know) you were coming, I would have baked a cake.
Gasta dinero como si tuviese una mina de oro.	She spends money as if she owned a gold mine (but she doesn't).

The contrary-to-fact construction may be used with a future action to indicate that it is considered unlikely.

Si me ofreciera un millón de dólares, no lo aceptaría.	If he were to offer me a million dollars, I wouldn't accept it.
Si hiciera mal tiempo mañana, no iríamos.	If it should rain tomorrow, we wouldn't go.
Si te lo pidiera, ¿le prestarías tu coche?	If he were to ask you, would you lend him your car?

B. Under no other circumstances will the subjunctive ever be used after the word **si.**[2]

Si vienes, las verás.	If you come, you will see them.
Si estuvo allí, no se aprovechó de ello.	If he was there (assuming that he was), he did not profit by it.

C. Note particularly that the present subjunctive is NEVER used after the word **si.** Note also that when **si** means *whether*, the indicative must be used.

No sé si llegan hoy o mañana.	I don't know whether (if) they are arriving today or tomorrow.

[1] The **-ra** and **-se** forms of the imperfect and pluperfect subjunctive are interchangeable except in three instances (cf. 72 C, D, and E). The **-ra** form is more common than the **-se** in Spanish America.

[2] **Si**, followed by the present tense, has the meaning *assuming that*, and therefore is not considered in Spanish as a conjunction of uncertainty.

EJERCICIOS

A. Cambie las frases siguientes para indicar una condición contraria al hecho:

1. Si lo sé a tiempo, no lo haré. 2. Si está enfermo, me avisará. 3. Si llueve mañana, no saldremos a la calle. 4. Si nos escribe antes de venir, le esperaremos. 5. Si hace buen tiempo, daremos una vuelta en coche. 6. Si te lo han ofrecido ya, no hay que insistir. 7. Si soy rica, compraré esta casa algún día. 8. Si caben tantas personas en el autobús, iremos todos juntos. 9. Si ensucias la casa, te castigará. 10. Si no nos cuesta nada, nos quedaremos.

B. Conteste en español:

1. ¿Qué haría Ud. si se hiciera rico de la noche a la mañana? 2. ¿Qué pensaría Ud. si su mejor amigo se negase a hacerle un favor? 3. ¿Qué habría ocurrido si los españoles hubiesen descubierto y conquistado Norteamérica en vez de Centro y Sudamérica? 4. ¿Qué habría hecho Ud. si no hubiera tenido dinero para continuar sus estudios? 5. ¿Qué pasaría si hubiera una guerra atómica?

C. Diga en español:

1. If you smoke too much, you'll get sick. 2. If I had the money, I would buy a new car. 3. He talks as if he knew it all. 4. Did they tell you whether they had seen him? 5. If we had gone with them, this wouldn't have happened. 6. If they should arrive early, what would we do? 7. If I said it, I'm sorry. 8. If he was sick, why didn't he tell us?

70. Purpose

Conjunctions indicating purpose are followed by the subjunctive. The idea of purpose is related both to the implied command (one's will that something be done) and to indefinite future (at the time of the main clause action, the goal for which it was performed could not possibly have been fulfilled).

A. **Para que** (in order that, so that) is always followed by the subjunctive, because by its very meaning it always states purpose.

Ahorra su dinero para que sus hijos puedan asistir a la universidad.	He is saving his money so that his children may go to college.
Se lo explicaré en pocas palabras para que no se confundan Uds.	I shall explain it to you in few words so that you won't be confused.

B. If there is no change of subject, there is no need for two clauses. The idea is then summed up in one clause, with the preposition **para** followed by the infinitive.

Ahorra su dinero para poder asistir a la universidad.	He is saving his money in order to be able to go to college.
Se lo explicó en pocas palabras para no confundirlos.	He explained it to them in few words in order not to confuse them.

C. **De modo que** and **de manera que** (so that) will be followed by the subjunctive when they imply purpose, and by the indicative when they denote result.

Levántelo de modo que (de manera que, para que) lo vean todos.	Lift it up so that everyone can see it.

But:

Llovió ayer, de modo que suspendieron el partido.	It rained yesterday, so (that) the game was called off.

EJERCICIOS

A. Cambie según las indicaciones:

1. Lo estoy haciendo ahora **para** no tener que trabajar después. (para que Julia, para que mis hijos, para que tú y Ana)
2. Nos lo dijo **para que** estuviéramos preparados. (de modo que, de manera que nuestros alumnos)
3. Se lo mandaré **para** estar seguro. (para que Ud., para que tú, para que Uds., para que todos)

B. Traduzca al español:

1. It was very sunny, so (that) we could see the mountains in the distance. 2. They stopped (in order) to rest a little. 3. They stopped so that the children could rest. 4. I must iron my dress so that it will be ready for tomorrow.

71. Impersonal Expressions with Subjunctive or Indicative

A. Impersonal expressions that contain subjunctive ideas will be followed by the subjunctive. Most impersonal expressions fall into these categories.

Indirect or Implied Command

Conviene	**que venga.**	It is advisable	that he come.
Es preferible		It is preferable	
Es mejor, más vale		It is better	
Urge		It is urgent	
Importa,[3] **es importante**		It is important	
Es necesario		It is necessary	

[3] **¿Importa...?** also is used with the meaning *Do you mind . . . ?* Since the implication of command still obtains, it is followed by subjunctive. **¿Le importa que abra la ventana?** Do you mind if I open the window?

Emotion

Es lástima	**que hayan ido.**	It is a pity	that they have gone.
Es de esperar		It is to be hoped	
¡Ojalá!		Would (if only)	
Es lamentable		It is regrettable	
Es sorprendente		It is surprising	

Unreality: Doubt,
Uncertainty, Indefiniteness, etc.

Es (im)probable	**que nos conozca.**	It is (im)probable	that he knows us.
Es fácil		It is likely	
Es difícil		It is unlikely	
Es (im)posible		It is (im)possible	
Parece mentira, es increíble		It is incredible	
Es dudoso		It is doubtful	
Puede ser		It may be	

B. When an impersonal expression indicates a certainty, it is followed by the indicative.

Claro está	**que lo sabe.**	It is clear	that he knows it.
Es verdad		It is true	
Es evidente		It is evident	
No cabe duda de		There is no doubt	

C. Note that an impersonal expression does not call for the subjunctive because it is impersonal but because it may represent a concept that produces the subjunctive. Thus, as in the case of **creer,** the attitude of certainty or doubt, of belief or disbelief in the speaker's mind will determine the use of indicative or subjunctive.

¿Es cierto que ha ganado? (I think so, or I have no opinion.)	Is it true that he has won?
¿Es cierto que haya ganado? (I doubt it.)	

D. When the sentence is completely impersonal, the infinitive is used. Note that there is no change of subject.

Es necesario hacerlo.	It is necessary to do it.
Es imposible estudiar aquí.	It is impossible to study here.

EJERCICIOS

A. Cambie:

1. Nos visitarán mañana.
   (Es posible que, Es mejor, Ojalá, Es difícil, Es verdad)
2. Tenían razón.
   (Era imposible que, Claro está, Puede ser, Parecía mentira)
3. Eso no se repetirá.
   (Es evidente que, Conviene, Importa mucho, Es dudoso, Ojalá)
4. Valía más de lo que pagamos.
   (Era probable que, Es de esperar, No cabía duda de)

B. Conteste en español:

1. ¿Es probable que haga mucho frío este mes? 2. ¿Importa que terminemos esta lección hoy? 3. ¿Es posible que haya muchos estudiantes extranjeros en esta escuela? 4. ¿Es necesario practicar mucho para tocar un instrumento musical? 5. ¿Es cierto que es Ud. un famoso millonario? 6. ¿No será mejor que acabemos este ejercicio ahora?

EJERCICIO DE REPASO

1. Sometimes I doubt that marriage is essential in life. —What!
2. If they had married later, they would have been happier.
3. It is possible that he'll take the step when he finds himself alone some day.
4. If bachelorhood were the ideal state, there would be more people who would say so.
5. If I were married, I wouldn't stop (**dejar de**) working, but I would work less than now.
6. He told me that it was impossible for an intellectual to be a good wife.
7. It will be very difficult for her to find a man who meets her conditions.
8. If you find a woman who is willing to marry you, you may consider yourself lucky. —Thanks a lot!
9. I promised to do what I could so that he might be happy.
10. It would be preferable that he reached a certain level of education before accepting that position.

REPASO DE VERBOS

Repase los verbos **tener** y **hacer** y después diga en español:

I have it. Have you done it? I hope they have them. We want you (**tú**) to do it. He wanted us to do it. She wouldn't have done that. Did you (**Uds.**) do this? Why didn't you (**vosotros**) have it ready? Do me a favor. Don't do it that way. Have patience (**tú**). Do it yourself (**tú mismo**).

PART B

72. Subjunctive in Principal Clauses

Aside from the appearance of subjunctive forms in polite and negative direct commands, there are several other instances of subjunctive usage in principal clauses.

A. Indirect commands

In certain common expressions and constructions, the indirect command is not preceded by **que** and apparently stands by itself in a main clause. Actually, this main clause is really a pseudo-main clause, and another main clause of volition or emotion is implied.

Dios le bendiga.	May God bless you.
¡Viva el Rey!	Long live the King!

B. Subjunctive after certain expressions of emotion and doubt

1. **Ojalá** (would that, if only, how I wish) is regularly followed by the subjunctive.

¡Ojalá se lo hubiera advertido!	If only I had warned him!

2. **Tal vez, quizá**(**s**)—perhaps—are followed either by the subjunctive or the indicative, according to the degree of doubt or certainty the speaker indicates.[4]

Quizá(s) **venga mañana.**	Perhaps he will come tomorrow (but I doubt it).
Quizá(s) **viene** (or **vendrá**) **mañana.**	Perhaps he will come tomorrow (I think he will).

C. Softened assertion

The **-ra** form of the imperfect subjunctive is used, mostly with the verbs **querer, deber,** and **poder,** to impart a milder, more polite tone to the statement.

Quisiera saber...	I should like to know . . .
Ud. debiera seguir su consejo.	You (really) should follow his advice.

D. Subjunctive in the result clause of contrary-to-fact sentences

Both in oral and written Spanish, the **-ra** form of the pluperfect subjunctive frequently replaces the conditional perfect in the result clause.

[4] **A lo mejor,** which is very common for *perhaps* in Spain, regularly takes the indicative. **A lo mejor nos lo dice hoy,** maybe he'll tell us today.

Si lo hubiese[5] sabido, lo hubiera hecho.	If he had known, he would have done it.

E. Subjunctive for the pluperfect indicative

In literary Spanish, the **-ra** form of the imperfect subjunctive at times replaces the pluperfect indicative. This is not a true subjunctive usage, however, since in this case, the **-ra** form merely points back to the Latin pluperfect indicative, from which it stems: **amaveram** (Latin pluperfect) > **amara.**

Perdonó al hombre que lo delatara a la policía.	He forgave the man who had denounced him to the police.

73. Indicative after **esperar** and **temer**

When **esperar** means *expect* and **temer** means *think*, these verbs lose much of their normal implication of emotion (hope—fear) and, under such circumstances, are followed by the indicative.

Espero que venga.	I hope (emotion) that he will come.
Espero que vendrá.	I expect (belief) that he will come.
Temo que esté enferma.	I'm afraid (worried) that she is sick.
Me temo que va a llover.	I'm afraid (I think—little emotion) that it is going to rain.

74. Unreality

Aside from the obvious cases of denial (*he denied that . . .*, etc.), there are many subtle instances in which the idea of the main clause, or the conjunction that introduces the subordinate clause, casts a cloak of unreality on the action of the subordinate clause.

A. Negative statements that deny the following assertion produce a subjunctive in the subordinate clause: **No quiero decir que...** *I don't mean that . . .*; **No es que...** *It isn't that . . .*, etc.

Eso no quiere decir que fuera culpable.	That doesn't mean that he was guilty.
No es que me guste verte sufrir, sino que no puedo ayudarte.	It isn't that I like to see you suffer, but that I can't help you.

B. Clauses introduced by **porque** (because) take the indicative if they make a positive assertion, the subjunctive if they deny or negate the reality of an assumption.

[5] When the **-ra** form of the subjunctive replaces the conditional in the result clause, the **-se** form is often preferred in the *if* clause.

No alabé su trabajo porque fuera original, sino porque lo había hecho con cuidado.	I praised his work not because it was original, but because he had done it carefully.

But:

Alabé su trabajo porque era muy original.	I praised his work because it was very original.

75. Indefinite Degree or Amount

A. **Por** + an adjective or adverb + **que...** means *no matter* or *regardless of how much* (*little*, *smart*, etc.). When it is followed by the subjunctive, it conveys the idea of an indefinite amount or degree.

Por lista que sea, no lo podrá engañar.	No matter how smart she is, she won't fool him.
Por mucho que ahorre, no tendrá para comprar aquella casa.	Now matter how much he may save, he won't have enough to buy that house.

B. If the degree or amount is definite, the indicative is used.

Por mucho que se esforzaba, no tenía bastante talento para ser grande.	No matter how much he tried, he did not have enough talent to be great.

76. Subjunctive after **el que, el hecho de que, que**

A. When a subordinate clause that begins with **el que, el hecho de que,** or **que** (the fact that,[6] the assumption or situation that) precedes the main clause, the subjunctive is generally used. Since the speaker begins the sentence without the element of certainty furnished by the principal clause on which it depends, he momentarily adopts an attitude of doubt.

El que estuviera con ellos esa noche indica que era cómplice suyo.	The fact that he was with them that night indicates that he was an accomplice of theirs.
El que te traicione Pablo es increíble.	The assumption (or possibility) that Paul will betray you is incredible.

[6] The English expression *the fact that* is frequently misleading, since this often refers to situations that are not actually factual (The fact that he may be rich . . .. The fact that they might have been there . . .). The insinuation of possible doubt implicit in this expression is heightened in Spanish, thus explaining the frequency of subjunctive usage in such cases.

B. **El hecho de que** and **el que** may be followed by the subjunctive even when the main clause precedes, since the Spanish construction often implies a suggestion of doubt.

Le ha ayudado más que nada el (hecho de) que asistiera a una buena escuela.	The fact that he attended (or may have attended) a good school has helped him more than anything else.

77. Infinitive vs. Subjunctive

A. Normally, when there is no change of subject, the prepositions **para, sin, antes de, después de, hasta, a menos de, con tal de,** and other such prepositions of purpose, time, and uncertainty, are used with the infinitive.

No saldré a menos de tenerlo.	I shall not go out unless I have it.
Es capaz de todo con tal de conseguirlo.	He is capable of anything provided he gets it.
Siga Ud. caminando hasta llegar al pueblo.	Keep walking until you reach the town.

B. Normally, when there is a change of subject, the equivalent conjunctions **para que, sin que, antes (de) que, a menos que, con tal que,** etc., are followed by a clause containing the subjunctive, and **después de que, hasta que,** etc., by a clause containing either indicative or subjunctive, depending upon their meaning in the sentence.

C. The following usages are alternates to the rule.

1. Use of conjunction + subordinate clause when there is no change of subject:

A menos que, con tal que, and **hasta que** may be used with a following clause even if there is no change of subject. The sentence acquires thereby a somewhat more emphatic or more graphic descriptive tone.[7]

No lo permitirá a menos que haya cambiado de parecer.	He will not permit it, unless he has changed his mind.
Siga Ud. caminando hasta que llegue al pueblo.	Keep walking until you reach the town.
Lo haré, con tal que reciba primero el dinero.	I will do it, provided I receive the money first.

[7] Remember that the prepositions **para**, **sin**, and **antes de** + the infinitive may not be substituted by a clausal construction when there is no change of subject.

2. Use of preposition and infinitive when there is a change of subject:

Even where there is a change of subject, the prepositions **sin, a menos de, con tal de, antes de,** and **después de** + the infinitive often take the place of the conjunction + clause construction. However, in such cases, the subject must follow the infinitive.

Llegaron todos los huéspedes antes de ponerse el sol.	All the guests arrived before the sun set.
Entraron en la casa sin oírlos nadie.	They entered the house without anybody's hearing them.

D. The infinitive may be used after certain impersonal expressions even when another personal subject is implied or stated. The infinitive construction makes an objective or factual statement. The subjunctive, which is more emphatic and subjective, expresses the speaker's opinion of the action.

Le es imposible hacerlo.	It is impossible for him to do it.
Es imposible que él lo haga.	It is impossible that he will do it.
Nos importa verlos en seguida.	It is important for us to see them at once.
Importa que los veamos en seguida.	It is important that we see them at once.

E. **De** + an infinitive may be used in place of a contrary to fact *if* clause.

De no haberla perdido, no tendría que comprarme otra ahora.	If I hadn't lost it, I wouldn't have to buy myself another one now.

EJERCICIOS

I. Tradúzcase al español.

A. May God protect them! I begged them to pay attention to the natives and not to go into the interior without the most thorough preparation, but they ignored me and set out for the unknown territory with only two guides, ten mules, and provisions for two weeks. Anyone who knows this region knows that this is insufficient. I hope they find what they are looking for and that none of my fears will be realized.

B. The two children, walking on tiptoe so that nobody should hear them, took the money from the chest and went downstairs. They left the house without anybody's seeing them, crossed the fields, and were (**se hallaron**) soon on the road. They decided to run toward the town, because, provided that they could catch the train, they would be out of the reach of their parents within an hour. It would take them half an hour to reach the town, and they were sure that their parents would not catch up with them unless they had already awakened and were following them. It was possible, of course, that there would be no train, because of the heavy snow which had been falling for a week (**estaba cayendo desde hacía una semana**) and which created an impassable obstacle on many sections of the track. If this should happen they would have to hide at an old abandoned farm until the trains resumed service.

II. Composicíon.

1. Lo que pasó en el interior
2. Por qué los niños quieren huir de casa y lo que les ocurrió

LECCIÓN DÉCIMA

SER AND ESTAR

Adaptado de

EXCELSIOR

México, D.F., 15 de noviembre de 1963

El Milagro del Doctor Verdoux

Eran las siete y cuarto de la tarde. El doctor había terminado su servicio y deseaba regresar a París a buena hora. En dos ocasiones intentó llamar por teléfono a un amigo para indicarle que visitaría a su hijo enfermo al día siguiente. Pero la línea estaba ocupada. Esos pocos minutos perdidos en los intentos para telefonear al amigo iban a convertir al Dr. Verdoux en el hombre del milagro quirúrgico del año.

Después del segundo intento de llamar por teléfono a su amigo, el Dr. Verdoux se dirigió a su coche, que estaba estacionado a la puerta de la clínica. En el momento de subir al vehículo, oyó sonar el teléfono. Dio media vuelta, en tanto que la enfermera contestaba a la llamada. En el otro extremo del hilo informaban de un accidente. Un marinero se había seccionado la pierna izquierda a la altura del muslo y se desangraba rápidamente.

Diez minutos después, una ambulancia llegaba al lugar del accidente. El marinero, Boudic, quien estaba a punto de perder el conocimiento, tuvo aún fuerzas para indicar al ambulante que su pierna izquierda estaba a tres metros del lugar donde él yacía. El ambulante envolvió la pierna en una frazada para llevarla, junto con el hombre, a la clínica del Dr. Verdoux en Poissy. Cuando llegó la ambulancia, lo primero que preguntó el Dr. Verdoux fue: "¿La pierna? ¿Dónde está la pierna?" En esos mismos momentos la secretaria de la clínica, presa de honda emoción, anunciaba: "Doctor, a la entrada hay un envoltorio con una pierna. ¿Qué hago con él?" En esos instantes, el Dr. Verdoux no sabía aún qué hacer.

Christian Verdoux es un cirujano de cuarenta y tres años de edad. Un hombre sereno, padre de cuatro hijos, es de la parte meridional de Francia. Su señora, que es ginecóloga, trabaja en la misma clínica que él. El Dr. Verdoux no es especialista en injertos en el cuerpo humano, y por eso, podría haberse limitado a contener la hemorragia y a suturar la herida del marinero, quien estaba tendido ya en la mesa de operaciones.

Eran exactamente las ocho menos siete cuando comenzó la operación, la que iba a prolongarse cerca de nueve horas. En muchas ocasiones el Dr. Verdoux se quitó los guantes para poder coser mejor los nervios más delgados. Dos veces mandó traer sangre al centro de Versalles. Fue necesario aplicar en transfusiones tres litros de sangre al herido para sustituir la que había perdido. Durante ocho horas la pierna injertada al marinero estuvo en peligro. Sin embargo, ese peligro fue vencido y el herido entró en franca convalecencia.

El Dr. Verdoux está seguro de que Boudic podrá caminar en un plazo de cinco a seis meses y está igualmente convencido de que la operación puede repetirse. Un hombre modesto, apenas puede creer que se califique de extraordinaria la operación que realizó en el marinero. Pero sí, la operación le ha traído una satisfacción complementaria e inesperada: su hija mayor, impresionada por la hazaña de su padre, ha decidido estudiar la medicina.

PREGUNTAS

1. ¿Por qué quiso el Dr. Verdoux telefonear a su amigo?
2. ¿Qué hizo después del segundo intento de llamar?
3. ¿Qué oyó en el momento de subir al coche?
4. ¿De qué accidente le informaban?
5. ¿Dónde estaba la pierna del marinero cuando llegó la ambulancia?
6. ¿Qué hizo con ella el ambulante?
7. ¿Cómo es el Dr. Verdoux y de dónde es?
8. ¿A qué hora comenzó la operación y cuántas horas se prolongó?
9. ¿De qué está seguro ahora el Dr. Verdoux?
10. ¿Qué otra satisfacción inesperada le ha traído la operación?

CONVERSACIÓN

1. ¿Le interesa a Ud. la medicina? ¿Le gustaría ser médico o enfermera? ¿Por qué?

2. ¿Cuál considera Ud. el descubrimiento médico más impresionante de nuestra época? ¿Y de todas las épocas?
3. ¿Cree Ud. que un médico debe cobrar más a sus pacientes ricos que a los pobres? ¿Qué le parece a Ud. la medicina socializada? ¿Cree Ud. que un médico tiene el derecho de negarse a visitar a un paciente muy enfermo si el paciente no puede pagar? En su opinión, ¿tienen los médicos el derecho de declararse en huelga, como hicieron los de Bélgica hace poco?
4. ¿Le gustaría a Ud. seguir la misma carrera o profesión que su padre?

PART A

78. General View of **ser** and **estar**

Ser and **estar** both mean *to be*. However, these two verbs are widely different in their concepts, and they can never be interchanged without a basic change of meaning. In most cases, they cannot be interchanged at all.

In general, **ser** tells *who* the subject is or *what* it is in its essence. **Estar** usually relates *where* or in what *condition* or *position* the subject is. The following are their principal uses.

79. **Ser** and **estar** with Adjectives

A. When the verb *to be* joins the subject with an adjective, **ser** is used to represent an essential characteristic or quality; **estar** is used to represent a state or condition or a semblance of being—what the subject looks like, seems like, feels like, tastes like, not what it actually is in essence.

Keep in mind the following nouns: **un ser** (a human being, an essence), **un estado** (a state), **los Estados Unidos** (the United States).

CHART OF THE USES OF *Ser* AND *Estar*

ser (who, what)	**estar** (where, how)
1. With Adjectives	
Characteristic, quality	State, condition, semblance of being
2. Subject = noun, pronoun	Location
3. Possession	**Estar** + present participle = progressive tense
4. Origin, material, destination	**Estar** + past participle = resultant state of an action
5. Time of day	
6. Passive voice	

Ser		Estar	
El hielo es frío.	Ice is cold.	**El café está frío.**	The coffee is cold.
El muchacho es pálido	The boy is (characteristically) pale.	**El muchacho está pálido.**	The boy is (looks, happens to be) pale.
¡Qué bonita eres!	How pretty you are!	**¡Qué bonita estás!**	How pretty you look!
Su sobrina es lista.	His niece is bright (alert).	**Su sobrina está lista.**	His niece is ready.
Mi hijo es bueno (**malo**).	My son is good (bad).	**Mi hijo está bueno** (**malo**).	My son is well—in good condition (ill—in bad condition).
¿Cómo es?	What is he like?	**¿Cómo está?**	How is he feeling?
Las uvas son verdes.	The grapes are green (their normal color).	**Las uvas están verdes.**	The grapes are green (unripe).

Important: The common notion that **ser** indicates a permanent situation and **estar** a temporary one is not entirely accurate. Of course, an essential characteristic or quality frequently is permanent, and a state or condition may often be temporary. But this is not necessarily so.

Youth is temporary. Wealth may come and go. Beauty may disappear. Size may change. Yet for the time that they last, they are sufficiently pervading to characterize a being.

Somos jóvenes.	We are young.
Era pobre.	He was poor.
Eran muy gordas.	They used to be very fat.

Conversely, a state may be fairly permanent: **Está muerto,** he is dead (the resultant *state* of the action of dying). Even the addition of the adverb *always* does not convert a state into a characteristic:

Esa ventana siempre está cerrada.	That window is always closed.

B. Age and financial position are regarded as characteristics of a person, and therefore the adjectives **joven, viejo, rico, pobre** normally take **ser.** However, when the speaker wishes to imply that the subject looks, seems, appears, feels (not is) young or old, **estar** is used.

El Sr. Colón es viejo.	Mr. Colon is old.
Cuando era joven, era muy rico.	When he was young, he was very rich.

But:

¿Ha visto Ud. al Sr. Colón? Está muy viejo.	Have you seen Mr. Colon? He looks very old.

C. **Ser** is used in almost all impersonal expressions.

Es (im)posible.	It is (im)possible.
Es evidente, importante, necesario, trágico, etc.	It is evident, important, necessary, tragic, etc.
Es de esperar.	It is to be hoped.

EJERCICIOS

A. Complete las frases siguientes usando **ser** o **estar**:

1. Ayer Luisa ______ muy guapa, ¿verdad? 2. Aunque ______ rico, nunca ______ contento. 3. ¿______ caliente el café? No, ______ algo frío. 4. Hoy el señor García tiene mala cara; ______ muy viejo. 5. Mis padres ______ jóvenes entonces. 6. ¿Qué le parece la chica? ¿______ guapa o no? 7. La sala ______ hermosa pero ______ sucia. 8. Desde que llegó a Sevilla, mi madre ______ mala. 9. Tus amiguitos no me gustan nada. ______ muy malos. 10. Su familia ______ muy pobre, su papá ______ enfermo, y por eso siempre ______ preocupado.

B. Diga en español:

1. How is the water today? —It's a little cool. 2. Wood is heavy. The Andes are high. The grass is tall. 3. What is in this trunk? It's very heavy. 4. Nothing. It's a heavy trunk. 5. Johnny was to be here too, but he's sick. 6. You must be very tired. You look pale. Are you hungry? 7. Joan, how slim you look! —I *am* slim! 8. Are you sad or are you angry with me? —No, it's that the book I'm reading is very sad.

80. Other Uses of **ser**

A. When *to be* links the subject with a noun or a pronoun

Somos entusiastas del tenis.	We are tennis fans.
No creo que sea Raúl.	I don't think it's Ralph.
¿Quién es? —Soy yo.	Who is it? —It's I.

B. To state possession

¿De quién es esa casa?	Whose house is that?
Es (la) mía.	It is mine.
Y ésta es (la) de mis suegros.	And this one is my in-laws'.

C. To indicate origin (the place from which the subject comes), material or destination

¿De dónde es? —Será de otro planeta.	Where is he from? —He must be from another planet.
Las paredes son de vidrio y el techo es de aluminio.	The walls are (made of) glass and the roof is (made of) aluminum.
El nuevo televisor es para mi cuarto.	The new television set is for my room.
Esta corbata es para Ud.	This tie is for you.

D. To express time of day

¿Qué hora es?	What time is it?
Es la una en punto.	It is exactly one o'clock.
Eran las tres y media.	It was 3:30.[1]
Serán las cinco menos cuarto.	It is probably (or about) a quarter to five.

Note that the verb is always plural, except when the hour is one o'clock.

E. To form the passive voice

Ser + past participle + **por** is used when the action of the verb is done to the subject by someone or something (cf. **139**).

Fue atropellado por un coche.	He was hit by a car.
La cosecha será destruida por la sequía.	The crop will be destroyed by the drought.

EJERCICIOS

A. Cambie:

1. Esas cajas son de **hierro.**
   (aluminio, acero, cobre, plata, oro, madera, vidrio)
2. No **es** la una y media. **Son** las dos.
   (será, era, sería)
3. Esta camisa será para ti.
   (traje, chaqueta, sombrero, zapatos, calcetines, medias)

[1] Recall that the imperfect is used to express time in the past.

B. Conteste en español:

1. ¿De dónde es su familia? 2. ¿De dónde eran sus abuelos? 3. ¿De qué es su casa? 4. ¿De qué serán los muebles de esta sala? 5. ¿De quién es la casa en que vive Ud.? 6. ¿De quién es el coche que usa Ud.? 7. ¿De qué color es su alcoba?

C. Traduzca al español:

1. Who is the lucky man? 2. This is a magnificent painting. 3. The fire was put out by the firemen. 4. Whose books are these? —They are my brother's. 5. Where is Mr. Campos from? —He is from Galicia. 6. What's that? —It's your supper, dear. 7. He was to come at half-past three. —Well, it's already 4:15. 8. According to my watch, it is twenty-five to five. 9. I thought the ring was for me, but he gave it to his wife. —He's a cad!

81. Other Uses of **estar**

A. To indicate location (where the subject *is*, not where he *came from*)

¿Dónde está tu novia?	Where is your girlfriend?
Está aquí conmigo.	She is here with me.
Sus padres están de vacaciones en Méjico.	His parents are on vacation in Mexico.

B. With the present participle, to form the progressive tense

Estar + present participle is frequently used to describe an action more graphically in its progress at a given moment[2] (cf. **179**A).

Estábamos discutiéndolo cuando entró.	We were discussing it when he came in.
El tenor está cantando ahora mismo.	The tenor is singing right now.
Ha estado trabajando todo el día.	He has been working all day.

Important: Note that **ser** is NEVER followed by a present participle.

C. With the past participle, to describe the resultant state of an action

Note that if the idea *already* can be inserted before the past participle, **estar** is normally indicated.

[2] **Estar** + present participle is not used with **ir** and **venir:**

I am going. **Voy.**

Están sentados a la mesa.	They are seated at the table.
La puerta estaba abierta.	The door was open.
El libro está bien escrito.	The book is well written.
Este teatro no estaba construido cuando salí de Lima.	This theater was not built when I left Lima.
Está muerto.	He is dead.

EJERCICIOS

A. Cambie:

1. He estado **cocinando** toda la tarde.
   (comer, trabajar, estudiar, prepararlos, discutirlo)
2. Estaban bailando cuando se apagaron las luces.
   (Las gitanas, Mi novia y yo, La artista)
3. **El niño** estaba dormido.
   (Nosotras, Todos, ¿Tú...?, ¿Vosotros...?, ¿Uds...?)
4. ¿Están **cerradas** las ventanas?
   (abrir, hacer, romper, lavar)

B. Diga en español:

1. The poet is from Soria, but he is here now. 2. He is visiting some relatives. 3. Where, oh where, can my husband's pen be? 4. I think it's lost —Don't say that. Oh, here it is. 5. Who is going to play that role? —I hope it's not Carmen. 6. The museum was closed when we arrived. 7. He'll be dead when they find him. 8. She said that she would try to be there on time.

82. *To be* in Expressions of Weather

A. Weather expressions that refer to phenomena that are *felt* (temperature, wind, etc.) use **hacer.**

Hace frío hoy. Pero mañana hará calor.	It is cold today. But tomorrow it will be warm.
Hacía mucho viento cuando salimos.	It was very windy when we went out.
Hace mucho sol.	It is (feels) very sunny.

Recall that a person's reaction to temperature requires the verb **tener.**

Tengo frío (calor).	I am cold (warm).

B. Weather expressions that refer to phenomena that are *seen* use **haber.**

Hay mucho sol.	It is very sunny. (The sun is out brightly.)
Hay luna.	The moon is out.
Hay mucho polvo (lodo) hoy.	It is very dusty (muddy) today.

EJERCICIO

Conteste en español:

1. ¿Qué tiempo hace hoy? 2. ¿Qué tiempo hizo ayer? 3. ¿En qué estaciones del año hace más calor? 4. ¿En qué estaciones hace fresco o frío? 5. ¿Dónde hace calor todo el año? 6. ¿Dónde hace mucho frío siempre? 7. ¿Qué ropa lleva Ud. cuando hace mucho frío? 8. ¿Y cuando hace calor? 9. ¿Qué comemos cuando hace calor? 10. ¿Y qué tomamos cuando hace frío?

EJERCICIO DE REPASO

1. It took him (**tardar... en**) three hours to return to Paris, and when he arrived it was 6 P.M.
2. I have been calling him for an hour, but the line is always busy.
3. He said that he would be there when he felt a little better.
4. His car was parked on the other side, so the policeman gave him a ticket.
5. The patient, who was quite (**bastante**) young, was on the verge of losing consciousness.
6. The doctor was from the south of France. He was considered the greatest specialist in this field.
7. For eight hours the grafted leg was in danger, but the danger was finally overcome.
8. This is really a miracle. You know, the leg had been entirely cut off.
9. Dr. Verdoux is now convinced that the operation can be repeated.
10. No, the doctor did not call you last night. It was I.

REPASO DE VERBOS

Estudie todos los tiempos del indicativo y subjuntivo de **ser** y **estar.**

PART B

83. The Psychology of **ser** and **estar** Used with Adjectives

A. The difference between **ser** and **estar,** when used with the same adjective, is often of a rather subtle nature, but is none the less important in its implication. In addition to the usual connotations of these verbs, **ser** may be said to indicate the normal, or objective attribute of the adjective, and **estar,** a subjective evaluation.

La sopa es rica.	The soup is rich. (It is full of rich ingredients.)
La sopa está rica.	The soup is delicious. (It tastes rich.)
Toñuelo es muy alto.	Tony is very tall. (The speaker is making an objective statement about his size.)
Toñuelo está muy alto.	Tony is very tall. (Here the speaker is describing Tony's height at a particular time, with the implication that Tony is still in the process of growing up.)
Estos zapatos son grandes.	These shoes are large.
Estos zapatos me están grandes.	These shoes are too large for me. (They may be small shoes, but my foot is smaller.)

B. Consider the difference implicit in the use of **ser** and **estar** with the various adjectives that mean *happy*.

1. **Feliz** refers to true happiness. It expresses an essential aspect of one's life rather than an emotional state. Therefore, it is most frequently used with **ser.**

Los habitantes de este pueblo son muy felices.	The inhabitants of this town are very happy.
¿Quién es verdaderamente feliz?	Who is really happy?

Estar feliz is synonymous with **estar contento.**

2. **Alegre** means *gay, joyful.* **Ser alegre** means *to be jovial, to be of a gay disposition.*

Ese Pablo es muy alegre, pero creo que no es feliz.	That Paul is a jovial fellow, but I think he isn't happy.

Estar alegre means *to be in a gay mood.*

Todos estuvimos muy alegres esa noche.	We all were very gay that night.

3. **Contento** means *pleased, satisfied,* and is used with **estar.**

No estoy nada contenta de su actitud.	I am not at all pleased with his attitude.

4. **Contentadizo** means *easily pleased.* Since it generally describes a person's characteristic disposition, it usually takes **ser.** The negative **descontentadizo** (malcontent, hard to please) is very frequent, and of course, follows the normal principle of usage.

No te quejes tanto. Eres muy descontentadizo.	Don't complain so much. You are very hard to please (a malcontent).

But:

¿Qué pasa hoy? Estás muy descontentadizo.	What's the matter today? You seem very grouchy.

C. The adjective **loco** (crazy) is more commonly used with **estar,** since it is viewed as expressing a state of mind rather than an inherent characteristic.

Está loco; no sabe lo que dice.	He's mad; he doesn't know what he is saying.

When **loco** is used with **ser,** it means *a madman.*

Lo han llevado al manicomio, porque es loco.	They have taken him to the asylum, because he is mad (a madman).

D. A few past principles may be use adjectivally with either **ser** or **estar.** Even though the English translation is the same, there is an implicit difference in meaning.

Estamos casados.	We are married. (This is our status.)
Somos casados.	We are married (people). We are man and wife.

84. Other Uses of **ser**

A. **Ser** is used when *to be* means *to take place.*

¿Dónde es la conferencia?	Where is the lecture? (Where does the lecture take place?)
¿Cuándo es el concierto?	When is the concert?
La escena es en Madrid.	The scene is in Madrid.

B. **Ser** and location

Occasionally, **ser** is used in sentences involving location when the place or site is really the implied predicate noun.

Aquí es donde vivo.	Here is (the place) where I live.
Nuestra casa es en Barcelona.	Our home is (in) Barcelona. (Barcelona is the site of our home.)

C. **Ser** is frequently found with the past participle **nacido** (born) in colloquial speech, particularly Spanish America.

Soy nacido en Panamá.	I was born in Panama. (I am a native of Panama.)

Nací en Panamá is more correct grammatically.

85. Other Uses of **estar**

A. To indicate the fit of clothing

Estos zapatos me están muy grandes.	These shoes are (too) big for me.
El abrigo te está muy ajustado.	The overcoat is too tight for you.

Notice the subjective evaluation implicit in this usage.

B. To express one's stand on an issue

Estoy contra la pena de muerte.	I am against capital punishment.
Están por ir.	They are for (in favor of) going.

C. **Estar para** means *to be about to.*

Estábamos para salir cuando llamaron.	We were about to leave when they called.

86. **Quedar** as a Substitute for **estar**

A. To describe the resultant state of an action

Quedar, which means *to remain,* lends a somewhat more graphic force to the resultant state.

Quedé muy sorprendido al oírlo.	I was very surprised to hear it.
El pobre quedó como aplastado.	The poor fellow was quite dismayed.

A consecuencia del combate, quedaron[3] heridos dos policías.	As a result of the fight, two policemen were wounded.
Ud. queda encargado del proyecto.	You are in charge of the project.

B. To indicate the fit or appearance of clothing

Me queda un poco grande la falda.	The skirt is a little big on me.
Le queda bien ese traje.	That suit looks good on you.

C. To denote location

¿Dónde queda la estación?	Where is the station?

87. Changes of Meaning with **ser** and **estar**

Aside from the difference of implication that always exists when the same adjective is used with **ser** or **estar,** there is very often an essential difference in translation as well. (Recall **bueno, malo, listo, verde** as illustrated in **79.**) The following are other important adjectives that also show marked differences in translation when used with **ser** or **estar.**

A. **Estar enfermo** means *to be sick.* **Ser enfermo** or **enfermizo** means *to be an invalid* or *to be sickly.*

El pobre Ramón siempre está enfermo. —Sí, es algo enfermizo.	Poor Raymond is always sick. —Yes, he is rather sickly.

B. **Estar cansado** means *to be tired.* **Ser cansado** means *to be tiresome.*

¡Qué cansada estoy!	How tired I am!
¡Qué cansado es ese profesor!	How tiresome that professor is!

C. **Estar aburrido** means *to be bored.* **Ser aburrido** means *to be boring.*

¿Está aburrido? —Hasta más no poder. El libro es muy aburrido.	Are you bored? —Terribly. The book is very boring.

D. **Estar seguro** means *to be certain, sure, positive* (one's state of mind), or *to be safe* (out of danger).

[3] In Spanish newspaper and radio reporting, **resultar** is most often used to describe the result of an accident: **En el accidente resultaron heridas tres personas.** Three people were injured in the accident.

Estoy seguro de que me vio.	I am sure that he saw me.
No te preocupes. Tu hijo está seguro.	Don't worry your son is safe.

Ser seguro means *to be a certainty* or *to be safe* (not dangerous), *trustworthy*, *reliable*, *accurate* (as an object, a method, etc.).

Eso es absolutamente seguro.	That is absolutely certain (an absolute certainty).
No te preocupes. La máquina es segura.	Don't worry. The machine is safe.

88. Other Translations of *to be*

A. **Hallarse** and **encontrarse** frequently are used with the meaning *to be* (*in a certain place or situation*). By their very meaning, they place a subtle emphasis on the temporary, chance, or unexpected nature of the situation. Although the two verbs are synonymous, **hallarse** is more frequent in current usage.

Se hallaban entonces en Buenos Aires.	They were (happened to be) in Buenos Aires at that time.
A veces, me hallo sin palabras.	At times, I am (find myself) at a loss for words.

B. **Verse** means *to be in a certain position* or *situation.* It stresses the person's awareness of his situation or his conviction about a course of action.

Me veo obligado a decirles...	I am obliged to tell you . . .

EJERCICIOS

I. Tradúzcase al español.

Spain is a country of many geographical regions. Its surface is furrowed by many rivers. One could (**pudiera**) almost say that it is many countries in one. The Castilian plateau, which is situated in the center of Spain, is high and arid; its soil is often of a reddish color; its winters are cold and its summers hot. Some of the Castilian plains, like La Mancha, are like deserts, others are sparsely covered with (**de**) shrubs and trees that never seem to have enough water. The character and behavior of the Castilians reflect the severity of the land and the climate. They are grave and austere and very hardworking.

The former province of Andalusia, in the south of the country, is more fertile than Castile, and its olive trees, which are planted on much (**gran parte**) of its soil, are one of its salient features. Andalusians are generally lively and gay and have a reputation for being great talkers (**tienen fama de habladores**). There is also much fertile soil in the region of Valencia on the Mediterranean coast, which produces the famous Valencian oranges. Catalonia, to the north of Valencia, is the most industrialized section of the country, and its capital, Barcelona, is the most important city in Spain from the economic point of view.

On the slopes of the formidable Pyrenees Mountains (**Montes Pirineos**) to the northwest are huddled the picturesque villages of the old province of Navarre. The Basque provinces (**Provincias Vascongadas**) to the west of Navarre have green mountains and valleys and a rainy climate. Their inhabitants still speak the mysterious and old Basque language (**vascuence,** *m.*) and are known for their love of independence. There are other sections, such as Aragon, Asturias, and Galicia, each one with its geographical and cultural characteristics and its own history.

II. Composicióno

1. Una descripción de mi pueblo o vecindad
2. Las distintas regiones de los Estados Unidos: sus rasgos salientes y su historia
3. Una vista inolvidable
4. Una viñeta íntima

LECCIÓN ONCE

THE ARTICLES

Adaptado de

PUEBLO

Madrid, 26 de abril de 1963

El Fraile Se Ha Hecho Torero

Este hombre de ojos brillantes, que está sentado frente a mí se llama Enrique Moreno, pero hasta hace poco se llamó fray Gerardo de las Palmas y fue fraile antes de ser torero. Enrique Moreno tuvo que dejar los hábitos de capuchino porque la misma llamarada de la vocación que tuvo para hacerse fraile, la ha sentido ahora para hacerse torero. La vida da unos saltos tremendos. Al igual que en las novelas hay un torero que se corta la coleta para hacerse monje, aquí, en la vida real —que no hay novela más grande que la vida misma— hay un hombre que fue fraile y que va a vestirse el traje de luces muy pronto.

Nació en Las Palmas de Gran Canaria. Sólo tenía en el mundo del toro un antecedente, su abuelo César Moreno, que había sido apoderado de Rafael el Gallo y que le había contado la historia del viejo, único y excepcional Rafael, el del sombrero alto, las puntas de brillantes en la camisa y la pañoleta de seda sobre el cuello.

Enrique Moreno sintió pronto la llamarada del toro en la sangre. Toreó mucho de muchacho hasta que un día le vino a las manos un libro con la vida de San Francisco de Asís. Y nuestro hombre, de la noche a la mañana, cambió los alamares por el pardo sayal de capuchino. Pasó ocho años en el convento, hasta que no pudo más. Un día salió a la calle, ya de paisano, con pantalón, el brillo en los ojos, afeitada la barba, un poco temeroso de lo que iba a hacer, pero dispuesto a todo. El día 1° de mayo, si Dios quiere, aquel fray Gerardo de las Palmas saldrá a torear de nuevo. El domingo eligió él mismo los toros que habrá de torear. Y pidió los más grandes y los de más cuerna.

Enrique Moreno ha pensado mucho en lo que quiere hacer. Quiere torear para ganar dinero que dar a la gente que lo necesite. Torear para remediar en algo a la gente que ha visto en los hospitales, o a la puerta misma del convento, pidiendo limosna, a la gente que tiene hambre, a la que no tiene trabajo, a la que va por el mundo con el saco de la tristeza a las espaldas. "Sólo para ellos y nada más que para ellos".

El hombre está triste a veces, contento en ocasiones. Pero siempre veo en sus ojos esa llama de algo que no sé comprender ni escribir. ¿La vocación? ¡Quién sabe! Que a Dios se le sirve de muchas formas. Y más vale torero bueno que fraile malo.

PREGUNTAS

1. ¿Qué fue Enrique Moreno antes de ser torero?
2. ¿Por qué tuvo que dejar los hábitos de capuchino?
3. ¿Cuál fue su único antecedente en el mundo del toro?
4. ¿Cómo vestía el gran torero Rafael el Gallo?
5. ¿Qué hizo Enrique de muchacho?
6. ¿Por qué decidió hacerse monje?
7. ¿Cuántos años pasó en el convento?
8. ¿Cómo salió un día a la calle?
9. ¿Qué toros escogió para su estreno en la corrida?
10. ¿Qué piensa hacer con el dinero que gane?

CONVERSACIÓN

1. ¿Qué piensa Ud. de Enrique Moreno? ¿Cree Ud. que hizo bien o mal al dejar el convento? En su opinión, ¿ha cometido un pecado?
2. ¿Le interesa a Ud. la corrida de toros? ¿Ha visto Ud. alguna vez una corrida? ¿Dónde? ¿Le gustó? ¿Cree que sería popular en los Estados Unidos?
3. ¿Para qué profesión u oficio se prepara Ud.? ¿Por qué ha escogido Ud. esa carrera? Si descubre más tarde que no le interesa ya, ¿tendrá valor para cambiar a otro oficio? ¿Y si tiene familia? ¿Qué carrera sigue su padre? ¿Cuándo la emprendió? ¿Le gusta todavía? ¿Cómo la escogió?

PART A

89. The Definite Article

These are the forms of the definite article:

el soldado the soldier	**los estudiantes** the students
la clase the class	**las señoras** the ladies

A. The article **el** is used before a feminine singular noun that begins with a stressed **a** or **ha.**

el alma the soul | **el ala** the wing
el agua the water | **el hambre** hunger

But:

las aguas the waters

B. Contractions

A + **el** is contracted to **al; de** + **el** becomes **del.**

Vamos al museo. Let's go to the museum.
La firma del Sr. Alas... Mr. Alas' firm . . .

C. The definite article is generally repeated before each noun.

la pluma y el lápiz the pen and pencil

D. When a plural noun refers to both masculine and feminine beings or things, the *masculine* plural article is used.

los hermanos de Estelita Stella's brothers and sisters
los hijos de Pérez the children, the sons and daughters of Pérez

E. The neuter article is used primarily before adjectives. It never appears before a noun.

Lo malo es... The bad part is . . .
Esto es lo mejor que puedo hacer. This is the best that I can do.

EJERCICIOS

A. Cambie:

1. No me gusta **el agua.**
(aguas minerales, arma de fuego, armas de fuego)
2. El pajarito se lastimó **el ala.**
(alas, pico, cabecita, ojo derecho, dos ojos)
3. Mañana iremos a la **feria.**
(estadio, clases, universidad, concierto, juegos olímpicos)
4. ¿Han llegado noticias del **frente**?
(capitán, misioneros, jefe, patrona)
5. Lo **mejor** sería esperar.
(peor, más difícil, más indicado, más fácil)

B. Traduzca al español:

1. Let's go to the hotel. —I prefer that we go first to Mr. Encina's house. 2. Hunger is the most serious problem of humanity. 3. The poor (fellow) fell into the water. 4. The waters had reached a dangerous point for the inhabitants of the village.

90. Special Uses of the Definite Article

Aside from its normal use, as in English, to designate a specific noun (*the* bread that I bought—**el pan que compré;** *the* house we live in—**la casa en que vivimos**), the definite article in Spanish has certain important functions that it does NOT have in English. It is used most frequently as follows:

A. With all titles, except **don** and **Santo,** when speaking *about* (not *to*) a person

El presidente Kennedy fue asesinado en 1963.	President Kennedy was assassinated in 1963.
El señor Ramos quiere hablar con Ud.	Mr. Ramos wants to speak with you.

But:

Adiós, señor Chips.	Goodby, Mr. Chips.
Don Juan fue un amante trágico.	Don Juan was a tragic lover.
San Francisco	Saint Francis

B. With nouns used in a general or abstract sense

El pan es el sostén de la vida.	Bread is the staff of life.
La historia se repite.	History repeats itself.
Las mujeres gastan más dinero que los hombres.	Women spend more money than men.

Notice especially that the definite article is NOT used when the partitive idea of *some* or *any* is implied.

Déme dinero para pan.	Give me (some) money for (some) bread.
No tuvieron tiempo.	They didn't have (any) time.

C. With days of the week and seasons of the year (except after **ser**), and with dates of the month

El otoño es hermosísimo en el norte.	Fall is beautiful in the North.
La tienda está cerrada los miércoles.[1]	The store is closed on Wednesdays.
Saldremos el diez y seis.[1]	We shall leave on the 16th.

But:

Hoy es martes.	Today is Tuesday.

D. With the time of day

Son las dos.	It is two o'clock.
Eran las siete y cuarto.	It was 7:15.

E. With the names of languages, except after **en** or **de,** or immediately after the verb **hablar**

El español no es difícil.	Spanish is not difficult.
El alemán lo es.	German is.
¿Habla bien[2] **el francés?**	Does he speak French well?

But:

Un libro en español...	A Spanish book . . .
Nuestro profesor de latín...	Our Latin professor . . .
¡Cómo! ¿Uds. no hablan japonés?	What! You don't speak Japanese?

After the verbs **comprender, estudiar, aprender, leer, oír, saber,** and **escribir,** the article may be used or omitted.

F. With parts of the body and articles of clothing, in place of a possessive adjective

Metió la mano en el cajón.	He put his hand in the drawer.
Ponte la camisa blanca.	Put on your white shirt.
Se quitarán Uds. el sombrero ante una señora.	You will take your hats off before a lady.

Note in the last sentence above, since each person is taking off *one* hat, the singular must be used.

[1] Spanish does not use any preposition to translate the English *on* when referring to days or dates.

[2] When any word other than the subject pronoun intervenes between **hablar** and the name of the language, the article is used.

G. With the names of certain countries

1. These are the most frequently used names that include the article. The article is disappearing, however, in newspaper and colloquial use.

(los) Estados Unidos the United States

(el) **Canadá**	(el) **Japón**
(el) **Perú**	(la) **China**
(el) **Paraguay**	(el) **Uruguay**
(el) **Ecuador**	(el) **Brasil**
(la) **Argentina**	(la) **Gran Bretaña**

2. The article is used with the names of all countries when that name is modified by an adjective or a phrase.

la Inglaterra isabelina	Elizabethan England
la España septentrional	Northern Spain
la Europa del siglo doce	twelfth-century Europe

H. When a noun is omitted

1. The article plus **de** means *the one(s) of* or *with*. Frequently it is translated in English as *that* or *those of* or *with*. (Recall the pseudo-demonstrative, **57**.)

Nuestra clase y las de 1960 y 1961...	Our class and those of 1960 and 1961 . . .
¿Ve Ud. a aquel hombre —el del pelo rojo?	Do you see that man—the one with the red hair?

It also stands in place of a noun that is modified by a possessive. The article serves to avoid repetition of the noun.

Mi abrigo y el de Diego son idénticos.	My coat and Jim's (coat) are identical.
Nuestra casa y la de mis padres...	Our house and my parents' . . .

2. The article plus **que** means *he who*, *the one(s) who* or *those who*.

El que me lo vendió ha desaparecido.	The one who sold it to me has disappeared.

I. With an infinitive to form a noun

Nos despertó el ladrar del perro.	The dog's barking woke us.
¿A quién no le gusta el bailar de los gitanos?	Who doesn't like the dancing of the gypsies?

EJERCICIOS

A. Póngase la forma apropiada del artículo definido siempre que sea necesario:

1. Tanto en _____ latín como en _____ alemán se declinan _____ sustantivos. 2. Me parece que _____ francés es más difícil que _____ español. 3. Se tarda muchos años en hablar bien _____ ruso. 4. Estuve en _____ Corea del Sur _____ año pasado, pero no aprendí _____ idioma. 5. Siempre viajo en _____ verano y me gustan mucho _____ vacaciones. 6. Hoy es _____ martes, _____ quince de abril. 7. Volverán a vernos _____ lunes a _____ una en punto. 8. Esperamos que nuestra tertulia resulte tan agradable como _____ de hoy. 9. _____ más interesante de estas reuniones es que se conoce a gente de otros países. 10. ¿Es tarde ya? —Sí, serán _____ diez.

B. Conteste en español:

1. ¿Qué naciones integran la Organización de los Estados Americanos? 2. ¿Qué país de Hispanoamérica le interesa más? 3. ¿Qué país europeo conoce Ud. mejor? 4. ¿Ha hecho Ud. alguna vez un viaje fuera de los Estados Unidos? ¿Adónde fue? 5. ¿Cuáles son las lenguas principales de Europa? ¿Y del Extremo Oriente? 6. ¿Cree Ud. que se puede vivir feliz sin dinero? 7. En su opinión, ¿es verdad que la historia se repite? 8. ¿Qué estación del año le gusta más? ¿Por qué? 9. ¿Qué día es hoy? ¿Qué hora será? 10. ¿Cuándo terminarán las clases este semestre?

C. Diga en español:

1. Money is the root of all evil. 2. The watch that you gave me doesn't work. 3. Gold is worth more than silver. 4. Friendship is worth more than both. 5. Is the book written in English? 6. Will you wait a moment, Mr. Masa? Dr. Vásquez is busy. 7. Have courage and faith. Life is good. 8. That one is my sister—the one with (**de**) the blue skirt and the red eyes. 9. May I (**Puedo**) put on the new shoes? 10. Come on Sunday at half past nine. 10. Where were you on June tenth at a quarter to seven?

91. The Indefinite Article:

These are the forms of the indefinite article

un joven	a young man	**unos lápices**	some (a few) pencils
una calle	a street	**unas monedas**	some (a few) coins

A. **Un** may be used before a feminine noun that begins with a stressed **a** or **ha.** If the first syllable is not stressed, the normal feminine article remains.

un ala a wing   **un hambre feroz** terrific hunger

But:

una hacienda   **una artista**

B. **Unos** means *several*, *a few*, or *about* (in the sense of *approximately*). Normally, however, the idea of *some* or *any* is conveyed by omitting the article.

¿Tiene Ud. dinero?	Do you have any (some) money?
Mi hermana tiene unos veinte galanes.	My sister has about twenty boy-friends.

92. Omission of the Indefinite Article

In Spanish, the indefinite article is NOT used in certain cases in which it does appear in English. It is generally omitted under the following circumstances:

A. After **ser,** with an unmodified noun of profession, occupation, religion, nationality, or political party

Su padre es polaco.	His father is a Pole.
Es profesor de lenguas extranjeras.	He is a professor of languages.

BUT when the noun is modified, the article is generally used.

Es un violinista excelente.	He is an excellent violinist.

B. With personal effects, when the numerical concept of *a*, *an* (*one*) is deëmphasized

Salió sin sombrero.	He went out without a hat.
Hoy no voy a llevar chaqueta.	Today I am not going to wear a jacket.
Ella escribe mal con lápiz, mucho mejor con pluma.	She writes badly with a pencil, much better with a pen.

C. With **otro** (another), **tal** (such a), **cien(to)** (a hundred), **mil** (a thousand), **cierto** (a certain), and **¡qué!** (what a!)

Ahora tenemos que buscar otro.	Now we have to look for another one.
Te lo he advertido cien veces.	I have warned you a hundred times.
¡Qué tonto!	What a fool!

EJERCICIOS

A. Póngase la forma apropiada del artículo indefinido siempre que sea posible:

1. No puedo escribir sin ______ pluma. 2. Eso no se debe hacer con ______ lápiz. 3. Mi novio es ______ abogado. 4. Es ______ abogado

muy conocido. 5. ¿Podría Ud. darme _______ fósforos? 6. Le tuve que prestar _______ otros cinco dólares. 7. No salgas hoy sin _______ bufanda. 8. Gana _______ mil pesetas semanales.

B. Conteste en español:

1. ¿Piensa Ud. seguir la misma carrera que su padre o sus hermanos? ¿Qué son ellos? ¿Qué piensa Ud. ser algún día? 2. ¿Lleva Ud. chaqueta casi todos los días? 3. ¿Cree Ud. que un caballero siempre debe llevar corbata, a menos que esté jugando a los deportes? 4. ¿Cree Ud. que una señora debe llevar sombrero y guantes cuando va a la ciudad? ¿Y medias?

EJERCICIO DE REPASO

1. Before becoming a Spanish professor, I was a bullfighter. —Ole!
2. Nowadays soccer is more popular in Spain than bullfighting.
3. Before he decided to become a monk, he had been a famous singer.
4. Tell him not to leave the house until he shaves off his beard.
5. They spoke no Spanish, though they had been living in Spain for six months.
6. Did you notice the young man dressed as (**de**) a bullfighter and the other one with the red hair and the guitar?
7. He said that he would give the money that he'd earn to those who needed it.
8. If they are good, bullfighters can earn a great deal of money, but they often die in the ring.
9. He really didn't want to fight (**torear**) any more, but pride forced him to show the public that he wasn't afraid.
10. A good bullfighter is better than a bad friar, he kept repeating a hundred, a thousand times. Do you think he regrets it now?

REPASO DE VERBOS

Estudie los verbos **dar** y **decir,** y después diga en español:

I gave it to him. They told us (it). If only he would tell the truth! You (**vosotros**) used to say that. Give them to me. (**Ud., Uds., tú, vosotros**). Don't give them to her. (**Ud., Uds., tú, vosotros**). Let's tell them (it) now. Let's not tell them.

PART B

93. Feminine Forms of Nouns Referring to Professions

In recent years, women have begun to enter professions to which they formerly did not belong. The Spanish language recognizes this by adding feminine forms to nouns which used to have only the masculine.

A. Nouns ending in **-ista** indicate gender by the article.

the newspaperwoman **la periodista**
the psychiatrist **la alienista**

B. Some nouns ending in **-o** or **-e** have new feminine forms ending in **-a**.

la estudianta	the student	**la médica**	the doctor
la arquitecta	the architect	**la cirujana**	the surgeon
la abogada	the lawyer	**la ingeniera**	the engineer

C. Traditionally, a man's wife may be called by a feminine form of his occupational name.

la alcaldesa the mayor's wife
la generala the general's wife

94. The Neuter Article **lo**

A. With adjectives and adverbs

1. **Lo** may be used with an adjective to create an abstract noun.

Lo hermoso no es siempre lo mejor.	The beautiful is not always the best.

2. It may translate *how*, indicating degree or extent. It is used with both adjectives and adverbs in this sense.

No se daba cuenta de lo cansados que estaban.	He didn't realize how tired they were.
Me maravillaba de lo bien que cantaba.	I was amazed at how well he sang.

The indirect exclamation **qué** may substitute for **lo... que** in this construction.

3. **Lo** appears in many common idiomatic expressions.

por lo tanto	therefore
por lo visto	apparently
a lo lejos	in the distance
por lo pronto	for the time being
a lo mejor	maybe, for all we know
por lo general	as a general rule

B. With **de**

Lo de means *the matter of*, *the incident about*, *the story of*, etc.

¿Qué pasó ayer? —Lo de siempre.	What happened yesterday? —The same old story.
Acabo de contarle lo de mi tía.	I have just told him the incident about my aunt.

95. The Definite Article with Nouns in Apposition

The definite article may be used or omitted before a noun in apposition. However, a slight difference of meaning results from the presence or absence of the article. English frequently follows the same usage.

Carlos Montoya, guitarrista	Carlos Montoya, (a) guitarrist
Carlos Montoya, el guitarrista	Carlos Montoya, the guitarrist
Madrid, capital de España	Madrid, (the) capital of Spain
Madrid, la capital de España	

In the first example of each group, the absence of the article gives the clause in apposition an explanatory nature, and intimates that the fact is not presumed to be universally known. In the second examples, the presence of the article implies that the fact is presumed to be well known.

96. Omission of the Definite Article

A. With nouns in a series

1. In a series of general or abstract nouns taken as a group, the definite article is often omitted.

¡Libertad, fraternidad, igualdad!	Liberty, fraternity, equality!
Naturaleza, hombres, animales, todo estaba dormido.	Nature, men, animals, everything was asleep.

This occurs especially in titles of books.

Guerra y paz *War and Peace*
Sangre y arena *Blood and Sand*

2. Less frequently, the article is omitted in a series of specific nouns.

Le dolían brazos, piernas y dientes.	His arms, legs, and teeth hurt.

3. When a series of nouns refers to one unit of activity or being, it is common to omit all but the first definite article.

Los servicios, programas y actividades de esta organización...	The services, programs, and activities of this organization . . .
La casa y finca de mi vecino han sido vendidas.	My neighbor's house and land (considered as a unit) have been sold.

But:

La casa y la finca de mi vecino...	My neighbor's house and his land (two separate units) . . .

B. Omission in idiomatic usage

In a number of idioms, the definite article is omitted. The noun in such cases is generally used in a figurative, rather than a literal sense.

Espero que en adelante pueda levantar cabeza.	I hope that from now on he will be able to raise his head (gain respect in society).
El joven decidió correr mundo.	The boy decided to see the world (travel about).

With the time of day, it is often omitted after **de** and **a** when referring to the duration of an event.

Mi clase es de una a dos.	My class is from one to two.

97. Use and Omission of the Indefinite Article

A. Before unmodified predicate nouns

1. The indefinite article is omitted before an unmodified predicate noun of religion, nationality, profession, political or social affiliation, etc., when the factor stressed is the category to which the subject belongs: "What is he?"[3]

¿Qué es ese señor? —Es médico.	What is that gentleman? —He is a doctor.
Soy católico.	I am a Catholic.

[3] Occasionally, it is omitted even before a modified predicate noun that emphasizes the subject's category:

Es antiguo servidor de su Majestad. He is an old servant of his Majesty.

2. The indefinite article is used before an unmodified predicate noun of religion, etc., when the element stressed is the person's identity, not his category: "Who is he?"

¿Quién es ese señor?	Who is that gentleman?
—Es un médico.	—He is a doctor.

It is also used to give special (and usually favorable) emphasis to the noun. The article is then also stressed with the voice.

¡Es un escritor!	He is some writer!
¡Eres un soldado!	You are a real soldier!

B. Before nouns in apposition

The use of the indefinite article with nouns in apposition generally follows the same rule as that for unmodified predicate nouns. When the category (occupation, etc.) is stressed, the article is omitted. When the subject's identity is stressed, the article is used.

El pleito fue defendido por García, conocido abogado de la capital.	The case was pleaded by García, a well-known lawyer of the capital.
El pleito fue defendido por García, un conocido abogado de la capital.	

98. Further Omission of the Indefinite Article

A. In negative sentences

The indefinite article is usually omitted in negative sentences, unless the numerical value of **uno** meaning *one* (*a single*) is strongly emphasized.

No han dicho palabra.	They haven't said a word.
No queremos piso sin calefacción.	We don't want an apartment without heating.
No dejaron huella.	They didn't leave a trace.

But:

No han dicho (ni) una palabra.	They haven't said a single word.

Note that **ni** is often used before the indefinite article in emphatic negative sentences.

B. After **tener** and **buscar**

The indefinite article is generally omitted in negative sentences with **tener** and **buscar,** and frequently in affirmative sentences, unless the concept of *one* is stressed.

No tengo llave.	I don't have a key.
¿Buscas piso?	Are you looking for an apartment?
Mi hermana tiene novio.	My sister has a fiancé.
Tengo clase a la una.	I have a class at one.

But:

No tiene (ni) un amigo.	He doesn't have one friend.

C. In proverbs

Many proverbs and adages omit the article.

Perro que ladra no muerde.	A barking dog doesn't bite.
Casa con dos puertas mala es de guardar.	A house with two doors is hard to guard.
Más vale pájaro en mano que buitre volando.	A bird in the hand is worth two in the bush (is better than a flying vulture).

D. Before nouns modified by **bueno** or **malo**

Frequently, when **bueno** or **malo** precedes the noun it modifies, the indefinite article is omitted. The adjective is regarded as a unit with the noun and there is little numerical connotation.

Es buen amigo mío.	He is a good friend of mine.
Es mala persona.	He is a bad person.
Hicieron muy mala impresión.	They made a very bad impression.
Ud. nos ha dado muy buen ejemplo.	You have given us a very good example.

But:

Hicieron una impresión muy mala.	They made a very bad impression.
Ud. nos ha dado un ejemplo muy bueno.	You have given us a very good example.

99. The Articles with **tal**

A. **Tal** (such a) is never followed by an article.

en tal caso	in such a case

B. **Tal** may be preceded by an article.

1. With the indefinite article, **tal** means *a certain*, *a so-called*, etc.

Vino a verme un tal don Joaquín Rima.	A certain Don Joaquín Rima came to see me.

2. With the definite article, **tal** means *the aforementioned*

El tal Sr. Rima me dijo...	The aforementioned Mr. Rima told me . . .

100. The Indefinite Article with **cierto**

A. When **cierto** precedes the noun and is used indefinitely, meaning *a certain*, it does not take the indefinite article.[4]

Nos lo ofreció cierto vendedor ambulante.	A certain peddler (some peddler) offered it to us.
En cierta ocasión...	On a certain occasion . . .

B. When **cierto** means *sure* (and in this sense, usually follows the noun), the article is used.

Se enfrentan con una derrota cierta.	They face a certain (sure) defeat.
Le prometo un ascenso cierto.	I promise you a sure promotion.

101. Collective Nouns

Collective nouns are singular in Spanish. However, when nouns that state a part (**mayoría, minoría,** etc.) of a plural whole are followed by that whole, the plural is used.

El pueblo ha triunfado.	The people have triumphed.
La mayoría no lo aceptará.	The majority won't accept it.

But:

La mayoría de las mujeres no lo aceptarán.	The majority of women won't accept it.
Gran parte de sus planes han fracasado.	A large number of his plans have failed.

EJERCICIOS

I. Traducir al español.

It was a holiday and it was very cold. There wasn't a person on the street, although it was midday. The apartment I was going to see was in a large old house which seemed to be on the point of collapsing. Although I am not a millionaire, I have always lived in large, modern houses and that old building made (**me produjo**) an unpleasant impression on me.

[4] **Un cierto**—*a certain*—used specifically, is synonymous with **un tal**:
Vino a verme un cierto D. Joaquín Rima.

I entered it and went up two flights. In my pocket I had the key, which the agent, a man of few words, had given me. I opened the door and found myself in a dark, small, and dirty apartment of three rooms. It had small windows, walls that had not been painted for years, and a kitchen without a refrigerator.

It did not take me long to (**no tardé mucho en**) decide that I would never take the apartment, and I was sorry that I had wasted (**haber perdido**) my time in this manner. I went to the door and tried to open it, but I couldn't. I tried (**Lo intenté**) again, but in vain. It was impossible to open it. Something had happened to the lock.

I went to the window that faced the street and leaned out of it, hoping to attract the attention of somebody in the street. But there were no passersby. I returned to the door and tried to open it again, but with the same result.

I was already on the point of breaking it down when I saw a fire escape outside of one of the windows in the back of the apartment. I took a board and broke the glass. I had never left an apartment by such a staircase, but this time it couldn't be helped (**no había más remedio**).

Five minutes later, I was on the street again, but now I had another problem. A policeman was approaching me with a curious look on his face . . .

II. Composición.

1. Lo que me pasó con el policía
2. Mi concepto de una casa (o apartamento) ideal
3. Por qué prefiero vivir en la ciudad (en las afueras, en el campo)

LECCIÓN DOCE

INTERROGATIVES, EXCLAMATIONS, INDEFINITES, NEGATIVES

Adaptado de un artículo por Luis Valeri

LA VANGUARDIA ESPAÑOLA

Barcelona, 13 de agosto de 1963

La Murmuración

Murmuración, la define el diccionario como "conversación en perjuicio de un ausente" o "noticia verdadera o falsa que se repite para indisponer a unas personas con otras o para desprestigiar a alguna". La tendencia humana a ocuparnos excesivamente de la vida de nuestros semejantes como simple conversación sin ninguna necesidad verdadera, no es sólo una torpeza, sino que puede producir graves disgustos. Y a veces lo peor no es traer o llevar chismes, sino expresarse con medias frases insidiosas que sin decir nada quieren decir mucho, y producen a veces más daño que la murmuración declarada:

—Sí, sí, fíate de fulana...

—¿Por qué dices esto?

—No me hagas hablar...

—¿Pero qué sabes de ella para decir esto?

—Ya te he dicho que no quiero hablar porque... en fin, dejémosla en paz.

—No, no, ¿qué pasa? ¿Ha hecho algo? Porque yo la tengo por buena persona...

—Sí, sí, fíate de las buenas personas...

Y así se alarga indefinidamente una conversación que sin decir nada, dice más que si se lanzara contra alguien una acusación.

Aun las personas murmuradoras son a su vez objeto de ella. "¡Qué lengua tiene fulana! Es peor que una víbora." Y realmente, nunca como en estos casos está tan bien aplicado este calificativo. Nadie está exento de la murmuración.

La murmuración no es algo peculiar de las mujeres. He concurrido a "peñas" de "amigos" y sé cómo se habla de un ausente. Recuerdo una vez que estaban despellejando a un buen hombre. En ese mismo momento entró él en la tertulia y llegó a oír su nombre acompañado de un epíteto poco favorable para él. Al verle, todos los contertulios, sorprendidos, se callaron. El buen hombre preguntó irónicamente:

—¿Conque os estabais ocupando de mí? ¿Y qué decíais de este "pobre hombre"?

—¡Nada de eso! —exclamó uno.

—Quita, quita, no creía que fueses tan suspicaz —repuso otro.

Y un tercero que estaba harto de oír tanta murmuración, contestó:

—Pues sí, te estaban poniendo verde. Pero consuélate, porque hoy te ha tocado a ti como ayer le tocó a fulano y mañana le tocará a mengano.

PREGUNTAS

1. ¿Cómo define "murmuración" el diccionario?
2. ¿Qué resultados puede producir?
3. A veces, ¿qué es peor que la murmuración abierta?
4. ¿Puede Ud. citar algunas de esas medias frases insidiosas?
5. ¿Quién está exento de la murmuración?
6. ¿Es algo peculiar de las mujeres la murmuración?
7. ¿Qué incidente recuerda el escritor del artículo?
8. ¿Qué dijo el buen hombre al entrar?
9. ¿Cómo contestaron los dos primeros "amigos" suyos?
10. ¿Qué dijo el tercero?

CONVERSACIÓN

1. ¿Conoce Ud. a una persona murmuradora? ¿Quién es? ¿De quién suele murmurar? ¿Tiene muchos amigos aquella persona? Y Ud., ¿ha murmurado Ud. alguna vez? ¿Lo hace frecuentemente?

2. ¿Recuerda Ud. un episodio mortificante que haya ocurrido como resultado de la murmuración? ¿Cuál ha sido el momento más mortificante de su vida?
3. En el caso referido por el autor de este artículo, ¿cree Ud. que hizo bien o mal el amigo que dijo la verdad al buen hombre? ¿Qué habría hecho Ud. en su lugar?

PART A

102. Interrogatives

An interrogative is a pronoun, adjective, or adverb that asks a question. It must always have a written accent. The following are the most common interrogatives:

A. **¿Quién(es)?** Who? Whom?

¿Quién es ese hombre tan guapo?	Who is that good-looking man?
¿Por quién(es) tañen las campanas?	For whom do the bells toll?

B. **¿Qué?, ¿Cuál(es)?** What? Which?

1. As a pronoun

¿Qué? asks for a definition or explanation and always means *what?*

Mamacita, ¿qué es un cocodrilo? —¿Qué dices?	Mommy, what is a crocodile? —What are you saying?

¿Cuál(es)? asks for a selection and may be translated as *which?* or *what?*

¿Cuál es la nueva edición?	Which is the new edition?
¿Cuáles de estos poemas le gustan más?	Which (ones) of these poems do you like best?
¿Cuál es su número de teléfono?	What (which one) is your telephone number?

2. As an adjective

¿Qué? means both *what?* and *which?*

¿A qué hora nos encontramos?	At what time shall we meet?

¿Qué programa presentan esta noche?	Which (or what) program are they presenting tonight?
¿Qué notas te dio?	What grades did he give you?

¿Cuál(es)? is popularly used also in this sense.

¿En cuál casa vive Ud.?	In which house do you live?
¿Cuáles libros compraremos?	Which books shall we buy?

C. **¿De quién(es)?** Whose?

¿De quién(es)? is the only interrogative of possession. It must never be confused with the relative adjective **cuyo,** which is translated as *whose* (cf. **164**).

¿De quién es esta pluma?	Whose pen is this?
¿De quiénes son aquellos asientos desocupados?	Whose seats are those unoccupied ones?

D. **¿Cómo?** and **¿Qué tal?** How?

1. **¿Cómo?** inquires as to the way in which something is done, or the situation in which something or someone is found.

¿Cómo se aprende a hablar un idioma extranjero?	How does one learn to speak a foreign language?
¿Cómo le gusta el café—con crema o con leche?	How do you like coffee—with cream or with milk?
¿Cómo está Ud.?	How are you?

2. **¿Qué tal?** asks for an evaluation.

¿Qué tal les pareció la comedia?	How did you like the play? (How did it seem to you?)
Hola. ¿Qué tal?	Hello. How are things?
¿Qué tal le gustó el café? —Muchísimo, gracias.	How did you like the coffee? —Very much, thank you.

E. **¿Dónde?** and **¿A dónde?** (**¿Adónde?**)

¿Dónde? inquires about the the location of the subject.

¿A dónde? (or **¿adónde?**) asks *in which direction?* and is used with verbs of motion.

¿Dónde está mi abrigo?	Where is my coat?
¿A dónde vas, hijo?	Where are you going, son?

F. **¿Cuánto?** How much? **¿Cuántos?** How many?

¿Cuánto tiempo nos queda?	How much time do we have left?
¿Cuántas piezas sabe Ud. tocar?	How many pieces can you play?

G. **¿Por qué?** and **¿Para qué?** Why?

¿Por qué? inquires about the reason, the motive for an action. **¿Para qué?** means *to what end? what for? what good will come of it?*

¿Por qué los ofendió Ud.?	Why did you insult them?
Debes trabajar más. —¿Para qué?	You should work harder. —Why? (What for?)

EJERCICIOS

A. Haga preguntas basadas en las frases siguientes. Por ejemplo:

Esto es una nevera.	**¿Qué es esto?**
Tu sombrero está aquí.	**¿Dónde está mi sombrero?**

1. Esta pluma es de María. 2. Nos gustó mucho la película. 3. Esto es un antiguo instrumento musical. 4. Juan es el mejor estudiante de la clase. 5. La casa más antigua de esta calle es la última. 6. A mí me gusta el café sin azúcar. 7. Quito es la capital del Ecuador. 8. La Coruña está en el noroeste de España. 9. He pasado la tarde estudiando. 10. Al Palacio Real se va por la Puerta del Sol. 11. Esta línea representa una carretera principal. 12. Son nuestros. 13. Porque no quise hacerlo. 14. Mi número de teléfono es el 254-63-89. 15. ¡No!

B. Diga en español:

1. Who is Silvia? What is she (like)? 2. To whom were you talking? —To a friend of mine. 3. Why did you have to give up your job? —What does it matter? 4. Whose is that blue car parked near the fire hydrant? —Who wants to know? —A policeman. —How much will it cost me? 5. What is your address? —What? —Where do you live? —What is he saying? —In which house do you eat and sleep? —Why didn't you ask me that before? —What for? You probably don't know.

103. Exclamations

A. All interrogatives may be used exclamatively, if the sense permits.

¡Cuántas haciendas tiene!	How many estates he has!
¡Quién lo haría sino él!	Who would do it but he!
¡Cómo! ¡Qué me dices! ¡Cómo miente!	What! What are you telling me! How he lies!

B. **¡Qué!** and **¡Vaya un!** What a . . .!

1. **¡Qué...!** followed by a noun, means *what a . . .!* Notice that the definite article is not used.

¡Qué muchacho!	What a boy!
¡Qué pelea!	What a fight!

¡Vaya un...! is synonymous with **¡qué!** in this sense, and always requires the indefinite article.

¡Vaya un muchacho!
¡Vaya una pelea!

2. **¡Qué...!** followed by an adjective or an adverb, means *how . . .!*

¡Qué simpático es!	How nice he is!
¡Qué bien canta!	How well he sings!

EJERCICIOS

A. Póngase el interrogativo o exclamativo apropiado:

1. ¿______ libro quiere Ud.? 2. ¿______ metros de largo tiene la estación? 3. ¡______ calor hace! 4. ¡______ niños quisieran tener una bicicleta como ésta! 5. ¡______ flores más hermosas! 6. ¡______ me alegro! 7. ¡______ hombre tan inteligente!

B. Diga en español:

1. What a day to go to the beach! 2. How (much) we like to dance! 3. How well they did, and how badly the others did! 4. What a good boy you are! 5. Who would believe it!

104. Indefinites

These are the most common indefinites:

algo something
alguien somebody, someone
algún, alguno (a) some, any or some (one of a group)
algunos (as) some, several (of a group)
algún día some day, some time
(en) alguna parte somewhere
(de) algún modo, somehow, in some way
(de) alguna manera
jamás ever (when a negative is implied)
alguna vez ever, at some time (no negative implication)

Tengo algo que contarte.	I have something to tell you.
Hay alguien en la cocina con Dina.	Someone's in the kitchen with Dinah.
¿Ha visto Ud. a alguno(s) de mis amigos?	Have you seen any of my friends?
Sí, he visto a algunos.	Yes, I have seen some.
¿Han oído Uds. jamás tal cosa?	Have you ever heard such a thing? (Negative reply expected)
¿Ha estado Ud. alguna vez en París?	Have you ever been in Paris?

EJERCICIOS

A. Conteste:

1. ¿Ha estado Ud. alguna vez en España? 2. ¿Le gustaría ir algún día al Japón? 3. ¿Cuáles son algunos de sus platos favoritos? 4. ¿Ha visto Ud. a algunos de sus amigos hoy? 5. ¿Tiene Ud. algo importante que hacer esta tarde? 6. ¿Ha leído Ud. algunas novelas interesantes recientemente? 7. ¿Le espera alguien después de la clase? 8. ¿Ha visto Ud. jamás un libro que le haga tantas preguntas personales?

B. Diga en español:

1. Some day, somewhere, somehow, I am going to find somebody who loves me. 2. That is something that *I* would like too. 3. Some people have luck at (**para**) cards. 4. Well, something is better than nothing.

105. Negatives

A. Negation in general

1. A sentence is made negative by placing **no** before the entire verb form, i.e., before **haber** in a compound tense, or before the auxiliary that precedes a present or past participle. This is contrary to English usage, which places the negative between the auxiliary and the participle.

No ha ido.	He has not gone.
No estaban gritando.	They were not shouting.
No hemos sido elegidos todavía.	We have not been elected yet.
El drama no está terminado.	The drama is not finished.

2. Only object pronouns—direct, indirect, or reflexive—may stand between the negative and the verb.

No les he hecho daño.	I have not hurt them.

B. These are the most common negatives:

nada nothing, not . . . at all
nadie nobody, no one
ningún, ninguno (a) none, no (one of a group)
ningunos (as) no; none (of a group) (*rare*)
nunca, never
jamás
de ningún modo, in no way, by no means, not at all
de ninguna manera
tampoco neither (opposite of *also*)
ni... ni neither . . . nor (opposite of *either . . . or*)

C. The double negative

1. Remember:

En español, no se omite nunca ningún negativo. Pues, casi nunca.	In Spanish, you (don't) never leave out no negative. Well, hardly never.

Two negatives, or as many negatives as the sentence requires, add up to a negative in Spanish.

No conozco a nadie en este pueblo. —Ni yo tampoco.	I don't know anyone in town. —Neither do I.
No lo han mencionado nunca a nadie.	They have never mentioned it to anyone.

2. When a negative such as **nunca, nadie, nada,** or **tampoco** precedes the verb, **no** is omitted.

No he estado nunca en París.	I have never been in Paris.
Nunca he estado en París.	
No se lo dijo nadie.	Nobody told him.
Nadie se lo dijo.	
No sabe leer tampoco.	Neither does he know how to read.
Tampoco sabe leer.	

D. Use of negatives after comparisons

After a comparative, indefinites take the negative form.

Le respeto a él más que a nadie.	I respect him more than anyone.
Ahora sabemos menos que nunca.	Now we know less than ever.
Más que nada.	More than anything.

Comparative Chart of Indefinites and Negatives

Indefinites	*Negatives*
algo something	**nada** nothing
alguien somebody, someone	**nadie** nobody, no one
algún, alguno (**a**) some, any or some (one of a group)	**ningún, ninguno** (**a**) none, no (one of a group)
algunos (**as**) some, several (of a group)	**ningunos** (**as**) no; none (of a group) (*rare*)
(**en**) **alguna parte** somewhere	(**en**) **ninguna parte** nowhere
(**de**) **algún modo,** somehow, in some way	(**de**) **ningún modo,** in no way
(**de**) **alguna manera**	(**de**) **ninguna manera**
jamás ever (negative implied)	**nunca, jamás** never
alguna vez ever, at some time	
	ni... ni neither . . . nor
	tampoco neither, not . . . either (opposite of *also*)

EJERCICIO

Conteste negativamente las preguntas siguientes:

1. ¿Ha visto Ud. hoy algo de interés especial? 2. ¿Ha viajado Ud. alguna vez en un helicóptero? 3. ¿Se ha encontrado con alguno de sus amigos esta mañana? 4. ¿Vamos a algún sitio? 5. ¿Me ha llamado alguien? 6. ¿Han terminado Uds. también? 7. ¿Lo harán ellos de algún modo? 8. ¿Habéis hecho algo para mí? 9. Por lo visto no ha venido María. ¿Y Luisa? 10. Será él o su hermano, ¿verdad?

EJERCICIO DE REPASO

1. What is gossip? Gossip is usually (**suele ser**) a conversation damaging the character of a person who is not present.
2. There was no reason (**motivo**) to believe that this would produce any serious unpleasantness.
3. He went out into the garden without anyone's saying anything.
4. Whose gloves are those they have just found on the bench?
5. What is the subject of that conversation? They don't seem to be saying anything interesting.
6. Have you ever seen a group of people who are more interested in gossiping than these old women?
7. Though women like to gossip more than men, there are some men who are real experts at gossiping. For example, do you know what Chalo said the other night . . . ?
8. What a party! All they do is rip the hide off (**poner verde**) their friends.
9. "So you were talking about me?" he said. "Surely there must be something more interesting to (**que**) say." —"No, nothing."
10. Is there anyone who hasn't done it at some time? I'm afraid we have all gossiped at times.

REPASO DE VERBOS

Estudie los verbos **poder** y **poner** y después diga en español:

They couldn't come. Where did you (**tú**) put it? I put it on the desk. We were afraid that he couldn't finish. Somebody put them there. I haven't put anything anywhere. Put it here. (**Ud., Uds., tú, vosotros**). Let's not put it (*f.*) there.

PART B

106. Interrogatives in Indirect Questions

Often, a question is included within another statement, or a sentence may be so phrased that it refers to a question either in the mind of the speaker or in that of the person addressed. In such cases, Spanish uses the interrogative pronoun, which thereby maintains its written accent.

Dime adónde vas y cuándo.	Tell me where you're going and when.
No quiere revelar quién es ese señor.	He won't reveal who that man is.
No sé qué pasó.	I don't know what happened.

107. The Pronouns **¿cuál? ¿qué? ¿quién?** to mean *which* (*one*)?

Although the normal function of **¿cuál?** is to indicate a selection, the pronouns **¿qué?** and **¿quién?** are also used at times to translate the English *which* (*one*)?

A. **¿Cuál?** is generally used when **ser** is followed by a predicate noun or pronoun.

¿Cuál es la mía?	Which is mine?
¿Cuál es el elemento más peligroso —el agua o el fuego?	Which is the more dangerous element —water or fire?

It must be used before a phrase introduced by **de.**

¿Cuál de las tres alternativas prefiere Ud.?	Which of the three alternatives do you prefer?

B. **¿Qué?** appears often instead of **¿cuál?** when the objects from which the selection is to be made are nouns used in the general or abstract sense.

¿Qué es más peligroso —el agua o el fuego?	Which (or what) is more dangerous—water or fire?
¿Qué prefiere Ud. —el fútbol o el básquetbol?	What do you prefer—football or basketball?

¿Cuál? remains when the objects are nouns used in a specific sense.

¿Cuál es más peligroso —este león o ése?	Which is more dangerous—this lion or that one?
¿Cuál prefiere Ud. —el nuestro o el de ellos?	Which do you prefer—ours or theirs?

C. **¿Quién?** appears frequently when the selection involves persons. It may be translated as *which* (*one*)? *who*? or *whom*?

¿Quién va a invitarle, María o Mercedes?	Who is going to invite him, Mary or Mercedes?
¿Quién es más inteligente — Juan o Pedro?	Who (which one) is more intelligent —John or Peter?
¿Quiénes son los líderes?	Who (which ones) are the leaders?

108. The Interrogative *Whose*?

A. When *whose*? is subject of *to be*, it is translated by **¿de quién**(es) + **ser...?**

¿De quién es aquel sombrero negro?	Whose is that black hat? (To whom does that black hat belong?)

B. But, when *whose*? is preceded by a preposition, or is used with a verb other than **ser,** it is translated in either of the following ways:

1. By **qué**

¿Con qué dinero se fue?	With whose money did he abscond?
¿En qué cuarto dormirás?[1]	In whose room will you sleep?
¿Qué sombrero tomó?	Whose hat did he take?

2. By using **¿De quién es...?** followed by a clause that describes the action.

¿De quién era el dinero con que se fue?	With whose money did he abscond?
¿De quién es el cuarto en que dormirás?[1]	In whose room will you sleep?
¿De quién era el sombrero que tomó?	Whose hat did he take?

109. Exclamations

A. **¡Qué!**

¡Qué + a noun, means *what a . . .*! When the noun is followed by an adjective, **tan** or **más** must precede the adjective.

¡Qué muchacho más (**o tan**) **guapo!**	What a handsome boy!
¡Qué obra más (**o tan**) **interesante!**	What an interesting work!

[1] There is a slight difference in connotation between **¿En qué cuarto dormirás?** and **¿De quién es el cuarto en que dormirás?** The first emphasizes selection of a room from among a group of rooms (a house) with which the speaker is familiar. The second sentence emphasizes the question as to the possessor: *To whom does the room that you will sleep in belong?*

When the adjective precedes its noun, **tan** or **más** is omitted.

¡Qué buena persona!	What a good person!
¡Qué guapo muchacho!	What a handsome boy!
¡Qué maravillosa vista!	What a magnificent view!

B. **¡Cuánto!** is used before a verb to correspond to the English *how* (*much*)!

¡Cuánto le quería Ana!	How (much) Anna loved him.
¡Pero cuánto le temía!	But how (much) she feared him!

Recall, however: **¡qué!** translates *how*! before an adjective or adverb (**¡Qué bien lo hace!** How well he does it!), and **¡cómo!** refers to the way in which the action is done (**¡Cómo dibuja!** How he draws!).

C. **¡Quién!**

¡Quién! followed by a verb in the **-ra** form of the imperfect subjunctive, has the meaning *how I wish . . . if only I could . . .*

¡Quién supiera escribir!	If only I could write!

110. *Someone* and *Anyone*

A. **Alguien** means *someone*—some specific person.

Alguien llama a la puerta.	Someone is at the door.
¡Alguien me lo pagará!	Someone will pay for it!

B. **Cualquiera** means *anyone at all.*

Cualquiera que me engañe lo sentirá.	Anyone who deceives me will regret it.
Cualquiera sabrá eso.	Anyone at all will know that.

1. **Un cualquiera** means *a nobody*, *an ordinary fellow*, a person who is just anybody at all.

No te dejaré casarte con un cualquiera.	I won't let you marry a nobody.

2. As an adjective, **cualquier**(**a**) means *any . . . at all*, *any . . . whatever*. When placed before a noun, it loses its final **a.** The plural form is **cualesquier**(**a**).

Me contento con un dibujo cualquiera.	I'll be satisfied with any sketch at all.
Cualquier vestido servirá para esa fiesta.	Any dress at all will do for that party.

111. *Some, Any, Several, A few*

A. The idea of *some* or *any* is most frequently implied in Spanish by merely omitting the article.

¿Tienes fósforos?	Do you have any matches?

B. **Algunos** and **varios** indicate *some* or *several*, and although indefinite in number, have a more numerical implication than the wholly indefinite omission of the article.

¿Tienes algunos fósforos?	Do you have some (a few, several) matches?

Varios is the less used of these adjectives. Aside from its meaning of *several*, it bears the further sense of *various* and *sundry*.

Vende varios tipos de cuadernos.	He sells several (different) kinds of notebooks.

C. **Unos cuantos** and **unos pocos** are synonymous and mean *a few, a small number of*.

Tengo sólo unos cuantos (o unos pocos).	I have only a few.

D. **Alguno que otro** means *a few, some*, in the sense of *an occasional*.

En el puerto se veía alguno que otro bote de vela.	In the port an occasional sailboat (a few sailboats) could be seen.

(For the difference between *little* and *a little*, see p. 276.)

112. Negatives

A. In certain cases, negatives are used although the sentence is not obviously negative.

1. After comparatives (see **105** D)

El sabe más que nadie.	He knows more than anyone.

2. In sentences where a negative meaning is implied

Me fue imposible hacer nada.	It was impossible (not possible) for me to do anything.

3. After **sin**

Sin dirigir palabra a nadie, salió del cuarto.	Without speaking to anyone, he left the room.
Eso me dejaría sin nada que ponerme.	That would leave me without anything to wear.

B. In other cases, affirmatives are occasionally used for negatives, often with special emphasis.

1. **Alguno,** following the noun, is an emphatic equivalent of **ninguno** (not) any, none.

No le hagas caso alguno.	Don't pay any attention at all to him.
No me dio indicación alguna.	He didn't give me any indication at all.

2. **En mi vida** is used very frequently to mean *never in my life.*

En mi vida he jugado a las cartas.	Never in my life have I played cards.
En su vida ha molestado a nadie.	Never in his life has he bothered anybody.

3. **En absoluto** means *absolutely not*!

¿Papá, me darás un coche? —¡En absoluto!	Dad, will you give me a car? —Absolutely not!

EJERCICIOS

I. Traducción.

I had never seen such a house in my life. It looked like a castle, for (**pues**) it had a round tower at each end, its roof was covered with battlements, and its windows were round and small.

"What a strange house!" exclaimed my wife when she first saw it (**al verla**). And although I didn't say anything, I didn't like it at all. If I had known what surprises were awaiting us in it, I would never have gone there for my vacation. But my uncle had written me from Europe, asking me whether I wanted to spend a few weeks in his house, since nobody lived there, and I had accepted his invitation.

Although the rooms were somewhat gloomy, they were comfortable, and after we had dusted the furniture, we began to feel at home. The first night passed without incident, but I shall never forget the second night.

Between one o'clock in the morning and four o'clock, there were strange noises on the upper floor. Doors opened, beds moved, and footsteps were heard in hallways and rooms. We knew that nobody could have entered the house without our knowing it. We didn't believe in ghosts, but what were we to think?

The noises stopped at dawn. We decided to stay one more night (**una noche más**). The same thing (**lo mismo**) happened that night—the same noises, the same footsteps. The next day, we packed out suitcases and left, swearing that we would never sleep in that house again.

—I would have stayed a little longer. A little noise never hurt anyone. And besides, the trip must have cost you so much.

—I know. But we felt that any place would be better than that. Tell me, which would you prefer: to lose sleep or to lose money?

—What a question! Do you know what I would do? Well, I'll tell you. . . .

II. Composición.

Cómo explico yo el incidente arriba referido y lo que haría en tal situación

LECCIÓN TRECE

ADJECTIVES

Adaptado de un artículo por Afranio Melo

AMÉRICAS

Unión Panamericana, noviembre de 1963

La Ruta del Siglo

La constitución brasileña de 1946 contiene providencias para promover el desarrollo económico del Amazonas y del nordeste, que son las dos zonas subdesarrolladas más extensas del país. El programa consiste especialmente en superar la pobreza extrema del habitante de la selva amazónica, que vive en precarias chozas de paja, crónicamente mal nutrido y analfabeto. Esa gente está desparramada sobre un área de más de 4,000,000 de kilómetros cuadrados y dedicada a labores de poca productividad material y monetaria. Su nivel de vida es de los más bajos del mundo.

Cuando se construyó Brasilia en las colinas del Estado de Goías, el centro político de la nación se trasladó tierra adentro. Renovado interés se mostró por tener una carretera que uniera la región del Amazonas con la nueva capital. A mediados de 1958 se comenzó la construcción de la carretera Belem-Brasilia, "la carretera del siglo". En algunas partes las dificultades para llegar al sitio donde se construía el camino obligaron a utilizar medios aéreos de acceso. Se construyeron nueve aeropuertos y numerosos puentes, entre ellos algunos de grandes dimensiones. También hubo que derribar árboles y limpiar de troncos un área de más de 16 millones de metros cuadrados.

Tres verdaderos milagros ocasionados por la construcción de la carretera muestran su significación como instrumento de progreso. El primero de esos milagros se llama Gurupí. Situada en la porción central de Goías, a unos 746 kilómetros de Brasilia, esta población tiene sólo cinco años de existencia y ya cuenta con más de 8,000 habitantes. Imperatriz es un segundo milagro. Desde hace 50 años, hasta que se construyó la carretera no se habían edificado casas. La ciudad vivía del pasado, del esplendor de la época del caucho. Ahora llegó el camino y con él multitud de obreros y diversas ocupaciones relacionadas con la construcción. La ciudad empezó entonces a crecer de nuevo y fue invadida por gente del nordeste. Esta gente es realmente trabajadora. El municipio de Imperatriz solía producir 40,000 sacos de arroz por cosecha y ahora produce más de 200,000.

El tercer milagro producido por la carretera fue el de Ceres. Hoy Ceres es una población de 10,000 habitantes y provee de cereales y vegetales a la parte sur del Estado y a Brasilia. Su desarrollo no se debe únicamente a la fertilidad de la tierra sino también a las facilidades de transporte que se le han abierto ahora.

Tal es la historia de la famosa "carretera del siglo" que puede transformar en el futuro todo el paisaje de una vasta porción del interior del Brasil. Abierta y construida por miles de brasileños anónimos, elogiada por unos y criticada por otros, este camino está dándole de hecho al Brasil regiones que anteriormente le pertenecían sólo en el papel.

PREGUNTAS

1. ¿Qué providencias contiene la constitución brasileña de 1946?
2. ¿Cómo vive la gente de la selva amazónica?
3. ¿Sobre qué área está desparramada esa gente?
4. ¿Dónde se construyó la nueva capital Brasilia?
5. ¿Qué tuvieron que construir como consecuencia?
6. ¿Cuándo se comenzó la construcción de la carretera Belem-Brasilia?
7. ¿Qué dificultades encontraron al construir el camino?
8. ¿Qué efecto ha tenido la carretera en el pueblo de Gurupí?
9. ¿Cómo era Imperatriz antes de la llegada del camino? ¿Cómo es ahora?
10. ¿A qué factores se debe el desarrollo de Ceres?

CONVERSACIÓN

1. ¿Conoce Ud. un pueblo o ciudad que haya nacido como consecuencia de la construcción de una carretera, un aeropuerto, una fábrica, etc.? ¿Conoce Ud. una población que haya muerto como resultado del traslado de una industria mayor?
2. ¿Ha cambiado en años recientes la condición económica del pueblo en que vive Ud.? ¿Cómo?
3. ¿Ha visto Ud. alguna vez un caso de verdadera pobreza? ¿Dónde fue? ¿Se ha hecho algo por remediarla?
4. ¿Cree Ud. que los Estados Unidos deben ofrecer ayuda económica a los países subdesarrollados? ¿Cree Ud. que la ayuda económica trae consigo el derecho de exigir ciertas reformas internas en el país recipiente?

PART A

113. Function and Forms of Adjectives

A. Use and agreement

1. An adjective is used to describe a noun. Therefore, it must always agree in gender and number with the noun it describes.

Está cansado.	He is tired.
Gloria es simpatiquísima.	Gloria is very nice.
Nuestros amigos italianos...	Our Italian friends . . .

2. If an adjective modifies two nouns of the same gender, the plural of that gender is used.

blusas y ropas muy bonitas very pretty blouses and dresses

3. If an adjective modifies both a masculine and a feminine noun, the masculine plural is used.

novelas y cuentos históricos historical novels and stories

B. The feminine singular

1. Adjectives ending in **-o** change the final **-o** to **-a.**

un día hermoso a beautiful day
una muchacha hermosa a beautiful girl

2. Adjectives ending in **-dor** or **-ón, -án, -ín,** and adjectives of nationality that end in consonant add **-a.**

un capataz muy trabajador a hardworking foreman
una mujer muy trabajadora a hardworking woman
el gobierno francés the French government
la poesía francesa French poetry

3. All other adjectives have the same form for both the masculine and feminine.

un libro fácil an easy book
una canción fácil an easy song
un tono suave a soft tone
una brisa suave a soft breeze
un chico cortés a polite boy
una persona cortés a polite person
mi amigo mejor my best friend
su obra mejor his best work

C. Plural forms

The plural of adjectives is formed exactly like that of nouns: **-s** is added to a singular form that ends in a vowel; **-es** is added to one that ends in a consonant. A final **-z** changes to **-c** before **-es.**

muchos cambios many changes
comidas deliciosas delicious meals
bailes encantadores charming dances
parejas felices happy couples

EJERCICIOS

A. Cambie:

1. un **hombre** hablador (mujer); un **chico** inteligente (chica); un **alumno** perezoso (alumna); un **libro** chiquitín (libreta); un **potro** andaluz (yegua); un **niño** preguntón (niña); un **joven** holgazán (una joven); el **cuarto** interior (la habitación); mi **amigo** francés (amiga); un **estudiante** superior (obra)
2. una **casa** azul (casas); la **luz** rojiza (luces); un **alma** ruin (almas); el **abrigo** gris (abrigos); un **acto** atroz (actos); una **criada** trabajadora (unas criadas); un **tigre** feroz (tigres); un **viejo** hablador (viejos); un **matrimonio** feliz (parejas)

B. Diga en español:

1. a blond child (*m.* and *f.*); a good opportunity; green lamps; difficult lessons; small portions
2. Japanese artists (*m.* and *f.*); young doctors; English literature; a lazy worker; a happy family

114. Shortening of Adjectives

A. A few adjectives drop the final **-o** when they precede a masculine singular noun.

primero, primer first
alguno, algún some
malo, mal bad
postrero, postrer last
bueno, buen good
tercero, tercer third
ninguno, ningún no, none

Ése es un buen ejemplo.	That is a good example.
No tengo ningún dinero.	I have no money.
El primer día de cada mes...	The first day of each month . . .

B. Three common adjectives lose their last syllable under certain conditions.

1. **Grande** (large, great) becomes **gran** before any singular noun.

   (**un**) **gran número** a large number
   una gran obra de arte a great work of art

2. **Ciento** (one hundred) becomes **cien** before all nouns and before the numerals **mil** and **millón.** It is not shortened before any other numeral.

Pío Baroja escribió cien obras.	Pio Baroja wrote a hundred works.
Recibió cien mil votos.	He got 100,000 votes.

But:

Hay ciento dos páginas.	There are 102 pages.

3. **Santo** (Saint) becomes **San** before all masculine names except **Domingo** and **Tomás.**

   San Francisco St. Francis
   San Agustín St. Augustine

But:

   Santo Domingo St. Dominick
   Santa Teresa St. Theresa

EJERCICIOS

A. Conteste en español:

1. ¿En qué página estamos ahora? 2. ¿De qué trata el primer capítulo de este libro? 3. ¿En qué página empieza la lección tercera? 4. ¿Qué ciudades norteamericanas llevan nombres de santos? 5. ¿Hay más de cien mil habitantes en el pueblo donde vive Ud.? 6. ¿Cuántos años hay en un siglo? 7. ¿Cuántos años hace que somos una nación independiente? 8. ¿Cree Ud. que tiene buen gusto en el vestir? 9. ¿A quién considera Ud. un gran hombre (o una gran mujer)? 10. ¿Cuántos centavos vale un dólar? ¿Y diez dólares?

B. Diga en español:

1. Some day; no time; some friends of mine. 2. His third wife; the first seat; the second story; the first of June. 3. A good possibility; bad taste; a great poet. 4. One hundred and fifty; a hundred years; a hundred million Americans; St. Andrew; St. Ann.

115. General View of the Position of Adjectives

Unlike English, Spanish does not have a fixed position for most adjectives. Spanish adjectives both precede and follow the noun. However, many adjectives do have a fairly specific position in normal use, and if that position is changed, the adjective acquires a special emphasis or a different connotation.

116. Placement of Adjectives After the Noun

A. The primary function of an adjective that is placed after the noun is to set that noun off from others of its kind.

una lámpara azul a blue lamp

(Blueness is not a general characteristic of lamps. Rather, it distinguishes the lamp it describes from lamps of other colors.)

B. The following are important categories of distinguishing adjectives that regularly follow the noun:

1. Adjectives of nationality and religion

   los perfumes franceses French perfumes
   la Reforma Protestante the Protestant Reformation

2. Adjectives of color and shape

   la Casa Blanca the White House
   una mesa redonda a round table

3. Adjectives referring to branches of learning, classifications, or scientific terminology

   un estudio psicológico (literario, geográfico, filosófico, etc.) a psychological (literary, geographic, philosophical, study etc.)
   ácido acético acetic acid

4. Adjectives modified by adverbs (especially those modified by **más** or **menos**)

   una canción muy triste a very sad song
   el autor más leído del año the most read author of the year

5. Participles used as adjectives

   una figura arrodillada a kneeling figure
   una causa perdida a lost cause

EJERCICIO

Cambie:

1. una situación peligrosa (interesante, nueva, difícil)
2. la revolución rusa (francesa, americana, hispanoamericana)
3. um drama psicológico (filosófico, contemporáneo, clásico)
4. mi tío rico (casado, mayor, peruano, neoyorquino)
5. sus zapatos viejos (nuevos, negros, gastados)

117. Placement of Adjectives Before the Noun

A. Demonstrative, unstressed possessive,[1] and indefinite adjectives (including **mucho** and **poco**), and cardinal numbers regularly precede the noun.

esta ciudad this city
tres ratones ciegos three blind mice
nuestros parientes our relatives
algún día some day
poca diferencia little difference

B. Certain common adjectives (**bueno, malo, joven, viejo, pequeño**) often precede, but may follow the noun.

Eres un buen muchacho (or **un muchacho bueno**).	You are a good boy.
Es un joven periodista (or **un periodista joven**).	He is a young newspaperman.

C. A usually distinguishing adjective may be placed before the noun if the speaker wishes to describe a normal characteristic of that noun, rather than to differentiate it from other nouns of its type (cf. **122**B).

la blanca nieve the white snow
la alta Sierra Nevada the lofty Sierra Nevada
la hermosa Escocia beautiful Scotland

D. In a question, the predicate adjective after **ser** or **estar** precedes the subject.

¿Está casada tu hermana?	Is your sister married?
¿Es muy rico su tío?	Is his uncle very rich?

[1] The stressed forms **mío, tuyo**, etc., of course, always follow the noun.

EJERCICIOS

A. Conteste en español:

1. ¿Tiene Ud. un hermano mayor (o una hermana mayor)? 2. ¿Tiene hermanos menores? 3. ¿Vive su familia en esta ciudad? 4. ¿Cuántos días hay en cada semana? 5. ¿Se considera Ud. un buen estudiante de lenguas? 6. ¿Es alto o bajo su padre? ¿Y su madre? 7. ¿Son ricos la mayor parte de sus parientes? 8. ¿Están casados ya algunos de sus amigos?

B. Diga en español:

1. Our town has five public libraries. 2. Is your brother slim or heavy? 3. The red blood was staining his white shirt. 4. He has written several historical novels in recent years. 5. Richard is the most intelligent boy I know. 6. A dazzling sun was coming in through the open windows.

118. Changes in Meaning According to Position

Many adjectives have a significant difference in meaning when they are placed before or after the noun. Note particularly the following:

un hombre grande a big man
un gran hombre a great man

un amigo viejo an old (elderly) friend
un viejo amigo an old (long-standing) friend

el muchacho pobre the poor (not rich) boy
el pobre muchacho the poor (pitiful) boy

119. Placement of Two or More Adjectives

There are two principal ways of handling two or more adjectives that modify one noun.

A. Place one adjective before the noun and one (or more) after the noun. The shorter, or the more subjective, adjective will precede.

Mi rico tío venezolano me mandó este anillo.	My rich Venezuelan uncle sent me this ring.
Un estupendo poeta contemporáneo francés...	A magnificent contemporary French poet . . .

B. When both (or all) adjectives are felt to be equal in their distinguishing force, place them after the noun, joining two by **y,** or separating them all by commas.

un muchacho listo y simpático
a bright, nice boy

una novela larga, aburrida, (y) **hueca**
a long, boring, and shallow novel

For a more poetic or dramatic effect, the adjectives may all be placed before the noun.

los largos, sombríos, (y) tortuosos corredores
the long, somber, winding corridors

EJERCICIOS

A. Conteste afirmativamente empleando los adjetivos indicados entre paréntesis:

1. ¿Está su casa de campo en un cerro? (muy alto). 2. ¿Acaba Ud. de hablar con esa chica? (simpática) 3. ¿Conoció Ud. ayer a este joven? (rico, americano) 4. ¿Estudian Uds. ahora literatura? (moderna, inglesa) 5. ¿Recuerda Ud. al huérfano que vimos allí? (pobre, ciego, enfermo) 6. ¿Es amigo de Ud. el señor García? (antiguo, mío) 7. ¿Te gustaría ahora un baño? (bueno, caliente) 8. ¿Le gustan las flores? (pequeñas, amarillas, azules) 9. ¿Tiene amigos ese muchacho? (algunos, interesantes) 10. ¿Ha escrito Ud. ya un estudio sobre España? (bueno, geográfico, cultural)

B. Escriba en español:

1. The young Argentinian author has just written a new psychological drama. 2. The poor woman fell down a long and winding staircase. 3. It was a magnificent afternoon, one of those clear, cool afternoons we always liked so much. 4. A black silent figure was hiding behind the back door of the little house.

120. Use of Prepositional Phrases Instead of Adjectives

When an English adjective denotes the material out of which something is made, Spanish generally uses a prepositional phrase (**de** + the material) instead of an adjective.

una casa de madera a wooden house
una pared de vidrio a glass wall
un techo de paja a thatched roof
un anillo de oro a gold ring

EJERCICIO

Diga en español:

a brick house, a diamond bracelet, leather shoes, a cotton dress, a silk robe, a Swiss watch (**¡Ojo!**), an aluminum table, a plastic toy, a straw hat, a steel beam, an electric light (!), nylon stockings, a wool suit, an iron pot

121. Adjectives Used as Nouns

A. An adjective is often used with a definite or indefinite article to form a noun.

un belga, los eslavos a Belgian, the Slavs
un viejo, la joven an old man, the young girl
algún insolente some fresh fellow

B. With the neuter article **lo,** the masculine singular form of the adjective becomes an abstract noun that describes the quality indicated by the adjective.

Lo bueno y lo malo...	Good and bad . . .
Lo curioso era...	The strange (thing or part) was . . .
Lo mejor del viaje era...	The best (part) of the trip was . . .

EJERCICIO DE REPASO

1. Concrete steps should be taken to improve the economic situation of the nation.
2. The collapse of the rubber industry resulted in a deep economic crisis.
3. The population of that jungle used to live in precarious straw huts.
4. The low standard of living of those poor people was reflected in their food and clothing.
5. The administrative structure of the federal government was transferred inland.
6. The old plan of a network of roads does not include an artery that crosses the Amazon jungle.
7. The official name of this great road was BR–14, but it also bore the name of a famous engineer who died in the teeming tropical jungle.
8. Among the numerous bridges that they will have to build, two will be of major dimensions.
9. I hope they will be able to adapt themselves to these new and difficult conditions.
10. They have been building this important highway for five years.

REPASO DE VERBOS

Estudie los verbos **ver** y **querer** y después diga en español:

I want you to see it. They wanted us to see them. He refused. Did you (**tú**) see her? Will they want to come? I doubt that he'll want (to). I should like to go.

PART B

122. Further Analysis of the Position of Adjectives

Although demonstrative, numerical, possessive, and indefinite adjectives normally precede the noun, and other adjectives—of color, shape, nationality, etc.—generally follow the noun (cf. **116**), the position of adjectives, on the whole, is quite flexible. Although it is impossible to give an overall rule covering every situation, the following considerations may serve as guides in determining the position of the adjective.

A. By being placed after the noun, the adjective is given a distinguishing force, thereby setting off the noun from other nouns of the same category.

Las mujeres hermosas no son necesariamente menos inteligentes que las feas.	Beautiful women are not necessarily less intelligent than homely ones.

B. By being placed before the noun, the adjective has one of two implications.

1. It expresses a characteristic or expected quality of the noun. There is no particular stress on the adjective in a distinctive sense.

Las hermosas modelos demostraban las últimas modas.	The beautiful models were demonstrating the latest fashions.
Los musculosos boxeadores entraron en el cuadrilátero.	The muscular boxers entered the ring.

Adjectives of size frequently precede the noun, since the qualities expressed are often felt to be inherent in the noun. When placed after the noun, these adjectives retain their distinguishing sense.

una pequeña casa a small house
una casa pequeña

un largo viaje a long trip
un viaje largo

2. It may acquire an emotional, intense, or often poetic value, stressing a subjective attitude on the part of the speaker.

Contrast this with the literal meaning of the adjective placed in its more usual position after the noun.

una histórica ocasión	an historic occasion (history-making, memorable)
una ocasión histórica	an historic occasion (belonging to history)
un fantástico cuento	a fantastic story (amazing, incredible)
un cuento fantástico	a fantastic story (full of fantasy)
sus dramáticas obras	his dramatic works (filled with dramatic impact)
sus obras dramáticas	his dramatic works (theatrical, for the stage)
una imposible tarea	an impossible task (a very difficult task magnified by the emphatic emotional reaction of the speaker)
una tarea imposible	an imposible task (a more objective distinction between this task and others that are feasible)

Even adjectives of color are occasionally placed before the noun to impart a more poetic flavor.

Sus negros ojos me seguían mirando.	His black eyes kept following me.
Me enamoré de sus rubios cabellos.	I fell in love with her blonde hair.

123. Changes of Meaning According to Placement

Aside from the significant changes in meaning already observed in the placement of the adjectives **grande, pobre,** and **viejo** (cf. **118**), the following differences of connotation should also be noted in other common adjectives.

A. **Medio,** before the noun, means *half*; after the noun, it means *average.*

medio indio half-Indian
el hombre medio the average man

B. **Mismo,** before the noun, generally means *same,* and less frequently *very*; after the noun, its normal meaning is the intensifying (*one's*) *self.*

el mismo día the same day
el rey mismo the King himself

C. **Nuevo,** before the noun, means *new* in the sense of *another*; after the noun, it retains the literal sense of *new* (*not old*).

un nuevo plan a new (another) plan
mis zapatos nuevos my new shoes (as contrasted with the old ones)

D. **Alguno,** before the noun, is the indefinite *some*; placed after the noun in a negative sentence, it becomes a very emphatic negative.

Tiene algún talento.	He has some talent.
No tiene talento alguno.	He has absolutely no talent at all.

E. **Ese,** the demonstrative *that,* acquires a derogatory implication when placed after the noun.

ese artista that artist
el artista ese that so-called artist

124. The Position of Ordinal Numbers

Ordinal numbers are generally not used beyond **décimo** (tenth). With the dates of the month, only **el primero** (the first) takes the ordinal.

A. With chapters of books and personal titles, ordinal numbers usually follow the noun.

Capítulo Segundo Chapter II
Carlos Quinto Charles V

But:

Luis Catorce Louis XIV

B. In all other cases, they usually precede the noun.

la tercera página the third page

C. When **primero** and a cardinal number modify the same noun, the cardinal number comes first. This is the opposite of English usage.

los tres primeros cuentos the first three stories

125. The Use of Adjectives in Place of Adverbs

Adjectives are frequently used in Spanish with the force of adverbs, especially in cases where the action described emphasizes the state or condition of the subject, not the manner in which the action is performed.

Salió silenciosa.	She went out silently. (She was silent as she went out.)
Viven felices a pesar de su pobreza.	They live happily in spite of their poverty.
Siempre me saludaban alegres.	They always used to great me gaily.

126. The English Prefix *un* with Adjectives

The English prefix *un* is usually translated in Spanish by placing the adverb **poco** before the adjective, unless the Spanish adjective has a negative form beginning with **in** (**infeliz**—unhappy; **infiel**—unfaithful, etc.).

Eso es poco importante.	That is unimportant.
Nos dieron una comida saludable, pero poco apetitosa.	They gave us a healthful, but unappetizing meal.

127. Replacement of Adjectives by Suffixes

Spanish often adds certain diminutive and augmentative endings to nouns in order to convey not only a feeling of size, but also a favorable or unfavorable connotation. Frequently, the use of such suffixes obviates the need for adjectives.

A. **-ito**

-ito, which sometimes takes the form **-cito,** gives the implication of smallness, plus a generally favorable evaluation. However, it may be used merely to imply affection, with no connotations of size.

una casita a (nice) little house
un hombrecito a small man
Juanito Johnny (no implication of size)
madrecita, mamacita Mom, Mommy
un chiquitito a tiny little boy

The diminutive **-uelo** is less favorable.

un chicuelo a boy, a kid
un tiranuelo a petty tyrant

B. **-illo**

-illo or **-cillo** is a warmly affectionate diminutive ending, but may be used sarcastically.

Juanillo Johnny-boy
una casilla a charming little cottage
un chiquillo a cute little boy (or baby boy)
un autorcillo a would-be author

C. **-ón**

-ón gives a general implication of largeness or impressiveness.

un caserón a mansion
un hombrón a big (impressive looking) man
una mujerona a large woman

D. **-ote**

-ote, -ota imply a derogatory evaluation and are often affixed to adjectives as well as to nouns.

un viejote a surly old man
una zagala grandota a big, hulking shepherd girl

E. **-azo**

-azo implies largeness, but often with a comic or derogatory effect; **-aco** also appears in this sense.

un hombrazo a huge (probably awkward) fellow
un pajarraco a big, ugly bird

F. **-uca, -ucha**

These suffixes, which are used only in the feminine, give a most derogatory connotation.

una mujeruca a slovenly, wretched woman
una casucha a hovel, a shack

128. Lo + Adjective + que

The neuter article **lo,** followed by an adjective and **que,** corresponds to the English *how* + adjective. In this sense, *how* refers to a degree or extent, and is not an exclamation.

No se da cuenta de lo bonita que es.	She doesn't realize how pretty she is.
¿Sabe Ud. lo divertidas que son esas comedias?	Do you know how amusing those plays are?

EJERCICIOS

I. Tradúzcase al español.

When we reached the top of the hill, we saw a magnificent panorama. In the distance some blue mountains, which formed the horizon, stood out against a sky even bluer than the mountains. To the right one could see a large lake surrounded by beautiful cypresses and elegant villas. Many sailboats were moving through the smooth water of that lake, which shimmered in the midday sun. In the center, green fields where a few cows were grazing, stretched out to the foot of the mountains. Some peasants were working in the fields and their white shirts formed a perfect harmony with the green of the grass. To the left there was a small village whose old houses clustered around a beautiful Gothic church. Beyond the village there was a mysterious wood in the midst of which stood an old castle. Everything seemed so peaceful and happy that we too began to feel at peace with the whole world. I don't think many people realize how profound can be the impression made by such a landscape. The view was so beautiful that we did not want to leave the hill and we remained there several hours. Have you ever felt the same sensation? If you have, you will know how happily one can live with nature, and that material things are sometimes unimportant.

II. Composición.

Un paisaje que me llamó la atención
Descripción de un cuarto
Un lugar interesante que he visitado

LECCIÓN CATORCE

ADVERBS AND COMPARISONS

Adaptado de

ESPAÑA SEMANAL

Madrid, 18 de agosto de 1963

Los Misterios Humanos

Cada día compramos alguna cosa. Casi nunca, sin embargo, nos hacemos la pregunta de por qué y cómo lo hacemos. En realidad, la adquisición de un producto no es más que la conclusión de una serie de procedimientos mentales, de impresiones y reflexiones. Y las técnicas comerciales se valen cada día más de la psicología para influir en el ritmo de las ventas. El problema, como oímos decir a muchos industriales, no está en producir, sino en vender.

Se ha visto por experiencia que se puede hacer una previsión más o menos certera en los productos alimenticios. Pero la predicción del gusto de los consumidores no es tan fácil en otros terrenos. Cuando las personas han satisfecho el hambre, el sueño y otras necesidades, tienen a su disposición productos que, hasta cierto punto, son superfluos y que permiten mayor libertad para escoger. Aquí es donde comienzan las dificultades para el psicólogo y para el vendedor.

Parece que sólo la menor parte de los compradores son capaces de valorar objetivamente una mercancía. Especialmente importante es la presentación de la mercancía, el ambiente de la venta y la personalidad del vendedor. Por ejemplo, para los paquetes de cigarrillos americanos se ha visto que eran particularmente eficaces figuras de jóvenes deportivos y de bronceadas muchachas. Figuras como éstas tanto se pueden enfocar hacia el público femenino como al masculino. Cuando se quiere abrir una brecha en el comprador masculino, se ha visto que la figura más eficaz es la de una muchacha que muestre, según un conocido psicólogo, "una cierta complacencia". Las mujeres, sin embargo, prefieren las figuras de una pareja feliz y afectuosa, un hombre elegante, o escenas de familia con niños pequeños.

A veces la presentación no tiene el menor efecto en la mentalidad de algunas personas. Muchas mujeres miran antes de todo la etiqueta con el precio y sólo compran artículos en reclamo. Unos carteles bien visibles que terminen con el número nueve tienen una acción sumamente persuasiva en muchas mujeres. Así, por ejemplo, anunciar un artículo a 99 pesetas tiene mucho más atractivo que si se pusiera el cartelito del precio en las 100 pesetas.

Personas sugestionables, con tendencias neuróticas, tienden a ser más receptivas a la propaganda y la presentación, pero en las compras intervienen también motivos más simples. Bajo el estímulo del hambre, las compras alimenticias son mayores. La miopía impide a muchos comprar en los supermercados, ya que la vista no alcanza las mercancías colocadas demasiado altas. En suma, el lugar de la venta es casi siempre una exposición estudiada científicamente y tiende a asemejarse a un laberinto lleno de sorpresas.

PREGUNTAS

1. ¿De qué se valen cada día más las técnicas comerciales?
2. ¿Cuál es el problema mayor de los industriales?
3. ¿En qué productos se puede hacer una previsión más o menos certera?
4. ¿Qué permiten los productos superfluos?
5. ¿Cuántos compradores son capaces de valorar realmente una mercancía?
6. ¿Qué es especialmente importante?
7. ¿Qué figuras son más eficaces para vender cigarrillos? ¿Por qué?
8. ¿Qué figuras prefieren en general las mujeres?
9. ¿Qué otras condiciones afectan las ventas?
10. ¿Quiénes son más receptivas a la propaganda y la presentación?

CONVERSACIÓN

1. ¿Le gusta ir de compras? ¿Con qué frecuencia va? ¿Qué compras ha hecho Ud. esta semana?
2. ¿Influyen en Ud. la presentación de la mercancía y el ambiente del almacén? ¿Recuerda Ud. haber comprado algo alguna vez porque el vendedor había sido muy amable con Ud.? ¿En qué orden de importancia pondría Ud. los siguientes: presentación, calidad, precio, ambiente?

3. ¿Ha comprado Ud. alguna vez una verdadera ganga? ¿Qué fue? ¿Compró el artículo porque era una ganga o porque lo necesitaba?
4. ¿Qué le parece a Ud. la propaganda comercial que se hace en la televisión y la radio? ¿Compra Ud. muchos de los productos presentados así? ¿Cuáles ha comprado? ¿Quedó Ud. satisfecho después? ¿Cree Ud. que sería mejor la televisión de circuito cerrado sin anuncios comerciales?

PART A

129. Adverbs

A. Function of adverbs

Adverbs are used to modify a verb, an adjective, or another adverb. They answer the questions *where*? *how*? *when*?

Viene a menudo a visitarnos.	He comes often to visit us.
Tienen algunas ideas muy buenas.	They have some very good ideas.
No canta tan mal.	He doesn't sing too badly.
Vivimos allá en la cuesta.	We live there on the hill.
¿A dónde vas?[1]	Where are you going?

B. Formation of adverbs

Most adverbs of manner (*how*?) are formed by adding **—mente** to the feminine singular form of the adjective.

lento slow	**lentamente** slowly
amargo bitter	**amargamente** bitterly
fácil easy	**fácilmente** easily
cortés polite	**cortésmente** politely

C. Position of adverbs

1. Although there is no rigidly fixed position for adverbs, it is generally good form to place the adverb immediately after the verb it modifies, and immediately before the adjective or adverb it modifies.

Escribe maravillosamente.	He writes wonderfully.
Ella sabe mucho más que yo.	She knows much more than I.
Viven muy cerca.	They live very near.

[1] **¿A dónde?** (or **¿adónde?**) must be used with verbs of motion.

2. In a phrase consisting solely of **no** and an adverb, Spanish places the adverb first.

Ahora no.	Not now.
Todavía no.	Not yet.

EJERCICIOS

A. Conteste negativamente, empleando adverbios de significado opuesto:

1. ¿Hablan **bien** el español? 2. ¿Quiere que escribamos **mucho**? 3. ¿Insiste en que leamos **rápidamente**? 4. ¿Vivís **cerca**? 5. ¿Le digo a Pablo que venga **temprano**? 6. ¿Protestaron **fuertemente**? 7. ¿Prefiere Ud. que me siente **aquí**? 8. ¿Se les puede ver **fácilmente**? 9. ¿Se lo decía a Ud. **siempre**? 10. ¿Está **arriba** tu padre? 11. ¿Trabajas **fuera** ahora? 12. ¿Ha llegado **ya** el correo?

B. Diga en español:

1. You can do better if you try. 2. Don't complain so much. 3. He always buys himself expensive suits. 4. Anita never does (**sale**) well on exams. 5. There is too much to (**que**) do here. 6. There's my car. Where is yours? 7. They speak very clearly, don't they?

130. Equal Comparisons of Adjectives and Adverbs

A. **Tanto... como** as much . . . as; in the *plural*, as many . . . as

1. Used as an adjective, **tanto** will agree in gender and number with the noun it modifies.

No tenemos tanto trabajo como ellos.	We don't have as much work as they.
¿Sabe Ud. tantos poemas como ella?	Do you know as many poems as she?

2. As an adverb, **tanto** never changes its ending.

No compra tanto aquí como antes.	He doesn't buy as much here as before.
Paco no come tanto como debiera.	Paco doesn't eat as much as he should.

B. **Tan... como** as . . . as

Tan is used only to modify an adjective or another adverb. It is NEVER used before **mucho.**

Es tan leal como valiente.	He is as loyal as (he is) brave.
Mi sobrino es tan alto como yo.	My nephew is as tall as I.
Hablan español tan bien como cualquier hispano.	They speak Spanish as well as any native.

But:

Ella sabe tanto como sus maestros.	She knows as much as her teachers.

Tan, used without **como,** means *so.*

Estamos tan contentos.	We are so pleased.

EJERCICIOS

A. Cambie las frases siguientes para expresar una comparación de igualdad:

1. No hay nadie **más** inteligente **que** Ricardo. 2. Tenemos **más** dinero **que** todos ellos juntos. 3. Debes tener **más** paciencia **que** tu hermana. 4. Estaban **menos** cansados **que** antes. 5. Mi coche es **más** nuevo **que** el suyo. 6. Habla **mejor que** nosotros. 7. No quiero estudiar **más.** 8. Habrá **menos** hombres **que** mujeres a bordo. 9. Gasta **menos que** Uds. 10. Tiene **más** discos **que** un almacén.

B. Diga en español:

1. I am so tired. —You can't be as tired as I. 2. The chief had as many enemies as friends. 3. You shouldn't smoke so much. —I don't smoke as much as you. 4. There were as many employees as clients at the reception. 5. She dances as well as a professional dancer. 6. Please. Don't do so many things at a time.

131. Unequal Comparisons of Adjectives and Adverbs

A. Regular comparatives

To form most comparatives, **más** (more) or **menos** (less) is placed before the adjective or adverb.

más enfermo sicker
más difícil more difficult
menos inteligente less intelligent
más despacio more slowly

Mi coche es más nuevo.	My car is newer.
—El mío es más hermoso.	—Mine is prettier.
Por favor, caminen Uds. más rápidamente.	Please walk faster.

B. Irregular comparatives

1. Six adjectives and four adverbs are compared irregularly in Spanish.

Adjectives		*Adverbs*		*Comparative*	
mucho	much; *pl.*, many	**mucho**	much, a great deal	**más**	more
poco	little (in amount or degree)	**poco**	little	**menos**	fewer, less
bueno	good	**bien**	well	**mejor**	better
malo	bad	**mal**	badly	**peor**	worse
grande	large			**mayor**[2]	older, larger
pequeño	small			**menor**[2]	younger, smaller

2. **Grande** and **pequeño** may also be compared regularly: **más grande, más pequeño,** etc. In this sense, the adjective refers only to size, not to age.

Pedro es mayor, pero Raúl es más grande.	Peter is older, but Ralph is bigger.

EJERCICIO

Lea con cuidado, y después conteste las preguntas:
1. Mario tiene veinte años. Juan tiene quince... ¿Quién es mayor? 2. Arturo tiene dos metros de alto. José tiene 1.80... ¿Quién es más bajo? 3. Andrés ha sacado una A en el examen, David una B... ¿Quién salió mejor? 4. Pedro recorre los cien metros en veinte segundos, Guillermo en catorce... ¿Quién corre más rápidamente? 5. El libro azul mide treinta centímetros de largo y veintidós de ancho. El libro rojo mide diecinueve de largo y trece de ancho... ¿Cuál es más pequeño? 6. Segovia está a cincuenta kilómetros, El Escorial a cuarenta... ¿Cuál está más lejos? 7. Yo llego en diez minutos, Carlos en doce... ¿Quién vive más cerca?

132. Translations of *than*

A. Que

When a direct comparison is made between two persons, things, or actions, *than* is translated by **que,** except before a number.

Paco es más alto que tú.	Frank is taller than you.
Hemos visto más películas este año que el año pasado.	We have seen more movies this year than last year.
Ahora sé menos que antes.	Now I know less than before.
Canta mejor que baila.	She sings better than she dances.

[2] To keep in mind the meaning of **mayor**—*older, larger*—and **menor**—*younger, smaller*—think of *major* and *minor*.

B. **De**

Before a number, *than* is translated by **de.**

El viaje dura menos de cuatro horas.	The trip takes less than four hours.
El gobierno ha gastado más de diez millones de dólares en eso.	The government has spent more than ten million dollars on that.
¿Cuánto dinero le queda? —No más de cinco dolares.	How much money do you have left?—No more than five dollars.

The idiom **no más que** means *only*.

No tengo más que cinco dólares.	I have only five dollars.

C. **De** + definite article + **que**

When the sentence has *two* stated verbs and *than* really means *than what*, *than the one(s) who or that*, etc., it is translated by **del que, de los que, de la que, de las que,** or **de lo que.**

1. If the object being compared by the two clauses is a noun, the article that corresponds to that noun follows **de.**

Tiene más amigos de los que puede invitar.	He has more friends than (those whom) he can invite.
María debe más dinero del que ganará en toda su vida.	Mary owes more money than (that which) she'll earn in her whole life.

2. When an adjective, an adverb, or a whole idea is being compared, the neuter article **lo** follows **de.**

Es más bonita de lo que esperábamos.	She is prettier than (what) we expected.
Canta mejor de lo que nos habían dicho.	He sings better than (what) we had been told.
Entienden más de lo que crees.	They understand more than (what) you think.

EJERCICIOS

A. Conteste en español con frases completas:

1. ¿Es Ud. más alto o más bajo que su mejor amigo? 2. ¿Es su madre mayor o menor que su padre? 3. En su opinión, ¿es más fácil el inglés que el español? 4. ¿Trabaja Ud. menos este semestre que el semestre pasado? 5. ¿Le gustan más sus cursos este año que el año pasado? ¿Por qué? 6. ¿Tiene Ud. más amigos ahora que cuando asistía a la escuela superior? 7. ¿Tiene Ud. menos de diez dólares en el bolsillo (o en la bolsa) hoy?

8. ¿Conoce Ud. a alguien que tenga más de ochenta años? 9. ¿Ha recibido Ud. alguna vez una nota mucho mejor de la que esperaba? 10. ¿Conoce Ud. a alguien que parezca mucho más joven de lo que es? ¿Quién es?

B. Traduzca al español:

1. "More than you know, more than I'd show, man of my heart, I love you so (much)." 2. My dear girl, you are much more in love than I. Why are you so silly? 3. It is better to attend to the more important things first. 4. Juliet is the younger and smaller, but she is much nicer than her sister. 5. I don't think she is as pretty as mine. 6. José received fewer calls than he expected. 7. He knows less than you think.

133. Superlatives

A. General function of superlatives

A superlative compares one person or thing with all others of the same category and states that the object of its comparison has the most or least of a certain quality. Even when the noun to which it is compared is not stated, it is always implied.

B. Formation of superlatives in Spanish

Superlatives are formed by placing the definite article before the comparative. If the definite article is already used before the noun, it is not repeated after it.

Son los mejores de la clase.	They are the best in the class.
Fue el concierto más impresionante del año.	It was the most impressive concert of the year.

Notice that **de** is used after a superlative to translate the English *in*.

EJERCICIOS

A. Conteste en español:

1. ¿A quién considera Ud. el mejor presidente de nuestro país? ¿Por qué? 2. ¿Cuál es la ciudad más grande de este estado? 3. ¿Cuál es la universidad más destacada de todas? 4. ¿Quién es el miembro más viejo de su familia? ¿Cuántos años tiene? 5. ¿Quién es el más joven de su familia? 6. ¿Quién es el mejor profesor (o la mejor profesora) de esta escuela? (!) 7. ¿Cuál fue la noticia más impresionante de este año?

B. Diga en español:

1. We carry a selection of the finest wines. 2. The most expensive products are not always the best. 3. My older brother is one of the best-known

(**más...**) painters in the country. 4. His least valuable works cost more than we can afford (spend).

134. The Pseudo-Superlative—**ísimo**

The intensifying ending **-ísimo,** added to an adjective, corresponds to the English *extremely*, *very*, or *most*. It is not a superlative, since there is no actual or implied comparison with anything else.

Es una persona simpatiquísima.	He is a very (or most) charming person.
Es un día rarísimo.	It's a most unusual day.

EJERCICIO

Diga más enfáticamente:

un joven simpático; un libro interesante; una discusión animada; una familia rica; unos viejos pobres; una charla importante

EJERCICIO DE REPASO

1. It will be more difficult to sell this product than you believe.
2. They explained to us that the greatest problem was not producing, but selling.
3. Every year we produce much more than we can consume.
4. It is possible that the most effective advertising of cigarettes is done on television.
5. Often advertising doesn't have the slightest effect on the mentality of some persons.
6. Labels that attract attention will always have an extremely persuasive effect on many women.
7. It is as important to present a product well as to manufacture it well. —I can't believe that that's true.
8. Easily influenced people are of course the most receptive to advertising.
9. Figures of young sporting men and bronzed girls appeal as much to men as to women.
10. His nearsightedness prevented him from buying more than four or five articles in the supermarket.

REPASO DE VERBOS

Estudie los verbos **salir** and **valer,** y después diga en español:

I'm going out now. It will be worth more some day. We hope it's worth so much. They said that they would go out soon. I'm afraid they're leaving right now. It wouldn't be worth while.

PART B

135. Adverbs

A. Shortening of adverbs

1. When two or more adverbs ending in **-mente** modify the same verb, **-mente** is omitted from all but the last.

Entraron silenciosa y misteriosamente.	They entered silently and mysteriously.

2. **Recientemente** is shortened to **recién** before a past participle used as an adjective.

El misionero recién llegado...	The newly arrived missionary . . .
Los recién casados...	The newlyweds . . .

B. Use of prepositional phrases in place of adverbs

Prepositional phrases are frequently used instead of adverbs of manner.

dulcemente, con dulzura sweetly
irónicamente, con ironía, de modo irónico ironically, sarcastically
sencillamente, con sencillez simply

C. **Lo** + adverb + **que**

The neuter article **lo** followed by an adverb and **que** corresponds to the English *how* + adverb, to indicate extent. It is not an exclamation.

Se quejó de lo despacio que íbamos.	He complained about how slowly we were going.

D. **Dondequiera** wherever

Dondequiera and **adondequiera** are used much as the English *wherever*. When its meaning is *every place*, it is followed by the indicative. When it refers to an indefinite place, it calls for the subjunctive.

Dondequiera (**que**) **trabajaba, le querían todos.**	Every place (wherever) he worked, everyone liked him.
Dondequiera (**que**) **estés, piensa en mí.**	Wherever you are (may be), think of me.

E. Position of adverbs

When an adverb begins the sentence, it is generally more emphatic and often causes an inversion of the subject and verb.

Ud. lo sabe bien. Bien lo sabe Ud.	You know (it) very well.
Su padre siempre le reñía cuando le veía con ella.	His father used to scold him whenever he saw him with her.
Siempre le reñía su padre cuando le veía con ella.	

136. Comparisons

A. **Cuanto... tanto**

Cuanto más (**menos**)**... tanto más** (**menos**) means *the more* (*less*) . . . *the more* (*less*).

Cuanto más estudio, tanto menos comprendo.	The more I study, the less I understand.
Cuanto menos sabe, tanto más grita.	The less he knows, the more he shouts.

B. The regular and irregular comparisons of **bueno** and **malo**

Bueno and **malo** may be compared regularly: **más bueno, más malo**; they may also be compared irregularly: **mejor, peor.** However, there is an important difference in the implication of the two usages.

1. **Mejor** and **peor** are used for all general qualities except personality traits.

Es el peor hotel de la ciudad.	It is the worst hotel in the city.
El mejor estudiante de la escuela...	The best student in the school . . .

2. **Más bueno** and **más malo** refer specifically to traits of character.

Es el hombre más malo del pueblo.	He is the worst (the meanest) man in town.
Es más buena que una santa.	She is better (kinder) than a saint.
Es más bueno que el pan.	He is better than bread. (He is as good as gold.)

C. **Tan** to translate *such* (*a*)

When *such* (*a*) modifies an adjective, **tan** must be used instead of **tal.**

En un día tan hermoso, ¿quién puede trabajar?	On such a nice day, who can work?
Son personas tan buenas.	They are such good people.

But:

En tal caso, tendríamos que ponerle pleito.	In such a case, we would have to sue him.

D. Agreement of **mucho** in comparisons

1. When **mucho más** (much more) or **mucho menos** (much less) is followed by a noun, **mucho** generally retains its function as an adjective, and thereby agrees with the noun.

Mi madre tiene mucha menos paciencia que mi padre.	My mother has much less patience than my father.
El conoce a mucha más gente que yo.	He knows many more people than I.

In the plural, **muchos** (many) always agrees with the noun compared.

Había muchos más hombres que mujeres.	There were many more men than women.
Hoy vinieron muchas más personas que ayer.	Today many more people came than yesterday.

2. When **mucho** precedes **mejor** or any other comparative, it usually functions as an adverb, and is invariable. This is especially true when the adjective comes after the noun it modifies.

Su idea es mucho mejor que la nuestra.	His idea is much better than ours.
Los nuevos planes son mucho más factibles que los originales.	The new plans are much more workable than the original ones.
La Sra. Colón es mucho más razonable que su marido.	Mrs. Colon is much more reasonable than her husband.
Son mucho mejores bailadores que los otros.	They are much better dancers than the others.

137. *Than* in Special Situations

A. **Que** in the comparison of two clauses

1. When two actions are being directly compared, **que** is used. (Recall 132 A.)

Descansa más que trabaja.	He rests more than he works.
Cantan aun peor que bailan.	They sing even worse than they dance.

2. When the subordinate clause begins with a relative pronoun, **que** again translates *than.*

Estos delegados son más liberales que los que vinieron antes.	These delegates are more liberal than the ones who came before.
Esto importa mucho menos que lo que nos dijo ella.	This matters much less than what *she* told us.

B. **De** before words that imply quantity

Even though a specific number is not mentioned, **de** is often used before words implying quantity.

Solía dormir mucho menos de lo normal.	He used to sleep much less than the normal amount.
No me quedan más de unos cuantos.	I don't have more than a few left.
Ése come más de la cuenta.	That fellow eats more than is proper.

EJERCICIOS

I. Traducir al español.

CHARLES: Now you (*fam.*) have to learn to speak Spanish better.

JOHN: Why?

CHARLES: Because, in the first place, it is extremely important to know how to speak foreign languages in order to be able to understand the culture of other peoples. And in the second place, in order to understand and feel the spirit of our Spanish-speaking (**de habla española**) neighbors, it is indispensable to understand and speak their tongue.

JOHN: I have just returned from Europe. Wherever I went I always spoke English and everybody understood me. There are more people than I thought who understand English. So if I go to Latin America, I will do the same. There are as many Latin Americans as Europeans who know English.

CHARLES: Who knows? But even though that may be so, you are not right in insisting that everybody speak to you in English. What would you say if a person from another country came here without knowing one word of English and insisted upon your speaking to him in his own language?

JOHN: But English is much more important. It is the most important language in the world.

CHARLES: Not by any means, according to statistics. There are other languages, especially Asiatic tongues, spoken by many more people. Besides, you know very well how important Spanish is today in the United States, and how frequently it is heard in cities like New York. It is used more and more in the courts, in hospitals, in stores . . .

JOHN: All right, all right. You have convinced me. Where do I learn it?
CHARLES: I shall give you private lessons.
JOHN: Very well. And how much do you charge?
CHARLES: I shall make you a special price: ten dollars an (**la**) hour.
JOHN: Now I understand why you want me to study Spanish.

II. Composición.

1. Por qué es importante (o no es importante) saber lenguas extranjeras en el mundo de hoy
2. El estudio de lenguas extranjeras como requisito universitario
3. Cómo enseñaría yo una lengua extranjera

LECCIÓN QUINCE

THE PASSIVE VOICE

Adaptado de

A B C

Madrid, 10 de agosto de 1963

Asalto al Tren Correo

Ayer a las cinco de la mañana un tren-estafeta fue asaltado en las cercanías de Londres. El botín que fue robado por los atracadores del tren pasa de cuatrocientos veinticinco millones de pesetas. Las recompensas que han sido ofrecidas por las compañías aseguradoras y por Correos ascienden a cuarenta y cuatro millones de pesetas. Toda la policía del país está movilizada, pero aún no tiene una pista segura que conduzca al tesoro. Cientos de detectives están inspeccionando almacenes, viviendas, vehículos y bosques. Otros agentes secretos acuden a los bares para tratar de recoger alguna conversación sospechosa. Se hablaba de una avioneta pintada de rojo que al parecer despegó de un campo de aviación que no está en uso y que se halla cerca del punto donde fue asaltado el tren. Esta tarde, sin embargo, informan que no hay confirmación de ese vuelo misterioso. En la cuneta de la carretera donde esperaba el camión de los bandidos, ha sido descubierta hoy la siguiente inscripción, hecha con tiza amarilla: "Len se fue al otro puente, camino de Cheddington." ¿Una pista, o una broma de algún entusiasta de las investigaciones policíacas?

La policía sospecha que los ladrones han tenido la ayuda de algunos funcionarios relacionados con el transporte de esa ingente suma de dinero. Para el atraco tuvieron que saber cuándo se iba a enviar el tesoro, qué vagones lo llevaban, el horario exacto del tren y la distribución interior de los empleados de Correos. La operación fue realizada por los atracadores sin el menor titubeo y con exactitud matemática.

El director general de Correos anunció esta tarde que será reforzada la protección física de los trenes-estafeta. Se instalarán redes telefónicas dentro de los vagones para asegurar la comunicación entre ellos, y va a ser montado un sistema de radio-teléfono para mantener contacto con el exterior. En ningún caso, sin embargo, los que viajen en esas estafetas irán armados. Según el director general, es preferible que los bandidos aligeren un tren antes de que se registren en el país las escenas de tiros que acreditan a las películas del Oeste. Para los bandidos es un factor muy agradable que el personal de escolta vaya sin armas, pero eso también implica que si aquéllos hacen uso de las suyas y matan a alguien, el punto de destino es la horca.

"¿Están las joyas de la Corona a salvo?", se pregunta hoy un diario. Buen signo es que esas joyas nunca salen de la Torre de Londres para viajar en tren-estafeta.

PREGUNTAS

1. ¿Dónde fue asaltado el tren-estafeta?
2. ¿A qué suma llega el botín que fue robado?
3. ¿Qué recompensas han sido ofrecidas?
4. ¿Qué medidas está tomando la policía?
5. ¿De dónde despegó la avioneta de que se hablaba?
6. ¿Qué fue descubierto en la cuneta de la carretera?
7. ¿Por qué sospecha la policía que los bandidos tuvieron la ayuda de algunos funcionarios?
8. ¿Cómo será reforzada la protección física de los trenes-estafeta?
9. ¿Por qué no quiere el director que el personal de escolta vaya armado?
10. ¿Qué les pasará a los bandidos que usen armas?

CONVERSACIÓN

1. ¿Qué noticia de las últimas dos semanas le impresionó más? ¿Qué noticia del último año? ¿Recuerda Ud. el asesinato del presidente Kennedy? ¿Cuántos años tenía Ud. entonces? ¿Cuáles fueron sus primeras impresiones?
2. ¿Ha ocurrido un robo en su vecindad recientemente? ¿Ha habido un robo alguna vez en su casa o en casa de un amigo o pariente suyo? ¿Cuándo? ¿Encontraron a los ladrones?
3. ¿Cree Ud. que la policía debe usar armas de fuego? ¿Por qué?

PART A

138. The Difference Between Active and Passive Voice

The active voice is a construction in which the subject does the action of the verb. In the passive voice, the subject does not do, but receives the action of the verb.

El presidente le nombrará embajador.	The President will appoint him ambassador. (The subject—President—is doing the appointing.)
Será nombrado embajador (por el presidente).	He will be appointed ambassador (by the President). (The subject—he—is receiving the appointing.)

139. The True Passive

A. The true passive voice in Spanish is formed exactly as in English.

Subject +	**Ser** +	*Past Participle* +	**por**
Nuestra escuela	**fue**	**fundada**	**por el estado.**
Our school	was	founded	by the state.
Estos libros	**serán**	**publicados**	**por Zigzag.**
These books	will be	published	by Zigzag.

Notice that the past participle agrees with the subject.

B. At times, **de** is used instead of **por** to indicate the agent (the doer of the action), particularly when the action is mental or emotional.

Son	**amados**	**de todos.**
They are	loved	by everyone.

C. IMPORTANT: The true passive construction must be used when the doer of the action is expressed.

When the agent is not mentioned, but strongly implied, the true passive (of course, without **por** or **de**) may still be used in many cases.

La Gioconda	**fue**	**pintada**	**entre 1500 y 1504.**
La Gioconda	was	painted	between 1500 and 1504.
Muchos árboles	**han sido**	**plantados**	**en esta vecindad.**
Many trees	have been	planted	in this area.
Juan	**será**	**enviado**	**a Nueva York.**
John	will be	sent	to New York.

D. Remember that the passive voice always involves an action that is being done to the subject. If the sentence expresses a state, not an action, **estar** is used and there is no passive voice. (See **81** C.)

La casa está rodeada de un hermoso jardín.	The house is surrounded by a beautiful garden. (No action.)
Estaban sentados cerca de la ventana.	They were seated near the window.

EJERCICIOS

A. Cambie las frases siguientes según los nuevos sujetos:
1. La presa fue destruida por el diluvio.
(presas, cosechas, árboles, granero)
2. Los folletos han sido confiscados por el gobierno.
(contrabando, drogas, sus obras, pasaportes)
3. La casa será reconstruida pronto.
(edificio, motores, casas, aparato)

B. Conteste afirmativamente las preguntas siguientes empleando en su contestación la voz pasiva:

1. ¿López y Hermanos construirán la casa? (**Sí, la casa será...**) 2. ¿Derribó muchos árboles el huracán? (**Sí, muchos árboles fueron...**) 3. ¿Cortarán la hierba hoy? 4. ¿Han vendido la casa ya? 5. ¿Tu tío escribió ese poema? 6. Miguel Angel pintó ese cuadro, ¿no? 7. Felipe II las invitó a la corte, ¿verdad? 8. ¿Han asaltado un tren-estafeta? 9. ¿La policía ha cogido al ladrón? 10. ¿La compró un famoso millonario? 11. ¿Le aman todos?

C. Diga en español:

1. Our house was built by Losada and Co. 2. It is very well built. 3. Her dresses will be designed by a famous Paris *couturier*. 4. The trunks were sent to a wrong address. 5. Suddenly, the window was opened. 6. He would have been run over by the car if she hadn't called him at (**en**) that moment. 7. The car knocked down an iron fence.

140. Alternates for the True Passive When the Agent Is *NOT* Expressed

A. The impersonal *they* as an alternate for the passive voice

Just as in English, the third person plural may be used in Spanish as a substitute for the passive voice when the agent is not expressed.

Dicen que no será candidato.	It is said (they say) that he will not be a candidate.
Le dieron el premio a María.	Mary was given (they gave Mary) the prize.
Acaban de construir un nuevo edificio.	A new building has just been erected. (They have just erected . . .)

B. The reflexive

A reflexive construction is often used in place of the true passive when the doer of the action is not stated.

1. If the subject of the passive sentence in English is not a person, it becomes the subject of a normal reflexive construction in Spanish (as if it had done the action to itself, or they, to themselves).

Se vendió la casa hace dos meses.	The house was sold two months ago.
Se han escrito muchas novelas sobre este tema.	Many novels have been written on this theme.

Notice that the reflexive verb will normally precede its subject when it is used passively.

2. If the subject of the passive sentence in English is a person (or an animate thing that plausibly could do the action to itself), Spanish uses an impersonal reflexive construction, which is always in the third person singular. *One* (indicated by the impersonal **se**) does the action, and the person to whom the action is done is the object of the verb.

Se la veía allí a menudo.	She was seen there often. (One used to see her there often.)
Se me ha dicho que no vienen.	I have been told that they are not coming. (One has told me . . .)
Se le mató al general.	The general was killed. (One killed the general.)

NOTE: The impersonal reflexive construction can take either a direct or an indirect object.

Se la mandó.	She was sent. (One sent her. *Direct object.*)
Se le ofreció un empleo.	She was offered a job. (One offered a job to her. *Indirect object.*)

However, only **le** and **les** may be used for a third person masculine object, direct or indirect.

Se le halló.	He was found.
Se les llevó.	They were taken.
Se le habrá dejado una fortuna.	He has probably been left a fortune.

EJERCICIOS

A. Cambie las oraciones siguientes por una construcción reflexiva:

1. La casa ha sido vendido ya. (**Ya se ha...**) 2. Los trabajos no han sido iniciados. (**No se han...**) 3. Las puertas fueron abiertas. 4. Mañana pintarán el piso. 5. Le ofrecieron un buen puesto. 6. La sentencia fue anunciada. 7. Así evitarán una catástrofe. 8. Los premios fueron entregados hoy. 9. Han cancelado todos los visados. 10. Dicen que va a llover.

B. Traduzca al español:

1. The article was published in every newspaper. 2. It is very badly written. 3. I am told that it will be very warm out tomorrow. 4. We have been given another chance. 5. Let's give them another chance. 6. Suddenly, the house was surrounded by police. 7. The mirror was broken during the quarrel. 8. The mirror was already broken when I came in. 9. The document has been signed. (3 ways) 10. "Poems are made by fools like me, but only God can make a tree."

141. Summary of the Passive Voice in Spanish

A. When the doer of the action is expressed, the true passive must be used.

***Don Quijote* fue escrito por Cervantes.**	*Don Quixote* was written by Cervantes.
Será recibido por el rey mismo.	He will be received by the king himself.

B. When the agent is not expressed, there are three possible ways of stating the passive idea.

1. The true passive, when an agent is strongly implied[1]

***Don Quijote* fue publicado en 1605.**	*Don Quixote* was published in 1605.
Será bien recibido.	He will be well received.

[1] The true passive construction without agent expressed should not be used when the person to whom the action is done is really the indirect object of the action (see **142** B1).

2. The impersonal *they* (third person plural)

   Publicaron *Don Quijote* en 1605.
   Le recibirán bien.

3. The reflexive
   a. Normal reflexive construction when the subject is not a person

      Se publicó *Don Quijote* en 1605.

   b. Impersonal reflexive (**se** *one*) when the subject of the English passive construction is a person

      Se le recibirá bien.

EJERCICIO

Conteste en español:

1. ¿Cree Ud. que los niños malos deben ser castigados mucho por sus padres? ¿En qué forma? 2. ¿Le castigaban a Ud. mucho cuando era niño? 3. ¿Cree Ud. que un alumno que se comporta mal en la escuela debe ser castigado corporalmente por el maestro? 4. ¿Le han acusado a Ud. injustamente alguna vez? 5. ¿Ha sido Ud. invitado a una fiesta esta semana? 6. ¿Se le ha ofrecido recientemente una buena oportunidad?

EJERCICIO DE REPASO

1. How much money was stolen by the bandits? —More than a million dollars.
2. The whole police force was already mobilized when the second train was attacked.
3. The vehicle has been discovered today in a ditch along (**de**) the road.
4. I hope this operation will be carried out without the slightest hesitation.
5. We have been told that telephones will be installed in the (railroad) cars.
6. I want a radio-telephone (communication) system to be set up as soon as possible.
7. Have you been taught to use these weapons? —Not yet.
8. We prefer that the train be attacked rather than having a single man killed.
9. He was hanged because he had made use of his weapon against one of the unarmed guards.
10. When they approached the building, it was already surrounded by many policemen.

REPASO DE VERBOS

Estudie los verbos **conocer, parecer, etc.,** y después diga en español:
I know him. We didn't know them. Did you deserve it? I'm rocking the baby. He is afraid that they'll perish. They appeared tired. I hope he knows her.

PART B

142. The True Passive Construction

A. Preferred usage

Aside from its required use when the agent is mentioned, the true passive construction is preferred when the agent is not stated, but is strongly implied or obvious.

Este cuadro es de Goya; fue pintado en 1814.	This painting is by Goya; it was painted in 1814.
***Hamlet* fue escrito después de *Julio César*.**	*Hamlet* was written after *Julius Caesar*.

B. Avoidance

1. When a person is the indirect recipient of the passive voice action, the true passive must be replaced by either the third person plural (*they*), *not* reflexive, or by the impersonal reflexive (*one*). The third person plural construction is somewhat more common in spoken language.

Me han dicho que...	I have been told that[2] . . .
Se me ha dicho que...	(It has been told *to* me.)
¿Nos darán otro examen?	Will we be given another exam?
¿Se nos dará otro examen?	(Will it be given *to* us?)
Deben ofrecerles un buen puesto.	They should be offered a good job.
Se les debe ofrecer un buen puesto.	(It should be offered *to* them.)

The true passive is correct when a person is the direct recipient of the passive action.

No fui invitado.	I was not invited.
Debe ser ascendido.	He should be promoted.

[2] **Me ha sido dicho,** though hypothetically correct, is very rarely used and should be avoided.

However, even here, it is being supplanted increasingly, especially in oral usage, by the third person plural construction.

No me invitaron.	I was not invited. (They didn't invite me.)
Deben ascenderle.	He should be promoted. (They should promote him.)

2. In the present and imperfect indicative, the true passive is normally replaced by an active construction when it describes an action in its progress.[3]

El muchacho abre (**está abriendo**) **la ventana.**	The window is (being) opened by the boy.
La guardia de honor izaba (**estaba izando**) **la bandera.**	The flag was being raised by the honor guard.

However, either a true passive or an active construction may be used in these tenses to express a mental or emotional attitude, or an habitual action.

Es temido de todos. **Todos le temen.**	He is feared by all.
Eran respetados hasta de sus enemigos. **Hasta sus enemigos los respetaban.**	They were respected even by their enemies.
Estos romances eran cantados por los gitanos. **Los gitanos cantaban** (**solían cantar**) **estos romances.**	These ballads used to be sung by the gypsies.

143. Preferred Usage of the Third Person Plural

When a verb has both a direct and an indirect object pronoun, the third person plural is used as a substitute for both the reflexive and the true passive constructions. Obviously the use of the reflexive would create the unlikely situation of having three consecutive object pronouns (reflexive, indirect, and direct), and the true passive would be cumbersome and abnormal with an indirect object that refers to a person.

[3] Only with the progressive tense (**estar** + present participle), does the true passive frequently appear: **La cuestión está siendo discutida por la junta.** *The matter is being discussed by the council.* Notice how the progressive emphasizes an action *in progress* at a particular moment.

No se lo han dicho.	He has not been told it.
Se lo preguntaron.	They were asked it.
Me los enseñarán de antemano.	I will be shown them in advance.

144. The Reflexive Passive

A. To imply an accidental or unexpected action (Recall **49** C.)

Se me han olvidado las gafas.	I forgot my glasses.
Se le perdió el dinero.	He lost the money.

B. The reflexive passive vs. the impersonal **se**

There is considerable confusion even in current literate usage between the reflexive substitute for the passive voice and the impersonal construction with **se**.

1. The normal reflexive passive used with persons

We have seen that when a person is subject of the passive sentence in English, and the agent is not mentioned, the proper reflexive construction in Spanish should be the impersonal **se** (one) followed by a verb in the third person singular. The English subject then becomes the object, direct or indirect, of the verb.

Se les veía en todas partes.	They were seen everywhere.

The impersonal third person plural, *not* reflexive, is an alternate: **Los veían en todas partes.**

However, the theoretically incorrect form—**Se veían en todas partes**[4]—is found so frequently in both oral and written Spanish, that it is difficult to dismiss it simply as an error. Moreover, this construction appears with many verbs other than **ver.**

Se oían cantar.	They were heard singing.
Se reclutaron muchos soldados.	Many soldiers were recruited.

2. The impersonal **se** instead of the normal reflexive

The normal reflexive construction is properly used as a substitute for the passive when the subject is not a person and the agent is not expressed.

[4] Strictly speaking, this sentence would be correct grammatically only if it were meant to convey: *They saw each other* or *They saw themselves.*

Ya se han vendido los libros.	The books have already been sold.

However, the technically incorrect—**Ya se ha vendido los libros.** *One has already sold the books.*—is found rather frequently in modern Spanish and is gradually gaining acceptance.

145. Passive and Pseudo-Passive in English

A. In Spanish, there can never be any doubt as to the passive or nonpassive quality of a sentence. In English, however, it is the context which often determines whether a sentence is passive or not. Thus difficulties may arise in the translation into Spanish of isolated sentences. It is important to keep in mind at all times that the passive voice speaks of an action that is done to the subject by an agent mentioned or unmentioned. If the sentence treats not of an action but of a state, **estar** is to be used.

La ventana fue cerrada. **Se cerró la ventana.** **Cerraron la ventana.**	The window was closed.

The Spanish here records the act of someone's closing the window.

La ventana estaba cerrada.	The window was closed.

Here the Spanish describes the condition of the window at a certain time. There is no reference to the act of its having been closed by anyone. If the word *suddenly* is added, the sentence becomes obviously passive.

De repente la ventana fue cerrada (se cerró la ventana, o cerraron la ventana).	Suddenly, the window was closed.

B. **Estar** + past participle to translate an English pseudo-passive

Estar is used at times with the past participle, even though the agent of the apparent action is expressed. Actually, the stress then lies on the state of affairs and not upon the description of an action.

El pueblo estaba gobernado por un general siciliano.	The town was governed by a Sicilian general.

The emphasis of the Spanish sentence is placed on the situation of the governed—*The town was in the hands of . . .*—rather than on the action involved in governing. Similarly:

Le revista está dirigida por el Sr. Ortiz.	The magazine is edited by (under the editorship of) Mr. Ortiz.
Estaba influido por su amigo.	He was influenced by (under the influence of) his friend.

146. The Use of **ser muerto**

Although **muerto** is the past participle of **morir** (to die), it is used in place of **matado** to express the action of being killed. **Ser matado** generally means *to be slaughtered* (as of animals) or *to be assassinated.*

El pobre fue muerto por el tranvía.	The poor fellow was killed by the streetcar.
El primer ministro ha sido matado (o asesinado) por la multitud.	The prime minister has been killed by the crowd.

Often, when the agent is not expressed, Spanish prefers the simple active verb, **morir.**

Murió en la guerra (**en el accidente, etc.**).	He was killed (He died) in the war (in the accident, etc.).

EJERCICIOS

I. Tradúzcase al español.

Have you seen the paper today? Well, listen to this. It's one of the most unusual cases I have ever heard. It seems that about ten years ago, a well-known Chilean engineer was accused of murder. He denied the crime, and although there was only circumstantial evidence, he was found guilty and sentenced to death. He appealed to all the higher courts, but in vain. Finally, he made a plan. If he wasn't pardoned by the last day, he would know how to save himself.

On the morning of the execution, the prisoner asked the guard to give him a cigarette. The guard gave it to him. He then asked him to light it for him, since his hands were trembling so (**tanto**). The guard assented. But when the guard approached, the condemned man grabbed him by (**de**) the throat, choked him, took the keys, and fled. His escape was discovered almost immediately and he was pursued by hundreds of police. But it seems that his plans were well made. He was taken by friends to a prearranged hideout, and disappeared.

A few years later, the police caught another man who confessed to the original crime for which (**por el cual**) the engineer had been condemned. There was no longer any doubt that he had been innocent of the first crime, but now he was being sought for the murder of the guard. Well, yesterday, they found him. For nine years he had been living in a country village. He had married, had three children, and was respected and liked by all his neighbors. His friends begged the police to let him go, but of course, they couldn't. After all, he had committed a premeditated murder. Now what do you think of that . . . ?

II. Composición.

1. Cómo yo decidiría el caso arriba referido
2. Mi concepto de la justicia

LECCIÓN DIECISÉIS

PREPOSITIONS

Adaptado de un artículo por Luis Moure-Marino

ABC

Madrid, 20 de junio de 1963

El Viaje a la Luna

La frase "prometer la luna" ya no sirve para expresar lo imposible. Efectivamente, en un discurso pronunciado en una fábrica de proyectiles, el presidente de los Estados Unidos ha prometido la luna a los americanos para fecha muy próxima, acaso para el año venidero: "Hemos decidido colocar un hombre en la luna —ha dicho—, no porque la empresa sea fácil, sino precisamente por ser difícil; porque esa empresa servirá para organizar y ponderar nuestras mejores energías y porque el reto de llegar a la luna es uno que no estamos dispuestos a aplazar..."

En relación con este entusiasmo popular por alcanzar la luna, leemos que para los niños americanos ha pasado la época de los vaqueros y el béisbol, pues también los juguetes infantiles simulan artefactos espaciales. La Administración de la Aeronáutica y del Espacio recibe a diario millares de cartas de niños menores de diez años en las que preguntan qué deben hacer para llegar a ser astronautas. Claro es que no todo es entusiasmo infantil en los programas espaciales estadounidenses. En los próximos años los Estados Unidos dedicarán exclusivamente a investigaciones espaciales una suma superior a todo lo gastado en investigación desde la revolución americana hasta el fin de la segunda guerra mundial. La fiebre por los proyectos espaciales ha provocado profundos cambios en la vida social. Han surgido nuevas industrias y ciudades. Todo hace presentir que una mañana cualquiera nos desayunaremos con la noticia de que un grupo de intrépidos astronautas americanos han "alunizado" felizmente.

Muy bien. Los americanos o los rusos habrán llegado a la luna... "¿Y qué?" —preguntaremos nosotros. "¿Qué beneficios derivarán para la humanidad de tan largo viaje?..." Se nos contesta que el que domine el espacio dominará la tierra. Y nosotros seguiremos preguntando: "¿Y qué?..." Porque, en efecto, cada vez se domina a los hombres menos con las armas y más con las ideas. Este colosal esfuerzo por alcanzar la luna resulta un tanto contradictorio cuando son tan numerosos y tan graves los problemas que tenemos en la tierra. El hambre azota a una gran parte del género humano; hierven en las sociedades terribles conflictos económicos; los humanos vivimos atormentados por la angustia del aniquilamiento atómico y acechados por terribles enfermedades. ¿Por qué no tratamos de superar estos graves problemas antes de viajar hacia las estrellas? Lo primero sería poner orden en nuestra revuelta casa y sólo después podríamos lanzarnos por los largos caminos siderales.

PREGUNTAS

1. ¿Qué significaba antes la frase: "prometer la luna"?
2. Según el presidente de los Estados Unidos, ¿para cuándo colocarán un hombre en la luna?
3. ¿Por qué decidieron los americanos tratar de llegar a la luna?
4. ¿Por qué dice el autor que ha pasado para los niños americanos la época del béisbol y de los vaqueros?
5. ¿Qué recibe a diario la Administración de Aeronáutica y del Espacio?
6. ¿Cuánto dedicarán los Estados Unidos a estudios espaciales en los próximos años?
7. ¿Cómo ha cambiado la vida social americana?
8. ¿Qué hace presentir todo esto?
9. Según el autor del artículo, ¿con qué se domina más a los hombres?
10. ¿Qué problemas dice el autor que debemos resolver antes de lanzarnos a la luna?

CONVERSACIÓN

1. ¿Qué piensa Ud. de las opiniones expresadas aquí por el autor de este artículo? ¿Está Ud. de acuerdo con la mayor parte de ellas? ¿Por qué? ¿Cree Ud. que el escritor entiende bien la filosofía de la vida americana? ¿Es verdad que el interés por la ciencia ocupa ahora en los Estados Unidos un puesto de primera importancia? ¿Le interesa a Ud. la ciencia? ¿Cree Ud. que debe tomar precedencia sobre las humanidades en el programa de estudios universitarios?
2. ¿Le interesaría a Ud. ser astronauta? Si se realiza la posibilidad de ir a la luna, ¿le gustaría ir? ¿Iría Ud. en la primera expedición?

3. ¿Cree Ud. que el hombre tiene derecho a salir de los límites de nuestro mundo? ¿Por qué?
4. ¿Cree Ud. que hay vida humana en otros planetas? ¿Qué evidencia hay hasta ahora?

PART A

147. Uses of **a**

A. The personal **a**

1. **A** must normally be used before a direct object that refers to a specific person or persons, except after the verb **tener.**

Encontré a un amigo mío en San Juan.	I met a friend of mine in San Juan.
Visitamos a los Romero la semana pasada.	We visited the Romeros last week.
¿A quién saludabas, a ella o a él?	Whom were you greeting, her or him?

But:

Tengo cinco tías, dos tíos y treinta y un primos.	I have five aunts, two uncles, and thirty-one cousins.

2. The personal **a** is also used when the direct object is one of the indefinites—**alguien, nadie, alguno**(**s**), **ninguno**(**s**) (when the latter two refer to persons).

No he llamado todavía a nadie.	I haven't called anyone yet.
¿Ha visto Ud. a alguno de ellos?	Have you seen any of them?

3. It may also appear when the direct object is the name of a country; at times it is used to personify an abstract noun or an animal.

¿Visitará (a) **Méjico este verano?**	Will he visit Mexico this summer?
Quería mucho a su perro.	He loved his dog very much.
Amar a la bondad es amar a Dios.	To love goodness is to love God.

B. After verbs of motion

A is used after all verbs of motion to introduce an infinitive, a noun, or a pronoun.

Vamos a ver.	Let's see.
Vino a oír el concierto.	He came to hear the concert.
Ven a mí, muchacho.	Come to me, boy.

Remember that a verb of motion is followed by **a** + the prepositional object pronoun. It does not (except in the most limited of circumstances) take an indirect object pronoun.

C. After verbs of beginning, learning, teaching

Ella le enseñó a bailar.	She taught him to dance.
Ahora empiezo a comprender.	Now I am beginning to understand.

D. **Al** + infinitive = *upon* (doing something)

Al salir de la iglesia, vimos que llovía.	Upon leaving the church, we saw that it was raining.
Al llegar a la cima, decidieron descansar.	Upon reaching the summit, they decided to rest.

EJERCICIOS

A. Conteste en español:

1. ¿Cree Ud. que conoce bien a sus profesores? 2. ¿A quiénes visitó Ud. la semana pasada? 3. ¿Quién le enseñó a nadar? 4. ¿Cuándo aprendió Ud. a bailar? 5. ¿Empiezan Uds. a hablar bien el español ahora? 6. ¿Adónde fue Ud. anoche? 7. ¿Cuántos amigos íntimos tiene? 8. ¿A quién recuerda Ud. mejor de su niñez? 9. ¿Qué va Ud. a hacer este verano? 10. ¿Qué hizo Ud. primero al despertarse esta mañana?

B. Diga en español:

1. We were going to buy it. 2. Go to him and ask him for it. 3. Upon realizing the truth, he turned pale. 4. Have you seen Mike today? —No, neither him nor his parents. 5. They are learning to draw and paint. 6. Does your father know the dean? 7. Does the dean know your father? —No, thank goodness.

148. Uses of **de**

A. To indicate possession

Marcela es la sobrina de la mujer del mayordomo del tío de mi padre.	Marcella is my father's uncle's butler's wife's niece.

B. After certain very common verbs, prepositions, and expressions

acabar de to have just
tratar de to try to
alegrarse de to be happy
enamorarse de to fall in love with
antes de before
olvidarse de to forget (about)
acordarse de to remember
darse cuenta de to realize
estar seguro de to be sure
después de after

EJERCICIOS

A. Conteste en español:

1. ¿De quién es la casa en que vive Ud.? 2. ¿Se ha olvidado Ud. recientemente de algo importante? ¿Qué fue? 3. ¿Se alegrará de terminar sus estudios universitarios? 4. ¿Qué cosas nuevas ha tratado Ud. de hacer este año? 5. ¿Ha estado Ud. enamorado de alquien alguna vez? ¿De quién?

B. Diga en español:

1. Don't forget to lock the door. 2. He tried to finish on time, but he couldn't. 3. Do you realize how late it is? 4. We had just left school when it began to snow.

149. Uses of **con**

A. As a substitute for an adverb of manner

con cuidado carefully
con impaciencia impatiently
con amargura bitterly
con mucho gusto gladly

B. After certain common verbs, such as

casarse con to marry
contar con to count on
soñar con to dream of

EJERCICIOS

A. Diga de otra manera:

1. Habló irónicamente. 2. Lloró amargamente. 3. Sonrieron tristemente. 4. Lo aceptan todo tranquilamente. 5. Escríbalo más cuidadosamente. 6. Debes hablar con más claridad.

B. Diga en español:

1. Marian is going to marry my brother. 2. Who would dream of such a thing? 3. I count on you to (**para**) keep the secret. 4. He enunciated his words clearly and carefully.

150. Uses of **en**

A. To indicate location—*at* (a certain place) or *in*

Estudiaremos en la Universidad de Madrid este verano.	We shall study at the University of Madrid this summer.
Estará en casa toda la tarde.	He will be at home all afternoon.

B. After certain common verbs, such as

pensar en	to think of, or about	**confiar en**	to trust
entrar en	to enter	**insistir en**	to insist upon
tardar en	to delay, to be long in, to take long	**convenir en**	to agree to
		consistir en	to consist of

EJERCICIOS

A. Conteste en español:

1. ¿Vive Ud. en la universidad misma o en casa de su familia? 2. ¿En qué está pensando en este momento? 3. ¿Cuánto tiempo tarda Ud. en llegar a la escuela por la mañana? 4. ¿En quién confía Ud. más? 5. ¿En qué consiste la Organización de los Estados Americanos?

B. Diga en español:

1. It is not permitted to enter the laboratory. 2. All I do is (**No hago más que**) think of you. 3. They agreed to deliver it next week. 4. How long does it take to get to Cádiz?

151. Uses of **para**

Para, which is translated most frequently in English as *for* or *in order to,* is characterized by looking ahead ⟶ toward the goal, the objective, the destination of the action.

para ⟶ goal / destination / objective

Almost all of its principal uses conform to this concept. Its important meanings are given below.

A. In order to ⟶ goal

Estudia para (ser) médico.	He is studying to be a doctor.
Ahorraremos para comprar una casa nueva.	We shall save in order to buy a new house.

B. Destined for ⟶ goal, destination

Esto es para ti.	This is for you.
Salen para Inglaterra mañana.	They are leaving for England tomorrow.

C. To be used for ⟶ objective

ropas para señoras ladies' clothes

un vaso para vino a wine glass

But:

un vaso de vino a glass of wine

D. By or for (a certain date or time) ⟶ objective

Para mañana, lean Uds. el capítulo diez.	For tomorrow, read Chapter X.
Estará de vuelta para la semana que viene.	He will be back by next week.

E. Considering, compared with, with respect to

Para un muchacho de diez años, sabe demasiado.	For a ten-year-old, he knows too much.
Para algunos estudiantes, esto será difícil; para Uds., es fácil, ¿verdad?	For some students, this may be hard; for you, it's easy, isn't it?

EJERCICIOS

A. Cambie según las indicaciones:

1. **Tengo** algo para ti. (No tengo...) 2. **Ahora** venden ropas para niños. (Antes) 3. Volverán para **fines** de marzo. (principios) 4. Salieron para Inglaterra **ayer.** (la semana que viene) 5. ¿Me quieres dar un vaso de **vino?** (cerveza) 6. **¿Estudian** para abogado? (vosotros) 7. **Dice** que lo tendrá para el miércoles. (Dijo)

B. Diga en español:

1. I have a present for your sister. 2. For an old man, he is very strong. 3. Please have them ready by ten o'clock. 4. They left for the station half an hour ago. 5. a water glass; a cup of tea; a clothes brush; a tooth brush; a cup of coffee. 6. To go to the city, you have to take the train.

152. Uses of **por**

Por has two general types of usages. One refers to tangible or physical actions: *by*, *through*, *around*, *along*, etc. The other type looks back ⟵ to the motive, the impulse of the action.

A. Tangible or physical uses (location, position, etc.)

1. By (an agent), by means of

La pared fue destruida por el incendio.	The wall was destroyed by the fire.
POR AVION	VIA AIRMAIL
Nos llamó por teléfono.	He telephoned us.

2. Through, along, around, in

Me paseaba por el parque un día...	I was strolling through (in) the park one day . . .
Les gusta andar por la orilla del río.	They like to walk along the river bank.
Estará por aquí.	It must be around here.

3. During, for (a period of time)

Mañana por la mañana...	Tomorrow morning . . .
Vámonos por la tarde.	Let's go during (in) the afternoon.
Se han ido a Quito por tres meses.	They have gone to Quito for three months.

4. In exchange for

Me dio su chaqueta por mi reloj.	He gave me his jacket for my watch.
Pagué dos dólares por esta corbata.	I paid two dollars for this tie.

5. Per[1]

Máxima velocidad: 80 kilómetros por hora	Maximum speed: 80 kilometers per hour
el noventa por ciento de los votantes	90 percent of the voters

B. Motive, impulse ←— **por**

1. Motive, impulse ←— out of, because of, through

Se casó con ella no por amor sino por compasión.	He married her not for love, but for pity.
Lo dijeron por miedo.	They said it out of fear.

[1] *Per* may also be translated by using the definite article: *Thirty cents a (per) dozen.* **Treinta centavos la docena.** This usage is especially common when quoting prices.

2. Motive, impulse ←— for the sake of, on behalf of

Haría cualquier cosa por su hijo.	He would do anything for his son.
¡Por Dios!	For heaven's sake!

3. Motive, impulse ←— in order to, in the hopes of

When **por** is used, the outcome is viewed as doubtful or uncertain, and the emphasis lies on the motive of the action.

Se esfuerza por alcanzar un puesto político.	He is trying hard to attain a political post.
Hizo lo posible por salvarlos, pero no pudo.	He did everything possible to save them, but he couldn't.

4. Motive, impulse ←— for, in quest of, in search of

Fue por agua.	He went for water.

Not *destined for* water, but *motivated by the desire to get* or *bring back* water.

Mandaron por el médico.	They sent for the doctor.

5. Motive, impulse, origin ←— pending, yet to be

In this case, the outcome is uncertain. The emphasis lies on the project that is planned, on the origin of the action.

El puente todavía está por concluir.	The bridge is yet to be completed.

EJERCICIO

Complete las frases siguientes con **por** o **para:**

1. _______ aprender bien, hay que estudiar mucho. 2. En estos países se ha hecho muy poco _______ los indios. 3. ¿Cuánto le cobraron _______ ese sombrero? ¿Veinte pesos? ¡Dios mío! 4. Vuelva mañana _______ la tarde, ¿está bien? 5. Pídale que tenga arreglado el reloj _______ el lunes próximo. 6. Habla muy bien el castellano _______ un extranjero. 7. El verano pasado salimos _______ Holanda en junio e hicimos un viaje _______ toda Europa. 8. Quiere que su hijo estudie _______ médico. 9. Esta tarjeta no es _______ ti. 10. Todas las casas del pueblo fueron quemadas _______ el enemigo. 11. Todavía quedan muchas cosas _______ hacer. 12. Dígale que vaya a la tienda _______ pan. 13. Me hacen falta unas cinco tazas _______ te. 14. Le pagarán diez dólares _______ hora. 15. ¿Por qué no la mandas _______

avión? 16. Ése nunca hace nada ______ nadie. 17. Este perro ha sido mordido ______ un hombre. —¡Cómo! 18. Demos una vuelta ______ la playa.

EJERCICIO DE REPASO

1. The project of placing a man on the moon cannot be carried out yet.
2. The undertaking attracted (*imperfect*) us precisely because it was difficult.
3. For American children, space exploration will soon be more important than baseball.
4. In order to reach the moon they will have to appropriate astronomical sums to space projects from now on.
5. Don't you think we should also appropriate money for other scientific investigations?
6. It is said that whoever (**el que**) controls space will also control the earth.
7. The enthusiasm for space exploration has caused deep changes in American social life.
8. To many people this colossal effort to reach the moon seems unrealistic.
9. How long would it take the astronauts to arrive on the moon?
10. Upon landing they realized that the rocket had been damaged.

REPASO DE VERBOS

Estudie **conducir, producir, traducir, etc.**, y después diga en español: He produced them. Did you (**tú**) translate it? He told us to conduct them there. Translate them (*f.*) into Spanish. (**Ud., Uds.**) They introduced a new topic. Do you (**Uds.**) produce wheat here?

PART B

153. Omission of the Personal a

A. The personal **a** is omitted before an object noun that does not refer to a specific person.

Busca un nuevo ayudante.	He is looking for a new assistant (no specific person).

But:

Busca a su nuevo ayudante.	He is looking for his new assistant (a specific person).

B. It is often omitted when both the direct and indirect objects are persons. The omission of the **a** thereby avoids confusion as to which of the objects is the indirect.

Mandó un mensajero al rey.	He sent a messenger to the king.

C. It may be omitted when **querer** means *to want.*

¡ Quiero mi mamá !	I want my mother!

But:

Quiero a mi mamá.	I love my mother.

154. Further Uses of the Preposition **a**

A. It may express the method by which an action is carried out.

Lo escribí a máquina.	I typed it. (I wrote it by machine.)
Lo cosen a mano.	They sew it by hand.

B. It may correspond to the English *for* or *toward,* to express an emotional attitude with respect to its object.

Demostró su odio a los extranjeros.	He showed his hatred for (or toward) foreigners.
Tengo gran afición a los deportes.	I am very fond of sports.

C. Very often, it denotes removal or separation.

Quitamos las armas a los rebeldes.	We took the weapons away from the rebels.

D. Occasionally, it may mean *at* (up *to* a certain point in space, but not within it)

Estaban sentados a la mesa.	They were sitting at the table.
Está a la puerta.	He is at the door.

But:

Está en casa.	He is at home (inside the house).
Estudian en la Universidad de Madrid.	They are studying at (within) the University of Madrid.

E. In expressions of time, it may mean *within.*

A los pocos días de llegar a Burgos...	Within a few days of arriving in Burgos . . .

155. Further Uses of **de**

A. **De** often translates *with* when referring to a characteristic of the subject described or to an item that is regarded as more or less inseparable from him. **De** must be used when the subject is a pronoun.

el muchacho del pelo rojo	the boy with the red hair
la niña de la falda azul	the girl with (wearing) the blue skirt
el de la guitarra negra	the one with the black guitar (he is identified with that guitar)

Notice how **con** retains the sense of a separable adjunct.

Ese hombre con la guitarra negra...	That man with (now holding) the black guitar . . .
¿Quién es esa niña con la falda azul?	Who is that girl with the blue skirt (in her hand, etc.)?

B. **De** may mean *in the capacity of*, and in this sense, corresponds to the English *as*.

Está en París de cónsul.	He is in Paris as a consul.
Trabaja de secretaria.	She works as a secretary.
¿Puedo servirle de guía?	May I serve as your guide?

C. **De** frequently refers to the practical purpose of a tool or a device.

una máquina de coser	a sewing machine
una máquina de escribir	a typewriter
herramientas de barrenar	boring tools

D. It may show the cause of an action or state, and corresponds then to the English *of* or *with*.

Me muero de sed.	I'm dying of thirst.
Está loco de amor.	He is mad with love.
Se matará de trabajo.	He will kill himself with work.

E. It is used in certain common idiomatic expressions.

Está de vacaciones.	He is on vacation.
Primero darán de comer al niño.	First they will feed the child.

F. **De** + infinitive may serve as a substitute for an *if* clause contrary to fact. (Recall 77 E.)

De haberle prevenido yo a tiempo, se habría salvado.	If I had warned him on time, he would have been saved.

156. En, sobre, (por) encima de

A. **En** means *in*, *at*, *on*, or *upon*.

1. In the sense of *on* or *upon*, it generally refers to an object that is resting upon or leaning against a surface.

La vajilla ya está en la mesa.	The silver is already on the table.
Los cuadros están colgados en las paredes.	The pictures are hanging on the walls.
Está sentado en una butaca.	He is sitting in an armchair.

2. **En** also translates the English *to* after an ordinal number, including **último** last.

Fue el primero en salir.	He was the first to leave.
Seré el último en rendirme.	I will be the last to surrender.

B. **Sobre** means *on*, *upon*, *about*, *over*.

1. It means *on* or *upon* in the sense of *on top of*. It refers to an object that is resting on a surface or that is placed above it.

Póngalo sobre (or **en**) **la mesa.**	Put it on the table.
La espada estaba suspendida sobre su cabeza.	The sword was suspended over his head.

2. It may mean *on* or *about* in the sense of *concerning*.

un discurso sobre política	a speech on (or about) politics

C. **Encima de** or **por encima de** means *over*, *above*.

Encima del edificio había un gran letrero.	Above the building was a large sign.
Volamos por encima de los Andes.	We flew over the Andes.

157. Para and por

A. With **trabajar**

1. **Trabajar para** means *to work for* (*to be employed by*) a company, an individual, etc.

Trabaja para el gobierno.	He works for the government.
Hace dos años que Ana trabaja para nosotros.	Anna has been working for us for two years.

2. **Trabajar por** means *to work on behalf of* (*for the sake* or *benefit of* someone) or *in place of* someone.

Trabajo sólo por ti.	I work only for your sake.
¿Por qué candidato estás trabajando?	For which candidate are you working?

B. In combination with other prepositions

Por + preposition accompanies verbs expressing movement.

Pasó por entre las carretas.	He passed among the carts.
Saltó por encima de la pared.	He jumped over the wall.
Se escapó por detrás del edificio.	He escaped in back of the building.

C. **Por** + noun or adjective

Por, followed by a noun or an adjective, may be used in place of a clause. **Ser** is then the implied object of **por.**

Le mandaron a presidio por (ser) falsario.	They sent him to prison for being (because he was . . .) a counterfeiter.
Ella le desprecia por (ser) pobre.	She scorns him because he is poor.

158. Por vs. de by

Por translates *by* when referring to a physical action or motion. **De** is used when referring to a state or condition, or to a mental or emotional attitude.

Fue rodeado por sus admiradores.	He was surrounded by his admirers. (At that moment they surrounded him.)
Estaba rodeado de sus admiradores.	He was (already) surrounded by his admirers.
Llegó acompañada por muchos reporteros.	She arrived accompanied by many reporters.
Llegó acompañada de muchos reporteros.	She arrived in the company of many reporters.
Fueron rechazados por el público.	They were rejected by the public.
Eran odiados de todos.	They were hated by all.

EJERCICIOS

I. Traducir al español.

You remember the North African campaign, don't you? Well, here is (**aquí tiene Ud.**) a true story that happened to us during one of the worst months of the fighting.

Our men occupied a hill near the abandoned village. The only well in that whole region was in the middle of the hill, and our enemies, who surrounded us, knew it. From their positions, (**a**) some two hundred yards from ours, they could see us drink water. They had very little water left, and the heat of the desert was driving them (**les volvía**) crazy. For them, the situation was desperate. What they didn't realize was that for us it was equally desperate.

They were three hundred and we fifty. And worse than anything, our well was almost dry and our only hope was the relief column that was supposed to arrive at the village any day (**de un día a otro**). But they didn't know this. And so, although they were sure that a direct assault on the hill would cost them at least half of their men, they decided that they would have to attack us and take our position as soon as possible.

Hour after hour, the tension mounted. The next day, we had (**no nos quedaba**) no water left, but to deceive them we pretended to be drinking almost all the time. At the same time, we shouted to them through a megaphone to surrender, promising them all the water they wanted. They couldn't see that there was nothing in our canteens and thought that the well was still full. This made them even more desperate (**los desesperó**) and they attacked with the fury of despair.

We repulsed the assault, but our ammunition almost ran out (**se nos acabaron**). Another attack would have finished us. But they did not try again. They came toward us without arms, their hands raised, and carrying a white flag, because they preferred to be prisoners and drink our water rather than (**antes que**) die of thirst in the desert. This was one victory that was won by psychology, and not by force. But that wasn't the end. There still were difficulties to overcome. . . .

II. Composición.

1. La conclusión de este episodio
2. ¿Debe haber reglas de conducta en la guerra? ¿Cuáles? ¿Por qué?

LECCIÓN DIECISIETE

RELATIVES AND CONJUNCTIONS

Adaptado de

EL ESPECTADOR

Bogotá, 1° de marzo de 1964

Enlace de Carlos Hugo e Irene

Londres. Los buenos cuentos de amor terminan con una frase que dice: "y se casaron y fueron felices para siempre". Los mejores cuentos de amor tienen príncipes y princesas, carrozas doradas y coronas de perlas. Todo el mundo quiere que el idilio de la princesa Irene sea así. Se trata de la princesa Irene de Holanda, segunda en la sucesión del trono, quien se enamoró de un príncipe español que pilotea aviones y en cuyo país impera un régimen que no es ni monarquía ni república ni nada que tenga definición concreta.

Los tulipanes pintarán la tierra de color cuando los novios reales digan que sí en una ceremonia religiosa católica. Sin embargo, en Holanda hay los que creen (y la reina Juliana entre ellos) que el príncipe Carlos no es el que puede hacer feliz a Irene. Y el sentimiento no tiene nada que ver con la cuestión religiosa. Tampoco tiene que ver con el hecho de que la familia de él no tenga mayores medios económicos y la de ella posea una cuantiosa fortuna. Algunos piensan que el matrimonio sólo le interesa al príncipe Carlos como medio de fortalecer sus aspiraciones al trono. Además, muchos holandeses están resentidos de que el príncipe Javier, padre de Carlos, haya hecho el anuncio del noviazgo por su cuenta, lo cual indica que considera a su familia más noble y más antigua que la que está gobernando a Holanda. El príncipe Javier, quien ha cumplido ya 74 años, voló a La Haya para asistir a las ceremonias de compromiso, durante las cuales los tórtolos estaban tan acaramelados que un técnico de televisión tuvo que toser para que prestaran algo de atención. La princesa dijo que lamentaba tener que irse a vivir fuera de Holanda, pero que eso no era decir "adiós", sino "hasta pronto".

La historia de los idilios reales está llena de cosas parecidas. El emperador Hirohito del Japón tuvo que romper con todas las tradiciones para aprobar el casamiento de su hijo Akihito con una plebeya. El Conde de Harewood, primo de la reina Isabel de Inglaterra se casó con la hija de un violinista refugiado. También se recuerda el caso de la princesa Isabel de Yugoeslavia, hija del ex-regente Pablo, la que contrajo matrimonio con un fabricante norteamericano y de la princesa Sandra Torlonia, nieta del rey Alfonso XIII de España, la que se casó con un plebeyo. El padre la desheredó, pero después la familia la aceptó de nuevo cuando tuvo el primer hijo.

Siempre pasa lo mismo. Las familias reales, doloridas, piensan en su historia y sus glorias pasadas, pero después se rinden ante el presente.

PREGUNTAS

1. ¿Cómo terminan los buenos cuentos de amor?
2. ¿De quiénes se trata ahora?
3. ¿Qué régimen impera en la patria del príncipe Carlos?
4. ¿Qué temen la reina Juliana y otros holandeses?
5. ¿Qué diferencia hay en la posición económica de las dos familias?
6. Según algunos, ¿qué le interesa más a Carlos?
7. ¿Por qué están resentidos muchos holandeses?
8. ¿Qué dijo la princesa durante las ceremonias de compromiso?
9. ¿Qué otros casos parecidos se encuentran en la historia reciente?
10. ¿Cómo se resolvió el caso de la nieta de Alfonso XIII?

CONVERSACIÓN

1. ¿Le interesa a Ud. la vida personal de las familias reales? ¿Cree Ud. que la existencia de una clase noble presta dignidad al país? ¿Por qué?
2. ¿Le gustaría a Ud. ser príncipe, princesa, monarca, etc.? ¿Cree Ud. que un príncipe tiene derecho a una vida privada? ¿Tiene el derecho de casarse con quien desee, a pesar de la opinión general del público?
3. ¿Qué le parece a Ud. el sistema monárquico constitucional de Inglaterra? ¿Cree Ud. que la monarquía absoluta tiene su razón de ser todavía en los países subdesarrollados? Si Ud. fuera rey de un país, ¿preferiría ser un monarca de poderes limitados o titulares, o uno que tuviera la responsabilidad de gobernar?

PART A

The main function of relatives and conjunctions is essentially similar: they both serve to join one clause with another. Their meanings, however, and their uses are very different. Relative pronouns and their functions are treated in **159** through **164**, conjunctions in **165** through **167**.

159. Que

Que is the most frequently used of the relative pronouns. It means *who*, *that*, or *which*, and, as direct object of a verb, *whom*. It refers to both persons and things, singular and plural, and its form is invariable.

El hombre que vino a cenar...	The man who came to dinner . . .
Los muebles que compramos el año pasado...	The furniture that (or which) we bought last year . . .
El muchacho que vieron corriendo calle abajo...	The child whom they saw running down the street . . .

160. Quien, quienes

Quien(**es**) means *who*, *whom*, and occasionally *the one*(*s*) *who*. It refers only to persons and has singular and plural forms. There is no special feminine form.

A. **Quien**(**es**) is used when a person (or persons) is object of a preposition. Its meaning in such cases is always *whom*.

Mamá, ésta es la muchacha de quien te he hablado tanto.	Mom, this is the girl about whom I have spoken to you so much.
Esos señores con quienes viajamos son famosos estadistas europeos.	Those gentlemen with whom we traveled are famous European statesmen.

B. It also appears frequently when the relative *who* is separated from the main clause by a comma, or when a distinction must be made between a person and a thing.

El general Díaz, quien encabezó las fuerzas revolucionarias, ha sido elegido presidente.	General Diaz, who headed the revolutionary forces, has been elected president.
El propietario de la hacienda Dos Robles, quien también es alcalde del pueblo...	The proprietor of Two Oaks Ranch, who is also mayor of the town . . .

EJERCICIOS

A. Cambie:

1. **El señor** que vive en la casa de al lado...
(La familia, los niños, el perro)
2. **La película** que vimos ayer...
(El cuadro, los policías, las modelos, los ejemplos)
3. El joven **de** quien hablo...
(con, a, por, ante)
4. **La señora** con quien vivía...
(La familia, los muchachos, los tíos, las primas)

B. Traduzca al español:

1. Have you seen the beautiful coffee pot that they bought in San Juan? 2. The couple with whom (*pl.*) we took the trip are newlyweds. 3. The little girl who goes to school with mine has the measles. 4. Mr. Alonso, who has a chain of shoestores in the city, will open another one here. 5. The contemporary author that I like best is Delibes. —Who?

161. El cual, la cual, los cuales, las cuales

These forms are used under certain conditions instead of **que** or **quien(es)** to mean *who*, *which*, or *whom*. The following are the circumstances in which they appear:

A. To clarify, in case of ambiguity

La hermana de Miguel, la cual sale mañana, llamará a nuestros amigos en París.	Michael's sister, who is leaving tomorrow, will call our friends in Paris.

NOTE: If Michael were going, the relative would be **el cual,** or frequently **que** or **quien,** since one would assume that the relative referred to the last named person.[1]

B. To translate *which*, after prepositions of two or more syllables, and after **por,**[2] **sin,** and all other prepositions which would normally form a conjunction by the addition of **que**

[1] Ambiguity still exists, of course, if both persons are of the same gender and if the relative *who* refers to the first. **Aquél**—*the former*—or some explanatory clause, may then be necessary.

[2] Obviously, **por** + **que**, especially in oral use, would give the immediate impression of *because* and would obliterate completely the real meaning of the sentence. **Sin que, después de que, antes de que**, etc., also would convey the idea of conjunctions.

De pronto, descorrió la cortina detrás de la cual estaba el ladrón.	Suddenly, he opened the curtain behind which the thief was standing.
La ventana por la cual había entrado todavía estaba abierta.	The window through which he had entered was still open.
He perdido mis gafas, sin las cuales no puedo ver casi nada.	I have lost my eyeglasses, without which I can hardly see anything.

162. El que, la que, los que, las que

A. **El que,** etc., means *he who, those who, the one(s) who.*

Los que no pudieron asistir a la boda pusieron telegramas.	Those who couldn't attend the wedding sent telegrams.
El que gritó no fue la víctima, sino un transeúnte.	The one who shouted was not the victim, but a passerby.

B. These forms also have the same uses as **el cual** (cf. **161**).

La hermana de Miguel, la que sale...	Michael's sister, who is leaving . . .
La cortina detrás de la que...	The curtain behind which . . .
Mis gafas, sin las que...	My eyeglasses, without which . . .

EJERCICIO

Póngase el pronombre relativo apropiado:

1. Las señoras ______ vinieron con mi tía son hermanas. 2. La mujer de ______ le estuve hablando es parienta mía. 3. La botella por ______ subí al desván estaba rota. 4. El libro ______ me trajo Juan es poco interesante. 5. ______ mucho habla, mucho yerra. 6. El guía con ______ fuimos a Toledo acaba de llamarme. 7. La tía de Roque, a ______ le gustan mucho los collares de perlas, se compró uno muy bonito. 8. Los otros libros, sin ______ no puedo preparar el examen, no han llegado todavía. 9. ______ estaban allí sabrán la respuesta. 10. La hija del juez, ______ (*f.*) es una persona simpatiquísima, le rogó que perdonara al ladrón. 11. La esposa del general, ______ (*f.*) ha escrito dos obras importantísimas, nos hablará mañana. 12. ______ te dijo eso mentía. 13. El hijo de mi vecina, ______ (*m.*) se va a graduar en junio, ya tiene un puesto maravilloso.

163. Lo que and lo cual

A. **Lo que** (not **lo cual**) corresponds to the English relative pronoun *what.*

Amigo mío, bien sé lo que quieres.	My friend, I know very well what you want.
Lo que hace es distinto a lo que dice.	What he does is different from what he says.

B. **Lo que** and **lo cual** may be used interchangeably to translate *which*, when referring back to a whole idea, not to a specific noun.

Anita baila bien, lo que (lo cual) la hace muy popular.	Ann dances well, which makes her very popular.
No le gustan nada las mujeres, lo que (lo cual) quiere decir que no te dará el empleo.	He doesn't like women at all, which means that he won't hire you.

EJERCICIO

Diga en español:

1. What she wants is impossible. 2. Those who took part in the fight told us what happened. 3. What are you looking at? —That. —I still don't know what you mean. 4. First we had breakfast, after which we went for a walk. 5. He still hasn't returned, which worries us a little. 6. Which do you prefer? —The one that I already have.

164. The Relative Possessive **cuyo**

Cuyo, cuya, cuyos, cuyas, an adjective meaning *whose,* is never used as an interrogative. It always agrees in gender and number with the noun it modifies.

El artista cuyos cuadros vimos ...	The artist whose paintings we saw ...
Éste es el muchacho cuyo ensayo ganó el premio.	This is the boy whose essay won the prize.

But:

¿De quién son estos libros?	Whose books are these?

EJERCICIOS

A. Cambie:

1. Mi amigo, cuyo **primo** vive cerca, vendrá con **él** esta tarde. (novia, tíos, primas)
2. Este es el Sr. Cárdenas, cuya primera **novela** se acaba de editar. (obras, drama, ensayos)

B. Diga en español:

1. Are you the gentleman whose daughter is getting married today? —Yes, but who are you? —Your son-in-law. 2. This staircase, whose second step is broken, was the cause of the accident. 3. Whose (!) house is that? 4. Even Professor González, whose patience has no limits, got angry with him today.

165. Conjunctions

A. **Y, e** and

Y becomes **e** before a noun that begins with **i** or **hi.**

Este semestre estudiamos historia y geografía.	This term we are studying history and geography.
El semestre que viene estudiaremos geografía e historia.	Next term we shall study geography and history.

Notice, however, that **y** remains before the diphthong **hie.**

plomo y hierro lead and iron **vino y hielo** wine and ice

B. **O, u** or

1. **O** becomes **u** before a noun that begins with **o** or **ho.**

Cualquier hombre o mujer de mediana inteligencia sabe eso.	Any man or woman of average intelligence knows that.
Esa mina dará plata u oro.	That mine will produce silver or gold.

2. **O... o** means *either . . . or.*

O sigues mi consejo, o lo sentirás mucho.	Either you follow my advice, or you'll be sorry.
Toma (o) té o café, pero nunca leche.	He takes either tea or coffee, but never milk.

3. **Ni... ni** means *neither . . . nor* (or *not . . . either . . . or*).

No tengo ni tiempo ni paciencia para eso.	I have neither time nor patience for that.
El pobre chiquito no tiene ni padre ni madre.	The poor boy doesn't have either a father or a mother.

C. **Pero, sino** but

Sino is used for *but* only when the first part of the sentence is negative, and the second part contradicts it. In all other cases, **pero** is used.

Es listo, pero no saca buenas notas.	He is smart, but he doesn't get good grades. (First part is affirmative.)
No es rico, sino pobre.	He is not rich, but poor. (First part is negative; second part contradicts it.)
No es rico, pero le gusta dar limosna.	He is not rich, but he likes to give alms. (First part negative, but *no* contradiction.)

Sino que generally replaces **sino** to introduce a clause.

No lo compró, sino que lo pidió prestado.	He didn't buy it, but he borrowed it.

EJERCICIOS

A. Cambie según las indicaciones:

1. Pronto vendrán Marta y **Elvira.** (Inés) 2. Tengo unos seis o **siete.** (ocho) 3. ¿Se han casado ya Carlos e **Irene?** (Sofía) 4. ¿Es de plata o **platino** el broche? (oro) 5. ¿Me puede prestar aguja y **tela?** (hilo) 6. Lo harán de cobre y **bronce.** (hierro) 7. Cualquier sanatorio o **clínica** la admitirá. (hospital)

B. Conteste negativamente las preguntas siguientes: (**ni... ni**)

1. ¿Es Ud. el mejor o el peor estudiante de la clase? (**No soy ni...**) 2. ¿Hace mucho calor o muchísimo frío hoy? 3. ¿Está alegre o triste en este momento? 4. ¿Me lo vas a dar o prestar? 5. ¿Estudias ambas filosofía y psicología este semestre? 6. ¿Sois riquísimos o pobres? 7. ¿Son jóvenes o viejos sus padres?

C. Diga en español:

1. He isn't smart, but lucky. 2. She is not only intelligent, but beautiful. 3. John isn't a good student, but he is very handsome. 4. We aren't brilliant, but we're not the worst in the class. 5. They have always worked hard, but they're still very poor. 6. There aren't a hundred, but about fifty. 7. He didn't steal the money, but he found it.

166. Formation of Conjunctions from Prepositions

Many conjunctions that serve to introduce subordinate clauses are derived by adding **que** to a preposition.

hasta, hasta que until
después de, después de que after
antes de, antes de que before
sin, sin que without

Remember always that only a relative pronoun or a conjunction can ever introduce a subordinate clause. *A preposition can not!*

Esperamos hasta las ocho.	We waited until eight o'clock.
Esperamos hasta que volvió.	We waited until he returned.

167. Position of the Subordinate Clause Verb After Conjunctions

The verb of the subordinate clause is usually placed immediately after the conjunction, and its subject then follows.

Vámonos antes de que vuelvan tus padres.	Let's leave before your parents come back.
Limpió toda la casa sin que se lo dijera nadie.	She cleaned the whole house without anyone's telling her to.

EJERCICIO DE REPASO

1. Everyone hopes that the love story of Charles and Irene will end happily like the old tales of princes and princesses.
2. This time it is a question of Princess Irene of Holland, who fell in love with a Spanish prince but whose family is opposed to their marriage.
3. At first they decided to wait until both families consented to the marriage, but then they realized that it was impossible.
4. There are those in Holland who doubt that Charles is the one who can make her happy.
5. They say that it has nothing to do with the fact that her family may be much richer than his.
6. Charles' father announced the engagement on his own, which also offended many of the Dutch.
7. Prince Xavier, who is more than seventy years old, attended the engagement party, during which the young lovers seemed completely absorbed in each other.
8. The princess said that she was not saying goodbye, but "so long".
9. There have been many other similar cases in royal families, among which we recall that of Princess Isabel of Yugoslavia.
10. Also there is the famous example of Alphonse XIII's granddaughter, who married a commoner and was at first expelled from the family.

REPASO DE VERBOS

Estudie los verbos **traer** y **caer** y después diga en español:
She fell down. Did you (**Uds.**) bring it? He told us to bring them (*f.*). Don't fall! (**tú, vosotros, Ud., Uds.**) I'm bringing it. They didn't fall.

PART B

168. Uses of **que**

A. In nonrestrictive clauses

Current usage, especially in the spoken language, tends more and more to use **que** instead of **quien, el cual,** or **el que** as subject of a clause set off by commas.

Ese señor, que es muy buen amigo mío, va a invitarle a la fiesta.	That gentleman, who is a very good friend of mine, is going to invite you to the party.
La Sra. Castro, que es argentina...	Mrs. Castro, who is an Argentinian...

B. To translate *whom* after the preposition **de**

Although **quien** is regularly used to translate *whom* after a preposition, **que** may also be found after the preposition **de.**

Voy a ver al pintor de que les hablé ayer.	I'm going to see the painter about whom I spoke to you yesterday.

C. Before **sí** and **no**

When **sí** or **no** are not direct answers, but are incorporated into another statement, they must be preceded by **que.**

Dijo que no.	He said no.
Creo que sí.	I think so. (I think "yes.")
¿Qué decidieron?	What did they decide?
—Que no.	—No.

169. **Que** vs. **de que**

After a noun, when the relative pronoun *that* means *stating that, to the effect that, consisting in that,* etc., it is translated by **de que.**

No nos gusta la idea de que venga tan temprano.	We don't like the idea that he's coming so early.
No creí la mentira de que tú lo hubieses dicho.	I didn't believe the lie that *you* had said it.
Acaba de recibir la noticia de que su padre ha muerto.	He has just received the news that his father has died.

When *that* means *which* or can be omitted in English, **que** is used.

No nos gusta la idea que propuso.	We don't like the idea he advanced.
No creí la mentira que dijo.	I didn't believe the lie (that) he told.
Acaba de recibir el mensaje que le dejaste.	He has just received the message you left him.

170. **Quien** as a Compound Relative

A. The pronoun **quien** may be used to mean *the one who*, *he who*, *whoever*. In this sense, it is synonymous with **el que.**

Quien te dijo eso mentía.	The one who (whoever) told you that was lying.
Quienes le conocían le amaban.	Those who knew him loved him.
o	or
Quien le conocía le amaba.	Whoever knew him loved him.

This usage occurs very frequently in proverbs.

Quien no se atreve no pasa la mar.	Faint heart never won fair lady. (Literally: He who doesn't dare doesn't cross the sea.)
Quien ríe después ríe más.	He who laughs last laughs best.
Quien mucho habla mucho yerra.	He who talks much errs much.

B. **Quien** followed by the subjunctive, means *anyone who*.

Quien no haya visto Sevilla no ha visto maravilla.	Anyone who hasn't seen Sevilla hasn't seen a marvelous thing.

El que may also appear in this construction.

El que se mueva morirá.	Anyone who moves will die.

171. Cuanto

Cuanto (a, os, as) means *all that* (*which*), *all those who* (or *which*). It is an exact synonym for **todo lo que, todos los que,** etc.

Sabe cuanto (o **todo lo que**) **hay que saber.**	He knows all there is to know.
Cuantos (o **todos los que**) **lo vieron tuvieron la misma impresión.**	All those who saw it had the same impression.

172. **Donde** as a Relative

Donde, en donde, and **por donde** may be used as relative pronouns in place of **en que, por el cual,** etc.

La tienda donde compro mis libros...	The store in which (or where) I buy my books . . .
La escalera de salvamento por donde huyó el ladrón...	The fire escape by which the thief escaped . . .

173. Agreement of the Subordinate Clause Verb

A. When **quien** is subject of the subordinate clause and its antecedent is a personal pronoun (was it *you who* . . . ? etc.), the verb of the subordinate clause generally agrees with the personal pronoun in gender and number.

¿Fuiste tú quien lo hiciste?	Was it you who did it?
Fui yo quien le vi.	It was I who saw him.
Somos nosotros quienes lo dijimos primero.	We are the ones who said so first.

B. When **el que** is used instead of **quien** in the above situation, the *third* person is preferred.

¿Eres tú el que lo hizo?	Was it you who did it?
Fui yo el que le vio.	It was I who saw him.
Somos nosotros los que lo dijeron.	We are the ones who said so. (It was we who . . .)

174. **El que** as Object of a Preposition

When **el que, la que,** etc., is object of a preposition, the preposition must precede the relative pronoun.

De lo que yo quisiera hablar es...	What I should like to talk about is . . .
Al que no le guste, que se vaya.	Let anyone who doesn't like it leave.

175. Special Use of **cuyo**

Occasionally, **cuyo** is used like the English adjective *which*.

Es posible que venga esta noche, en cuyo caso iremos juntos.	It is possible that he will come tonight, in which case we'll go together.
Salió del cuarto, en cuyo momento se oyó un tiro.	He left the room, at which moment a shot was heard.

176. Use of **que** in a Quasi-Prepositional Function

Que appears at times before an infinitive. Its actual function is to give a passive meaning to the infinitive: *to be done*, *seen*, etc. This usage is especially common after the impersonal **hay** and after **tener.**

Hay mucho que analizar en este libro.	There is a great deal to analyze (to be analyzed) in this book.
Tiene algo que confesar.	He has something to confess (to be confessed).
Esto deja mucho que desear.	This leaves much to be desired.

177. **Por que** and **para que** + Subjunctive

A. The conjunction **por que,** followed by the subjunctive, emphasizes the motive or reason for which an action is done. The outcome of the action is in doubt at the time of its initiation.

Se mata de trabajo por que su esposa pueda tener un abrigo de pieles.	He is killing himself with work so that (in the hope that) his wife may have a fur coat.

B. **Para que,** which is always followed by the subjunctive, merely indicates purpose. The result is viewed as the logical consequence of the action.

Lo hará para que su familia pueda ir al campo.	He will do it so that his family may go to the country.

EJERCICIOS

I. Tradúzcase al español.

The professor whom we liked most was our professor of history. It was he who awakened our interest in the Middle Ages and who showed us how important that period is in the history of Western Europe. His wife, who was a very intelligent woman, always received us with her charming smiles when we visited him.

The little house in which he lived was situated at the other end (**al otro extremo**) of town. It was one of those old cottages which had been in fashion at the end of the last century, but which were no longer built when I went to college. The professor had a daughter, a pretty girl of eighteen, who from time to time joined us in our discussions.

Once, in September, we gathered at his house at about five in the afternoon. A long discussion on politics began almost at once and continued for several hours. We did not notice the heavy rain which began a little after seven, and when we were ready to leave, the storm had turned into a hurricane.

The hurricane continued until early morning (**hasta de la madrugada**) and we could not leave the professor's house until after eight o'clock. Ann, his daughter, who had stayed up chatting with us all night, made breakfast. It was perfectly delicious. I think that all of us who were (**todos los que estábamos**) there fell in love with her then.

"And what happened?"

"I was the one whom she married."

"What luck! And does she still cook so well?"

"Cook? Never! In fact, I make my own breakfast, and sometimes, hers too. But I must admit, it's worth the trouble. She still is the prettiest woman I know. And what she knows about politics and medieval history!"

II. Composición.

Mi concepto de una mujer (o de un hombre) ideal

LECCIÓN DIECIOCHO

PARTICIPLES AND INFINITIVES

Adaptado de

EL TIEMPO

Bogotá, 27 de enero de 1964

Aprenda a Dibujar
¡En Su Casa Por Correo!
Historietas Caricaturas Publicidad
Dibujos Animados
¡No Importa Su Edad!

Conociendo los secretos de nuestro acreditado método de instrucción, cualquier persona —hombre, mujer, o niño— puede, sin estudios cansadores y sin perder tiempo, dinero, ni energías, aprender a dibujar toda clase de historietas, caricaturas, dibujos animados, figuras femeninas, etc. Al terminar nuestro curso, queda Ud. preparado para gozar de brillantes posibilidades de éxito inmediato.

PUBLICIDAD

El comercio y la industria del mundo entero necesitan cada vez más dibujantes para la preparación de anuncios publicitarios, catálogos, carteles, y material gráfico en general. Este campo ofrece maravillosas oportunidades para personas de ambición y talento.

DIBUJOS ANIMADOS

Especializarse en esta profesión significa prepararse para una carrera de creciente desarrollo e ilimitadas perspectivas. El advenimiento de la televisión ha intensificado la demanda de buenos animadores.

INSTÁLESE POR SU CUENTA

Haga como muchos de nuestros alumnos que se han instalado por su propia cuenta y ahora ganan mucho dinero creando historietas y colaborando desde su propia casa con diarios y revistas de todo el mundo.

Complementando su aprendizaje, recibe desde el primer mes valiosas instrucciones especiales con "Ideas para Ganar Dinero", donde se describen infinidad de fáciles tareas para realizar en su tiempo libre mientras estudia, y que venderá a buen precio. Nosotros le indicaremos cómo hacerlo, a quién venderlo, y cuánto cobrar por su trabajo.

VIAJE GRATIS A ESTADOS UNIDOS

Venga a los Estados Unidos y sea huésped de nuestra escuela. Conozca y vea cómo se filma una película, conozca personalmente a los astros y estrellas que Ud. tanto admira en la pantalla. Conozca los fabulosos clubes nocturnos de Hollywood. Diviértase sin que le cueste un sólo centavo. ¡¡¡GRATIS!!! Si quiere más información, escriba a:

ESCUELA CONTINENTAL, S.A.
Carrera 8a No. 17–50.
Bogotá, Columbia

Nombre —————————————— Edad ————

Dirección ——————————————————

Ciudad o Pueblo ————————————————

Provincia, Departamento, o Estado ——————————

PREGUNTAS

1. ¿Qué puede hacer cualquier persona conociendo los secretos de este método?
2. ¿Para qué está preparado el estudiante al terminar el curso?
3. ¿Qué necesitan cada vez más el comercio y la industria?
4. ¿Qué significa especializarse en la profesión de los dibujos animados?
5. ¿Qué ha hecho el advenimiento de la televisión?
6. ¿Qué han hecho muchos alumnos de esta escuela?
7. ¿Con quiénes colaboran desde su propia casa?
8. ¿Qué más recibe el alumno complementando su aprendizaje?
9. ¿Qué le indicarán en el folleto?
10. ¿Qué más le ofrece al alumno la Escuela Continental?

CONVERSACIÓN

1. ¿Qué piensa Ud. de este anuncio comercial? ¿Hasta qué punto cree Ud. que dice la verdad? ¿Qué aspectos no cree Ud.? ¿Cómo se compara este anuncio con los que aparecen regularmente en los periódicos y revistas de los Estados Unidos?
2. ¿Cuál es el anuncio más cómico que haya visto Ud.? ¿Cómo era? ¿Cuál es el más ofensivo que recuerde Ud.? ¿Y el mejor?
3. ¿Sabe Ud. dibujar? ¿Le interesa a Ud. el arte? ¿Quiénes son sus artistas favoritos? ¿Cuáles le gustan menos? ¿Por qué?

PART A

178. The Past Participle

A. Irregular past participles

The following common verbs have irregular past participles:

abrir, abierto opened
decir, dicho said, told
escribir, escrito written
hacer, hecho done
morir, muerto dead
poner, puesto put
ver, visto seen
volver, vuelto (re)turned

B. Uses of the past participle

1. To form compound tenses

Recall that the past participle does not change its ending when it is used with **haber.**

Hemos vuelto.	We have returned.
Las muchachas lo habían leído.	The girls had read it.
Uds. habrán terminado.	You will have finished.

2. In the passive voice, after **ser**

The past participle must agree with the subject in this construction.

Fue calumniado por la prensa.	He was libeled by the press.
Las tropas serán mandadas al frente.	The troops will be ordered to the front.

3. As an adjective

Most past participles may be used as adjectives, if the meaning permits.

un orador apasionado an impassioned orator
una niña cansada a tired little girl
horas perdidas wasted hours

4. With **estar** or **quedar,** to describe the resultant state of an action

Están sentados.	They are seated.
Ya estaba muerto.	He was already dead.
Quedamos aturdidos por la noticia.	We were (left) stunned by the news.

5. In place of a clause

The past participle may be used independently to take the place of a clause beginning with *when, as soon as,* or *after* when referring to a completed action. It agrees with the noun or pronoun subject of the implied clause.

Vendida la casa, tendremos para el viaje.	When the house is sold, we'll have enough for the trip.
(**Apenas**) **llegados al aeropuerto, fueron a telefonear.**	As soon as they reached the airport, they went to telephone.
Sentados a la mesa, pidieron el menú.	After they were seated at the table, they asked for the menu.

EJERCICIOS

A. Cambie:

1. Fueron **perseguidos** por la policía.
(detener, registrar, encontrar, socorrer)
2. Quedé muy **sorprendida** al verle.
(agitar, asustar, impresionar, emocionar)
3. El niño no ha **hecho** nada.
(decir, escribir, devolver, romper, abrir)

B. Cambie las oraciones siguientes según el modelo:

Cuando hubieron llegado a Bogotá... **Llegados a Bogotá...**

1. Así que terminaron la comida... **(Terminada...)** 2. En cuanto hubieron comprado las entradas... 3. Después de echar las cartas... 4. Después de hacer las maletas... 4. Habiendo pintado las paredes... 5. Habiendo muerto el Sr. García...

C. Traduzca al español:

1. It had happened on repeated occasions. 2. This building wasn't (**estar**) finished when I left the city. 3. As soon as the letter was written, he went to the post office. 4. The children, led by the oldest brother, were discovered hiding (hidden) in the forest. 5. When the East coast was conquered, the explorers headed West. 6. Have you taken off those soiled clothes? I have found others to (**que**) give you.

179. The Present Participle (Gerund)

The present participle, also called the gerund, has several important functions:

A. The progressive tense

The present participle, used after **estar, seguir,** or a verb of motion, gives a more graphic picture of an action in its progress at a given moment.

Estábamos leyendo cuando se apagaron las luces.	We were reading when the lights went out.
Siguió comiendo como si no hubiera pasado nada.	He continued eating as if nothing had happened.

Ir and **venir** imply motion away from or toward the speaker.

Iban hablando.	They were (walking along) talking.
El niño venía cantando.	The child was (coming toward us) singing.

B. Independent usage

1. Used alone, the present participle may mean *by* (*doing something*).

Hablando se entiende la gente.	By speaking, people understand each other.
Leyendo mucho, aprenderás a hablar.	By reading a great deal, you'll learn to speak.

2. It may also replace a clause beginning with *when*, *since*, or *while*, when referring to a continuing action.

Conociéndole ya, no quise prestárselo.	Since I knew how he was, I wouldn't lend it to him.
Estando en la Florida, decidieron ir a San Juan.	While (when, since) they were in Florida, they decided to go to San Juan.

IMPORTANT: The present participle is never used as a noun or an adjective[1] in Spanish.

El cantar me alegra el corazón.	Singing gladdens my heart.
La bella durmiente...	Sleeping beauty . . .

EJERCICIOS

A. Substituya las palabras subrayadas por una construcción con el gerundio:
1. Me **seguían** los chicos. 2. **¡Mientes!** 3. **Comen** ahora. 4. **Arreglaba** las flores en el florero. 5. **Porque es** un alumno aprovechado, saldrá bien. 6. **Si hay** turistas, habrá quien nos compre estas baratijas. 7. **Cuando nos acercamos** a la valla, pudimos ver los toros. 8. **Porque me encontraba** solo, me puse a gritar. 9. **Ya que vivían** cerca, nos vinieron a visitar. 10. **Si trabajas mucho,** lo terminarás a tiempo.

B. Diga en español:
1. By eating too much and sleeping very little, he got sick. 2. Since he was an experienced actor, he applied for the role. 3. They were crossing the street when the siren sounded. 4. The child came running. 5. Having said it, he refused to retract. 6. What were you doing when the storm began? —I was sleeping.

180. The Infinitive

The infinitive has a variety of very important functions. These are the most salient.

A. As object of a verb

Just as in English, an infinitive that depends on a verb acts somewhat as object of that verb.

Quiero ir.	I want to go.
Puede caminar ahora.	He can walk now.
Sabe hacerlo.	He knows how to do it.

B. After prepositions

All prepositions are regularly followed by the infinitive. This is contrary to English usage, which generally employs the present participle.

después de salir after leaving
antes de detenerlos before arresting them
sin quitarse el sombrero without taking off his hat

[1] Except for these two words: **ardiendo** *burning*; **hirviendo** *boiling*.

C. As a noun

The infinitive is the only part of a verb that can ever be used as a noun. It appears frequently as a subject, object, or after **ser.** This, too, is contrary to the English, which uses the present participle.

El hacer bien a otros es su propia recompensa.	Doing good unto others is its own reward.
Escuchaba el cantar de los pájaros.	He was listening to the singing of the birds.
Ver es creer.	Seeing is believing. (To see is to believe.)

D. After verbs referring to the senses

¿Has oído cantar a Tomás?	Have you heard Tom sing?
Los vi morir.	I saw them die.
Le sentían acercarse.	They felt him approaching.

E. After verbs of ordering, forcing, permitting, preventing

Le mandaron salir.	They ordered him to leave.
Déjame comprarlo.	Let me buy it.
Les hicimos volver.	We made them return.
No deben impedirle casarse.	They shouldn't prevent him from marrying.

A clause containing the subjunctive may also follow these verbs, but after **mandar, hacer,** and **dejar,** the infinitive is more common.

F. **Al** + Infinitive = Upon (doing something), When (+ clause)

Al ver lo que pasaba, se asustó.	Upon seeing what was happening, he got frightened. (When he saw . . .)

EJERCICIO

Conteste en español:

1. ¿Qué hará Ud. primero al volver a casa esta tarde? 2. ¿Cuáles fueron sus primeras impresiones al entrar en esta universidad? 3. ¿Han cambiado esas primeras impresiones? 4. ¿Cree Ud. que el fumar mucho daña la salud? ¿Fuma Ud.? 5. ¿Ha oído cantar o tocar recientemente a un buen artista musical? ¿Quién fue? 6. ¿Qué piensa Ud. hacer cuando termine todos sus estudios? 7. ¿Sabe Ud. tocar un instrumento musical? 8. ¿Sabe Ud. dibujar

bien? 9. ¿Le gustaría aprender a hablar otra lengua extranjera? 10. ¿Le gustaría terminar este ejercicio ahora mismo? ... Muy bien.

EJERCICIO DE REPASO

1. By using our method of instruction, any person can learn how to draw well and without tiring studies.
2. Upon finishing our course, you will be prepared to enjoy a brilliant career and marvelous opportunities.
3. Specializing in this field means preparing oneself for a constantly growing perspective.
4. The advent of television has intensified the demand for animators, cartoonists, and artists of all kinds.
5. Many of our students have gone out on their own and are making large sums of money by collaborating with magazines all over the world.
6. Complementing your apprenticeship, you will receive a valuable booklet with ideas for earning money.
7. We shall tell you also how to make (**sacar**) profit from your free time and how much to charge for your work.
8. Knowing how to draw is important also in your personal and social life.
9. Our best students are invited every year to go to the United States and meet famous movie stars.
10. If you want further information, write to us without wasting one more moment. If you hurry, the future is yours.

REPASO DE VERBOS

Estudie **oír, construir, leer** y otros verbos parecidos, y después diga en español:

I don't hear you. Are they building it already? They built it last year? He read it in the paper. Don't destroy anything. When are they concluding? She wants us to read her poem. He fled with the money. She begged him not to flee. Listen. (**tú, vosotros, Ud., Uds.**) Don't build it there. (**tú, vosotros, Ud., Uds.**)

PART B

181. The Past Participle

A. With verbs other than **estar** to indicate a state or condition

A number of verbs, such as **tener, verse, hallarse, sentirse,**

encontrarse, are used with the past participle to lend a more subjective tone to the description of a state or condition.

Tengo pintada de rojo la mesa.	My table is painted red. (I have it painted red.)
Se vio obligado a salir.	He was (found, or felt himself) obliged to leave.
Nos hallábamos muy ocupados.	We were very busy.
Se sienten avergonzados.	They are (feel) ashamed.

B. To translate an English present participle

When the present participle in English refers to a state or condition, and not to an action in its progress at a given moment, the past participle must be used in Spanish.

Estaban sentados alrededor de la hoguera.	They were sitting around the bonfire.
La encontramos arrodillada ante el altar.	We found her kneeling before the altar.
Me saludó tendido en la cama.	He greeted me (while) lying on the bed.
El ladrón estaba escondido debajo del sofá.	The thief was hiding (hidden) under the sofa.

In all the examples above the use of the present participle in Spanish would mean *in the act of* (being seated, kneeling down, etc.). The verb then would be reflexive.

182. The Present Participle

A. After the preposition **en**

The only preposition that may precede a present participle in Spanish is **en.** However, this construction, which is synonymous with **al** + infinitive, is used rather infrequently.

En volviendo a casa, me eché en un sillón.	Upon returning home, I threw myself into a big chair.
En saliendo del cuarto se cayó de bruces.	Upon leaving the room, he fell down headlong.

B. To describe a resulting or accompanying action

In written or formal Spanish, the present participle, without any preposition, is often used to indicate an action that accompanies or results from another action or situation. It is similar to an English construction that is often prefaced by *with* or *there*.

Ayer hubo tres accidentes resultando dos muertos y cuatro heridos.	Yesterday there were three accidents, with two (being) killed and four injured.
Las elecciones se celebraron en diciembre, siendo elegido el candidato liberal.	The elections were held in December, with the liberal candidate being elected (there being elected . . .).

C. Spanish translations of English present participles used as adjectives

1. The only present participles that may be used as adjectives in Spanish are **ardiendo** and **hirviendo.**

agua hirviendo boiling water
una casa ardiendo a burning house

2. Spanish has many adjectives ending in **-dor** or **-ante, -iente** (gerundive forms) that correspond to a present participle in English.

un pájaro hablador a talking bird
un sermón inspirador an inspiring sermon
agua corriente running water
un caballero andante a knight errant (wandering)

3. When there is no corresponding adjective in Spanish, a clause must be used.

Tomamos el camino que conducía al castillo.	We took the road leading to the castle.

183. The Infinitive with Passive Force

The infinitive is employed with passive force in the following situations.

A. After **mandar, dejar, hacer**

Nos mandaron encarcelar.	They ordered us (to be) imprisoned.
Se deja llevar de su entusiasmo.	He lets himself be carried away by his enthusiasm.
Hice pintar las paredes.	I had the walls painted.

B. After **ser de**

1. In certain impersonal expressions

Es de esperar que se mejore de salud.	It is to be hoped that his health improves.
Es de suponer que no lo consentirán.	It is to be assumed that they will not permit it.
Es de notar que...	It is to be noted that . . .
Era de verse...	It was worth seeing . . . (You should have seen . . .)

2. When **ser... de** is preceded by an expressed or implied subject.

Esa pieza es fácil de tocar.	That piece is easy to play (to be played).
El chocolate era imposible de obtener durante la guerra.	Chocolate was impossible to get (to be gotten) during the war.
Es difícil de explicar.	It is difficult to explain (to be explained).

But, when the infinitive that follows **ser** is really its subject, the passive force is lost and **de** is omitted.

Es fácil tocar esa pieza.	It is easy to play that piece.
Era imposible obtener chocolate.	It was impossible to get chocolate.
Es difícil explicarlo.	It's difficult to explain it.

184. Infinitive Substitutes for a Clause

A. **Al** + infinitive is often used as a substitute for a clause beginning with *when.*

Al entrar ella en el cuarto, la saludamos todos.	When she entered the room, we all greeted her.
Al acercarse cualquier forastero, el perro empezaba a ladrar.	When any stranger approached, the dog began to bark.

Notice that the subject of the implied clause follows the infinitive.

B. **De** + infinitive may serve as a substitute for an *if*-clause contrary to fact, especially in the compound tenses.

De haberla visto antes, se lo habría advertido.	If I had seen her sooner, I would have warned her.

C. Other prepositions + infinitive may also be substituted.

Hasta, sin, and certain other prepositions may be followed by the infinitive, whether or not there is a change of subject. Thus, they often replace subordinate clauses. Recall that the subject of the omitted clause must then *follow* the infinitive.

Se fueron sin saberlo nadie.	They went away without anyone's knowing it.
No lo deje hasta acabarlo.	Don't leave it until you finish it.

185. The Infinitive as an Imperative

As we have noted, this usage occurs mainly in short sentences that serve as written directions or public notices.

No Fumar	No Smoking; DO NOT SMOKE
Traducir al español las frases siguientes.	Translate the following sentences into Spanish.

186. The Infinitive to Translate an English Past Participle

When a past participle in English is preceded by the prefix *un*, Spanish generally uses **sin,** or at times **por,** followed by the infinitive.

El piso está todavía sin (or **por**) **pintar.**	The apartment is still unpainted.
Potros sin domar...	Untamed horses . . .

EJERCICIOS

I. Traducir al español.

Most of the students in our class used to study only for approaching final exams, and never paid any attention to the professor all semester. I don't know why, because he was really an inspired man, and inspiring too. For example, he would repeat to us constantly, "Only by studying does one learn." Or then, he would add, "Besides, studying is necessary for the mind." Wasn't that brilliant? On certain days, when he felt especially moving, he would remind us, "Only by working all the time can one achieve success. Without working, the mind is like a plant without water."

I decided to follow his advice, and I spent the rest of the year studying every night until my eyes closed (**se me cerraban los ojos**) with fatigue. One day, since I was so tired from all that studying, it was impossible for me to resist the lulling rhythm of his voice. I fell asleep in class. Suddenly, I heard someone shout into my ear (**al oído**), "Sleeping students don't pass courses."

When the course was finished, I knew that I deserved the D that I received. Today I realize more than ever that the professor was right; for I have learned that only by working and studying all the time without playing, without resting, can one find true happiness—if not in this world, certainly in the other!

II. Composición.

Mi concepto de un buen profesor
El profesor que me gustó más (o menos)
Por qué quiero (o no quiero) ser profesor

REFERENCE GUIDES

A

WHAT'S THE DIFFERENCE BETWEEN . . . ?

"What's the Difference Between . . . ?" contains an analysis of one hundred and fifty common English words whose varied translation(s) in Spanish often cause confusion. Use the word list below to help you find "the difference between." The Spanish words and expressions are treated in the section that follows, on pages 247 through 313; the numbers beside each of the words (below) indicate the paragraph(s) in which they appear.

1. about

sobre, acerca de about, concerning, dealing with (usually a topic)
Sobre is used somewhat more frequently.

Es un libro sobre (acerca de) la revolución francesa.	It is a book about the French Revolution.

de about, concerning (usually, though not necessarily, concerning a person)

He oído hablar mucho de él.	I have heard a great deal about him.
No sé nada de su familia.	I don't know anything about his family.
No hablemos de eso.	Let's not talk about that.

a eso de about, approximately (used before a number, and generally refers to time of day)

Llegaron a eso de las once y media.	They arrived about 11:30.

Sobre is often used colloquially in this sense.

Nos veremos sobre las ocho, ¿eh?	We'll meet around eight, OK?

cerca de about, nearly, almost (used primarily with numbers or hours of the day)

La China tiene cerca de quinientos millones de habitantes.	China has about (close to) five hundred million inhabitants.

unos about, approximately (used before numbers, but not to express time of day)

Mi tía tiene unos cincuenta años.	My aunt is about fifty years old.

más o menos more or less; may also be translated *about*

Tiene cincuenta años, más o menos.	He is about fifty years old.

2. above

arriba (*adv.*) above, overhead (unlimited, not necessarily relative to the position of another object) OPPOSITE: **abajo** below

Arriba, un cielo nublado y tormentoso; abajo, un torbellino de aguas turbulentas.	Above, a cloudy, stormy sky; below, a whirlpool of turbulent waters.

encima (*adv.*) above, on top (usually relative to the position of another object) OPPOSITE: **debajo** underneath

Primero pondrás el ungüento, y encima, la venda.	First you'll apply the ointment, and on top (above), the bandage.
Se me cayó encima.	It fell right on top of me.
Debajo hay miles de corrientes; encima no se ve nada.	Underneath there are thousands of currents; on top (above), nothing is visible.

encima de (*prep.*) (piled) on top of; suspended above

Lo puse encima del armario.	I put it on top of the wardrobe.
¿Por qué no lo colgamos encima del sofá?	Why don't we hang it above the sofa?

sobre (*prep.*) above, over: on top of

Sobre, though essentially synonymous with **encima de,** implies a closer position to the object, a feeling often of almost touching, resting upon it. Also, **sobre** may be used figuratively.

Sobre todo, cuide de no ofenderlos nunca.	Above all, take care never to offend them.

3. actual(ly)

The English word *actual* has two meanings: (1) real (2) present, current.

actual present, current, contemporary

La situación actual de la economía peruana...	The present situation of the Peruvian economy . . .
El presidente actual es el Sr. Domínguez.	The current president is Mr. Domínguez.

verdadero, real, efectivo actual (in the sense of real or true)

El jefe verdadero (**real** or **efectivo**) **es García.**	The actual (real) leader is García.
La razón verdadera fue...	The actual (real) reason was . . .

en la actualidad, actualmente nowadays, currently at present

En la actualidad vive en Chile.	At present, he is living in Chile.

en realidad, a decir verdad actually, really, truthfully

En realidad, ella no era su madre.	Actually, she wasn't his mother.
A decir verdad, no sabía la respuesta; la adiviné.	Actually (to tell the truth), I didn't know the answer; I guessed it.

4. after

después de (*prep.*) after (in sense of time)

Después de poner la mesa, metió las chuletas en el horno.	After setting the table, she put the chops in the oven.

tras (*prep.*) after (in a sequence or series); after, right behind (location)

Día tras día, hora tras hora...	Day after day, hour after hour . . .
Corrió tras él.	She ran after him.

después de que (*conj.*) after (introduces a clause referring to time)

Después de que se gradúe su hermano mayor, Pepe asistirá también a la universidad. After his older brother graduates, Joe will attend college too.

después (*adv.*) afterwards, later, then

Primero, llamó a la policía. Después, salió en busca de los ladrones él mismo. First, he called the police. Then he went out in search of the thieves himself.

5. again

otra vez again, another time (as before)

Repita otra vez. Repeat again.

¿No quieres cantármela otra vez? Won't you sing it for me again?

de nuevo again, anew (from a fresh start), all over again

Hágalo de nuevo. Do it over again.

Cinco minutos después se presentó de nuevo con otra demanda. Five minutes later he turned up again with another demand.

una vez más one more time, once again

Por favor, diga una vez más: *perro, perro, perro...* Please, say once more: *perro, perro . . .*

volver a (+ *infinitive*) to do (something) again

Me volvió a llamar a medianoche. ¿Qué te crees? He called me again at midnight. How about that?

6. (to) agree

estar de acuerdo to be in agreement on an issue; to agree with someone

En eso estamos de acuerdo todos. On that we all agree.

Pues yo no estoy de acuerdo con Uds. Well, I don't agree with you.

estar conforme to agree to something; to go along with

Creo que debiéramos invitarlos. —Estoy conforme. I think that we ought to invite them. —I agree. (It's all right with me.)

convenir en, quedar en to agree to do something

Convinieron en reunirse todos los martes.	They agreed to meet every Tuesday.
Quedamos en vernos al día siguiente.	We agreed to see each other on the following day.

7. ahead

adelante (*adv.*) up ahead, farther on; onward, forward OPPOSITE: **atrás**

No importa. Seguiremos adelante.	It doesn't matter. We'll keep going ahead.
Los encontrarás un poco más adelante.	You'll find them a little farther up ahead.

adelantado (*adj.*) ahead, advanced

Mi reloj anda algo adelantado.	My watch is running a little ahead (fast).
Está muy adelantada para su edad.	She is far ahead for her age.

más adelantado que, más adelante que, delante de ahead of

Este niño está más adelantado que (más adelante que, delante de) los demás de su clase.	This boy is ahead of the other pupils in his class.

8. anyone

cualquiera, cualquier persona anyone (at all)

Cualquiera (Cualquier persona) podría hacer eso.	Anyone at all could do that.

alguien anyone (in a question), someone

¿Hay alguien que me pueda ayudar?	Is there anyone (someone) who can help me?

nadie anyone (after a negative)

No hay nadie hoy.	There isn't anyone here today.

9. anyway

en fin well, to sum up, anyway, so

En fin, decidió ir con nosotros al campo.	Anyway he decided to go with us to the country.

en todo caso anyway, in any case or event

En todo caso partirán antes del quince. Anyway (in any event) they'll leave before the fifteenth.

a pesar de todo, de todos modos anyway, despite everything

A pesar de todo (De todos modos), nos tendrá que pagar. He'll have to pay us anyway.

10. appointment

cita a date—a social, or (less frequently) business, appointment

¿Tienes cita con Juan el sábado? Do you have an appointment (date) with John Saturday?

compromiso an appointment—sometimes social, often business or professional

No hay tiempo para más compromisos hoy. There is no time for more appointments today.

hora a doctor's appointment

¿Me puede dar hora mañana el Dr. Ulcera? Can Dr. Ulcera give me an appointment tomorrow?

nombramiento appointment (to a position)

¿Quién conseguirá el nombramiento ante las Naciones Unidas? Who will get the appointment to the United Nations?

11. around

alrededor (*adv.*) round about, all around, on all sides

Alrededor había fuentes y árboles y hermosas flores. All around were fountains and trees and beautiful flowers.

alrededor de (*prep.*) around, in a circle about

Formaron un círculo alrededor del campeón. They formed a circle around the champion.

por (*prep.*) around, in the vicinity of, through the general area of

Tiene que estar por aquí. It has to be around here.

¿Por qué no damos una vueltecita por el parque? Why don't we take a little turn around (in) the park?

a eso de, sobre around (referring to time of day) (*see* about, p. 248)

unos, más o menos around, about, approximately (*see* about, p. 248)

12. (to) ask

pedir to ask for (to ask to be given something, etc.); to make a request to someone

No le pediré nada aunque me muera de hambre.	I won't ask him for anything even if I starve to death.
Pídale que vuelva.	Ask him to come back.

preguntar to ask (a question), to inquire

Pregúntale cuándo volverá.	Ask him when he'll come back.

hacer una pregunta to ask a question

No me hagas tantas preguntas.	Don't ask me so many questions.

preguntar por to ask for (about), to inquire about

Acabo de ver a Carmen y ella preguntó por ti.	I have just seen Carmen and she asked for you.

• at **en, a** (*see* **154** D, p. 209)

13. (to) attend

atender a to attend to (a matter, a person, etc.)

Atiende a sus propios asuntos sin interesarse por otra persona.	He attends to his own affairs without taking an interest in anyone else.
La dependienta está atendiendo a su primer cliente.	The clerk is attending to her first customer.

asistir a to attend (a school, a function, etc.)

Asistimos al Instituto.	We attend the Institute.

IMPORTANT: **Asistir** does not normally mean *to assist, help*. **Ayudar** is used in this sense.

Ayuda a su padre en el negocio.	He assists his father in the business.

NOTE:

Los asistentes...	Those in attendance . . .
El ayudante del general...	The assistant (aide) to the general . . .

• (to) be (*see* **ser-estar,** Chap. X)

14. (to) be cold

hacer frío to be cold (refers to climate, weather, or room temperature)

Hace mucho frío, ¿no?	It's very cold (out here, or in here), isn't it?

tener or **sentir frío** to be cold (describes a person's reaction to cold). **Sentir** implies a sudden chill.

Tengo (siento) frío. —Y yo siempre tengo calor.	I am (feel) cold. —And I am always warm.

ser frío to be cold (depicts a characteristic of a person or thing); to be distant, aloof, impassive

No me gusta ese hombre. Es demasiado frío.	I don't like that man. He's too cold (distant, frigid).
La nieve es fría.	Snow is cold.

estar frío to be in a cold state or condition

Lo olla ya está fría.	The pot is already cold.
Mi sopa está fría.	My soup is cold.

15. because

porque (*conj.*) because (+ *clause*)

No le interesa porque no lo entiende.	It doesn't interest him because he doesn't understand it.
No van a comer de eso porque no les gusta.	They won't eat that because they don't like it.

a causa de (*prep.*) because of, due to (+ *a noun or pronoun*)

A causa del aumento de los precios, se trasladarán a otra ciudad.	Because of the increase in prices, they will move to another city.
No pudimos acabarlo a causa de él.	We couldn't finish it because of him.

debido a (*prep.*) because of, due to (+ *a noun*)

Debido a is synonymous with **a causa de,** except that it usually refers only to nonpersonal nouns.

Debido a circunstancias fuera de nuestro control....	Due to circumstances beyond our control . . .

por (*prep.*) because of, for the sake of; out of, motivated by

Trabaja sólo por ella.	He works only for her sake (because of her).
Lo hizo por miedo.	He did it because of (out of) fear.

16. (to) become

llegar a ser to become (something—usually as the culmination of a series of events)

Después de diez y ocho años en el Senado llegó a ser presidente.	After eighteen years in the Senate, he became president.

hacerse to become (usually a member of a profession or trade); to become (rich); to change into

Su hijo se ha hecho cura.	His son has become a priest.
El agua se hace hielo a los treinta y dos grados.	Water becomes ice at 32°.

ponerse (+ *adj.*) to become (to adopt, acquire, assume, take on a certain condition or state—usually a person)

Si no te cuidas, te pondrás enfermo.	If you don't take care of yourself, you'll get sick.
Se puso pálido (rojo, enojado).	He became pale (red, angry).

Frequently, a transitive verb used reflexively conveys the same meaning as **ponerse** (+ adjective).

Se enojó, se enfadó.	He became angry.
Se alegrará cuando oiga las noticias.	He will be (become) happy when he hears the news.

volverse to become (as by a sudden change); to turn (into)

El pobre se ha vuelto loco.	The poor fellow has become (gone, turned) crazy.

convertirse en to become, turn into, change into (a physical change)

La cera se convierte en sustancias gaseosas cuando se quema.	Wax turns into (becomes) gaseous matter when it burns.
De noche, el ilustre Doctor Jekyll se convertía en (o se hacía) un monstruo diabólico.	At night, the illustrious Dr. Jekyll became a diabolical monster.

meterse a to become, to set one's mind on a new course of activity or plunge into a new endeavour. **Meterse a** often has somewhat derogatory implications or connotations of impermanence.

Ahora se ha metido a pintor. ¿En qué va a pensar después?	Now he has become a painter (taken up painting). What will he think of next?

ser de, hacerse de to become of, to happen to

¿Qué será de mí?	What will become of me?
¿Qué se ha hecho de Felipe?	What has become of Phil?

quedarse to become, be left in a certain condition (usually a thing)

La casa se ha quedado muy sucia.	The house has become very dirty.

17. before

antes de (*prep.*) before (referring to time)

Antes de ponerte la nueva camisa, no dejes de quitarle todos los alfileres.	Before putting on your new shirt, be sure to take out all the pins.

antes (*adv.*) before (in time), first

El cantó antes, ella después.	He sang first, she afterwards.

antes de que (*conj.*) before (introduces a clause referring to time, and is always followed by the subjunctive)

Vámonos ahora mismo antes de que llueva.	Let's go right now, before it rains.

antes que (*prep.*) before, rather than (does not stress time)

Se dejaría echar a la calle antes que pedir prestado a nadie.	He would let himself be thrown out into the street rather than borrow from anyone.

delante de before, in front of, ahead of (refers to location, not time)

Tiene una labor tremenda delante de ella.	She has a tremendous job before her.
Estaban sentados delante del hogar.	They were seated in front of (before) the fireplace.

ante before, in front of (a person, an altar, a court, etc.)

Ante usually implies some relation of deference.

Se arrodilló ante el altar (el rey, el juez, etc.)	He kneeled before the altar (the king, the judge, etc.)
Hay que quitarse el sombrero ante una señora.	One must remove his hat before a lady.

18. behind

detrás de (*prep.*) behind, in back of (something) OPPOSITE: **delante de**

Los niños estaban escondidos detrás del sofá.	The children were hiding behind the sofa.

tras (*prep.*) behind, following, after

Pedrito se fue corriendo, y tras él, todos los demás muchachos.	Little Pete went off running, and behind him, all the other children.

atrás (*adv.*) behind, in back (not specifically relative to the position of another object) OPPOSITE: **adelante**

Los heridos se han quedado atrás.	The wounded have remained behind.
Dio tres pasos hacia atrás.	He took three steps back(wards).

atrasado (*adj.*) behind, backward

El proyecto anda un poco atrasado.	The project is a little behind (schedule).
El reloj está atrasado.	The clock is behind (slow).

19. below

abajo (*adv.*) below, underneath (not relative to the position of something else) OPPOSITE: **arriba**

Abajo corría una corriente tumultuosa.	Below there ran a tumultuous current.
No mire nunca hacia abajo; siempre, hacia arriba.	Don't ever look below (down); always look up.

debajo (*adv.*) below, under (with respect to something else) OPPOSITE: **encima**

Ahí lo puso debajo.	He put it there underneath.
Encima se veía una cara sonriente; debajo, una mueca terrible.	On the surface one saw a smiling face; below, a terrible grimace.

debajo de, bajo (*prep.*) under, below, underneath (*see* under, **137**, p. 308)

Debajo de la superficie hay valiosas minas de plata.	Below the surface there are valuable silver mines.

20. beside(s)

además de beside, aside from

Además de su mucho trabajo en casa, estudia de noche.	Beside the great amount of work she does at home, she studies at night.

al lado de, a su lado beside, next to, at one's side (location)

Joaquín está al lado de su madre.	Jack is beside his mother.
A su lado estaban todos sus hijos y nietos.	Beside him were all his children and grandchildren.

además besides, moreover, furthermore

Además, nunca había salido de su pueblecito.	Besides, he had never left his his village.

21. boat

barco, buque large boat, ship

un barco (buque) de guerra	a warship

vapor steamship, boat, steamer

El vapor entrará en muelle a las siete.	The steamship will dock at 7 o'clock.

bote a small boat, usually a rowboat

Se metieron los dos en el bote y empezaron a remar.	The two got into the boat and began to row.

barca a fairly small ship, used for fishing, etc.

La barca abandonada había servido para llevar contrabando.	The abandoned boat had been used for carrying contraband.

lancha a small boat (often with a motor), launch

Fuimos conducidos a tierra en lanchas.	We were taken ashore in launches (boats).

ir por mar or **en barco** to travel by boat or ship

¿Iréis en avión o por mar (en barco)?	Will you go by plane or by boat?

22. (to) burn

arder to be on fire, to be burning

La casa estaba ardiendo.	The house was burning.

quemar to burn, scorch, sear (something or someone); to destroy by fire

¡Ay, por Dios! Me he quemado los dedos.	Ouch! I have burnt my fingers.
La quemaron viva.	They burnt her alive.

quemarse (*intransitive*) to burn down (or up)

Se quemó el establo.	The stable burned down.

pegar (o **poner**) **fuego a** to set on fire, burn down

El loco pegó (o puso) fuego a la barraca.	The madman set fire to (burned) the cabin.

23. but

sino but, on the contrary

Sino is used only when the first part of a sentence is negative, and the second part contradicts it. **Sino que** introduces a clause.

No es valiente, sino cobarde.	He is not brave, but cowardly.
No estudia, sino que pasa el tiempo jugando.	He doesn't study, but spends his time playing.

pero but (in all its uses except that noted for **sino**)

Es cobarde, pero todos creen que es valiente.	He is a coward, but every one thinks he is brave.

Mas is a literary synonym for **pero.**

menos but, except

Nadie lo sabe menos yo.	No one knows but I.

si no fuera por but for, except for, if it weren't for

Si no fuera por él, todos habrían muerto.	But for him, they would all have died.

24. by

por by (an agent); by means of (in which the physical nature of the action itself is stressed)

Las velas fueron apagadas por el viento.	The candles were blown out by the wind.
Nos llamó por teléfono.	He called us by (on the) telephone.

de by (an agent or accompanying factor) **De** implies an emotional or mental attitude, or a physical state already achieved.

Era muy amado de sus empleados.	He was very much loved by his employees.
Está rodeada de amigos y parientes.	She is surrounded by friends and relatives.

en by (a means of transportation, but referring almost exclusively to persons)

Iremos en avión, no en barco.	We'll go by plane, not by ship.
But: **Mandaron la carta por avión.**	They sent the letter by (via) airmail.

para by a future time

Para mañana deben terminarlo.	They ought to finish by tomorrow.

25. can

poder can (to be able, physically capable); may, can (colloquial English—to be allowed)

Puedes hacerlo si quieres.	You can do it if you want to.
No puedo levantarlo.	I can't lift it up.
Mi madre dice que puedo ir.	My mother says that I can (may) go.

saber can (in the sense of *to know how to*)

Sabe hablar siete lenguas.	He can speak seven languages.
¿Sabe Ud. tocar el piano?	Can you play the piano?

26. clerk

dependiente, dependienta generally a salesclerk
contador a bank clerk; bookkeeper
empleado usually a nonselling clerk; an employee of a store, office, etc.

Le expliqué el caso al empleado de Correos.	I explained the case to the postal clerk.

escribano a clerical worker; court clerk

El escribano apuntará su nombre y dirección.	The clerk will take down your name and address.

mozo a general helper (grocery clerk, etc.)

27. confidence

confianza confidence, faith, reliance, trust

Tengo la mayor confianza en Uds.	I have the greatest confidence in you.

confidencia a confidence, something that is being confided; confidence, secrecy

Me lo dijo en confidencia.	He told me it in confidence.
Nunca se debe revelar una confidencia.	One should never reveal a confidence.

28. corner

esquina street corner (sidewalk); an outside corner

Te esperaremos en la esquina, ¿está bien?	We'll wait for you on the corner, all right?

rincón (*m.*) (an inside) corner; nook

La mesa nueva cabrá ahí en el rincón.	The new table will fit there in the corner.

bocacalle (*f.*) street corner (intersection, in the road)

El policía dirigía el tránsito en la bocacalle. The policeman was directing traffic on the corner.

29. country

país country, nation

Hay muchos países que no tienen puertos de mar. There are many countries that don't have seaports.

campo the country (as opposed to the city)

Pasamos el verano en el campo. We spent the summer in the country.

patria country, fatherland, homeland (often emotional or poetic)

Murió por su patria. He died for his country.

tierra native land, home province, etc.

Tierra is also used figuratively to mean *the land, earth, world*, etc.

Mi tierra es Andalucía. My land is Andalucía.

terreno country, lay of the land, topography, terrain

El terreno era áspero y escabroso. The country was rough and rugged.

30. dark

oscuro dark (in color); not lighted

Mi nuevo traje es de un verde oscuro. My new suit is dark green.

Vive en una calle oscura. He lives on a dark street.

a oscuras (in the) dark, with the lights out (**a oscuras** is also used figuratively)

El cuarto estaba a oscuras. The room was dark.

Están tanteando a oscuras. They're groping in the dark.

31. date

fecha a date of the month or year

No se sabe la fecha exacta de su nacimiento. The exact date of his birth is not known.

¿Qué fecha es hoy? What is today's date?

The idioms **¿A cuántos del mes estamos?** and **¿Qué fecha tenemos?** also ask: What is today's date?

cita a date, an appointment to meet somebody (usually socially)

Tengo una cita con él mañana. I have a date with him tomorrow.

compromiso a date, an appointment, an engagement (either social or business)

Ya tiene compromiso para esta tarde.	He already has an appointment for this afternoon.

citarse to make a date

Nos citamos para hoy.	We made a date for today.

32. (to) destroy

destruir to destroy completely, to annihilate

No se puede destruir nunca el alma del hombre.	Man's soul can never be destroyed.

destrozar to destroy, ruin, devastate

La tormenta destrozó gran parte del edificio.	The storm destroyed (wrecked) a large part of the building.

33. ear

oído (inner) ear; hearing

Tiene una herida en el oído.	He has an injury in his ear.
Me lo susurró al oído.	He whispered it into my ear.

oreja (outer) ear

Le cortaron una oreja.	They cut off his ear.
Tenía vendada la oreja derecha.	His right ear was bandaged.

34. (to) enjoy

divertirse, pasarlo bien to enjoy, amuse oneself, to have a good time

Nos divertimos mucho en el club.	We enjoy ourselves very much at the Club.
Lo pasé muy bien anoche.	I had a very good time last night.

gozar de to enjoy, take pleasure or pride in, reap satisfaction from; to enjoy the benefits of (good health, etc.)

Siempre ha gozado de buena salud.	He has always enjoyed good health.
Goza de sus nietos.	She enjoys her grandsons.
Gozan de mucha fama en su pueblo.	They enjoy a great reputation in their home town.

disfrutar (de) to enjoy, take pleasure and advantage from

Disfruta de la vida.	He enjoys life.

gustarle (mucho) a uno to enjoy (a book, show, etc.)

¿Qué tal le gustó el concierto?	How did you enjoy the concert?
No me ha gustado nunca su compañía.	I have never enjoyed his company.

35. even

hasta, aun, incluso (*adv.* and *prep.*) even, furthermore (surprisingly); in addition; including

Although these are usually interchangeable, **aun** is less emphatic than **hasta** or **incluso,** and **incluso** is less frequent as an adverb.

Hasta (**Aun**) **sabe leer y escribir japonés.**	He even knows how to read and write Japanese.
Hasta (**Aun, Incluso**) **los niños iban armados por las calles.**	Even the children went about armed in the streets.
Todos han aprobado el examen, incluso tú.	Everyone passed the exam, even (including) you.

(**ni**) **siquiera** (not) even

No tiene (**ni**) **siquiera un amigo.**	He doesn't have even one friend.
Ni siquiera gasta para la comida.	He doesn't even spend for food.

par (*adj.*) even (of a number)

Primero vamos a decir los números pares.	First let's say the even numbers.

justo, exacto, igual even (in quantity, size, etc.)

Córtelo en pedazos iguales (**justos**), **¿está bien?**	Cut it into even pieces, all right?
Quedó exacto por todos lados.	It came out even on all sides.

36. (to) fail

fracasar to fail, not to succeed, to make a fiasco

Esta vez no voy a fracasar.	This time I won't fail.

suspender to fail (somebody in a course)

Le suspendieron por haber faltado al examen final.	He was failed for having missed the final exam.

ser (**quedar**) **suspendido** to fail (a course)

Han sido (**o quedado**) **suspendidos sólo dos estudiantes este año.**	Only two students have failed this year.

Fracasar is also used in the sense of to fail a course:

El único que fracasó fue Miguel. Mike was the only one who failed.

dejar de to fail to (do something)

No dejes de cerrar la puerta cuando salgas. Don't fail to shut the door when you go out.

faltar (a) to fail, disappoint, deceive (somebody); to fail in

Yo no te faltaré nunca. Te lo prometo. I'll never fail you. I promise you.

No debes faltar a tus obligaciones. You shouldn't fail in your obligations.

The preterite of almost any verb may translate *failed to* when the English implies merely a simple past action.

Prometió venir, pero no se presentó. He promised to come, but he failed to appear.

37. fair

justo fair, just

Eso no es justo. That's not fair.

mediano, regular; así así fair, so-so, average

Carlos es un estudiante mediano (regular). Charles is a fair student.

¿Cómo estás hoy? —Regular. (Así así.) How are you today? —Fair. (O.K., So-so.)

claro fair, light in color

Elda tenía unos ojos clarísimos. Elda had very light (fair) eyes.

blanco fair (skin)

Su cutis blanco contrastaba con el pelo oscuro. Her fair skin contrasted with the dark hair.

rubio fair (haired and/or skinned)

A él le gustan sólo las mujeres rubias. He likes only fair women.

38. fear

temor (*m.*) (a specific) fear, or (plural) fears

Todos sus temores resultaron infundados. All his fears turned out unfounded.

Le estremeció un temor repentino. A sudden fear shook him.

miedo fear (as an abstraction)

El miedo representa un peligro en sí.	Fear represents a danger in itself.
Lo hizo por miedo.	He did it out of fear.

Notice that **miedo** is never plural.

tener miedo de or **a** (**una persona**) to be afraid of, to be in fear of

No tengas miedo. Ese perro no muerde... ¡Ay! Disculpa.	Don't be afraid. That dog doesn't bite . . . Oh, my! I'm sorry.

temer to fear; to be concerned or worried (**temer** is usually less emphatic, less emotional than **tener miedo**)

Teme las consecuencias de su acción.	He fears the consequences of his action.
El niño temía (tenía miedo a) su padrastro.	The boy feared (was afraid of) his stepfather.
Temo que llueva mañana.	I'm afraid it will rain tomorrow.

39. (to) feel

sentir to feel (something); to feel (to sense, to believe) that . . .

No le sentimos ninguna compasión.	We don't feel any compassion for him.
Sentía su presencia en todas partes.	He felt her presence everywhere.
Siento que todo va a salir bien.	I feel that everything will turn out all right.

sentirse (+ *adj.*) to feel (in a certain condition or state)

Me siento honrado...	I feel honored . . .
Se sintió avergonzado delante de sus parientes y amigos.	He felt ashamed in front of his relatives and friends.

40. few

pocos few, not many (**Pocos** always has a negative implication)

Ese tiene pocos amigos.	That fellow has few friends.

unos pocos, unos cuantos a few, several, some (positive implication)

¿Cuadernos? Sí, quedan unos pocos (unos cuantos).	Notebooks? Yes, there are a few left.

41. finally

al fin finally, at last, in the end

Al fin, decidimos telefonearles.	Finally, we decided to telephone them.

por fin finally, at (long) last

Por fin is more exclamatory than **al fin,** and implies a feeling of relief.

Por fin lo han acabado.	At last, they have finished it! (They have finally finished it.)

en fin finally, in short, to sum up

En fin, recobraron lo perdido y se acabó el asunto.	Finally (in short), they recovered what had been lost and the matter was concluded.

42. (to) find

hallar, encontrar to find, locate (someone or something)

Lo hallamos (encontramos) en su casa.	We found it in his house.
La hallaron (encontraron) dormida en el bosque.	They found her asleep in the woods.

descubrir to find, discover, uncover (usually a physical object, a territory, etc.)

Han descubierto un tesoro de diamantes y perlas.	They have found (discovered) a treasure of diamonds and pearls.

hallarse, encontrarse to be (to find oneself)

Hallarse is more frequent when the verb is followed by an adjective.

Al día siguiente, se hallaban (encontraban) en Sevilla.	On the following day, they were in Seville.
Me hallo obligado a advertirles que...	I am obliged to advise you that . . .

43. fix

arreglar, componer to fix (an apparatus, etc.); arrange

¿Han arreglado (compuesto) ya el televisor?	Have they fixed the television set yet?
No te preocupes. Yo te lo arreglaré todo.	Don't worry, I'll fix everything for you.

fijar to affix, to fix, fasten, make fast

Fijen bien la araña para que no se caiga, ¿está bien?	Fix the chandelier so that it won't fall, all right?

44. (to) fly

ir en avión to fly, take a flight, go by air

¿Cómo iréis? —En avión.	How will you go? —We'll fly.

volar to be in flight; to fly (over some place, etc.)

Volamos sobre los Andes.	We flew over the Andes.

pilotear (un avión) to fly (a plane)

tripular to fly (pilot) a commercial plane, head the crew

Mi sobrino pilotea su propia avioneta.	My nephew flies his own little plane.
Hacía años que tripulaba aviones de chorro.	He had been piloting jets for years.

45. free

libre free, independent; open, accessible

Garantizan el libre acceso a la frontera.	They guarantee free access to the border.
Así debe actuar un hombre libre.	That's how a free man should act.

gratis (*adv.*) free, without demanding payment

¿Cuánto te cobró? —Nada. Me lo dio gratis.	How much did you pay? —Nothing. He gave it to me free.

gratuito (*adj.*) free of charge

Esta tarde habrá un número de entradas gratuitas para la ópera.	This afternoon there will be a number of free admissions to the opera.

46. from

de from (emanating from a place, person, etc.); from (a point in time or space)

El humo proviene de las muchas fábricas.	The smoke comes from the many factories.
La carta es de mi hermano.	The letter is from my brother.
De aquí a Nueva York hay 100 millas.	It is 100 miles from here to New York.

desde from, since (a certain point in time); from (a certain place)

Desde places greater emphasis on location or position in time or space. Frequently, it is followed by **hasta** until.

Nos gritó desde la colina.	He shouted to us from the hill.
Vive con nosotros desde el primero de marzo.	He has been living with us since the first of March.
Estarán aquí desde junio hasta septiembre (o de junio a septiembre).	They will be here from June to September.

47. funny

gracioso funny, comical; witty, charming

Un chiste muy gracioso	A very funny joke
Su marido es tan gracioso.	Her husband is so funny (witty).

hacerle gracia a uno to strike someone as being funny

No sé por qué, pero eso siempre me hace gracia.	I don't know why, but that always strikes me funny.

tener gracia to be funny, humorous, witty (applied especially to ideas, etc.)

Todo lo que dice tiene mucha gracia ¿no?	Everything he says is very funny (witty), don't you think so?

divertido funny, amusing, witty (persons, situations, etc.)

La comedia es divertida en extremo.	The play is extremely funny.

cómico comical, laughworthy

No veo nada cómico en eso.	I don't see anything funny in that.

curioso, extraño, sorprendente funny (strange, odd, curious, surprising)

Es curioso que lo dijera *ella*, y no *él*.	It's funny that *she* should say it, and not *he*.

48. game

juego a type of game; gaming, gambling; play

Han popularizado un nuevo juego de naipes.	They have popularized a new card game.
Un juego de palabras	A play on words

partido a specific performance of a game, a contest, match

El partido se celebra a las tres.	The game starts at three o'clock.

deporte (*m.*) a sport, an athletic game (*not* contest)

Mi deporte favorito es el fútbol.	My favorite sport is soccer.

49. glance

mirada a glance (at someone or something); a way of looking

Me echó una mirada curiosa.	He gave me a curious glance.
Con una mirada tal, se podría enfriar el sol.	With a look like that, the sun could freeze over.

ojeada a glance (through a book, etc.), a rapid perusal

Hoy le puedo dar sólo una ojeada rápida.	Today I can give it only a quick glance.

50. (to) go

ir to go

Voy a verle mañana.	I am going to see him tomorrow.
Va con nosotros.	He is going with us.

irse, marcharse to go away

Ya se ha ido (marchado). Llegaste tarde.	He has already gone away. You came too late.

salir (de) to leave, to go out (of)

Salió hace media hora.	He went out half an hour ago.
Saldrán del edificio al mediodía.	They will leave (go out of) the building at noon.

salir a to go out into (the street, the hall, etc.)

Acaba de salir a la calle.	He has just gone out into the street.

salir para to leave for, to go away to

Salimos para la capital mañana.	We are leaving for the capital tomorrow.

bajar to go down

No bajes la escalera tan aprisa.	Don't go down the stairs so rapidly.

subir (a) to go up or aboard

Ha subido a su cuarto.	He has gone up to his room.
Subieron al tren.	They went aboard the train.

entrar en to go into (in Spanish America, **entrar a**)

Entraron en (or **a**) **aquella tienda.**	They went into that store.

51. half

medio (*adj.* and *adv.*) half

Son las cinco y media.	It is half-past five.
Es medio indio, medio blanco.	He is half Indian, half white.
Está medio loco de hambre.	He is half-crazy with hunger.

mitad (*n.*) a half

La dividieron en dos mitades.	They divided it into two halves.
Una mitad para ti, la otra para mí.	Half for you, the other half for me.

52. (to) hang

colgar to hang up (something)

Colgaron su retrato en el salón.	They hung his portrait in the living room.

estar colgado to be hanging (up)

El nuevo abrigo estaba colgado de un gancho.	The new coat was hanging on a hook.

pender to be hanging or suspended (from something); to be pending

La espada pendía de un solo hilo de seda.	The sword was hanging from a single thread of silk.

ahorcar to hang, to execute (someone)

Lo ahorcaron sin darle oportunidad para defenderse.	They hanged him without giving him a chance to defend himself.

53. happy

feliz basically happy (a characteristic)

un matrimonio feliz	a happy marriage or couple
un desenlace feliz	a happy ending

alegre happy, gay, joyous, jovial (either a characteristic or a chance state of mind or disposition)

Estuvieron muy alegres anoche.	They were very gay last night.

contento happy, satisfied, content, pleased

Estaría muy contenta de pasar toda mi vida allí.	I would be very happy to spend my whole life there.
¿Quién puede estar contento siempre de sí mismo?	Who can always be satisfied with himself?

54. (to) hear

oír to hear (to perceive and recognize sound); listen (in a command)

¿Oyes lo que te digo?	Do you hear what I'm saying to you?
Oye, Juan...	Listen, John . . .

oír decir que to hear (it said) that . . . (as news, a fact, etc.)

He oído decir que el estado va a rebajar los impuestos.	I have heard that the state is going to lower taxes.

oír hablar de to hear about (a person, an event, etc.)

Hemos oído hablar de su tío y de su mucha riqueza. We have heard about his uncle and his great wealth.

escuchar to hear, listen to

Me gusta escuchar los programas musicales que se presentan por la tarde. I like to listen to (hear) the musical programs that are presented in the afternoon.

¿Me escuchas, hijo? Are you listening to me, son? (Do you hear me?)

55. (a) here

aquí here (near me)

Su madre vive aquí cerca. His mother lives around here.

acá here (toward me)

Acá is used with verbs of motion, particularly with **venir.**

Ven (para) acá, Manuel. Come this way, Manuel. (Come here.)

(b) here is, here are

aquí está(n) here is, are (located, situated)

Aquí está mi mesa. Here is my desk. (It is located in this spot.)

aquí tiene Ud. here is, are (I am handing you, offering you . . .)

Aquí tiene Ud. su reloj. Here is your watch. (Here it is. Take it.)

he aquí here is, are (behold, witness); this is, these are

He aquí appears in a list of names or addresses, in newspaper captions, radio announcements, and in limited literary usage.

He aquí las estrellas que participarán en nuestra próxima presentación... Here are (these are) the stars who will take part in our next presentation . . .

aquí es here is the place (where) . . .

Aquí es donde vivo. Here is where I live.

56. (to) hire

emplear to hire, employ (a person)

Dicen que van a emplear dos mil obreros más. They say they're going to hire 2000 more workers.

alquilar to hire, rent (a car, hall, apartment, etc.)

En Cali alquilaremos un coche. In Cali we'll hire a car.

57. hit

pegar to hit, strike (someone)

No lo pegues, por favor.	Don't hit him, please.

golpear, abofetear to hit, beat (someone)

Los golpearon (**abofetearon**) **hasta que quedaron sin sentido.**	They hit (beat) them until they were unconscious.

acertar to hit (the mark); get the right answer, get the point, etc.

La bala le acertó en el muslo izquierdo.	The bullet hit him in the left thigh.
¡Felicitaciones! Has acertado otra vez.	Congratulations! You've done it again.

chocar to hit, crash into, collide with

El automóvil chocó con un árbol.	The car hit a tree.

58. hot

caliente hot; warm (**caliente** refers to the temperature of objects, liquids, etc., not to persons)

No hay agua caliente hoy.	There's no hot water today.
Vive en un clima caliente.	He lives in a hot (warm) climate.

cálido hot (and often humid or moist)

En los países cálidos, la vida es más difícil.	In hot (humid) countries, life is more difficult.

caluroso hot (giving off heat, as the weather, a day, etc.); ardent, warm (figurative)

Hemos sufrido unos días calurosísimos este verano.	We've had some very hot days this summer.
Me dio un saludo caluroso.	He gave me a warm greeting.

acalorado hot, heated, impassioned, enthusiastic (a discussion, fans, etc.)

Parece que interrumpíamos una discusión acalorada.	It seems we were interrupting a heated argument.

picante hot, spicy (food)

La comida mejicana es más picante que la española.	Mexican food is hotter than Spanish.

But: **hacer calor** to be hot out

Ayer hizo mucho calor, ¿verdad?	It was very hot yesterday, wasn't it?

tener calor to be (feel) hot (a person)

¿Tienes calor? —No, estoy bien. Are you hot? —No, I'm all right.

59. (a) how!

¡cómo! how, how well, how badly! (describes the manner in which something is done)

¡Cómo canta! ¡Cómo baila! How she sings! How she dances!

¡cuánto! how, how much!

¡Cuánto te quiero! How (much) I love you!

¡qué (+ *adj.* or *adv.*) how (good, bad, smart, tired, fast, etc.)

¡Qué amable es! How nice he is!

¡Qué bien recita! How well he recites!

(b) how?

¿cómo? how, in what way or manner?

¿Cómo puedo explicártelo? How can I explain it to you?

¿Cómo te gusta el café —con crema o con leche? How do you like coffee—with cream or with milk?

¿qué tal? how, what do you think of?

¿Qué tal? asks for an evaluation.

¿Qué tal estuvo la charla? How was the talk?

Hola. ¿Qué tal? Hello. How goes it?

60. (to) hurry

tener prisa, estar de prisa to be in a hurry

No te puedo hablar más ahora. I can't talk to you any more now.

Tengo mucha prisa. (Estoy de prisa.) I'm in a real hurry.

darse prisa, apresurarse; apurarse (in Spanish America) to hurry up

¡Date prisa! (¡Apresúrate! ¡Apúrate!) No hay tiempo que perder. Hurry up! There's no time to waste.

de prisa, aprisa in a hurry, hurriedly

Resultó mal porque lo hizo de prisa (aprisa). It turned out badly because he did it in a hurry.

61. (to) ignore

no hacer caso de or **a** (a person) to ignore, not to pay attention to (something or what someone is saying or doing)

No le hagas caso. Ignore him. (Don't pay any attention to him.)

pasar por alto to ignore, overlook (usually a statement or an action)

Sí, lo dijo, pero yo lo pasé por alto. Yes, he said it, but I ignored it.

desconocer to ignore (someone)

Le saludé, pero me desconoció. I greeted him, but he ignored me.

ignorar not to know, to be ignorant or unaware of

Se ignora la verdadera causa del accidente. The real cause of the accident is not known.

62. (to) introduce

introducir to introduce (a new subject, etc.), to bring in(to) or up

Introdujo la nueva resolución en el Senado. He introduced the new resolution in the Senate.

presentar to introduce (somebody to someone)

¿Quieres presentarme a tu prima? Will you introduce me to your cousin?

63. just

justo just, fair; exactly right, fitting or enough.

Hay que ser justo siempre. One must always be just.

Lo midieron tan bien que salió justo. They measured so well that it came out just right.

sólo just, only

Te pido sólo un día más. I ask you for just one more day.

¿Quién vive aquí? —Sólo mi hermano y yo. Who lives here? —Just my brother and I.

64. (to) know

saber to know (something, a fact, etc.); to know by heart or thoroughly; to know how to do something

No sé si ha vuelto todavía. I don't know whether he has come back yet.

¿Sabe Ud. este poema? Do you know this poem (by heart or thoroughly)?

Sabe tocar la guitarra. He knows how to play the guitar.

conocer to know (a person, a city, etc.); to be acquainted or familiar with

¿Conoce Ud. a mi hermano?	Do you know my brother?
No conozco ese poema.	I don't know (am not familiar with) that poem.

65. last

último last, final one (of a series); last (month) (*business*)

El último rey borbónico...	The last Bourbon king . . .
Ahora cursamos el último año del bachillerato.	Now we are in our last year of college.
Su favor del último...	Yours of last month . . .

pasado last, recently past (the series is still continuing)

la semana pasada	last week
el semestre pasado	last semester

But: **anoche** last night

Nos telefoneó anoche.	He phoned us last night.

66. (to) leave

salir (de) to leave (a place), to go out (of), depart (from)

Salió de la Habana en el "Emperatriz de Egipto."	He left Havana on the *Empress of Egypt.*
¿A qué hora sales?	At what time are you leaving?

salir para to leave for (a destination)

Saldrán para la capital el viernes que viene.	They will leave for the capital next Friday.

dejar to leave (something or someone) behind (either on purpose or through an oversight)

Lo dejé olvidado en casa.	I left it (forgotten) at home.
Raúl, no me dejes sola.	Ralph, don't leave me alone.

Recall: **Dejar** also means *to let, allow, permit.*

No le dejarán hacerlo.	They won't let him do it.

abandonar to leave (something or someone) behind (intentionally), to abandon

Tuvieron que abandonar el coche en medio del camino.	They had to leave the car in the middle of the road.

67. (to) let

dejar to let, allow, permit

Déjale ir, si quiere.	Let him go, if he wants to.

In the sentence above, one person is requesting permission of another.

No nos dejarán verla.	They won't let us see her.

Vamos a (+ *inf.* or *1st pers. pl. pres. subj.*) Let's (do, go, buy, see, etc.)

This is a direct command involving *you* and *me.*

Vamos a ver.	Let's see.
Sentémonos aquí. **Vamos a sentarnos aquí.**	Let's sit down here.

que (+ *3rd pers. pres. subj.*) let (permit, allow)

This is an indirect command, in which one person expresses his will that someone else do something. There is no implied request for permission.

Que lo haga Jorge.	Let George do it. (I want George to do it.)
Que se diviertan mientras puedan.	Let them enjoy themselves while they can. (May they enjoy themselves, I want them to . . .)

68. (to) like

gustarle a uno to find pleasing, to have certain inclination toward (persons, things, activities)

Me gusta viajar.	I like to travel.
¿Le gustó la película?	Did you like the film?
No nos gustan nada esos hombres.	We don't like those men at all.

querer to like (a person, or at times, an animal), to feel affection for

Quiero mucho a Juanito.	I like Johnny very much.

69. little

pequeño little, small in size

Una casa pequeña	A little house

poco (*adj.*) little (in amount), not much; (*pl.*) few, not many

Tiene poca astucia.	He has little shrewdness.
Es hombre de pocas palabras.	He is a man of few words.

poco (*adv.*) little, not much

Come poco para su edad.	He eats little for his age.

un poco de (*n.*) a little (bit of)

Con un poco de paciencia, se alcanza lo imposible.	With a little (bit of) patience, one can achieve the impossible.

70. (to) look

parecer to look, appear, seem to be, resemble

Pareces cansado hoy. You look tired today.

Parece no estar conforme. He seems to disapprove.

estar to look, seem, be

Estar gives a more subjective evaluation than does **ser** to the quality described by the adjective. However, it still retains its primary sense of *to be* and is not wholly synonymous with **parecer.**

Estás muy bonita esta noche. You look (are) very pretty tonight.

Parecer could not be used in this sentence.

mirar to look at

Me miró con verdadero odio. He looked at me with real hatred.

buscar to look for

Busco a mi marido. ¿Le ha visto Ud.? I'm looking for my husband. Have you seen him?

Notice that the English *for* is included within the meaning of **buscar,** and so Spanish uses no preposition.

parecerse a to look like, resemble

Se parece a su padre. He looks like his father.

ver to see, occasionally means *to look at*

Debieras verle con los ojos, no con el corazón. You should look at him (see him) with your eyes, not your heart.

tener buena (mala) cara, verse (mal) to look well (bad)

Tiene Ud. muy mala cara hoy. You look very bad today.
Se ve muy mal hoy.

71. (to) love

querer to love (a person or, occasionally, an animal)

Querer includes most of the concepts of *to love.*

Te quiero con toda el alma. I love you with all my heart.

amar to love (with great affection or passion)

Amar is somewhat more ardent than **querer.**

No podré amar nunca a otro. I will never be able to love any other man.

Ama a sus padres. He loves his parents.

enamorarse de to fall in love with

Se ha enamorado locamente de su profesor de historia.	She has fallen madly in love with her history teacher.

enamorar to make someone fall in love with one, to court

A don Juan le gustaba enamorar a las mujeres sólo para abandonarlas después.	Don Juan liked to make women fall in love with him just to abandon them afterwards.

72. matter

materia substance, (physical) matter

La materia no se puede destruir; toma otra forma.	Matter cannot be destroyed; it takes another form.

asunto (a) matter, question (at hand)

¿Por qué no hablamos primero de otro asunto?	Why don't we talk first about another matter?

Se trata de... It is a matter of . . . This matter deals with . . .

Ahora se trata de una princesa que se quiere casar con...	Now it is a matter (question) of a princess who wants to marry . . .

Da lo mismo. It doesn't matter. (Either way is equally all right.)

¿Quieres ir al cine o al teatro esta noche? —(Me) da lo mismo.	Do you want to go to the movies or to the theater tonight? —It doesn't matter. (I like both.)

No importa. It doesn't matter. (It's not important, nothing to be concerned about.)

¿Sabes? Se me olvidó traer la pluma que me prestaste. —No importa.	You know? I forgot to bring the pen you lent me. —It doesn't matter.
¿Qué tienes? ¿Qué te pasa?	What's the matter (What's wrong) with you?
¿Qué pasa?	What's up? (What's going on? What's the matter?)

73. (to) make

hacer to make (something); **hacer** (+ *infinitive*) to make (someone) do something; have something done

Te haré pasar todo el día en tu cuarto.	I'll make you stay in your room all day long.
La hicieron construir en el mismo sitio.	They had it built on the same site.

dar (hambre, sed, miedo, etc.) to make (someone) hungry, thirsty, afraid, etc.

El aroma que sale de esa olla me da un hambre feroz.	The smell that's coming from that pot is making me ravenously hungry.
Ese hombre nos da miedo.	That man scares us.

74. may

poder may

Poder is used to translate *may* when the meaning indicates *to be allowed to* or *able to.*

Puedes irte ahora, si quieres.	You may go now, if you want to.

Notice that the indicative of **poder** is used, since **poder** is the main verb of a principal clause.

Poder may also be used to indicate uncertainty, either in a main clause or after an expression of belief. Notice again that the indicative of **poder** is used in these circumstances.

Pueden tener razón.	They *may* be right.
Admitió que podía estar equivocado.	He admitted that he *might* (could) be mistaken.
Creo que puede ser él.	I think it *may* be he.

The subjunctive of any verb is used to translate *may* after conjunctions indicating uncertainty or indefiniteness. *May* then has the meaning *to be possible, but not certain.*

Aunque le vea, no hablaré con él.	Although I may see him, I won't speak to him.

Puede que, Es posible que may

Puede que or **Es posible que** is used in a main clause to translate *may* meaning possibility or uncertainty and must be followed by the subjunctive.

Puede que vengan. **Es posible que vengan.**	They *may* come.

75. (to) mean

significar to mean (as a word, etc.); to have the meaning, or significance

¿Qué significa esta palabra?	What does that word mean?
Eso significa que pronto llegarán a un acuerdo.	That means that soon they'll come to an agreement.

querer decir to mean (to say); to signify

Notice that although **querer decir** is often synonymous with **significar,** only **querer decir** can have a personal subject.

¿Qué quiere decir (**significa**) **eso?**	What does that mean?
Iremos en seguida... quiero decir, tan pronto como sea posible.	We'll go at once . . . I mean, as soon as it's possible.
¿Qué quiso decir el profesor?	What did the professor mean?

76. (to) meet

encontrar (**a**) to meet (someone or something), either by appointment or by chance

Vamos a encontrar el barco en Gibraltar.	We're going to meet the ship at Gibraltar.
Encontré a tu amiga Clara en el centro hoy.	I met your friend Claire downtown today.

conocer to meet (someone) for the first time, to be introduced to

Conocí a tu cuñado ayer.	I met (was introduced to) your brother-in-law yesterday.

verse con to meet by appointment, to have a meeting with

Me veo con él mañana por la mañana para discutirlo.	I'm meeting him tomorrow morning to discuss it.

dar con, tropezar con, encontrarse con to meet (by accident), to happen upon, "bump into," come across

Di con ellas en el tren.	I met them (bumped into them) on the train.
Tropezamos con el autor de esta novela cuando estábamos en Cádiz.	We met (came upon) the author of this novel when we were in Cadiz.

If **conocimos** were used in the last sentence above, it would mean *we were introduced to, made the acquaintance of . . .*

reunirse to meet (as a group, a club, etc.)

El Centro Hispano se reúne todos los viernes a las dos.	The Spanish club meets every Friday at two o'clock.

buscar to go to meet (someone at a station, etc.)

Tengo que buscarle en el aeropuerto.	I have to meet him at the airport.

77. middle

medio (*n.*) (the) middle; (*adj.*) middle, average

Estamos en el medio de la página 179.	We are in the middle of page 179.
La clase media es la que domina.	The middle class is the one that rules.

a mediados de around the middle of (a month, century, etc.)

Volverán a mediados de agosto.	They'll return around the middle of August.

en medio de in the midst of, surrounded by

No puedo ahora. Estoy en medio de un montón de trabajo.	I can't now. I'm in the middle of a pile of work.

mediano (approximately) middle; average, mediocre

Es de edad mediana.	He is middle-aged.
Poseía una inteligencia mediana.	He had an average (mediocre) intelligence.

78. (to) miss

perder to miss (a train, etc.)

Escucha, querida. Vendré un poco tarde. Acabo de perder el tren.	Listen, dear. I'll be a little late. I've just missed the train.
No pierdas la ocasión de hablar con él.	Don't miss the chance to talk with him.

echar de menos, extrañar to miss, to long for the presence of (someone or something)

Parece echar más de menos (o extrañar más) a su perro que a sus padres.	He seems to miss his dog more than his parents.

faltar a to miss (a class, lecture, performance, etc.), not to be present at a specified occasion

Faltó a la clase dos veces la semana pasada.	He missed class twice last week.

errar el tiro to miss (a target)

Apuntó con cuidado, pero erró el tiro.	He aimed carefully, but missed.

no coger to miss, to fail to catch (a train, a ball, etc.), to fail to meet

Me tiró la pelota, pero no la cogí.	He threw me the ball, but I missed it.

no encontrar to miss, fail to catch (a person)

Pasé por su oficina, pero no le encontré. I went to his office, but I missed him.

79. must

hay que one must (impersonal)

Hay que tener cuidado siempre. One must always be careful.

tener que to have to (indicates strong personal necessity or compulsion)

Tuve que dárselo. I had to give it to him.

deber should (moral obligation)

At times **deber** acquires the force of *must.*

Debo ir con ellos. I should (must, have to) go with them.

deber (**de**) must (in the sense of probability); the **de** is not required, however.

Debe (**de**) **haber cantado ya.** He must have sung already.

Future of probability must (in the sense of conjecture or probability)

Será Juanita. It must be (probably is) Joan.

80. neither

ni... ni neither . . . nor

Ni, when used alone, means *nor* or *not* (even).

Ni él ni su hermano han sido bautizados. Neither he nor his brother has been baptized.

Ni siquiera ella lo sabe. Not even she knows.

¡Ni por pienso!
¡Ni mucho menos! Not by any means!

tampoco neither (also . . . not), either (in negative sentences)

Yo no voy tampoco. I'm not going either. (I also am not going.)

Ni nosotros tampoco. Nor we either. (We too aren't going.)

81. next

siguiente next, immediately following

Al día siguiente, se hallaban en París. (On) the next day, they were in Paris.

próximo next (though not necessarily immediately following), future

La próxima vez que te vea hacerlo, llamaré a tu madre.	The next time I see you do it, I'll call your mother.

que viene next, forthcoming (usually refers to periods of time—weeks, months, etc.)

Le veremos la semana que viene.	We shall see him next week.

junto a next to, adjacent to

Estaba sentado junto al hogar.	He was sitting next to the fireplace.

de al lado, contiguo next to, adjoining (as a house)

Viven en la casa de al lado.	They live in the house next door.

82. Office

oficio office, position (public, professional, etc.), occupation, trade (viewed as an abstract entity)

No le considero calificado para el oficio.	I don't consider him qualified for the office.
El oficio de sacristán...	The office of sexton . . .

Cargo is used frequently when referring to a specific office or position: **el cargo de subdirector** the job (office) of assistant manager.

oficina office, place of doing business, government office, etc. (now in general usage for almost all types of office)

No me gustaría trabajar en una oficina.	I wouldn't like to work in an office.
La oficina del Ministerio de la Guerra.	The office of the Ministry of War.

bufete a lawyer's office

Mi marido piensa abrir bufete en Barcelona.	My husband is planning to open an office in Barcelona.

consulta, sala de consulta doctor's office

La sala de consulta estaba llena de gente.	The doctor's office was full of people.
Horas de consulta: 9 a 12:30	Office hours: 9 to 12:30

clínica dentist's or doctor's office

Mi dentista tiene su clínica en la calle Armando.	My dentist has his office on Armando Street.

Gabinete is also used in this sense.

83. (a) old

viejo old (applied to persons or things); when placed before the noun, it may mean *long-standing*

un profesor viejo	an old (elderly) professor
un viejo amigo	an old (long-standing) friend

antiguo old, ancient, antique

Recall: **antigüedades** antiques. When it is placed before the noun, **antiguo** may mean *former*. This adjective is generally not applied to persons, except when it means *ancient*, *former*, or *long-standing*.

una silla antigua	an old (antique) chair
los antiguos iberos	the ancient Iberians
el antiguo Ministro de Hacienda	the former Secretary of the Treasury
un antiguo amigo mío	an old friend of mine

anciano old, of very advanced age (applies only to persons and lends a rather poetic or affectionate connotation)

El anciano estaba sentado junto al hogar.	The old man was sitting by the fireplace.

(b) older

mayor older (establishes a comparative relationship between two persons, regardless of whether they are young or old)

Es mayor que yo. Tiene unos veinticinco años.	He is older than I. He is about twenty-five.

más viejo older, more aged (compares the adjective *old*)

Es más viejo que Matusalén.	He is older than Methuselah (both are old!).

más antiguo more ancient, most ancient

La catedral más antigua del Nuevo Mundo.	The oldest cathedral in the New World.

84. on

en on, resting upon or leaning against

Su retrato estaba colgado en la pared.	His portrait was hanging on the wall.
La vajilla ya está en la mesa.	The silverware is already on the table.

sobre upon, on top of, resting upon or suspended above

Sobre su cabeza apareció una aureola de luz.	Over his head there appeared a halo of light.
La puso sobre la vitrina.	She put it on the showcase.

NOTE: **En la vitrina** might imply *in* the showcase.

85. only

sólo, solamente (*adv.*) only (applies to persons, things, numbers, etc.)

Notice that the accent mark on **sólo** differentiates it from the adjective **solo** alone.

Sólo él y yo lo sabemos.	Only he and I know.
Habla sólo (solamente) con sus amigos.	He speaks only with his friends.
Nos quedan sólo cinco doláres.	We have only five dollars left.
But: **Estaba solo.**	He was alone.

no... más que (*adv.*) only; (to do, have, etc.) nothing but

No tiene más que diez dólares.	He has only ten dollars.
No hace más que llorar.	She does nothing but cry.
No me dejes. No tengo más que a ti.	Don't leave me. I have only (nothing but) you.

único (*adj.*) only (one), single, unique

Un hijo único es un hijo consentido.	An only child is a spoiled child.
Es la única esperanza que le queda.	It's the only hope he has left.

Solo also appears in this sense.

86. (a) order (*n.*)

la orden order, command; also, a religious or military order

Dio la orden de retirarse.	He gave the order to withdraw.
Las órdenes dominicana y franciscana...	The Dominican and Franciscan orders . . .

el orden order, orderliness, system, arrangement

El gobierno ha restablecido el orden.	The government has reestablished order.
Todo está en perfecto orden.	Everything is in perfect order.

pedido business order

(b) (to) order

mandar to order (someone to do something)

Le mandó darnos la llave.	He ordered him to give us the key.

pedir to order (something in a restaurant, store, etc.)

¿Qué vas a pedir? —Un bisté.	What are you going to order? —A steak.

hacer un pedido to order, place an order (for merchandise)

Le haremos un pedido si rebaja el precio.	We'll give you an order if you lower the price.

encargar to order (merchandise)

Se lo encargaremos a otra firma.	We shall order it from another company.

87. (to) pay

pagar to pay somebody; to settle an account; to pay for

¿Pagaste al médico?	Did you pay the doctor?
Ya pagué el alquiler.	I already paid the rent.
Nos pagará lo que hizo ayer.	He will pay us for what he did yesterday.

Notice that Spanish requires no preposition to translate *for*, unless the amount is mentioned or implied.

pagar... por to pay (a certain amount of money) for something

Pagó diez dólares por esa corbata. —¡Qué barbaridad!	He paid ten dollars for that tie. —How awful!

hacer una visita to pay a visit

Mañana haré una visita a mi tía Clara.	Tomorrow I shall visit my Aunt Claire.

prestar atención to pay attention, to fix one's mind on

No prestábamos atención a lo que decía el orador.	We weren't paying attention to what the speaker was saying.

hacer caso de (or **a**) to pay attention to; to heed, listen to

The preposition **a** is more frequent than **de** when referring to a person.

No le haga caso. No sabe nada.	Don't pay any attention to him. He doesn't know anything.

88. people

gente people (in general—as an abstraction or as a group)

NOTE: **La gente** is a collective noun.

La plaza estaba llena de gente.	The square was filled with people.
Hablando se entiende la gente.	By speaking, people understand each other.

personas people (as individuals), persons

Only **personas** can be used with specific numbers.

Hay muchas personas que no saben leer.	There are many people who don't know how to read.
Caben setenta personas en ese café.	That cafe holds seventy people.

gentes people (as a group, but with some implication of their individual identities within the whole)

Gentes is not used as frequently as **gente** or **personas.**

Las gentes se arremolinaban fuera del palacio.	The people were milling outside the palace.

pueblo the people, the masses; a people, a race, a nation

Los pueblos de Asia.	The peoples of Asia.
El pueblo no lo consentiría nunca.	The people would never consent to it.

público the people, the public

Está tratando de engañar al público.	He is trying to deceive the public (people).
Eso no se debe hacer en público.	That shouldn't be done in public.

89. (a) plan (*n.*)

plan (*m.*) a plan, scheme

Se me ocurre un plan maravilloso.	I've just thought of a great plan.

plano plan, sketch, diagram (of a house, etc.)

¿Nos deja ver el plano de la casa?	Will you let us see the plan of the house?

(b) (to) plan

planear to plan, make plans or designs for

En el futuro planeamos para este sitio un nuevo sanatario.	In the future we're planning a new sanatarium on this site.

pensar (+ *infinitive*) to plan (to do something), intend

¿Adónde piensas ir este verano? Where are you planning to go this summer?

90. (to) play

jugar to play (a game, sport, etc.)

jugar a las cartas to play cards
jugar al tenis to play tennis

tocar to play (an instrument)

¿Sabe Ud. tocar el violín? Do you know how to play the violin?

91. position

posición physical position; relative position (social, business, etc.), stature, status; condition

La posición del satélite indica que muy pronto va a agotarse. The position of the satellite indicates that it will expend itself very soon.

Quiso mejorar su posición social, pero sólo se creó enemigos. He tried to improve his social position, but he only made enemies.

Estamos en una posición poco envidiable. We are in an unenviable position.

puesto, cargo a position, post, situation, job

Van a ofrecerle un puesto (cargo) importantísimo. They are going to offer him a very important position.

92. (to) put

poner to put or place (in almost all senses)

Puso una moneda en el mostrador. He put a coin on the counter.

ponerse to put on (an article of clothing, etc.)

Se puso el sombrero y salió sin más ni más. He put on his hat and left without further ado.

meter to put within or inside of

Se metió la mano en el bolsillo y sacó la cartera. He put his hand in his pocket and took out his wallet.

colocar to put, to place, to arrange (in a specific order, position, or location)

Colocó la vasija de modo que todos pudieran verlo al entrar. She placed the vase in such a way that everyone could see it upon entering.

93. quality

cualidad a quality (of character, etc.)

Tiene muchas buenas cualidades.	He has many good qualities.

calidad quality (of merchandise, etc.)

Esta tela es de la mejor calidad.	This cloth is of the finest quality.

The plural **calidades** may be used synonymously with **cualidades** in referring to moral traits, etc.

94. question

pregunta a question, an inquiry

Me hizo muchas preguntas personales que no quise contestar.	He asked me many personal questions that I refused to answer.

cuestión a question, an issue, a matter

La cuestión que tenemos que decidir es si es culpable o inocente el acusado.	The question (issue) that we must decide is whether the accused is guilty or innocent.

tratarse de to be a question or matter of, to concern

Se trata del derecho de los estudiantes a protestar.	It is a question of (concerns) the student's right to protest.

95. quiet

callado quiet, silent, hushed, not speaking; laconic (with **ser**)

¿Quién puede quedarse callado cuando oye tantos disparates?	Who can remain quiet when he hears so much nonsense?

quieto quiet, unmoving, still

Todo estaba quieto, como si el mundo hubiera dejado de respirar.	Everything was quiet, as if the world had stopped breathing.

sereno, tranquilo quiet, peaceful, serene

Era una noche serena (tranquila), llena de paz y de amor.	It was a quiet night, filled with peace and love.

poco hablador quiet, laconic, reserved, unaccustomed to talking much

Mi hermano es muy poco hablador (muy callado) pero inteligentísimo.	My brother is quiet (doesn't talk much) but very intelligent.

bajo quiet, soft, not loud

Hablen en voz más baja, por favor.	Speak more quietly, please.

96. (to) raise

levantar to lift up, pick up

Levanten la mano derecha.	Raise your right hands.
La levantó en sus brazos.	He picked her up in his arms.

subir to raise, carry, bring or take up; raise (price, quality, etc.)

Tengo que subir un poco esta falda. Me queda muy larga.	I have to raise this skirt a little. It's very long on me.
¿Me hace el favor de subir la celosía?	Will you please raise the blind?
Ese siempre sube los precios.	That fellow always raises his prices.

criar to raise (a baby or child); to raise animals

Lo crió desde niño y ahora no la reconoce siquiera.	She raised him from a child and now he doesn't even recognize her.
Criamos ovejas y cabras.	We raise sheep and goats.

educar to raise, bring up, educate (in courtesy, etc.), rear

Ese niño está muy mal educado.	That boy is very badly raised.

cultivar to raise (crops)

Por aquí cultivan trigo y maíz.	Here they raise wheat and corn.

97. rather

algo rather, somewhat, a bit

Creo que el examen será algo difícil para ellos.	I think the exam will be rather difficult for them.

bastante rather, quite, considerable, considerably

Hace bastante calor en junio.	It is rather (quite) warm in June.

más bien rather, instead

Yo diría más bien la evolución, no la revolución tecnológica.	I would say rather (instead) the technological evolution, not revolution.

antes que rather than

Decidieron morir luchando antes que rendirse.	They decided to die fighting rather than surrender.

preferir, gustarle más a uno prefer, would rather

Preferiría (me gustaría más) arriesgarme con ellos que esperarlos en casa.	I would rather take a chance with them than wait for them at home.

Antes... que may also be used in this case.

Antes que esperarlos en casa me arriesgaría con ellos.

98. (to) reach

llegar a to reach, arrive at (a certain point or destination)

Llegamos a Córdoba por la mañana.	We reached Cordoba in the morning.

alcanzar to attain; to reach for; catch up with

Salieron temprano pero los alcanzaremos para mediodía.	They left early, but we'll reach them by noon.
Ha alcanzado un nuevo nivel de perfección.	He has reached a new level of perfection.
¿Me puedes alcanzar aquella cajita?	Can you reach that little box for me?

99. (to) realize

realizar to realize, make real, fulfill, put into effect

Nadie puede realizar todos sus sueños.	Nobody can realize all his dreams.

darse cuenta de to realize (a fact, etc.), to become aware of, to take into account

No se daba cuenta de las consecuencias de su conducta.	He didn't realize the consequences of his behavior.

100. (to) refuse

negarse a to refuse to do something

Se negó a hincarse de rodillas ante el rey.	He refused to kneel before the king.

no querer (*pret.*) to refuse, to be unwilling to do something

No quiso ir con nosotros.	He refused (didn't want) to go with us.

rechazar to refuse (an offer, a suitor, etc.)

No debes rechazar una oportunidad como ésa.	You shouldn't refuse an opportunity like that.

rehusar to refuse (something), to refuse to do (something)

Rehusó la oferta.	He refused the offer.
Se lo pidieron, pero rehusó.	They asked him, but he refused.

101. (to) remain

quedar to remain (in a certain state or condition); to be remaining or left over

Quedó pasmado por la noticia.	He remained shocked by the news.
Quedan unos cuantos libros de poesía.	A few books of poetry remain (are left).

quedarse to remain, stay on or behind

Se quedó todo el día en la cama.	He stayed (remained) in bed all day.
¿Cuánto tiempo te quedarás allí?	How long will you remain there?

102. respect

respeto respect, deference, admiration

Le tratábamos siempre con el mayor respeto.	We always treated him with the greatest respect.

respecto respect, aspect, sense

A este respecto, es un perfecto ignorante.	In this respect, he is a total ignoramus.

103. rest

el resto, lo demás the rest, remainder, balance, what is left over (applied to objects, ideas, etc., rather than to persons)

El resto (lo demás) será para Uds., si quieren.	The rest will be for you, if you wish.

Note, however: **los restos** the (mortal) remains.

los demás the rest, the others (both persons and things)

Los demás han quedado en volver mañana.	The others (the rest) have agreed to return tomorrow.

descanso rest, respite from fatigue

Lo que necesitas más que nada es descanso.	What you need more than anything else is rest.

104. (to) return

volver to return, come back

¿Cuándo piensan volver sus padres?	When do your parents intend to return?

devolver to return (something)

¡Ay de mí! Se me olvidó devolverle el dinero que me prestó.	Oh my! I forgot to return the money he lent me.

105. right

el derecho right (lawful, moral), privilege

Tengo el derecho de hacer lo que me dé la gana.	I have the right to do anything I feel like doing.

NOTE: **El derecho** also means *law*.

el bien, lo bueno (what is) right

Hay gente que no sabe distinguir entre el bien y el mal (lo bueno y lo malo).	There are people who can't distinguish between right and and wrong.

derecho (*adj.*) right (direction); (*adv.*) right, straight (to)

a la derecha	on the right
el pie derecho	the right foot
Se fue derecho al alcalde.	He went right to the mayor.

recto (*adj.*) right (angle); right (as opposed to evil)

Tracemos un ángulo recto.	Let's draw a right angle.
Hay que seguir el camino recto.	One must follow the right (good) road.

tener razón to be right (to have reason or logic on one's side)

NOTE: This idiom applies only to persons.

Tu papá tiene razón.	Your father is right.

ser justo, estar bien to be right, just, fair (referring to actions, statements, etc.)

Eso no es justo. **Eso no está bien.**	That isn't right.
No está bien lo que hizo.	What he did isn't right.

ser correcto to be right, correct (as a calculation, answer, piece of information, etc.); to be correct, proper

Su respuesta no es correcta (no está bien).	Your answer is not right.
No es correcto comer con las manos.	It is not right (correct, proper) to eat with one's hands.

106. same

Mismo and **igual** are synonymous when they mean *just like*. Only **mismo** may be used to mean *one and the same*.

Yo tengo los mismos aretes. Yo tengo unos aretes iguales.	I have the same earrings.
Tienen la misma cantidad (igual cantidad) que nosotros.	They have the same (equal) quantity as we.
Vive todavía en la misma casa.	He still lives in the same house.
¿El mismo profesor enseña las dos materias?	The same professor teaches both subjects?

107. (to) save

salvar to save, rescue

Le salvaron la vida, pero no se mostró nada agradecido.	They saved his life, but he didn't act at all grateful.

ahorrar to save (money, time, trouble, etc.), to hoard

Ahorra todo su dinero como si pudiera gastarlo allá en el otro mundo.	He saves all his money as if he could spend it in the other world.
A ver si puedo ahorrarte la molestia.	Let's see whether I can save you the trouble.

108. season

estación season of the year

La estación del año que me gusta más es el verano.	The season of the year that I like best is summer.

temporada season, period of time in which certain events, etc., take place

La temporada de las carreras coincide con nuestras vacaciones este año.	The racing season coincides with our vacation this year.

sazón season, point of maturity

Los melones no están en sazón ahora.	Melons aren't in season now.

109. set

juego a set (of furniture, tools, etc.)

Juego usually refers to a set of physical, though nonmechanical objects, often of household or personal use, and comprehends most groups of objects that have a joint function.

¡Liquidación! **Juegos de cocina.** **Juegos de salón.**	Sale! Kitchen sets. Living room sets.

un juego de botones a set of buttons

aparato a mechanical or electrical set (television, air conditioning, etc.)

El aparato no funciona. The set isn't working.

However, specific words have come into use for most appliances:

televisor, televisión television set.

servicio a set (of dishes or tableware)

Buscamos un nuevo servicio de porcelana. We are looking for a new set of china.

colección a set (of books)

una colección de las obras de Dickens a set of Dickens' works

terno a set (often of three objects, such as jewelry, clothes, etc.)

Me regaló un terno de aretes, pulsera y collar de perlas. He gave me a set of pearl earrings, bracelet, and necklace.

110. short

bajo short (in height)

Es un hombre bajo pero fuerte. He is a short, but powerful man.

corto short (in length)

Esas cortinas quedan un poco cortas. Those curtains are a little short.

Vive a corta (poca) distancia de aquí. He lives a short distance from here.

breve short, brief, succinct

Nos escribió una carta muy breve (or **corta**). He wrote us a very short letter.

Estuvo muy breve aquella noche. He was very short (brief) that night.

111. (to) sign

señal a sign, distinguishing mark, marker (not in writing); an indication; a signal

Cuando llegue a la cima, deje una señal en una piedra.	When you get to the top, leave a sign on a rock.
Te lo doy en señal de nuestra amistad.	I am giving it to you as a sign of our friendship.
Hizo la señal de la cruz.	He made the sign of the cross.

muestra, indicio a sign, an indication, evidence

¿Qué muestra puede darnos de su lealtad?	What sign (evidence) can he give us of his loyalty?
Esto es un indicio de su gran conocimiento del campo.	This is an indication (a sign) of his great knowledge of the field.

seña a sign, indication; a signal; a distinguishing mark or characteristic (often of a person)

Daba señas de gran impaciencia.	He gave signs of great impatience.
Descríbale. ¿Qué señas tenía?	Describe him. What did he look like? (What distinguishing signs did he have?)
Le hacía señas desde lejos.	He would make signs to him from afar.

signo a sign, signal; an indication; a mathematical sign

el signo ×	the sign ×

letrero a written or printed sign

El letrero rezaba: **Está prohibido fumar.**	The sign said: Smoking forbidden.

huella a sign, trace, vestige, clue

Desapareció sin dejar huella.	He disappeared without leaving a sign.

firmar to sign

Firmó el documento.	He signed the document.

112. since

desde (*prep.*) since (a certain time)

Estamos casados desde abril.	We've been married since April.

desde que (*conj.*) since (a certain time) (+ *clause*)

Desde que vive en la ciudad, no conoce a sus parientes.	Since he has been living in the city, he doesn't know his relatives any more.

ya que (*conj.*) since, now that

Ya que estás aquí, ¿por qué no te quedas toda la semana?	Since (now that) you're here, why don't you stay the whole week?

puesto que (*conj.*) since, because (**pues** is used synonymously)

No quiere salir del pueblo, puesto que su familia vive allí.	He doesn't want to leave the town, since his family lives there.

113. (to) sleep

dormir to sleep

No puedo dormir cuando hace calor.	I can't sleep when it is hot out.

estar dormido to be sleeping or asleep

¿Puedo hablar con María? —Ahora no. Está dormida.	May I speak to Mary? —Not now. She is sleeping (or asleep).

dormirse to fall asleep, to go to sleep

Duérmete, mi nene.	Go to sleep (fall asleep), my baby.

acostarse to go to bed, to lie down, to go to sleep (but *not* to fall asleep)

Me acosté a las diez, pero no me dormí hasta las once y media.	I went to bed at ten, but I didn't fall asleep until half-past eleven.

tener sueño to be sleepy

¿Qué tienes? —Nada. Tengo sueño.	What's the matter with you? —Nothing. I'm sleepy.

114. smooth

suave smooth, soft (to the touch, ear, etc.); gentle, suave

Es una tela muy suave.	It's a very smooth (soft) fabric.
Tiene una voz tan suave que da gusto oírle hablar.	He has such a smooth (gentle) voice that it's a pleasure to hear him speak.

liso smooth and shiny (as of a harder surface)

El suelo era tan liso que nos deslizábamos al bailar.	The floor was so smooth that we slid as we danced.
Tiene el pelo muy liso.	She has very smooth (and straight) hair.

plano smooth, flat, level

Hace falta una superficie más plana.	We need a smoother (more level) surface.

115. so

tan so (tired, tall, busy, slow, quickly, etc.)

Tan always modifies an adjective or an adverb, but never modifies **mucho.**

Estamos tan cansados hoy.	We are so tired today.
Se enoja tan rápidamente que me da miedo.	He gets angry so quickly that it frightens me.

tanto so much; (*pl.*) so many

Riñen tanto con sus vecinos.	They quarrel so much with their neighbors.
Tengo tantos problemas.	I have so many problems.

así so, thus, in this way; so, true

El patrón quiere que lo hagas así.	The boss wants you to do it so (in this way).
Dime, ¿es así?	Tell me, is it so?

Así is also used in the colloquial expression **así así** *so-so.*

de modo que so (that), and so . . ., so you say that . . .

NOTE: **De modo que** always introduces a clause; it may also mean *in order that.*

¿De modo que te despidió sin más ni más?	So he fired you just like that?
Se arañó la cara de modo que (para que) todos le tuvieran lástima.	He scratched his face so that everyone would feel sorry for him.

De manera que, which is synonymous with **de modo que,** is used somewhat less frequently.

para que so that, in order that (always indicates purpose)

Lo colocó en el estante más alto para que (de modo que) nadie pudiera tocarlo.	He placed it on the highest shelf so that nobody could touch it.

A fin de que may be used with the same meaning, but is less common than **para que.**

en fin, conque, así que so, well, to sum up

En fin (Conque, Así que) todo queda resuelto, ¿no? So everything is settled, isn't it?

En fin, ¿qué me cuentas? So what do you say?

116. some

Omission of the article: Spanish indicates the partitive idea *some, any,* by omitting the article.

¿Quieres café? Do you want (some) coffee?

No tengo fósforos. I don't have any matches.

unos some, a few, several; some, approximately

Me dio unas (o algunas) ideas muy buenas. He gave me some very good ideas.

La compañía tiene unos dos mil quinientos empleados. The company has some 2500 employees.

algunos some, several, a few

Algunos, although an indefinite, has a slightly stronger numerical connotation than **unos.** It does not have the meaning *approximately.*

Conocí a algunos amigos tuyos ayer. I met some (a few) friends of yours yesterday.

unos cuantos, unos pocos some, a few, a couple of

¿Te quedan muchos? Do you have many left?
—Unos cuantos, nada más. —Just a few (some).

117. (to) spend

gastar to spend (money, effort, etc.)

Gastó todo su dinero el primer día de la feria. He spent all his money the first day of the fair.

pasar to spend (time)

Pasamos el verano en el Canadá. We spent the summer in Canada.

118. sport

deporte *m.* an athletic sport

¿Qué deporte le gusta más? Which sport do you like best?

juego, broma sport, playfulness, jest

Lo dijo de broma. He said it in sport.

sport *adj.* sport (shirt, etc.) The English word is very frequent in this sense.

una camisa sport a sport shirt

119. step

paso a step (in a certain direction); also used figuratively

Dio tres pasos hacia adelante y se paró.	He took three steps forward and stopped.
Eso sería un paso definitivo.	That would be a definitive step.

medida a step, measure, act

Tendrán que tomar unas medidas más fuertes.	They will have to take some stronger steps (measures).

escalón (*m.*), **peldaño** step (of a stairway)

Se cayó en el segundo peldaño (escalón).	He fell on the second step.

120. still

todavía, aún (*adv.*) still; yet, as yet

Todavía (aún) vive con sus padres.	He is still living with his parents.
No ha hablado todavía (aún) el rector.	The president hasn't spoken yet.
¿Existe aún (todavía) la catedral?	Does the cathedral still exist?

Notice that **aun** without a written accent usually means *even.*

Aun yo lo sé.	Even I know it.

callado (*adj.*) still, quiet, not speaking

Permaneció callado durante toda la discusión.	He remained still during the whole discussion.

quieto, sereno, tranquilo still, not moving, tranquil

Las aguas quietas (serenas) pueden ser profundas.	Still waters may be deep.

121. (to) stop

detener to stop (something), to bring to a halt

Detuvo el tren al último momento.	He stopped the train at the last moment.

detenerse to stop (amidst an action), to come to a stop

Note that the implication here is one of an action that has been halted temporarily and will be resumed.

Se detuvo en el umbral.	He stopped on the threshold.

parar(se) to stop; to come to a rest

Note that **parar** is both transitive and intransitive: to stop (something), to come to a stop; to stop (at a hotel).

Se ha parado el trabajo en todas las fábricas.	Work has stopped in all factories.
Paramos en el Hotel Caribe.	We stopped at the Hotel Caribe.

dejar de to stop (doing something); in the negative, it also means *to fail to*

Deja de preocuparte.	Stop worrying.
No deje de telefonearle.	Don't fail to phone him.

122. straight

recto straight (as a line, posture, etc.)

Una línea recta es la distancia más corta entre dos puntos.	A straight line is the shortest distance between two points.
Siempre se tenía recto.	He always stood (held himself) straight.

derecho straight to, right to; straight ahead

Dijo que iría derecho a la policía.	He said he'd go straight to the police.
Siga derecho hasta llegar al semáforo.	Go straight until you get to the traffic light.

liso straight and smooth (as hair, a board, etc.)

Me gusta el pelo liso más que el muy rizado.	I like straight hair better than the very curly.

123. strange

extraño strange, unusual, curious

Me dirigió una mirada extraña.	He gave me a strange look.

extranjero strange, foreign

¡Cuánto me interesaría viajar a países extranjeros!	How I'd like to travel to strange (foreign) lands!

desconocido strange, unknown

Se nos acercó un desconocido.	A strange man approached us.
Van a explorar tierras desconocidas.	They are going to explore strange (unknown) lands.

124. (to) succeed

tener éxito to be successful, to succeed (in business, in a project, etc.)

Ha tenido tanto éxito en el extranjero que no piensa volver a América.	He has been so successful abroad that he doesn't intend to return to America.
El plan tendrá éxito, sin duda alguna.	The plan will succeed, without any doubt.

lograr to succeed (in doing something); to accomplish, achieve, fulfill

Logró escalar la pared.	He succeeded in scaling the wall.
Siempre logran todos sus propósitos.	They always accomplish all their ends.

suceder to succeed (in order), to follow in succession

Los Borbones sucedieron a los Hapsburgos.	The Bourbons succeeded the Hapsburgs.

125. such

tal (*adj.*) such a; **tales** (*pl.*) such

Tal is normally used *only* to modify a noun.

Tal libro (un libro tal) debe ser prohibido.	Such a book should be prohibited.
En tales circunstancias, yo habría hecho lo mismo.	In such circumstances, I would have done the same.

tan (*adv.*) such a (used before an adjective)

Es un hombre tan cosmopolita.	He is such a sophisticated man.
Acabo de leer un cuento tan divertido.	I have just read such a funny story.

126. suggestion

sugerencia a suggestion, recommendation

Aquí tiene Ud. una sugerencia interesantísima.	Here is a very interesting suggestion.

sugestión (the power of) suggestion

La hipnosis obra por medio de la sugestión.	Hypnosis works by means of suggestion.

127. (to) support

sostener to support (a family, etc.); to support, sustain (a theory, etc.); to support (in a physical sense)

No puedo sostener a mi familia con tan poco dinero.	I can't support my family with so little money.
Esto sostiene mi teoría.	This supports my theory.
Aquellas vigas sostienen el techo.	Those beams support the roof.

mantener to support (a family, etc.), to maintain

Mantiene además a sus padres.	He also supports his parents.

soportar to support (as a column); to tolerate, endure, put up with, stand

Aquellos débiles palitos no podrán soportar tanto peso.	Those weak little sticks will not be able to support so much weight.
No puede soportar a su mujer.	He can't stand his wife.

128. (a) (to) take

llevar to take (a person); to carry from one place to another

Te llevo al museo mañana.	I'm taking you to the museum tomorrow.

tomar to take, seize, grasp; to take (food or drink)

Tomó la carta y la hizo trizas.	He took the letter and tore it to bits.
¿Qué toma Ud. —café o té?	What do you take—coffee or tea?

dar un paso to take a step

El nene acaba de dar su primer paso.	The baby has just taken his first step.

dar un paseo (o una vuelta), pasearse to take a walk

Demos un paseo esta tarde.	Let's take a walk this afternoon.

hacer un viaje to take a trip

Hicimos un viaje al Oriente el año pasado.	We took a trip to the Orient last year.

tener lugar to take place

La reunión tendrá lugar a las tres.	The meeting will take place at three o'clock.

tardar (en) to take long (to); to be long; to take (a certain length of time)

No tardes en volver.	Don't take long to return.
El viaje tarda dos horas.	The trip takes two hours.

(b) (to) take away

quitar to take away or off, to remove from (someone or something)

Me quitó un gran peso del alma.	It took a great burden off my heart (away from me).
No les quiten Uds. lo poco que les queda.	Don't take away from them the little they have left.

llevarse to take away with one, to make off with

Se llevó el anillo de oro.	He took the gold ring (away with him).

129. then

entonces then, at that time; then, so

Vivíamos entonces en la Calle de la Independencia.	We were living then on Independence Street.
Entonces nos vemos mañana, ¿verdad?	Then we'll meet tomorrow, right?

luego then, next

Pensamos pasar la tarde con los niños; luego, iremos al cine.	We intend to spend the afternoon with the children; then we'll go to the movies.

después then, next, afterwards, later

¿Y qué hiciste después?	And what did you do then?

en aquel entonces then, in those days, in that period, back then

En aquel entonces no había automóviles.	Then there were no automobiles.

pues bien well then (no implication of time)

Pues bien, si ya se han decidido Uds...	Well then, if you have already decided . . .

130. (a) there

ahí there (near you)

Ahí corresponds somewhat to the demonstrative **ese** that.

Ahí está.	There it is.

allí (over) there

Allí corresponds roughly to **aquel.**

Viven allí desde hace muchos años.	They have been living there for many years.

allá (toward) there; yonder, far off

Allá is used primarily with verbs of motion, or to indicate remoteness in either time or space.

Se fue para allá.	He headed off yonder.
Se ha establecido un nuevo pueblecito allá en el bosque.	A new town has been established way off there in the forest.

(b) there is, are

hay there is (are), there exist(s)

Hay makes *no* reference to location.

Hay mucho que ver en todas partes.	There is a great deal to see everywhere.

allí está, ahí está there is (located)

Allí está nuestra casa.	There is our house.

allí es there is the place (where)

Allí es donde trabajo.	There is where I work.

131. (to) think

creer to think, believe

NOTE: **Un creyente** a believer.

Creo que va a llover.	I think it is going to rain.

pensar to think, meditate, use reasoning processes

Hay que pensar antes de hacer cualquier cosa.	One must think before doing anything.

pensar en to think about, occupy one's thoughts with

Paso todo el día pensando en ti.	I spend the whole day thinking of you.

pensar de to think of, have an opinion of

¿Qué piensa Ud. de mi suegra?	What do you think of my mother-in-law?

pensar (+ *infinitive*) to think of (doing something), to intend to, plan to

Pensamos ir a París el año que viene.	We plan to go (are thinking of going) to Paris next year.

132. (to) throw

echar to throw (without special effort or strength); to throw out, expel (often a person)

Échalo en la cesta, ¿está bien?	Throw it in the basket, all right?
Lo echaron de casa por haberlos avergonzado.	They threw him out for having shamed them.

arrojar, lanzar, tirar to throw (with strength, violence, or for distance) Notice: **el lanzador** pitcher (baseball)

Lo arrojaron (tiraron, etc.) por la ventana.	They threw it out of the window.

botar to throw out, expel forcibly (often an object)

Ya no sirve para nada. Botémoslo.	It's worthless now. Let's throw it out.

133. time

tiempo a period of time; duration of time; time (as an abstraction)

El tiempo vuela.	Time flies.
¿Tienes tiempo ahora?	Do you have time now?
No voy a quedarme mucho tiempo allí.	I won't stay there long.

hora time of day, hour; the proper or appointed time

¿Qué hora es?	What time is it?
Es hora de comer.	It's time to eat.

vez (a single) time, an instance

Me llamó dos veces ayer.	He called me twice (two times) yesterday.
Lo hemos leído muchas veces.	We have read it many times.

ocasión (*f.*) time, occasion, opportunity

Habrá otra ocasión.	There will be another time.

divertirse to have a good time

Nos divertíamos mucho con ellos.	We used to have a very good time with them.

134. too

también too, also

Yo le vi también.	I saw him too.

demasiado too (followed by an adjective or adverb); too much; **demasiados(as)** (*pl.*) too many

Es demasiado alto.	He is too tall.
Ella fuma demasiado.	She smokes too much.
Tenemos demasiadas deudas.	We have too many debts.

135. (to) try

tratar de, intentar, procurar (+ *infinitive*) to try to, attempt

Trataré de acabar a tiempo.	I'll try to finish on time.
Intentó (Procuró) fugarse, pero lo cogieron.	He tried to escape, but they caught him.

ensayar to try out; rehearse; try, test

Mañana ensayan la comedia nueva.	Tomorrow they're trying out (rehearsing) the new play.
Ensayemos la máquina, a ver cómo funciona.	Let's try the machine and see how it works.

probar to try out, test; to try on (clothes, etc.)

Pruebe la puerta. Tal vez esté abierta.	Try the door. Maybe it's open.
¿No te lo vas a probar?	Aren't you going to try it on?

The preterite of **querer** (+ *infinitive*) also means *tried to*, but the emphasis falls more on the intention than on the attempt.

Quise llamarte, pero la línea estaba ocupada.	I tried to call you, but the line was busy.

136. (to) turn

volver to turn (a page, one's back, the other cheek, etc.); to turn over; to turn upside down

No me vuelvas la espalda cuando te hablo.	Don't turn your back on me when I talk to you.
Ahora vuélvalo al otro lado.	Now turn it over on the other side.

volverse to turn (oneself) around

Oyó el silbido y se volvió en el acto.	He heard the whistle and turned around immediately.

doblar to turn (a corner)

No debes doblar la esquina tan aprisa.	You shouldn't turn the corner so fast.

dar vuelta (or **doblar**) **a la derecha** (**a la izquierda**) to turn right (left)

Cuando llegues a la esquina, da vuelta a la derecha. When you get to the corner, turn right.

apagar to turn out (a light, a radio, etc.)

Apagan las luces a medianoche. They turn out the lights at midnight.

poner to turn on (a radio, television set or other apparatus)

¿Se puede poner la radio? May I turn on the radio?

rechazar to turn down, reject (an offer, a suitor, etc.)

Lo rechazó sin pensarlo siquiera. He turned it down without even thinking it over.

137. under

debajo de under, below, underneath

Hay ríos que corren debajo de la tierra. There are rivers that run under the ground

bajo under, below, located in a lower position; under (in a figurative sense)

Estaban sentados bajo el árbol. They were sitting under the tree.

El pueblo adelantó mucho bajo la dominación islámica. The people advanced a great deal under the Islamic domination.

138. (to) understand

comprender to understand (the surface meaning, a word, phrase, a language, etc.)

¿Comprendes italiano? Do you understand Italian?

Muy bien. Te comprendo. All right. I understand you (what you're saying).

entender to understand (a language, etc., as **comprender**); to understand the surface meaning and the reason behind it; to be given to understand

Ya te entiendo perfectamente. I understand you perfectly (and why you're doing it).

Entiendo que no va a ser candidato en noviembre. I (am given to) understand that he won't be a candidate in November.

139. until

hasta (*prep.*) until (time); until, up to a certain place (used before an infinitive, a noun, or a number)

Esperemos hasta las tres.	Let's wait until three o'clock.
Le acompañarán hasta la próxima estación.	They will accompany him until (up to) the next station.

hasta que (*conj.*) until (must introduce a clause)

Siga Ud. caminando hasta que llegue a la plaza mayor.	Keep walking until you reach the central square.

140. (to be) used to

soler to be used or accustomed to (doing something), to do habitually

Soler is used only in the present and imperfect tenses.

Suelo visitarla todos los domingos.	I usually go to visit her every Sunday.
Solían cenar a las diez.	They used to eat at ten.

The imperfect of **soler** (+ *infinitive*) corresponds to the simple imperfect **(Cenaban a las diez)**, but emphasizes a bit more the habitual nature of the action.

acostumbrarse a to get used to

No me puedo acostumbrar al calor.	I can't get used to the heat.
Me he acostumbrado a su mirar.	I've grown accustomed to her face (look).

estar acostumbrado a to be used to, inured to, trained to

Ya están acostumbrados a levantarse a las seis.	They're now used to getting up at six.

141. (to) want

querer to want (something or to do something); to wish, will; negative, to refuse

Quiero llevarla conmigo.	I want to take her with me.
Quiere que le llamemos en seguida.	He wants us to call him immediately.
Dice que quiere más dinero.	He says he wants more money.
No quieren aceptarlo.	They don't want (wish) to accept it. (They refuse to, will not.)

desear to want, desire, wish

Desear is used much less frequently than **querer.** It is somewhat more literary, rhetorical, or impassioned.

Deseamos paz y prosperidad para todos.	We want peace and prosperity for all.
Les deseo un feliz año nuevo.	I wish you (desire for you) a happy new year.
La desea por su esposa.	He desires (wants) her for his wife.

142. warm

caliente, calientito warm, warmish

Tómese un baño caliente (calientito).	Take a nice warm bath.

templado warm, temperate (climate)

Prefieren vivir en un clima más templado.	They prefer to live in a warmer (but not hot) climate.

afectuoso, cariñoso, caluroso warm, affectionate

Me dio un abrazo cariñoso (afectuoso).	He gave me a warm embrace.

encarecido, expresivo warm, heartfelt (thanks, wishes)

Les ruego aceptar mis más encarecidas (expresivas) gracias.	I beg you to accept my warmest thanks.

abrigado warm, protected, snug; warm (as clothing)

Busquemos un rincón bien abrigado.	Let's look for a nice warm corner.
Hoy debes ponerte ropa bien abrigadita.	Today you should put on good warm clothes.

143. (to) waste

perder to waste (time)

Estoy perdiendo tiempo hablando contigo.	I'm wasting time talking to you.

desperdiciar to squander, waste

Desperdició toda su herencia.	He wasted his whole inheritance.

echar a perder to waste, spoil, ruin

Echa a perder todas las oportunidades que se le presentan.	He wastes all the opportunities that are presented to him.

144. way

manera, modo way, manner, method

Su manera de hablar nos impresionó mucho.	His way of speaking impressed us very much.
Voy a mostrarle un modo más fácil de hacer media.	I'm going to show you an easier way to knit.

cómo how, the way (to do something)

¿Quién sabe cómo se hace?	Who knows the way it's done?
No comprendo cómo lo hicieron.	I don't understand the way (how) they did it.

así, de este modo, de esta manera in this way

Primero, hay que cortarlo así (de esta manera).	First, you must cut it this way.
Así se hace mejor.	It is done best in this way. (This is the way it is done best.)

camino, way, road

Este es el camino de la ciudad.	This is the way to the city
Siga el camino de la virtud.	Follow the way (path) of virtue.

dirección way, direction

¿En qué dirección queda la estación?	Which way is the station?

¿Por dónde se va a la estación? may also be used.

camino de on the way to

Camino del pueblo, perdieron una llanta.	On the way to the village, they lost a tire.

145. why

¿Por qué? Why? What's the reason?

¿Por qué llama a toda hora?	Why does he call at all hours?

¿Para qué? Why? What for? What good will it do? To what end?

¿Para qué llorar? Eso no remedia nada.	Why cry? That doesn't help anything
¿Para qué estudias? —Para ingeniero.	What are you studying for? —To be an engineer.

146. (to) wish

desear to wish (success, happiness, etc.); to want, wish

Os deseo toda felicidad.	I wish you both every happiness.
Desea ir, pero no puede.	He wants (wishes) to go, but he can't.

¡Ojalá...! Oh, how I wish (+*subjunctive*)

¡Ojalá (que) venga pronto!	How I wish he comes soon!
¡Ojalá (que) no lo hubiera dicho!	How I wish he hadn't said it!

147. work

obra a work (of art, etc.); a deed (of charity, creation, etc.)

Las buenas obras perduran siempre.	Good works last forever.

trabajo work, labor

El trabajo descansa el alma, si no el cuerpo.	Work rests the soul, if not the body.

labor work, labor, effort (generally used in a figurative or poetic sense)

una labor de caridad humana	a work (an effort, labor of love) of human charity

148. worker

obrero factory worker, skilled or semiskilled worker

Los obreros se han declarado en huelga.	The workers have declared a strike.

trabajador worker (more general classification that includes most types); member of the proletariat (in social reference); workman, artisan, craftsman

Sindicato de Trabajadores Metalúrgicos	Union of Metallurgical Workers
¡Trabajadores del mundo...!	Workers of the world . . .!
Es muy buen trabajador.	He is a very good worker (workman, craftsman).

jornalero day laborer; wage earner, hired hand; proletarian

No hacen falta jornaleros en el invierno.	There is no lack of workers in the winter.

labrador farm worker; farm hand

Los labradores segaban bajo un sol calcinante.	The farm laborers were sowing under a scorching sun.

149. yet

Yet has two meanings in English: *still* (which refers to an action or state that is continuing after a certain period of time), and *already*.

todavía still

NOTE: **Todavía** translates the English *yet* most frequently in negative sentences.

Todavía tenemos que hallar alguien que pueda llenar el puesto.	We have yet to find someone who can fill the position.
¿Han llegado? —Todavía no.	Have they come? —Not yet (still not).

ya yet (in the sense of *already*)

¿Ya está aquí?	Is he here yet (already)?

ya no no longer, not . . . any longer, not . . . any more

Ya no vive con nosotros.	He doesn't live with us any more. (He no longer lives with us.)

por yet to be

La nueva carretera está por concluir.	The new road is yet to be completed.

150. younger

menor younger

Menor establishes a comparative relationship between two persons, irrespective of their actual age.

El hermano menor tenía sesenta años; el mayor casi ochenta.	The youngest brother was sixty; the eldest, almost eighty.

más joven younger, more youthful (compares the adjective *young*)

Ella es aun más joven que mi mujer.	She is even younger than my wife (both are young).

B

VERBS

REGULAR VERBS

Infinitive

hablar to speak	**comer** to eat	**vivir** to live

Present Participle

hablando speaking	**comiendo** eating	**viviendo** living

Past Participle

hablado spoken	**comido** eaten	**vivido** lived

SIMPLE TENSES

Indicative Mood

Present

I speak, am speaking	*I eat, am eating*	*I live, am living*
hablo	**como**	**vivo**
hablas	**comes**	**vives**
habla	**come**	**vive**
hablamos	**comemos**	**vivimos**
habláis	**coméis**	**vivís**
hablan	**comen**	**viven**

Imperfect

I was speaking, used to speak	*I was eating, used to eat*	*I was living, used to live*
hablaba	**comía**	**vivía**
hablabas	**comías**	**vivías**
hablaba	**comía**	**vivía**
hablábamos	**comíamos**	**vivíamos**
hablabais	**comíais**	**vivíais**
hablaban	**comían**	**vivían**

Preterite

I spoke, did speak	*I ate, did eat*	*I lived, did live*
hablé	**comí**	**viví**
hablaste	**comiste**	**viviste**
habló	**comió**	**vivió**
hablamos	**comimos**	**vivimos**
hablasteis	**comisteis**	**vivisteis**
hablaron	**comieron**	**vivieron**

Future

I shall (will) speak	*I shall (will) eat*	*I shall (will) live*
hablaré	**comeré**	**viviré**
hablarás	**comerás**	**vivirás**
hablará	**comerá**	**vivirá**
hablaremos	**comeremos**	**viviremos**
hablaréis	**comeréis**	**viviréis**
hablarán	**comerán**	**vivirán**

Conditional

I should (would) speak	*I should (would) eat*	*I should (would) live*
hablaría	**comería**	**viviría**
hablarías	**comerías**	**vivirías**
hablaría	**comería**	**viriría**
hablaríamos	**comeríamos**	**viviríamos**
hablaríais	**comeríais**	**viviríais**
hablarían	**comerían**	**vivirían**

SUBJUNCTIVE MOOD

Present

(*that*) *I* (*may*) *speak*	(*that*) *I* (*may*) *eat*	(*that*) *I* (*may*) *live*
hable	**coma**	**viva**
hables	**comas**	**vivas**
hable	**coma**	**viva**
hablemos	**comamos**	**vivamos**
habléis	**comáis**	**viváis**
hablen	**coman**	**vivan**

Imperfect (**-ra** form)

(*that*) *I might speak*	(*that*) *I might eat*	(*that*) *I might live*
hablara	**comiera**	**viviera**
hablaras	**comieras**	**vivieras**
hablara	**comiera**	**viviera**
habláramos	**comiéramos**	**viviéramos**
hablarais	**comierais**	**vivierais**
hablaran	**comieran**	**vivieran**

Imperfect (**-se** form)

(that) I might speak	*(that) I might eat*	*(that) I might live*
hablase	**comiese**	**viviese**
hablases	**comieses**	**vivieses**
hablase	**comiese**	**viviese**
hablásemos	**comiésemos**	**viviésemos**
hablaseis	**comieseis**	**vivieseis**
hablasen	**comiesen**	**viviesen**

IMPERATIVE MOOD

speak	*eat*	*live*
habla	**come**	**vive**
hablad	**comed**	**vivid**

COMPOUND TENSES

Perfect Infinitive	Perfect Participle
to have spoken, eaten, lived	*having spoken, eaten, lived*
haber hablado, comido, vivido	**habiendo hablado, comido, vivido**

INDICATIVE MOOD

Present Perfect

I have spoken	*I have eaten*	*I have lived*
he hablado	**he comido**	**he vivido**
has hablado	**has comido**	**has vivido**
ha hablado	**ha comido**	**ha vivido**
hemos hablado	**hemos comido**	**hemos vivido**
habéis hablado	**habéis comido**	**habéis vivido**
han hablado	**han comido**	**han vivido**

Pluperfect

I had spoken	*I had eaten*	*I had lived*
había hablado	**había comido**	**había vivido**
habías hablado	**habías comido**	**habías vivido**
había hablado	**había comido**	**había vivido**
habíamos hablado	**habíamos comido**	**habíamos vivido**
habíais hablado	**habíais comido**	**habíais vivido**
habían hablado	**habían comido**	**habían vivido**

Future Perfect

I shall have spoken	*I shall have eaten*	*I shall have lived*
habré hablado	**habré comido**	**habré vivido**
habrás hablado	**habrás comido**	**habrás vivido**
habrá hablado	**habrá comido**	**habrá vivido**
habremos hablado	**habremos comido**	**habremos vivido**
habréis hablado	**habréis comido**	**habréis vivido**
habrán hablado	**habrán comido**	**habrán vivido**

Conditional Perfect

I should (would) have spoken	*I should (would) have eaten*	*I should (would) have lived*
habría hablado	**habría comido**	**habría vivido**
habrías hablado	**habrías comido**	**habrías vivido**
habría hablado	**habría comido**	**habría vivido**
habríamos hablado	**habríamos comido**	**habríamos vivido**
habríais hablado	**habríais comido**	**habríais vivido**
habrían hablado	**habrían comido**	**habrían vivido**

SUBJUNCTIVE MOOD

Present Perfect

(that) I (may) have spoken	*(that) I (may) have eaten*	*(that) I (may) have lived*
haya hablado	**haya comido**	**haya vivido**
hayas hablado	**hayas comido**	**hayas vivido**
haya hablado	**haya comido**	**haya vivido**
hayamos hablado	**hayamos comido**	**hayamos vivido**
hayáis hablado	**hayáis comido**	**hayáis vivido**
hayan hablado	**hayan comido**	**hayan vivido**

Pluperfect (**-ra** form)

(that) I might have spoken	*(that) I might have eaten*	*(that) I might have lived*
hubiera hablado	**hubiera comido**	**hubiera vivido**
hubieras hablado	**hubieras comido**	**hubieras vivido**
hubiera hablado	**hubiera comido**	**hubiera vivido**
hubiéramos hablado	**hubiéramos comido**	**hubiéramos vivido**
hubierais hablado	**hubierais comido**	**hubierais vivido**
hubieran hablado	**hubieran comido**	**hubieran vivido**

Pluperfect (**-se** form)

(*that*) *I might have spoken*	(*that*) *I might have eaten*	(*that*) *I might have lived*
hubiese hablado	**hubiese comido**	**hubiese vivido**
hubieses hablado	**hubieses comido**	**hubieses vivido**
hubiese hablado	**hubiese comido**	**hubiese vivido**
hubiésemos hablado	**hubiésemos comido**	**hubiésemos vivido**
hubieseis hablado	**hubieseis comido**	**hubieseis vivido**
hubiesen hablado	**hubiesen comido**	**hubiesen vivido**

RADICAL CHANGING VERBS

A radical change means a change in the root (stem) of a verb. Specifically, in Spanish, it refers to a change in the *vowel* of the root.

1. The **-ar** and **-er** Radical Changing Verbs

Radical changing verbs that end in **-ar** or **-er** change the stressed vowel **e** to **ie,** the stressed **o** to **ue.**

-Ar or **-er** radical changing verbs change *only* in the present indicative and present subjunctive. All other tenses are conjugated regularly. (Recall that the imperative singular is the same as the third person singular of the present indicative.)

PATTERN OF THE PRESENT INDICATIVE

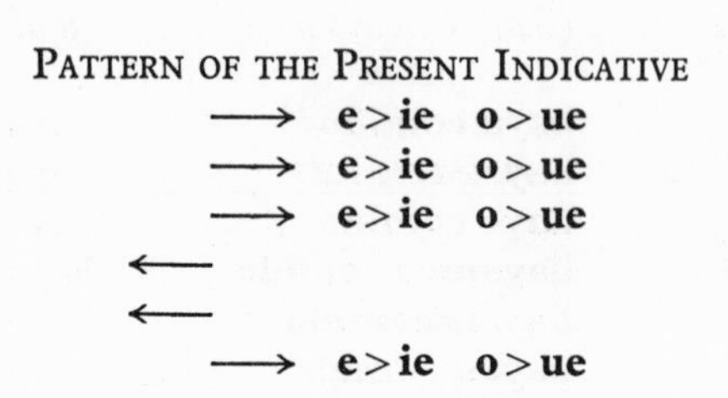

pensar	perder	contar	mover
pienso	**pierdo**	**cuento**	**muevo**
piensas	**pierdes**	**cuentas**	**mueves**
piensa	**pierde**	**cuenta**	**mueve**
pensamos	**perdemos**	**contamos**	**movemos**
pensáis	**perdéis**	**contáis**	**movéis**
piensan	**pierden**	**cuentan**	**mueven**

The present subjunctive follows exactly the same pattern, except that **-a** endings change to **-e, -e** endings to **-a.**

Common Verbs of This Type

acordarse	**empezar**	**pensar**
acostarse	**encender**	**perder**
atravesar	**encontrar**	**probar**
comenzar	**entender**	**recordar**
contar	**jugar**	**mover**
costar	**llover**	**sentar**(se)
despertar(se)	**negar**	**volver**

2. The **-ir** Radical Changing Verbs

Radical changing verbs that end in **-ir** are of two types:
Type I: Those whose stressed **e** changes to **ie,** whose stressed **o** changes to **ue.** Common verbs of this type are

advertir	**dormir**	**morir**
convertir	**mentir**	**sentir**

Type II: Those whose stressed **e** changes to **i.** Common verbs of this type are

concebir	**repetir**	**servir**
pedir	**seguir**	**vestir**(se)

A. The Present Indicative of **-ir** Radical Changing Verbs

The pattern is exactly the same as that of all other radical changing verbs.

Type I (**e**>**ie, o**>**ue**)		Type II (**e**>**i**)
siento	**duermo**	**pido**
sientes	**duermes**	**pides**
siente	**duerme**	**pide**
sentimos	**dormimos**	**pedimos**
sentís	**dormís**	**pedís**
sienten	**duermen**	**piden**

B. The Present Subjunctive of **-ir** Radical Changing Verbs

The pattern of the present indicative is maintained. But a *second* radical change is added. The *unstressed* **e** of the first and second persons plural becomes **i**; the unstressed **o** becomes **u**:

sienta	**duerma**	**pida**
sientas	**duermas**	**pidas**
sienta	**duerma**	**pida**
sintamos	**durmamos**	**pidamos**
sintáis	**durmáis**	**pidáis**
sientan	**duerman**	**pidan**

C. The Preterite of **-ir** Radical Changing Verbs

In the third person, singular and plural, the unstressed **e** becomes **i**, the unstressed **o** becomes **u**:

sentí	**dormí**	**pedí**
sentiste	**dormiste**	**pediste**
sintió	**durmió**	**pidió**
sentimos	**dormimos**	**pedimos**
sentisteis	**dormisteis**	**pedisteis**
sintieron	**durmieron**	**pidieron**

REMEMBER: The preterite of **-ar** and **-er** verbs has no radical change.

D. The Imperfect Subjunctive of **-ir** Radical Changing Verbs

The **e > i, o > u** change governs the entire imperfect subjunctive.

sintiera (**sintiese**)	**durmiera**(**iese**)	**pidiera**(**iese**)
sintieras	**durmieras**	**pidieras**
sintiera	**durmiera**	**pidiera**
sintiéramos	**durmiéramos**	**pidiéramos**
sintierais	**durmierais**	**pidierais**
sintieran	**durmieran**	**pidieran**

REMEMBER: The imperfect subjunctive of **-ar** and **-er** verbs has no radical change.

The present participle of **-ir** radical changing verbs changes the stem vowel **e > i, o > u: sintiendo, durmiendo, pidiendo.**

SPELLING CHANGING VERBS

Many verbs undergo a change in spelling in some tenses in order that the sound of the final consonant of the stem or the normal rules of Spanish spelling may be preserved. Recall:

1. **g** before **e** or **i** is pronounced like the Spanish **j.**
2. **g** before **a, o,** or **u** is hard.
3. **g** before **e** or **i** may be kept hard by placing **u** after the consonant.
4. **c** before **e** or **i** is pronounced like the English *th* (throughout Spain, except Andalusia) or like **s** (in Spanish America and Andalusia).
5. **c** before **a, o,** or **u** is pronounced like the English **k.**
6. **c** changes to **qu** before **e** or **i** to keep the sound hard.
7. **z** changes to **c** before an **e** or **i.**
8. Unstressed **i** between vowels changes to **y.**
9. Two consecutive unstressed **i**'s merge into one.
10. Two consecutive **s**'s are reduced to one.
11. A word that begins with a diphthong must be preceded by **h** or the initial **i** of the diphthong changes to **y.**
12. Unstressed **i** before **e** or **o** disappears after **ll, ñ,** and **j.**

The following are important types of verbs that are regular in their conjugation, but undergo necessary changes in spelling.

1. Verbs Ending in **-car** Change **c** to **qu** Before **e**

sacar to take out

Preterite	Present Subjunctive
saqué	**saque**
sacaste	**saques**
sacó	**saque**
etc.	**saquemos**
	saquéis
	saquen

2. Verbs Ending in **-gar** Change **g** to **gu** Before **e**

pagar to pay

Preterite	Present Subjunctive
pagué	**pague**
pagaste	**pagues**
pagó	**pague**
etc.	**paguemos**
	paguéis
	paguen

3. Verbs Ending in **-zar** Change **z** to **c** Before **e**

gozar to enjoy

Preterite	Present Subjunctive
gocé	**goce**
gozaste	**goces**
gozó	**goce**
etc.	**gocemos**
	gocéis
	gocen

4. Verbs Ending in **-cer** or **-cir** Preceded by a Consonant Change **c** to **z** Before **o** and **a**

vencer to conquer

Present Indicative	Present Subjunctive
venzo	**venza**
vences	**venzas**
vence	**venza**
etc.	**venzamos**
	venzáis
	venzan

5. Verbs Ending in **-ger** or **-gir** Change **g** to **j** Before **o** and **a**

coger to catch

Present Indicative	Present Subjunctive
cojo	**coja**
coges	**cojas**
coge	**coja**
etc.	**cojamos**
	cojáis
	cojan

dirigir to direct

Present Indicative	Present Subjunctive
dirijo	**dirija**
diriges	**dirijas**
dirige	**dirija**
etc.	**dirijamos**
	dirijáis
	dirijan

6. Verbs Ending in **-guir** Change **gu** to **g** Before **o** and **a**

distinguir to distinguish

Present Indicative	Present Subjunctive
distingo	**distinga**
distingues	**distingas**
distingue	**distinga**
etc.	**distingamos**
	distingáis
	distingan

7. Verbs Ending in **-quir** Change **qu** to **c** Before **o** and **a**

delinquir to commit an offense

Present Indicative	Present Subjunctive
delinco	**delinca**
delinques	**delincas**
delinque	**delinca**
etc.	**delincamos**
	delincáis
	delincan

8. Verbs Ending in **-guar** Change **gu** to **gü** Before **e**

averiguar to ascertain

Preterite	Present Subjunctive
averigüé	**averigüe**
averiguaste	**averigües**
averiguó	**averigüe**
etc.	**averigüemos**
	averigüéis
	averigüen

9. Verbs Ending in **-eer** Change Unstressed **i** to **y** Between Vowels

leer to read

Preterite	Imperfect Subjunctive		Participles: Present, Past
leí	**leyera**	**leyese**	**leyendo**
leíste	**leyeras**	**leyeses**	**leído**
leyó	**leyera**	**leyese**	
leímos	etc.	etc.	
leísteis			
leyeron			

10. Verbs Ending in **-eír** Are Radical Changing Verbs That Lose One **i** in the Third Person of the Preterite, Imperfect Subjunctive, and Present Participle

reír to laugh

Present Indicative	Preterite	Imperfect Subjunctive		Present Participle
río	**reí**	**riera**	**riese**	**riendo**
ríes	**reíste**	**rieras**	**rieses**	
ríe	**rio**	**riera**	**riese**	
reímos	**reímos**	etc.	etc.	
reís	**reísteis**			
ríen	**rieron**			

11. Verbs whose Stem Ends in **ll** or **ñ** Drop the **i** of the Diphthongs **ie** and **ió**

bullir to boil

Preterite	Imperfect Subjunctive		Present Participle
bullí	**bullera**	**bullese**	**bullendo**
bulliste	**bulleras**	**bulleses**	
bulló	**bullera**	**bullese**	
bullimos	etc.	etc.	
bullisteis			
bulleron			

reñir to scold (also radical changing)

Preterite	Imperfect Subjunctive		Present Participle
reñí	**riñera**	**riñese**	**riñendo**
reñiste	**riñeras**	**riñeses**	
riñó	**riñera**	**riñese**	
reñimos	etc.	etc.	
reñisteis			
riñeron			

CHANGES IN ACCENTUATION

1. Verbs Ending in **-iar**

Some verbs ending in **-iar** bear a written accent on the **i** in all singular forms and in the third person plural of the present indicative and subjunctive, and in the imperative singular.

enviar to send

Present Indicative	Present Subjunctive	Imperative
envío	**envíe**	
envías	**envíes**	**envía**
envía	**envíe**	
enviamos	**enviemos**	
enviáis	**enviéis**	**enviad**
envían	**envíen**	

2. Verbs Ending in **-uar**

Verbs ending in **-uar** (except those ending in **-guar**) bear a written accent on the **u** in the same forms listed above.

continuar to continue

Present Indicative	Present Subjunctive	Imperative
continúo	**continúe**	
continúas	**continúes**	**continúa**
continúa	**continúe**	
continuamos	**continuemos**	
continuáis	**continuéis**	**continuad**
continúan	**continúen**	

IRREGULAR VERBS

NOTE: Only the tenses containing irregular forms are given. The conjugation of verbs ending in **-ducir** may be found under **conducir;** those ending in a vowel +**cer** or +**cir** are found under **conocer;** and those ending in **-uir** are under **huir.**

andar to walk, go

Preterite	**anduve, anduviste, anduvo, anduvimos, anduvisteis, anduvieron**
Imperfect Subjunctive	(**-ra**) **anduviera, anduvieras, anduviera, anduviéramos, anduvierais, anduvieran**
	(**-se**) **anduviese, anduvieses, anduviese, anduviésemos, anduvieseis, anduviesen**

asir to seize

Present Indicative	**asgo, ases, ase, asimos, asís, asen**
Present Subjunctive	**asga, asgas, asga, asgamos, asgáis, asgan**

caber to be contained in

Present Indicative	**quepo, cabes, cabe, cabemos, cabéis, caben**
Preterite	**cupe, cupiste, cupo, cupimos, cupisteis, cupieron**
Future	**cabré, cabrás, cabrá, cabremos, cabréis, cabrán**
Conditional	**cabría, cabrías, cabría, cabríamos, cabríais, cabrían**
Present Subjunctive	**quepa, quepas, quepa, quepamos, quepáis, quepan**
Imperfect Subjunctive	(**-ra**) **cupiera, cupieras, cupiera, cupiéramos, cupierais, cupieran**
	(**-se**) **cupiese, cupieses, cupiese, cupiésemos, cupieseis, cupiesen**

caer to fall

Present Indicative	**caigo, caes, cae, caemos, caéis, caen**
Preterite	**caí, caíste, cayó, caímos, caísteis, cayeron**
Present Subjunctive	**caiga, caigas, caiga, caigamos, caigáis, caigan**
Imperfect Subjunctive	(**-ra**) **cayera, cayeras, cayera, cayéramos, cayerais, cayeran**
	(**-se**) **cayese, cayeses, cayese, cayésemos, cayeseis, cayesen**
Present Participle	**cayendo**
Past Participle	**caído**

conducir to conduct (similarly, all verbs ending in **-ducir**)

Present Indicative	**conduzco, conduces, conduce, conducimos, conducís, conducen**
Preterite	**conduje, condujiste, condujo, condujimos, condujisteis, condujeron**
Present Subjunctive	**conduzca, conduzcas, conduzca, conduzcamos, conduzcáis, conduzcan**
Imperfect Subjunctive	(**-ra**) **condujera, condujeras, condujera, condujéramos, condujerais, condujeran**
	(**-se**) **condujese, condujeses, condujese, condujésemos, condujeseis, condujesen**

conocer to know (similarly, all verbs ending in a vowel +**cer** and +**cir,** except **cocer, hacer, mecer,** and their compounds)

Present Indicative	**conozco, conoces, conoce,** etc.
Present Subjunctive	**conozca, conozcas, conozca, conozcamos, conozcáis, conozcan**

creer (*see* **leer,** p. 323)

dar to give

Present Indicative	**doy, das, da, damos, dais, dan**
Preterite	**di, diste, dio, dimos, disteis, dieron**
Present Subjunctive	**dé, des, dé, demos, deis, den**
Imperfect Subjunctive	**(-ra) diera, dieras, diera, diéramos, dierais, dieran**
	(-se) diese, dieses, diese, diésemos, dieseis, diesen

decir to say, tell

Present Indicative	**digo, dices, dice, decimos, decís, dicen**
Preterite	**dije, dijiste, dijo, dijimos, dijisteis, dijeron**
Future	**diré, dirás, dirá, diremos, diréis, dirán**
Conditional	**diría, dirías, diría, diríamos, diríais, dirían**
Present Subjunctive	**diga, digas, diga, digamos, digáis, digan**
Imperfect Subjunctive	**(-ra) dijera, dijeras, dijera, dijéramos, dijerais, dijeran**
	(-se) dijese, dijeses, dijese, dijésemos dijeseis, dijesen
Present Participle	**diciendo**
Past Participle	**dicho**
Imperative	**di, decid**

errar to err

Present Indicative	**yerro, yerras, yerra, erramos, erráis, yerran**
Present Subjunctive	**yerre, yerres, yerre, erremos, erréis, yerren**
Imperative	**yerra, errad**

estar to be

Present Indicative	**estoy, estás, está, estamos, estáis, están**
Preterite	**estuve, estuviste, estuvo, estuvimos, estuvisteis, estuvieron**
Present Subjunctive	**esté, estés, esté, estemos, estéis, estén**
Imperfect Subjunctive	**(-ra) estuviera, estuvieras, estuviera, estuviéramos, estuvierais, estuvieran**
	(-se) estuviese, estuvieses, estuviese, estuviésemos, estuvieseis, estuviesen
Imperative	**está, estad**

haber to have

Present Indicative	**he, has, ha, hemos, habéis, han**
Preterite	**hube, hubiste, hubo, hubimos, hubisteis, hubieron**
Future	**habré, habrás, habrá, habremos, habréis, habrán**

Conditional	**habría, habrías, habría, habríamos, habríais, habrían**
Present Subjunctive	**haya, hayas, haya, hayamos, hayáis, hayan**
Imperfect Subjunctive	(**-ra**) **hubiera, hubieras, hubiera, hubiéramos, hubierais, hubieran**
	(**-se**) **hubiese, hubieses, hubiese, hubiésemos, hubieseis, hubiesen**

hacer to do, make

Present Indicative	**hago, haces, hace, hacemos, hacéis, hacen**
Preterite	**hice, hiciste, hizo, hicimos, hicisteis, hicieron**
Future	**haré, harás, hará, haremos, haréis, harán**
Conditional	**haría, harías, haría, haríamos, haríais, harían**
Present Subjunctive	**haga, hagas, haga, hagamos, hagáis, hagan**
Imperfect Subjunctive	(**-ra**) **hiciera, hicieras, hiciera, hiciéramos, hicierais, hicieran**
	(**-se**) **hiciese, hicieses, hiciese, hiciésemos, hicieseis, hiciesen**
Past Participle	**hecho**
Imperative	**haz, haced**

huir to flee (similarly, all verbs ending in **-uir,** except those ending in **-guir** and **-quir**)

Present Indicative	**huyo, huyes, huye, huimos, huís, huyen**
Preterite	**huí, huiste, huyó, huimos, huisteis, huyeron**
Present Subjunctive	**huya, huyas, huya, huyamos, huyáis, huyan**
Imperfect Subjunctive	(**-ra**) **huyera, huyeras, huyera, huyéramos, huyerais, huyeran**
	(**-se**) **huyese, huyeses, huyese, huyésemos, huyeseis, huyesen**
Present Participle	**huyendo**
Imperative	**huye, huid**

ir to go

Present Indicative	**voy, vas, va, vamos, vais, van**
Imperfect Indicative	**iba, ibas, iba, íbamos, ibais, iban**
Preterite	**fui, fuiste, fue, fuimos, fuisteis, fueron**
Present Subjunctive	**vaya, vayas, vaya, vayamos, vayáis, vayan**
Imperfect Subjunctive	(**-ra**) **fuera, fueras, fuera, fuéramos, fuerais, fueran**
	(**-se**) **fuese, fueses, fuese, fuésemos, fueseis, fuesen**
Present Participle	**yendo**
Imperative	**ve, id**

oír to hear

Present Indicative	**oigo, oyes, oye, oímos, oís, oyen**
Preterite	**oí, oíste, oyó, oímos, oísteis, oyeron**
Present Subjunctive	**oiga, oigas, oiga, oigamos, oigáis, oigan**
Imperfect Subjunctive	(**-ra**) **oyera, oyeras, oyera, oyéramos, oyerais, oyeran**
	(**-se**) **oyese, oyeses, oyese, oyésemos, oyeseis, oyesen**
Present Participle	**oyendo**
Past Participle	**oído**
Imperative	**oye, oíd**

oler to smell

Present Indicative	**huelo, hueles, huele, olemos, oléis, huelen**
Present Subjunctive	**huela, huelas, huela, olamos, oláis, huelan**
Imperative	**huele, oled**

poder to be able

Present Indicative	**puedo, puedes, puede, podemos, podéis, pueden**
Preterite	**pude, pudiste, pudo, pudimos, pudisteis, pudieron**
Future	**podré, podrás, podrá, podremos, podréis, podrán**
Conditional	**podría, podrías, podría, podríamos, podríais, podrían**
Present Subjunctive	**pueda, puedas, pueda, podamos, podáis, puedan**
Imperfect Subjunctive	(**-ra**) **pudiera, pudieras, pudiera, pudiéramos, pudierais, pudieran**
	(**-se**) **pudiese, pudieses, pudiese, pudiésemos, pudieseis, pudiesen**
Present Participle	**pudiendo**

poner to put, place

Present Indicative	**pongo, pones, pone, ponemos, ponéis, ponen**
Preterite	**puse, pusiste, puso, pusimos, pusisteis, pusieron**
Future	**pondré, pondrás, pondrá, pondremos, pondréis, pondrán**
Conditional	**pondría, pondrías, pondría, pondríamos, pondríais, pondrían**
Imperfect Subjunctive	(**-ra**) **pusiera, pusieras, pusiera, pusiéramos, pusierais, pusieran**
	(**-se**) **pusiese, pusieses, pusiese, pusiésemos, pusieseis, pusiesen**

Past Participle	**puesto**
Imperative	**pon, poned**

querer to wish

Present Indicative	**quiero, quieres, quiere, queremos, queréis, quieren**
Preterite	**quise, quisiste, quiso, quisimos, quisisteis, quisieron**
Future	**querré, querrás, querrá, querremos, querréis, querrán**
Conditional	**querría, querrías, querría, querríamos, querríais, querrían**
Present Subjunctive	**quiera, quieras, quiera, queramos, queráis, quieran**
Imperfect Subjunctive	(**-ra**) **quisiera, quisieras, quisiera, quisiéramos, quisierais, quisieran**
	(**-se**) **quisiese, quisieses, quisiese, quisiésemos, quisieseis, quisiesen**

(**reír** *see* p. 323)

saber to know

Present Indicative	**sé, sabes, sabe, sabemos, sabéis, saben**
Preterite	**supe, supiste, supo, supimos, supisteis, supieron**
Future	**sabré, sabrás, sabrá, sabremos, sabréis, sabrán**
Conditional	**sabría, sabrías, sabría, sabríamos, sabríais, sabrían**
Present Subjunctive	**sepa, sepas, sepa, sepamos, sepáis, sepan**
Imperfect Subjunctive	(**-ra**) **supiera, supieras, supiera, supiéramos, supierais, supieran**
	(**-se**) **supiese, supieses, supiese, supiésemos, supieseis, supiesen**

salir to go out, leave

Present Indicative	**salgo, sales, sale, salimos, salís, salen**
Future	**saldré, saldrás, saldrá, saldremos, saldréis, saldrán**
Conditional	**saldría, saldrías, saldría, saldríamos, saldríais, saldrían**
Present Subjunctive	**salga, salgas, salga, salgamos, salgáis, salgan**
Imperative	**sal, salid**

ser to be

Present Indicative	**soy, eres, es, somos, sois, son**
Imperfect Indicative	**era, eras, era, éramos, erais, eran**

Preterite	**fui, fuiste, fue, fuimos, fuisteis, fueron**
Present Subjunctive	**sea, seas, sea, seamos, seáis, sean**
Imperfect Subjunctive	**(-ra) fuera, fueras, fuera, fuéramos, fuerais, fueran**
	(-se) fuese, fueses, fuese, fuésemos, fueseis, fuesen
Imperative	**sé, sed**

tener to have

Present Indicative	**tengo, tienes, tiene, tenemos, tenéis, tienen**
Preterite	**tuve, tuviste, tuvo, tuvimos, tuvisteis, tuvieron**
Future	**tendré, tendrás, tendrá, tendremos, tendréis, tendrán**
Conditional	**tendría, tendrías, tendría, tendríamos, tendríais, tendrían**
Present Subjunctive	**tenga, tengas, tenga, tengamos, tengáis, tengan**
Imperfect Subjunctive	**(-ra) tuviera, tuvieras, tuviera, tuviéramos, tuvierais, tuvieran**
	(-se) tuviese, tuvieses, tuviese, tuviésemos, tuvieseis, tuviesen
Imperative	**ten, tened**

traer to bring

Present Indicative	**traigo, traes, trae, traemos, traéis, traen**
Preterite	**traje, trajiste, trajo, trajimos, trajisteis, trajeron**
Present Subjunctive	**traiga, traigas, traiga, traigamos, traigáis, traigan**
Imperfect Subjunctive	**(-ra) trajera, trajeras, trajera, trajéramos, trajerais, trajeran**
	(-se) trajese, trajeses, trajese, trajésemos, trajeseis, trajesen
Present Participle	**trayendo**
Past Participle	**traído**

valer to be worth

Present Indicative	**valgo, vales, vale, valemos, valéis, valen**
Future	**valdré, valdrás, valdrá, valdremos, valdréis, valdrán**
Conditional	**valdría, valdrías, valdría, valdríamos, valdríais, valdrían**
Present Subjunctive	**valga, valgas, valga, valgamos, valgáis, valgan**
Imperative	**val(e), valed**

venir to come

Present Indicative	**vengo, vienes, viene, venimos, venís, vienen**
Preterite	**vine, viniste, vino, vinimos, vinisteis, vinieron**
Future	**vendré, vendrás, vendrá, vendremos, vendréis, vendrán**
Conditional	**vendría, vendrías, vendría, vendríamos, vendríais, vendrían**
Present Subjunctive	**venga, vengas, venga, vengamos, vengáis, vengan**
Imperfect Subjunctive	(**-ra**) **viniera, vinieras, viniera, viniéramos, vinierais, vinieran**
	(**-se**) **viniese, vinieses, viniese, viniésemos, vinieseis, viniesen**
Present Participle	**viniendo**
Imperative	**ven, venid**

ver to see

Present Indicative	**veo, ves, ve, vemos, veis, ven**
Imperfect Indicative	**veía, veías, veía, veíamos, veíais, veían**
Present Subjunctive	**vea, veas, vea, veamos, veáis, vean**
Past Participle	**visto**

C

GLOSSARY OF GRAMMATICAL TERMS

Active voice: A construction in which the subject does the action of the verb. *John buys the book.*

Adjective: A word that is used to describe a noun: *high* mountain, *interesting* book.

Adverb: A word that modifies a verb, an adjective, or another adverb. It answers the questions "Where?" "How?" "When?": He will be *there*. They do it *well*. I will see you *soon*.

Agree (agreement): A term generally applied to adjectives. An adjective is said to agree or show agreement with the noun it modifies, when its ending changes in accordance with the gender and number of the noun. In Spanish, a feminine, singular noun, for instance, will require a feminine, singular ending in the adjective that describes it: **camisa blanca;** and a masculine, plural noun will require a masculine, plural ending in the adjective: **zapatos rojos.**

Apposition: When a noun or a pronoun is placed after another noun or pronoun in order to explain it, it is said to be in apposition to that noun or pronoun: John Smith, *president* of the company.

Article: See *Definite article* and *Indefinite article.*

Auxiliary verb: A verb which *helps* in the conjugation of another verb: I *have* spoken. We *will* play. They *were* called.

Clause: A group of words that includes at least a subject and a verb and forms part or the whole of a sentence. The following sentence consists of two clauses: We saw the boy *who set fire to the house.*

Comparison: The change in the endings of adjectives and adverbs to denote degree. There are three levels of comparison: the *positive* (warm), the *comparative* (warmer), and the *superlative* (warmest).

Compound tense: A tense formed by the auxiliary verb *have* and the past participle: *We will have eaten.*

Conjugation: The process by which the forms of the verb are given in their different moods and tenses: *I am, you are, he is,* etc.

Conjunction: A word which serves as a link between words, phrases, clauses, or sentences: *and, but, that, because*, etc.

Definite article: A word standing before a noun and indicating a definite person and thing: *The* house.

Demonstrative: A word *pointing* to a definite person or object: *this, that, these*, etc.

Dependent (**or subordinate**) **clause:** A clause which by itself has no complete meaning, but depends on an independent, or principal, clause: I did not know *that he was ill.*

Dependent infinitive: An infinitive that follows a verb or, in Spanish, a preposition: He wants *to rest.*

Diphthong: A combination of two vowels forming one syllable. In Spanish, a diphthong is composed of one *strong* vowel (**a, e, o**) and one *weak* vowel (**u, i**) or two weak vowels: **ai, oi, ui.** Remember: *U* and *I* are weak, and everyone else is strong.

Exclamation: A word used to express emotion: *How* beautiful! *What* grace!

Finite verb form: Any form of the verb except the infinitive and the present and past participles.

Gender: A distinction of nouns, pronouns, or adjectives, based on sex denoted. In Spanish, there are only two types of nouns, *masculine* and *feminine*, but there are neuter pronouns.

Gerund: In English, a noun which is formed from a verb and shows the ending *-ing*: *Drinking* is bad for the health. In Spanish, the infinitive takes the place of the gerund in this sense. The present participle in Spanish is also called the gerund.

Indefinite adjective and pronoun: Words which refer to an indefinite person or thing. Important indefinite adjectives are *any* and *some*, and important indefinite pronouns are *somebody, someone, nobody*, and *no one.*

Indefinite article: A word standing before a noun and indicating an indefinite person or object: *A* man, *an* article.

Independent (**or principal**) **clause:** A clause which has complete meaning by itself: *I shall tell it to him* when he comes.

Infinitive: The form of the verb generally preceded in English by the word *to* and showing no subject or number: *to speak, to sleep.*

Interrogative: A word used in asking a question: *Who? What? Which?*

Intransitive verb: A verb which cannot have a direct object: The man *goes* away.

Modify: To describe a noun, adjective, or adverb, or the action expressed by the verb: A *good* man (adj.), he drives *poorly* (adv.).

Mood: A change in the form of the verb, showing the manner in which its action is expressed. There are three moods: *indicative, subjunctive*, and *imperative.*

Nonrestrictive clause: A clause which is not essential to the meaning of a sentence and is generally set off from the rest of the sentence by commas: My friend Joe, *who has just returned from Europe*, will come to see me tomorrow.

Noun: A word that names a person, place, thing, etc.: *Henry*, *Paris*, *table*, etc.

Number: Number refers to *singular* and *plural*.

Object: Generally a noun or a pronoun that is the receiver of the verb's action. A direct object answers the question "What?" or "Whom?": I see *him*. Do *it*. An indirect object answers the question "To whom?" or "To what?": Give *Mary* the ball. Nouns and pronouns can also be objects of prepositions: This book is *for Mary*. He was speaking *of you*.

Passive voice: A construction in which the subject receives the action of the verb: *The window was broken by Charles.*

Past participle: That form of the verb having in English the endings *-ed*, *-t*, *-en*, etc. (*raised*, *wept*, *eaten*, etc.), and in Spanish, usually the ending **-do** (**hablado**).

Person: The form of the pronoun and of the verb that shows the person referred to. There are three persons: *I*, *we*, *me*, *us*, *mine*, *our*, etc. (first person); *you*, *thou*, *your*, etc. (second person); *he*, *she*, *it*, *they*, *him*, *her*, *their*, etc. (third person). In Spanish, the polite forms **Ud.** and **Uds.** (*you*) are in the third person.

Phrase: A group of two or more words used together to form a part of speech, but not containing a subject and verb. Most phrases are introduced by prepositions: They stayed *in the hotel.*

Possessive: A word that denotes ownership or possession: *My* hat is bigger than *hers*.

Predicate: That part of a sentence which contains the verb and states something about the subject: The students of this class *have been studying very hard.*

Predicate adjective: An adjective which is used after many verbs of being (*to be*, *to seem*, *to become*, etc.) and which describes the subject: My friend is *poor*.

Predicate noun: A noun which is used after a number of intransitive verbs (*to be*, *to seem*, *to become*, etc.) and which is the equivalent of the subject: That man is an engineer.

Preposition: A word that introduces a noun, pronoun, adverb, infinitive, or present participle, and which indicates their function in the sentence. The group of words so introduced is known as a prepositional phrase: I plunged *into the water.*

Present participle: In English, an invariable verb form ending in *-ing*; They were *singing*. It may also be used as an adjective or a noun: The *singing* birds. *Singing* is fun. In Spanish, the present participle may be used only as a verb.

Pronoun: A word that is used to replace a noun: *he*, *us*, *them*, etc. A subject pronoun refers to the person or thing that is spoken of: *He* eats. *It* is beautiful. An *object pronoun* receives the action of the verb: He sees *us* (direct object pronoun). He spoke to *them* (indirect object pronoun).

A pronoun can also be the object of a preposition: They went with *me*.

Reflexive pronoun: A pronoun that refers back to the subject: *myself*, *yourself*, *himself*, etc. A reflexive pronoun is the object of a verb (he punished *himself*) or of a preposition (I prepared it for *myself*).

Relative pronoun: A pronoun that introduces a dependent clause and refers back to a previously mentioned noun: I saw the man *who* did it. In this sentence the antecedent is the word *man*.

Restrictive clause: A clause that is essential to the meaning of the whole sentence and cannot be dispensed with. I asked for the room *which I had occupied two years before*.

Simple tense: A tense which is not formed with the auxiliary verb *to have*: I *go*, we *saw*, etc.

Subject: The person, place, or thing that is spoken of: *John* sleeps, The *tree* is old.

Subordinate clause: See *Dependent clause*.

Superlative: See *Comparison*.

Tense: The group of forms in a verb which serves to show the time in which the action of the verb takes place.

Transitive verb: A verb that may have a direct object: Henry *eats* the apple.

Verb: A word that expresses an action or a state: He *works*. The rose *is* red. In Spanish, *regular* verbs follow a set pattern in which the stem (the infinitive minus the ending) remains unchanged (except for a *patterned* change in the case of radical changing verbs) and only the endings show a change determined by the person and the tense. *Irregular* verbs show deviations from the set pattern in the stem as well as in the endings. In *radical changing* verbs the stem vowel changes when *stressed* or in certain other situations, but a systematic pattern is always followed. The endings are regular.

D

NUMBERS, NAMES, AND GENDER

CARDINAL NUMBERS

0 **cero**
1 **uno** (*m.*), **una** (*f.*)
2 **dos**
3 **tres**
4 **cuatro**
5 **cinco**
6 **seis**
7 **siete**
8 **ocho**
9 **nueve**
10 **diez**
11 **once**
12 **doce**
13 **trece**
14 **catorce**
15 **quince**
16 **dieciséis (diez y seis)**
17 **diecisiete (diez y siete)**
18 **dieciocho (diez y ocho)**
19 **diecinueve (diez y nueve)**
20 **veinte**
21 **veintiuno, -a (veinte y uno, -a)**
22 **veintidós (veinte y dos)**
23 **veintitrés (veinte y tres)**
24 **veinticuatro (veinte y cuatro)**
25 **veinticinco (veinte y cinco)**
26 **veintiséis (veinte y seis)**
27 **veintisiete (veinte y siete)**
28 **veintiocho (veinte y ocho)**
29 **veintinueve (veinte y nueve)**
30 **treinta**
31 **treinta y uno, -a**[1]
40 **cuarenta**
50 **cincuenta**
60 **sesenta**
70 **setenta**

[1] Above 29, the one-word forms are not used.

80	**ochenta**	1100	**mil ciento**
90	**noventa**	1200	**mil doscientos, -as**
100	**ciento** (**cien**)	2000	**dos mil**
101	**ciento uno, -a**	100,000	**cien mil**
110	**ciento diez**	200,000	**doscientos,** (**-as**) **mil**
200	**doscientos, -as**	1,000,000	**un millón**
300	**trescientos, -as**	2,000,000	**dos millones**
400	**cuatrocientos, -as**	5,637,215	**cinco millones seiscientos** (**-as**) **treinta y siete mil doscientos** (**-as**) **quince**
500	**quinientos, -as**		
600	**seiscientos, -as**		
700	**setecientos, -as**		
800	**ochocientos, -as**		
900	**novecientos, -as**		
1000	**mil**		

Note that **uno** becomes **un** before a masculine noun; that **ciento,** which in the plural shows agreement in gender, becomes **cien** before a noun and before **mil** and **millones;** that **millón** is a masculine noun preceded in the singular by the indefinite article and followed by the preposition **de** before a following noun.

treinta y un libros thrity-one books
ciento dos[2] **mesas** one hundred and two tables
cien mujeres one hundred women
cien mil hombres one hundred thousand men
trescientas treinta copias three hundred and thirty copies
un millón de habitantes one million inhabitants

Beyond nine hundred the form **mil** must be used:

mil novecientos cincuenta y siete	Nineteen (hundred) fifty-seven
Gana tres mil seiscientos dólares al año.	He earns thirty-six hundred dollars per year.

ORDINAL NUMBERS

1st	**primer(o), -a**	6th	**sexto, -a**
2nd	**segundo, -a**	7th	**séptimo, -a**
3rd	**tercer(o), -a**	8th	**octavo, -a**
4th	**cuarto, -a**	9th	**noveno, -a**
5th	**quinto, -a**	10th	**décimo, -a**

Note that **primero** and **tercero** drop the **o** before a masculine singular noun, that with dates of the month only **primero** may be used, and that beyond **décimo** cardinal numbers are generally used.

[2] Note the omission of **y**.

el primer soldado the first solider
el tercer presidente the third president
el primero de abril April first
el dos de marzo March second
la Quinta Avenida Fifth Avenue
la Calle Ochenta y Seis Eighty-Sixth Street
Carlos Tercero[3] Charles the Third
Alfonso Doce Alfonso the Twelfth

When the ordinal number has a descriptive function, it precedes the noun. When its purpose is to distinguish one thing from another, it follows the noun.

FRACTIONS

Through *tenth*, ordinal numbers are used, except in the case of *half* and *third*, where **medio** and **tercio** are used respectively. **Medio,** used with a noun, is an adjective[4] and therefore shows agreement. No article appears before it, nor before the accompanying noun. Above *tenth*, **-avo** is usually added to the cardinal number, though there are some irregular forms. The feminine noun **mitad,** which is preceded by the article **la** and followed by the preposition **de** before a noun, is used to indicate half of a definite amount.

un medio one-half
dos tercios two-thirds
tres cuartos three-fourths
un octavo one-eighth
un décimo one-tenth
siete quinzavos seven-fifteenths
un décimosexto one-sixteenth
un décimonono one-nineteenth
un veintavo one-twentieth
media taza half a cup
hora y media an hour and a half
la mitad de sus discos half of his records

La tercera parte, la quinta parte, la décima parte, etc. may be used when the upper numeral of the fraction is *one*: one-third, one-fifth, one-tenth, etc.

TIME OF DAY

Time of day is expressed by the cardinal numbers preceded by the article **la (las)**. The verb *to be* is translated by **ser.**

¿Qué hora es?	What time is it?
¿Qué hora era?	What time was it?
Es la una.	It is one o'clock.
Son las dos.	It is two o'clock.
Era la una.	It was one o'clock.

[3] Note the omission of the definite article with titles of royalty, rulers, etc.
[4] **Medio** can also be used as an adverb: **No estaba más que medio despierto.** *He was only half-awake.*

Eran las cinco.	It was five o'clock.
Es la una y cuarto.	It is a quarter past one.
Son las tres y media.	It is half-past three.
Eran las nueve menos cuarto.	It was a quarter to nine.
Eran las ocho y veinte.	It was twenty past eight.
Son las diez menos diez.	It is ten to ten.
A las siete en punto	At seven o'clock sharp
A las diez de la mañana	At ten o'clock in the morning
A las cuatro de la tarde	At four o'clock in the afternoon
A las once de la noche	At eleven o'clock at night
A mediodía	At noon
A medianoche	At midnight

DAYS OF THE WEEK

lunes Monday
martes Tuesday
miércoles Wednesday
jueves Thursday
viernes Friday
sábado Saturday
domingo Sunday

el lunes on Monday
los jueves on Thursdays

MONTHS OF THE YEAR

enero January
febrero February
marzo March
abril April
mayo May
junio June
julio July
agosto August
se(p)tiembre September
octubre October
noviembre November
diciembre December

el primero de febrero February 1st
el dos de marzo March 2nd
el diecisiete de junio June 17th

SEASONS

la primavera spring
el verano summer
el otoño fall
el invierno winter

GENDER

All nouns in Spanish are either masculine or feminine. There are no neuter nouns.

A. Masculine nouns

The following types of nouns are generally masculine.

1. Nouns that refer to a masculine person

el hijo the son — **el padre** the father
el dentista the dentist — **el policía** the policeman

2. Nouns ending in **o**

el fonógrafo the phonograph — **el suelo** the floor

The most common exception is

la mano the hand

3. Certain nouns (of Greek origin) ending in **-ma, -ta, -pa**

el mapa the map — **el poeta** the poet
el clima the climate — **el sistema** the system
el programa the program — **el déspota** the despot

4. Infinitives used as nouns

El vivir aquí cuesta mucho. Living here costs a great deal.
El comer demasiado es peligroso. Eating too much is dangerous.

B. Feminine Nouns

The following categories are generally feminine.

1. Nouns that refer to a female being

la mujer the woman — **la escritora** the writer
la emperatriz the empress — **la artista** the artist

2. Nouns ending in **-a,** except if they refer to a male being

la barba the beard — **la ropa** the dress
la mejilla the cheek — **la periodista** the newspaperwoman

The most important exceptions to this rule are the Greek nouns ending in **-ma, -pa, -ta,** referred to above and **el día** the day.

Note also that **la persona** and **la víctima** are always feminine, even when referring to male beings. Nouns ending in **-ista** are either masculine or feminine, according to the person to whom they refer.

el turista, la turista the tourist
el artista, la artista the artist

3. All nouns ending in **-ción, -tad, -dad, -tud,** and **-umbre,** and most nouns that end in **-ie** and **-ión**

   The endings **-ción** and **-ión** correspond regularly to the English *-tion* and *-ion*, **-dad** and **-tad** to the English *-ty* and **-tud** to the English *-tude*.

   la nacíon the nation — **la libertad** liberty
   la unión the union — **la multitud** the multitude
   la ciudad the city — **la costumbre** the custom
   la serie the series

PLURAL OF NOUNS

Nouns are made plural by adding **-s** to a final vowel, **-es** to a final consonant or to a stressed final **-í** or **-ú.** Nouns that end in **-z** change the **-z** to **-c** before **-es.**

casa, casas — **rubí, rubíes**
mujer, mujeres — **lápiz, lápices**
lección, lecciones — **bambú, bambúes**

Notice that the addition of another syllable often makes the accent mark on the singular form unnecessary.

E

PUNCTUATION, CAPITALIZATION, AND SYLLABICATION

PUNCTUATION AND CAPITALIZATION

1. An inverted question mark is placed at the beginning of the interrogative part of the sentence and an inverted exclamation point is placed at the beginning of the exclamatory part of the sentence:

¿Cómo está Ud.?	How are you?
Es buen estudiante, ¿verdad?	He is a good student, isn't he?
¡Por Dios!	For Heaven's sake!
Está vivo, ¡gracias a Dios!	He is alive, thank God!

2. Instead of quotation marks, a dash is generally used in Spanish to indicate a change of speaker in a dialogue:

—¿Cuánto valen estos zapatos, señor García?	"How much are these shoes, Mr. García?"
—Se los dejo en diez pesos.	"I'll let you have them for ten pesos."

3. In Spanish, the names of languages, nationalities, days of the week, and months are not capitalized. The names of countries *are*.

Hablamos francés.	We speak French.
Es un escritor alemán.	He is a German writer.
La reunión tendrá lugar (**el**) **viernes, el dieciséis de marzo.**	The meeting will take place on Friday, March 16th.

But:

La reina de Inglaterra...	The Queen of England . . .

4. **Usted(es), señor(es),** and **don** are capitalized only when abbreviated.

Siéntese Ud. (usted).	Sit down.
Muy señores míos:	Dear Sirs:
Buenos días, Sr. Blanco.	Good morning, Mr. Blanco.
Acabo de hablar con D. Fernando Plaza.	I have just spoken with Don Fernando Plaza.
¿Has visto ya a don Enrique?	Have you seen Don Enrique yet?

5. Accent marks need not appear on capital letters. The *tilde*, however, because it signals a separate letter, cannot be deleted from capitals.

MEJICO, ESPAÑA	Mexico, Spain

SYLLABICATION

1. A single consonant, including the combinations **ch, ll, rr,** must go with the following vowel: **pa-lo-ma, ca-ba-llo, mu-cha-cho.**
2. Consonant groups between vowels are usually separated: **cas-ta, sal-do, mar-ca.**
3. If the second consonant is **l** or **r,** the combination cannot usually be separated: **Pa-blo, po-tro, o-tra.**
4. In groups of more than two consonants, only the last consonant (or inseparable combination of consonant followed by **l** or **r**) goes with the next vowel: **cons-tan-te, des-pren-der, den-tro.**

VOCABULARIES

Spanish–English

English–Spanish

The gender of all nouns, except masculine nouns ending in **-o** and feminine nouns ending in **-a,** or nouns that refer to a masculine or feminine person, is indicated by *m.* or *f.* Parts of speech are abbreviated as follows: *n.* noun; *v.* verb; *adj.* adjective; *adv.* adverb; *conj.* conjunction; *prep.* preposition; *pron.* pronoun; *refl.* reflexive; *part.* participle; *rel.* relative; *dem.* demonstrative. Radical changing verbs are followed by the change that the verb undergoes placed in parentheses. Thus: **perder** (**ie**), **pedir** (**i**), **contar** (**ue**). Irregular verbs that appear in full in the verb reference guide are marked with an asterisk. Verbs derived from these are also marked with an asterisk. Thus: ***componer, *detener.** The conjugation of verbs ending in **-ducir** may be found under **conducir.** Thus: ***producir, *traducir.** Verbs of the types of **huir** and **conocer,** and those that have a change in accentuation are followed by the ending of the first person singular of the present indicative placed in parentheses. Thus: **destruir** (**uyo**), **merecer** (**zco**), **enviar** (**ío**). Spelling-changing verbs show the affected consonant in italics: **co*g*er, sa*c*ar.** The Spanish-English vocabulary includes all verbs and idioms that appear in the reading passages and exercises, except for exact or close cognates. The English-Spanish vocabulary includes all words and idioms that are used in the exercises.

SPANISH–ENGLISH VOCABULARY

A

a to; at
abandonar to leave; abandon, give up
abierto open, opened
abismo abyss
abogado lawyer
abrigo (over)coat
abuelo grandfather
acabar to finish; **— de** (+ *infin.*) to have just (*present and imperfect only*)
acaramelados engrossed in each other
acaso perhaps
acceso access, approach
acción *f.* action; effect; share (of stock)
acechar to waylay, ambush
aceptar accept
acer*c*ar(se) to approach
acero steel
acompañar to accompany
aconsejar to advise
acostar(se) (**ue**) to lie down, go to bed
acreditar to accredit; enhance
actitud *f.* attitude
actual present, current
actuación *f.* conduct, action
actuar (**úo**) to act
acudir to hasten
acuerdo agreement; ***estar de —** to agree
adentro inside, within; **tierra —** inland
adhesión *f.* adherence
adivino fortuneteller
adquisición *f.* acquisition
advenimiento advent
aéreo aerial
afectivo emotional
afecto affection
afectuoso affectionate
afeitar(se) to shave
afirmar to state, affirm
afueras *f. pl.* suburbs, outskirts
agitado upset; rough (sea)
agradable pleasant
agua water
aguja needle
ahí there (near you)
ahora now
al + *infin.* upon or in (doing something)
ala wing
alamares *m. pl.* bullfighter's adornments
alargar(se) to stretch out, extend
alcoba bedroom
alegar to allege
alcaldesa mayor's wife
alcan*z*ar to reach; attain
alegrarse (**de**) to be happy
alegría joy
alejarse to go away, move off
alemán German
alfombra rug
algo something; **en —** in some way, to some extent; **— de** a little bit of
algodón *m.* cotton
algún (**alguno, a, os, as**) some
aligerar to hold up (*colloq.*)
alimenticio *adj.* (referring to) food
alma soul
almacén *m.* store; warehouse
almor*z*ar to have lunch
alto tall; high; loud; **en voz alta** aloud
altura height
aluminio aluminum
alumno student
aluni*z*ar to land on the moon
allí there
amable nice (a person)
amarillo yellow
ambicionar to hope to
amado beloved
amargamente bitterly
amargo bitter
Amazonas *m. sing.* Amazon
ambiente *m.* atmosphere
ambulante *n.* ambulance attendant
amenaza threat
amena*z*ar to threaten
amigo friend
amistad *f.* friendship
amor *m.* love
ampliar(ío) to amplify, enlarge; extend
amplio ample; full
analfabeto illiterate
andaluz Andalusian
***andar** to walk (about); go
anciano aged
angustia anguish
animar to animate
aniquilamiento annihilation

anoche last night
ante before; faced with
anteriormente previously
antes *adv.* before(hand); **— de** *prep.* before; **— de que** *conj.* before (+ *clause*)
antiguo old; ancient; former
anunciar to announce
anuncio announcement; **— comercial** or **publicitario** advertisement
añadir to add
año year
apagar to turn off or out; extinguish
aparato apparatus, machine; vehicle; plane
aparecer (zco) to appear
apasionado passionate, ardent
apasionar to excite, impassion
apenas hardly
aplazar to postpone
aplicar to apply
apoderado (bullfighter's) manager
apoyo support
aprender (a) to learn (to)
aprendizaje *m.* apprenticeship
aprobar (ue) to approve
apropiado *adj.* appropriate
aprovechado outstanding
aprovechar to take advantage of
apto apt; pertinent
aquel (aquella, os, as) that; those (yonder)
aquello that (neuter)
aquí here; **por —** around here
aeródromo airport
árbol *m.* tree
arqueólogo archeologist
arreglar to arrange; fix
arrepentirse (ie) to repent
arriba above; upstairs
arroz *m.* rice
artículo article
asaltar to assault, attack
asalto assault
ascender (ie) to rise up to, reach
asegurador insuring; **compañía —a** insurance company
asegurar to assure; say for certain
asemejarse to resemble
asequible within the grasp (of)
asesinato murder; assassination
así thus; so; this way; **— que** as soon as; so (+ *clause*)
asignatura course, subject
asistir a to attend
astro star; male movie star
astrólogo astrologist
asunto matter
asustar to frighten
atormentar to torment
atracador holdup man, robber
atraco holdup
atractivo *n.* charm
atrás behind
aumentar to increase
aun even
aún still
aunque although; even though
ausente *adj.* absent; *n.* absentee, absent person
autobús *m.* bus
autodeterminación self-determination
automovilista driver
aventurar(se a) to risk
avanzar to advance
averiguar (güe) to ascertain
avión *m.* airplane; **en** *or* **por —** by plane
avioneta small plane
avisar to advise; warn
ayer yesterday
ayuda *n.* help
ayudar to help
azotar to last
azúcar *m.* sugar
azul blue

B

bachillerato Bachelor's degree
bailar to dance
bajar to lower; go down
bajo *adj.* low; short (in height); *prep.* under
bandido bandit
banquero banker
baño bath
baratija trinket
barato cheap(ly)
barba beard
barco ship
barrer to sweep
barrio district, neighborhood
basar to base
base *f.* base; basis
bastante enough, quite, rather
beber drink
bebida *n.* drink
beca scholarship
béisbol *m.* baseball
bello beautiful (*poetic*); **bellas artes** fine arts

***ben*decir** to bless
bien well; **Está —.** All right.
bolsa purse
bolsillo pocket
bolso purse
bombilla light bulb
bordo: a — on board
bosque *m.* forest
botar to launch
botella bottle
botín *m.* booty, loot
botijo jug, pitcher
brasileño Brazilian
brecha gap; **abrir una —** make an inroad
brillante *adj.* brilliant; shining; *m.* diamond
brillo glow, shine
broche *m.* broach
broma joke
bronceado bronzed, suntanned
buen(o) good
bufanda scarf
burlar to trick, fool; **—se de** to make fun of
busca search
bus*c*ar to look for

C

caballo horse
***caber** to fit; **No cabe duda (de)...** There is no doubt . . .
cabeza head
cacería hunt
cada each, every; **— vez más** more and more
***caer** to fall; **—se** to fall down
café *m.* coffee; cafe
caja box, crate
cajón *m.* drawer
calcetín *m.* sock
calidad *f.* quality
caliente hot
califi*c*ar (de) to classify, consider (as)
calificativo term, name
calor *m.* heat, warmth; **hacer —** to be warm (out); **tener —** to be (feel) warm
caluroso heated (*fig.*)
callar(se) to hush; stop talking
calle *f.* street
cama bed
cambiar to change; exchange
cambio change; **en —** on the other hand
camino road; **— de** on the way to
camión *m.* truck
camisa shirt
campo field; country (*opp. of* city); **casa de —** summer house
canción *f.* song
cansado tired
cansador tiring
cansar(se) to tire (oneself); get tired
cantar to sing
cantidad *f.* amount
capaz capable
capítulo chapter
capuchino Capuchin monk
cara face; **tener mala —** to look bad
carne *f.* meat
carrera career; profession; race
carretera highway; road
carroza carriage
carta letter
cartel *m.* sign; poster
cartelito: — del precio price tag
cartera wallet
casa house; **a —** (to) home; **en —** at home
casamiento marriage; wedding
casar(se con) to marry
casi almost
caso case; **en — de que** in case
castellano Castilian
casti*g*ar to punish
caucho rubber
causa cause; (law) case; demand
cautela caution
cautiverio captivity
cazador hunter
ca*z*ar to hunt
celebrar to take place; celebrate
cenicero ashtray
censura censure, reprimand
centavo cent
centro center; middle; city
cepillar to brush
cerca *adv.* near(by); **— de** *prep.* near; nearly
cercanías *f. pl.* outskirts
cerco siege; enclosing circle
cerrar (ie) to close
cerro hill
certero sure, accurate
cerveza beer
ciego blind
cien(to) one hundred; **por —** percent **al seis por —** at six percent
ciencia science
cincuenta fifty

científico scientific
cierto certain; a certain
cigarrillo cigarette
cine *m.* movies; movie theater
circo circus
círculo circle
cirugía surgery; **— estética** plastic surgery
cirujano surgeon
citar to cite; quote
ciudad *f.* city
claridad *f.* clarity
claro clear; fair (light); **¡Claro está!** Of course!
clase *f.* class; classroom; class, kind, type
clínica doctor's office; clinic
cobrar to charge
cobre *m.* copper
coche *m.* car
cocinar to cook
co*g*er to catch
coleta (hair) queue; **cortarse la —** to leave the bullfighting profession
colina hill
colo*c*ar to place
collar *m.* necklace
comer to eat; **— se** eat up
cometer to commit; **— una falta** to do wrong
como as; like
¿Cómo? How? What did you say?
comparación *f.* comparison
comparar to compare
compensar to compensate
complacencia complacency
complementario additional
comportarse to behave
compra purchase
comprador purchaser
comprar to buy
comprobar (ue) to prove
compromiso engagement
compuesto compound
común common
comunicado communiqué
con with
concluir (uyo) to conclude
concurrir a to attend
condenar to sentence; condemn
condición *f.* condition (*often pl.*); quality, trait
con*ducir to lead
confiar (ío) to confide; trust
confirmar to confirm
conformación *f.* conformation, shape
conocer (zco) to know (a person); to be familiar or acquainted with; (*preterite*) met
conocimiento knowledge (*often pl.*); consciousness
conque so (+ *clause*)
conquistar to conquer
consagrar to uphold; consecrate
conse*gu*ir (i) to obtain, get
consejo(s) advice
conservador conservative
consigo with him(self)
consistir (en) to consist (of)
consolar (ue) to console
construir (uyo) to construct
consumidor consumer
contar (ue) to count; tell, relate; **— con** to count on; have
contemplar to contemplate
contemporáneo contemporary
con*tener to contain
contertulio person present at a social gathering
contestar to answer
continuar (úo) to continue
continuamente continually
contra against
con*traer to contract; **— matrimonio** marry
contrariedad *f.* reverse
contratiempo reverse, upset; disappointment
contrato contract
contribuir (uyo) to contribute
convencer (a) to convince
con*venir to be suitable, wise, fitting
convertir (ie) to convert; **—se en** to become
convento convent; monastery
copa goblet, glass; (a) drink
corbata tie
corona crown
corrector(a) corrective
correo mail
Correos the Post Office
corrida bullfight
cortar to cut; cut off
corte *f.* court
corto short (in length)
cosa thing
cosecha crop
coser to sew
costar (ue) to cost; **— trabajo** to be difficult
costilla rib
costumbre *f.* custom

crear to create
crecer (zco) to grow
creciente increasing; growing
***creer** to believe
criada maid, servant
criadero animal farm; kennel
criado servant
cristalizarse to come to a head
criticar to criticize
crueldad *f.* cruelty
cuaderno notebook
cuadro picture; painting
¿Cuál? Which?
cualquier(a) any; anyone (at all)
cuanto all that; **en —** as soon as
¿Cuánto (a, os, as)? How much? How many? **¿Cuántos años tiene Ud.?** How old are you?
cuarenta forty
cuarto fourth; quarter; room
cubierto (de) covered (with)
cubrir (*past part.* **cubierto**) to cover
cuello neck; collar
cuando when; **de vez en —** from time to time
¿Cuándo? When?
cuantioso large; numerous
cuenta bill; account; **darse — de** to realize; **por su —** on his (your) own
cuerna horns
cuerpo body
cuidado care; carefulness; **con —** carefully
cuidar (de) to take care (of); care (for); **—se** to be careful
culpa guilt
cumplir to complete; fulfill
cuneta roadside ditch

CH

chaqueta jacket
charla speech, talk
chico *n.* boy; *adj.* small
chiquitín *adj.* very small
chisme(s) *m.* (*pl.*) gossip, stories
chocar to shock; collide
choza hut
chuleta(s) cribbing, cheating (*colloq.*)

D

dado que granted that
dañar to injure
daño damage; **hacer —** to hurt; **daños y perjuicios** damages (law)
***dar** to give; to hit (the mark); **— a conocer** to reveal; **— media vuelta** turn half around; **miedo** frighten; **— muerte** kill; **— un paso** take a step; **— una vuelta** take a ride, walk, turn, etc.; **—se cuenta de** realize
de of; from; since; as; **— muchacho, — niño** as a boy; **— repente** suddenly
deber to be obliged to; should, ought to; *m.* duty
decepción *f.* deception; disappointment
decidir(se a) to decide (to)
***decir** to say; tell; **oír — a alguien** to hear (someone) say; **querer —** to mean, imply
declarado open, overt
declarar to declare
declinarse to be declined (a word)
dedicar to dedicate
definido definite
dejar to let, allow; leave (behind); **— de** to stop (doing something); to fail to
delgado thin; slim
demás: lo — the rest (what is left); **los, las —** the rest, the others
demasiado *adv.* too much; *adj.* too much; *pl.* too many
demorar to delay; **—se** take a long time
demostrar (ue) to show, demonstrate
dentro *adv.* inside, within; **— de** *prep.* inside, within
denunciar to inform of
depender (de) to depend (on)
deportivo sporting, athletic
derecho *adj.* right; *n.* right, privilege; law profession
derribar to knock down; overthrow
derrota defeat
desangrar(se) to bleed
desaparecer (zco) to disappear
desparramado scattered
desarrollar(se) to develop
desarrollo development
desayunar(se) to eat breakfast
descubrimiento discovery
descubrir (*past part.* **descubierto**) to discover
desde *prep.* from; since; **— que** *conj.* since (time)
desear to desire; wish
desempeñar to fill (a job, etc.); **— un papel** to play a role

desgracia misfortune
desgraciado unfortunate
desheredar to disinherit
despacho office
despegar to take off (a plane)
despellejar to skin alive (*fig.*)
después *adv.* after(wards), later; **— de** *prep.* after; **— de que** *conj.* after (+ *clause*)
despertar(**se**) (**ie**) to awaken
desprestigiar to take down (a reputation)
destacado outstanding
destinar to destine
destino destiny, fate; **punto de —** fate, outcome
destruir (**uyo**) to destroy
desván *m.* attic
detalle *m.* detail
*__de__*tener* to stop; arrest; **—se** stop
determinado a certain; determined
determinar to determine
devolver (**ue**) (*past part.* **devuelto**) to return (something), give back
día *m.* day; **hoy** (**en**) **—** nowadays
diario *adj.* daily; **a —** each day; *n.* newspaper
dibujante artist, sketcher
dibujar to draw
dibujo sketch
dicho aforesaid
diecinueve nineteen
diente *m.* tooth
diez ten
diferenciar(**se**) to differ
difícil difficult; unlikely
diluvio flood, deluge
dinero money
diputado delegate
dirección *f.* address; direction
director principal; director
dirigir to direct; **—se** (**a**) address; go toward
disco (phonograph) record
discurso speech
discutir to discuss; argue
disgusto unpleasantness
disparo shot; **hacer un —** fire a shot
dispuesto ready; willing
distar to be distant
distinguir to distinguish
*__dis__*traer*__se__ to amuse oneself
divertirse (**ie**) to enjoy oneself; have a good time
dolor *m.* pain
dolorido sorrowful
domingo Sunday
dominar to dominate
donde where
¿Dónde? Where?
dorado golden; gilded
dormir (**ue**) to sleep; **—se** to fall asleep
droga drug
duda doubt
dudar to doubt
dudoso doubtful
dueño (**a**) owner
durante during, for (a period of time)
durar to last

E

e and (*before words beginning with* **i** *or* **hi**)
edad *f.* age
edificar to construct
edificio building
editar to publish
efectivamente in fact
eficaz effective
egoísta selfish
ejemplo example
ejercicio exercise; **realizar —s** answer exam questions
elegir (**i**) to elect; choose
elogiar to praise
embargo: sin — nevertheless, however
emisor *m.* sending apparatus, transmitter
emitir to issue; emit
emocionar to excite
emperador emperor
empleado employee
emplear to employ; use; **—se** to be used
emprender to undertake
empresa company; undertaking, job
en in; at (a certain place)
enamorado *n.* lover; *adj.* **— (de)** in love (with)
enamorarse de to fall in love with
encontrar (**ue**) to find; meet; **—se con** to happen upon
encuesta poll
enemigo enemy
enérgico energetic
enfadar to anger; **—se** get angry
enfermedad *f.* disease

enfermera nurse
enfermo sick
enfocar to focus; **—se hacia** to be directed toward
ensayo attempt; essay
enseñanza teaching; education
enseñar to teach
ensuciar to dirty
entablar to establish, initiate
entender (ie) to understand
enterarse (de) to find out
entonces then
entrada entrance; ticket
entrar (en), — (a) (*Span. Amer.*) to enter
entre between; among; **—tanto** in the meantime
entrenar to train
entresemana midweek; **días de —** weekdays
entrevista interview
entrevistar to interview
entusiasta fan
enviar (ío) to send
envoltorio package
envolver (ue) (*past part.* **envuelto**) to wrap
epíteto epithet
época epoch, period
equipo team
equivocarse to be mistaken
errar (yerro) to err
escalerilla stepladder
escena scene
escoger to choose
escolta escort
esconder(se) to hide
escribir (*past part.* **escrito**) to write
escritor writer
escuchar to listen (to)
escuela school; **— superior** high school
ese (a, os, as) *adj.* that; those (near you); **ése, etc.** *pron.* that one, those, etc.
esforzarse por (ue) to strive to
esfuerzo effort
eso that (*neuter*); **por —** therefore
espacial (referring to) space
espacio space
espalda shoulder; back
espectáculo spectacle
esperanza hope
esperar to hope; wait for, expect
espía spy
esplendor *m.* splendor
esposa wife
estabilidad *f.* stability
establecer (zco) to establish
estación *f.* station; season
estacionar to park (a car)
estadio stadium
estadística statistic
estado state
estadounidense American (USA)
estafado cheated
***estar** to be (located or in a certain position, condition, or state); **— de acuerdo** to agree
estético aesthetic; **cirugía —** plastic surgery
enlace *m.* union, joining
estimular to stimulate
estímulo stimulus
esto this (*neuter*)
estratagema stratagem
estratégico strategic
estrecho *adj.* narrow; close; tight
estrella star
estreno debut
estudiante (a) student
estudiantil scholastic; student (*adj.*)
estudiar to study
estudio study
etiqueta tag; label
europeo European
evitar to avoid
evocar to evoke, bring back
evolucionar to evolve, change
examen *m.* exam(ination)
exento exempt
exigente demanding
exigir to demand
éxito success; **tener —** to succeed
expectativo expectant
explicar to explain
explicación *f.* explanation
explorar to explore
***exponer** to expose
extendido widespread; extensive
extenso extensive
exterior *adj.* external, outside; foreign; *m.* the outside
extranjero *adj.* foreign; *n.* foreigner; **en el —** abroad
extremo *n.* end; *adj.* far

F

fábrica factory
fabricante manufacturer
fácil easy; likely

fácilmente easily
falta fault; mistake
faltar to be lacking, missing; **— a** to miss (a class, etc.); to fail in (an obligation)
familiar *adj.* (of the) family; *pl.* relatives, kin
fecha date
feliz happy
feria *n.* fair
feriado: día — holiday
feroz fierce
fervientemente ardently
fiarse de (ío) to trust; rely on
fiebre *f.* fever
fiel faithful
fiesta party
fijar to fix; set, affix; **—se en** notice
fin *m.* end; purpose; **para fines de** by the end of
finca farm land
firmar to sign
fisonomía physiognomy, features
flor *f.* flower
florero vase
folleto pamphlet
forma form
fortalecer (zco) to fortify; strengthen
fósforo match
fracasar to fail
fraile monk
francés French
franco *adj.* frank; open; evident *n.* franc
frase *f.* sentence; phrase
fray Friar
frazada blanket
frente *m.* front; **— a** in front of; faced with; **en — de** in front of
fresco cool; fresh; **hacer —** to be cool out
frío *n.* cold(ness); **hacer —** to be cold (out); **tener —** to be (feel) cold; *adj.* cold
fructerífero fruitful
fuego fire
fuera *adv.* outside; **— de** *prep.* outside of
fuerte strong
fuga flight, escape
fulano fellow, guy
fumar to smoke
funcionar to work (a mechanism)
funcionario public official
fútbol *m.* soccer; football

G

gallo cock
gana desire
ganar to win; earn; **—(se) la vida** earn a living
ganga bargain
gastado worn out
gastar to spend (money)
gasto expense
género species
genio genius
gente *f. sing.* people
ginecólogo gynecologist
gitano gypsy
gobernar (ie) to govern
gobierno government
gozar (de) to enjoy
graduarse (úo) to graduate
gran(de) big, large; great
granero granary
grave serious
gris grey
gritar to shout
grueso thick
guante *m.* glove
guapo handsome; beautiful
guardar to keep; **—se de** to keep from, refrain from
guardia guard
guerra war
guía *m.* guide
guisar to cook
gustarle (algo a alguien) to like (something)
gusto pleasure; taste; **tener — en** to be pleased to

H

***haber** to have (*auxiliary verb to form compound tenses*); **— de** to be supposed or expected to; must (*probability or mild necessity*)
habitación *f.* room
habitante inhabitant
hábito(s) vestments
hablador talkative
hablar to speak, talk
habrá there will be; there probably is or are
hace (+ *verb in past*) ago
***hacer** to make; to do; **— frío, calor** to be cold, warm (out); **— un disparo** shoot (at); **— una maleta** pack a suitcase; **— una pregunta** ask a question; **— un viaje** take a

trip; **— una visita** pay a visit; **—se** to become
hacia toward
hacienda estate; finance
hallar to find; **—se** to be, find oneself
hambre *f.* hunger; **tener mucha —** to be very hungry
harto sated, tired (of)
hasta *prep.* until; even; **— que** *conj.* until (+ *clause*)
hay there is, there are;**— que** one must, it is necessary
hazaña feat, deed
He aquí Here is, Behold
hecho (*past part. of* **hacer**) done; made; *n.* fact; **el — de que** the fact that; **de —** in fact
hemorragia hemorrhage
herida wound
herido *n.* and *adj.* wounded (man)
hermano brother; *pl.* brothers and sisters
hermoso beautiful
hervir (ie) to boil
hierba grass
hierro iron
hijo son; *pl.* children, son(s) and daughter(s)
hilo wire; thread
historia history; story
historieta comic strip
hogar *m.* home (*fig.*); hearth
holandés Dutch(man)
holgazán lazy
hombre man; **el —** man(kind)
hondo deep
hongo mushroom
hora hour; **a buena —** early; **¿Qué — es?** What time is it?
horario schedule
horóscopo horoscope
hoy today
huelga strike (labor)
huérfano orphan
huerta vegetable patch, garden
huésped guest
húmedo wet, humid
huracán *m.* hurricane

I

idilio idyll, love story
idioma *m.* language
igual equal; same, similar, (a)like; **al — que** just as
igualdad *f.* equality
igualmente likewise; equally
ilimitado unlimited
ilustrado educated
impedir (i) to prevent
imperar to rule
implicar to imply
***im*poner** to impose
importar to matter, be important; import
impresionante impressive
impresionar to impress
incluso including
increíble incredible
indefinido indefinite
indicar to indicate
indio Indian
***indis*poner** to indispose; set against
individuo *n.* individual
industrial *adj.* industrial; *n.* industrialist
inesperado unexpected
infierno Hell
influir (uyo) en to influence
ingeniero engineer
ingeniosísimo very ingenious
ingente enormous
Inglaterra England
iniciar to begin, initiate
injertar to graft
injerto graft
injustamente unjustly
injustificable unjustifiable
inmediato immediate
inmenso immense
insistir en to insist on
inspeccionar to inspect
instalar to install; **—se por su cuenta** to go into business on one's own
integrar to compose, make up
intensificar to intensify
intentar to attempt to
intento attempt
intercambiar to exchange, interchange
interés *m.* interest
interesante interesting
interesar to interest
interrogar to question
intervención *f.* intervention; **no —** nonintervention
***inter*venir** to intervene
íntimo close, intimate
***ir** to go; **—se** go away
irónicamente sarcastically
izquierdo left

J

jaula cage
jardín *m.* garden
jefe chief, leader; boss
joven young; young person
jovencita little young thing (*f.*)
joya jewel
juego game; gambling
jueves Thursday
juez judge
jugar (ue) a to play (a game, sport)
juguete *m.* toy
juncal *m.* area filled with rushes
junto (a) *adv.* next, to, near; **— con** along with; *adj. pl.* together
justificar to justify

K

kilómetro kilometer (approx. ⅝ of a mile)

L

laberinto labyrinth, maze
lacónicamente succinctly
lado side; **la casa de al —** the house next door
ladrón thief
lago lake
La Haya The Hague
lamentar to regret
lámpara lamp
lanzar to hurl; throw; launch
lápiz *m.* pencil
largo long (length); **tener... metros de —** to be . . . meters long
lástima pity; **Es —** It's a pity
lastimar to hurt
lavar(se) to wash
***leer** to read
lejos *adv.* far; **— de** *prep.* far from; **a lo —** in the distance
lengua language; tongue
lento slow
letrero sign
levantar to raise, lift; **—se** get up, rise
ley *f.* law
libertad *f.* liberty
libreta pad; notebook
libro book
lid *f.* fight
ligero light (*adj.*)
limosna alms; **pedir —** to beg alms
limpiar to clean
línea line
listo smart; ready
litro liter (slightly more than a quart)
local *m.* site
localidad *f.* locality
localizar to locate
lógico logical
Londres London
luchar to fight; struggle
luego then; later; **desde —** of course
lugar *m.* place
luna moon
lunes Monday
luz *f.* light
llama flame
llamada call; calling
llamar to call; **— a la puerta** knock on the door; **— por teléfono** to telephone; **—se** to be named
llamarada flame, fire
llegada arrival
llegar to arrive; **— a** reach (a destination); **— a** (+ *infin.*) to succeed in, manage to; **—a ser** to become
llenar to fill
lleno de filled with, full of
llevar to carry; bring; take (a person); wear; **— vendada una oreja** to have a bandaged ear
llorar to cry
llover (ie) to rain

M

madera wood
madre mother
madrugada dawn; **hasta de la —** early morning
maduro mature
magistrado magistrate
mal *m.* evil; **de — en peor** from bad to worse; *adv.* badly; wrongly
mal(o) bad; wrong
maleta suitcase; **hacer una —** to pack a suitcase
mandar to send; order; **— traer** to have (something) brought
mandato, mando command
manera manner; **de — que** so (that); **de todas —s** in any case
mano *f.* hand
***man*tener** to maintain; support (a family); **—se** stay
manifestar (ie) to manifest
manzana apple
mañana tomorrow; morning; **por la —** in the morning

máquina machine; **— de escribir** typewriter
mar *m.* sea
marcharse to go away
marinero sailor
marzo March
matar to kill
martes Tuesday
más more; most; **— de** more than (+ *a number*); **no — que** only; **— que nunca** more than ever; **cada vez —** more and more
materia subject
matrimonio marriage; married couple
mayor greater; older; major; greatest; oldest
mayoría majority
media stocking
mediados: a — de around the middle of
médico doctor
medida measure
medio *adj.* half; *n.* middle; means; **por — de** by means of
medir (i) to measure
mejor better; best
mengano another fellow, or guy; **fulano y —** one guy and another
menor younger; smaller; lesser; minor; youngest; smallest; least
mentir (ie) to (tell a) lie
mentira lie; **Parece —** It's incredible
menudo: a — often
mercancía merchandise
merecer (zco) to deserve
merendar (ie) to have a snack (about 6 P.M.)
meridional southern
mes *m.* month
método method
meta aim, goal
meter to put
metro meter (approx. 39 inches)
miedo fear; **tener —** to be afraid
miembro member; limb
mientras (que) while; **— tanto** meanwhile
miércoles Wednesday
mil thousand
milagro miracle
militar *adj.* military; *n.* soldier
millares thousands
mínimo minimum
ministerio Ministry; **— de Hacienda** Ministry of Finance
ministro (cabinet) minister
minúsculo tiny
miopía nearsightedness
mirar to look at
misionero missionary
mismo itself; same; very
misterio mystery
moda fashion
modo way, manner; **de — que** so (that); **de algún —** in some way
molestar to bother, annoy; **—se** to take the trouble
molestia annoyance; bother
monarca monarch
monje monk
monologar to talk to oneself
montaña mountain
montar to set up
morder (ue) to bite
morir (ue) (*past part.* **muerto**) to die
mortificante embarrassing
mostrar (ue) to show; **—se** appear, seem
mover(se) (ue) to move
movilizar to mobilize
muchacho, a boy; girl
mucho much; **hacer — calor** to be very hot out; **tener — frío, mucha hambre** to be (feel) very cold, hungry
muebles *m. pl.* furniture
muerte *f.* death
mujer woman
mundial *adj.* (of the) world
mundo world; **todo el —** everybody
municipio town
murmuración *f.* gossip(ing)
murmurador gossip(er)
murmurar to gossip
museo museum
muslo thigh
muy very

N

nacer (zco) to be born
nada nothing, (not) anything; **¡Nada de eso!** What do you mean! Go on!
nadar to swim
nadie nobody, no one, (not) anybody
naturaleza nature
navegar to sail; navigate
necesitar to need
negar (ie) to deny; **—se a** to refuse to
negocio (a) business; business matter; *pl.* business

negro black
neoyorquino New Yorker
nervio nerve (*anat.*)
nevar (ie) to snow
nevera refrigerator
ni not (even); **— siquiera** not even; **ni... ni** neither . . . nor
nieto, a grandson; granddaughter; *pl.* grandchildren
ningún (ninguno, a, os, as) no, none
niñez *f.* childhood
niño, a boy; girl
nivel *m.* level; standard; **— de vida** standard of living
nobleza nobility; nobleness
nocturno *adj.* night; nocturnal
noche *f.* night; **esta —** tonight; **de la — a la mañana** overnight, suddenly
nordeste Northeast
noroeste Northwest
nota grade
noticia news(item); *pl.* news
novia sweetheart, fiancee
noviazgo engagement
nuevo new; **de —** again
número number; **hacer —s** to calculate
nunca never
nutrir to nourish

O

o or
objeto *n.* object
obligar to force, oblige
obra work (of art, etc.); creation
obrero worker
obstante: no — nevertheless
ob*tener to get, obtain
ocasionar to cause
ocultar to hide
ocupado busy
ocupar(se de) to occupy (oneself with); talk about
ocurrir to occur
ochenta eighty
odiar to hate
OEA (Organización de los Estados Americanos) OAS (Organization of American States)
oeste West
oficial *n.* officer; *adj.* official
oficio occupation
ofrecer (zco) to offer
oído inner ear; sense of hearing
***oír** to hear; **— decir a** to hear (someone) say
ojal *m.* buttonhole
¡Ojalá! If only! How I wish!
ojo eye; **¡Ojo!** Watch out!
olvidar(se de) to forget (about)
operar to operate (on someone)
opinar to have the opinion
***o*poner*se a** to oppose
opuesto opposite
oración *f.* sentence; prayer
orden *f.* order, command; *m.* order(liness); succession
oreja (outer) ear
oro gold
ortográfico *adj.* spelling
otro other; another

P

paciente patient
padecer (zco) to suffer
padre father; *pl.* parents
pagar to pay (for)
página page
pago payment
paisaje *m.* countryside; landscape
pájaro bird
país *m.* country (nation)
paisano civilian
paja straw
palabra word
pan *m.* bread
pantalla screen
pantalón (*generally pl.*) trousers
pañoleta neckerchief
papel *m.* paper
paquete *m.* package
par *m.* pair
para for; in order to; by or for (a certain date or time); considering, with respect to; **— que** in order that, so that
pardo brown
parecer (zco) to seem, look, appear; **—se a** to resemble (each other); **al —** apparently
parecido similar
pared *f.* wall
pareja couple; pair
parienta, pariente relative
parisiense Parisian
parte *f.* part; **la menor —** the minority; **la mayor —** most, the majority
pasado past

pasaje *m.* passage
pasajero passenger
pasar to pass; happen; spend (time); **— a** go into; **— de** exceed; **— de los treinta años** be more than 30 years old; **—se de listo** outsmart oneself
pasatiempo pastime
patria homeland, country
patrón, patrona boss
paz *f.* peace
pecado sin
pedir (i) to ask for, request; **— prestado** borrow
peine *m.* comb
película film
peligro danger
peligroso dangerous
pelota ball
pensar (**ie**) to think; — (+ *infin.*) to intend, plan to; **— de** to think of, have an opinion of; **— en** to think about
pensativo pensive(ly), wrapped in thought
peña bull session
peor worse; worst
pequeño small, little (in size)
perder (**ie**) to lose; waste (time, etc.); **— una asignatura** fail a course; **—se** get lost
perfeccionar to perfect
periodista journalist
perjuicio harm, ill effect; **daños y —s** damages (law)
perla pearl
permanecer (**zco**) to remain
perro dog
perseguir (**i**) to pursue
persona person; *pl.* people
personal *m.* personnel; **— de escolta** police escort; *adj.* personal
perspectiva prospect; perspective
pertenecer (**zco**) to belong
peruano Peruvian
pesar *m.* grief; **a — de** in spite of
peso unit of currency in Mexico and several other Spanish American countries
pico beak
pictórico *adj.* (of) art
pie *m.* foot; **a —** on foot; **en —** standing; **ponerse de —** to stand up
piel *f.* fur; **abrigo de pieles** fur coat
pierna leg
pilotear to pilot
pintar to paint
pintura painting
piso apartment; floor
pista trail; clue; lead
plata silver; money (*colloq.*)
platino platinum
plato plate; dish (of food)
playa beach
plaza (a) place, space; village square, plaza
plazo period (of time)
plebeyo *n.* commoner
plenamente fully
pluma pen
población *f.* population; town
pobre poor; poor man
pobreza poverty
poco *adj. and adv.* little, not much; **un —** (before and *adj.*); *pl.* few; **unos —** a few, several; *n.* **un — de** a little (bit) of; **hace —** recently
***poder** to be able; can; **no — más** not to be able to stand any more; *m.* power
policía *f.* police force; *m.* policeman
policíaco *adj.* police
ponderar to weigh, assess
***poner** to put; place; **—se** put on (clothes); **—se de pie** stand up
por by; for; per; during, in; through; along; for the sake of; on behalf of; on account of; in quest of; instead of; because of; in exchange for
porque because
¿Por qué? Why?
portátil portable
porvenir *m.* future
***poseer** to possess
posibilidad *f.* possibility
potencia power (nation)
potente powerful
potro stallion
precario precarious
precio price
predilecto favorite
preferir (**ie**) to prefer
pregunta question
preguntar to ask (a question), inquire
preguntón inquisitive
premio prize
prender to light (a cigarette, etc.)
prensa press (newspapers)
preocupar(**se de**) to worry (about)
presa dam

presentar to present; introduce (a person); **—se** appear
presentir (ie) to have a presentiment; **todo hace —** everything forebodes
preso de filled with, choked with
prestar to lend; **— atención** pay attention
previsión *f.* estimate; preplanning
primer(o) first
primo cousin
príncipe prince
principio beginning; principle; **para** or **a —s de** by or toward the beginning of
probar (**ue**) to try; taste; test; **—se** try on
procedimiento process; procedure
*__pro*ducir__* to produce
profundidad *f.* depth
profundo profound
prohibir to prohibit, forbid
prolongarse to last, be prolonged
prometer to promise
prometida fiancee
promover (**ue**) to promote
pronombre *m.* pronoun
pronunciar to pronounce; give (a speech)
propaganda advertising; propaganda
propietario owner
propio even; himself
propósito purpose; **a —** by the way; **de —** on purpose
protegido pet
*__pro*veer__* (*cf.* **ver**) to provide
providencia provision
provisto de supplied, provided with
provo*c*ar to provoke, produce
próximo next; close, near
proyectar to plan
proyectil *m.* missile
proyecto *n.* project
psicólogo psychologist
psicosis *f.* nervous tension
público *n. and adj.* public
pueblo (a) people; town
puente *m.* bridge
puerta door
pues *adv.* well (then) . . ., so
puesto job, post
pulsera bracelet; **reloj de —** wrist watch
punta (shirt) stud
punto point; **a — de** about to; **en —** sharp

Q

que *rel. pron.* that, who, which; *prep.* **—** (+ *infin.*) to (do, etc.); **algo — hacer** something to do
¿Qué? What? Which?
¡Qué! What a . . .!
quedar to be remaining or left over; to remain (in a certain condition); **—se** stay
quejarse de to complain about
quemar to burn
***querer** to want; like, love (a person); **— decir** to mean, imply
quien(es) who, whom; he who; **No hay —...** There is no one who (can . . .)
¿Quién(es)? Who?
quince fifteen
quirófano operating room (*med.*)
quirúrgico surgical
¡Quita! Go on! Come now!
quitar to take away; remove; **—se** to take off (one's clothing, etc.)

R

radioyente listener (to the radio)
rama branch
raptar to abduct; elope with
Raúl Ralph
razón *f.* reason; **tener —** to be right; **— de ser** reason for being
reaccionar to react
real *adj.* real; royal; *n.* *real* (a small unit of the old Spanish currency)
realidad *f.* reality; **en —** actually
reali*z*ar to put into effect, realize, accomplish; **—se** to take place
reanudar to renew
rebajar to reduce
receptor *m.* receiver
recibir to receive
recibo receipt
recién, reciente recent
reclamar to claim
reclamo: en — on special, on sale
reco*g*er to pick up
recomendar (**ie**) to recommend
recompensa reward
recordar (**ue**) to remember; remind (of)
recorrer to run (over a course)
recorrido run (of a ship, etc.)
recuerdo memory; souvenir; *pl.* regards
recurso resort, recourse; resource

red *f.* network; net
redoblar to redouble
*__reducir__ to reduce
referente a referring to
referir(se a) (ie) to refer to
reflejo reflex; reflection
reforzar (ue) to reenforce
refrescar to refresh; cool
refugiado refugee
regalar to give as a gift
regalo gift
régimen *m.* regime
registrar to search; register; **—se** to take place
registro register
regla rule
regresar to return
regular regular; fair, mediocre
reintegrarse a to rejoin
***reír (ío)** to laugh; **—se de** laugh at
reiterar to repeat
relativamente relatively
reloj *m.* clock; watch; **— de pulsera** wristwatch
remediar to remedy
remedio alternative, choice; remedy
rencor *m.* anger
rendirse (i) to surrender
renovar (ue) to renew
reparador *adj.* reparative
repasar to review
repente: de — suddenly
repetir (i) to repeat
*__reponer__ to replace; retort, reply
representante *n.* representative
requisito requirement
resentido resentful
resolver (ue) (*past part.* **resuelto**) to resolve; solve
respecto *n.* respect, aspect, regard; **— a** concerning, with respect to
respuesta answer
restablecer (zco) to restore
resuelto resolved, solved
resultado result; **dar —** succeed, work out
resultar to turn out
reto challenge
retrato portrait
reunión *f.* meeting
reunir (úno) to gather together; **—se** meet
revelar to reveal; develop (film)
revista magazine
revuelto *adj.* upset
rey king
rico rich
riesgo risk
ritmo rhythm; pace
robar to rob; steal
robo robbery
rogar (ue) to beg; pray
rojizo reddish
rojo red; **pintado de —** painted red
romper (*past part.* **roto**) to break
ropa (*generally pl.*) clothing
roto broken
ruido noise
ruin lowly, mean, terrible
ruso Russian

S

sábado Saturday
***saber** to know (a fact); know how; (*preterite*) found out, learned
sacar to take out; get, receive
saco sack, pack
sacudir to shake; dust (furniture)
seco dry
sala room; living room
***salir** to leave, go out; come out; **— para** to leave for
salón hall, large room
salto jump
salud *f.* health
salvar to save (a life, etc.)
salvo: a — safe
San Saint; **— Francisco de Asís** St. Francis of Assisi
sanatorio private hospital
sangre *f.* blood
sano healthy
santo saint
***satisfacer** (*cf.* **hacer**) to satisfy
satisfecho (de) satisfied (with)
sayal *m.* monk's robe
seccionar to cut off
sed *f.* thirst; **tener —** to be thirsty
seda silk
seguida: en — at once, immediately
seguir (i) to follow; continue, keep on (+ *present part.*)
según according to
segundo second; secondary
seguridad *f.* security; safety
seguro sure; secure; safe
selva jungle
semanal weekly, per week
semejante *adj.* similar; *n.* fellow man
sencillamente simply

sentarse (**ie**) to sit down
sentir (**ie**) to feel; feel sorry; regret; **—se** (+ *adj.*) to feel (tired, sad, etc.)
semana week
sentimiento sentiment; feeling
***ser** to be; *n.* being
sereno calm
servicio service; **en —** at work
serie *f.* series
servir (**i**) to serve; be useful
setenta seventy
si if, whether
sí *refl. pron.* himself, herself, yourself, itself, themselves, yourselves
sideral of the stars; starry
siempre always; **— que** whenever; **para —** forever
siglo century
siguiente following; next; **al día —** on the following day
significación *f.* significance
simpático nice
simular to simulate
sin *prep.* without; **— que** *conj.* without (+ *clause*)
sino but (on the contrary) (*after a negative*); except
sitio place
sobre about; over, above; on
sobresaliente excellent
sobrina niece
sobrino nephew
socorrer to rescue
soler (**ue**) to be accustomed to; to be usually
solo alone; mere
sólo only
soltería bachelorhood
soltero single, unmarried
solucionar to solve
sombrero hat
sonar (**ue**) to sound; ring
soneto sonnet
sonreír (**ío**) to smile
soplón *m.* squealer (*colloq.*)
sorprender to surprise; **—se** be surprised
sorpresa surprise
sospechar to suspect
sospechoso suspicious
sos*tener to sustain; support
su(**s**) his, her, your (**Ud., Uds.**), their
subdesarrollado underdeveloped
subir to go up; rise; raise up; get into (a car, etc.)
subrayar to underline
substituir (**uyo**) to substitute
suceder to happen; succeed (in order) **¿Qué le sucede?** What's the matter?
sucio dirty
sueño sleep; dream; **tener —** to be sleepy
suerte *f.* luck
sugerir (**ie**) to suggest
sugestionable easily suggestible
suicidarse to commit suicide
Suiza Switzerland
suizo Swiss
sujeto subject
suma sum; **en —** in short
sumamente extremely
sumergible *m.* underwater craft
sumergir(**se**) to submerge
superfluo superfluous
supermercado supermarket
supuesto: por — of course
surgir to arise, surge up
suspender to suspend; expel
superar to improve; overcome; surpass
suspicaz suspicious-minded
sustantivo noun
suturar to sew up (*med.*)
suyo (**a, os, as**) his, hers, yours, theirs

T

tal such (a); **— vez** perhaps
también also, too
tampoco neither (*opp. of* also)
tanto *adv.* as much, so much; **— yo como...** I as well as . . . **en — que** while; *adj.* **tanto** (**a, os, as**)**... como** as much, many . . . as; *n.* **un —** a bit, somewhat; **entre —** in the meantime, meanwhile
tardar en to take (a certain length of time) to; to be delayed in
tarde *f.* afternoon; early evening; **por la —** in the afternoon; *adv.* late **más —** later, afterwards
tarea task, job
tarjeta card
taza cup
té *m.* tea
técnica technique
técnico *n.* technician, mechanic; *adj.* technical
tela cloth
tema *m.* theme; subject
temer to fear
temeroso fearful
temprano early

tender (ie) a to tend to
tendido stretched out
telefonear to telephone
***tener** to have; **—... años de edad** to be . . . years old; **— calor** to be (feel) hot; **—... años de existencia** to have been in existence for . . . years; **—... de alto, largo, ancho** to be . . . high, long, wide; **— frío** to be cold; **— ganas de** to feel like (doing something); **— hambre** to be hungry; **— miedo** to be afraid; **— que** (+ *infin.*) to have to; **— que ver con** to have to do with; **— por** to consider, take (someone) for; **— razón** to be right; **— sueño** to be sleepy
tercer(o) third; **un —** a third person
terminar to end, finish
terreno area; field
tertulia social gathering
tesis *f.* thesis
tesoro treasure
tiempo (period of) time; weather; tense (*gram.*); **a —** in time; on time; **con —** beforehand; **hacer buen —** to be good weather
tienda shop, store
tierra land; **— adentro** inland
tigre *m.* tiger; jaguar
tío uncle
tiro (gun) shot; **escenas de —s** shooting scenes
titubeo hesitation
tiza chalk
tocar to play (an instrument); **— le a uno** to be someone's turn
todavía still, yet
todo *adj.* all; every; whole; **— el día** the whole day; **todos los días** every day; *n.* all; everything
tomar to take, seize; eat; drink
torear to fight bulls
torero bullfighter
toro bull
torpeza stupidity
torre *f.* tower
tórtolo turtledove (male)
toser to cough
trabajador *adj.* hardworking
trabajar to work
trabajo work; job
tra*ducir to translate
***traer** to bring; **— consigo** bring about; bring with one
traje *m.* suit; **— de luces** bullfighter's costume
trampa trap
tranquilidad *f.* tranquillity
tranquilo calm; tranquil
transmisor *m.* transmitter
transmitir to transmit
transportar to transport
transporte *m.* transportation
trasladar(se) to move; transfer
traslado transfer
trastorno *n.* upset
tratar to treat; **— de** try to; deal with; **—se de** be a matter or question of
través: a — de across; through
trece thirteen
treinta thirty
tren *m.* train; **— correo, — estafeta** mail train
treta trick
triste sad
tristeza sadness
triunfar to triumph
triunfo triumph
tronco (tree) trunk
trono throne
tropas *f. pl.* troops
trozo piece; chunk; fragment
tulipán *m.* tulip
turbación *f.* confusion
turístico *adj.* tourist

U

u or (*before words beginning with* **o** *or* **ho**)
ubicado located
últimamente lately
un, una a, an; *pl.* some; about, approximately
único only, sole; unique
unánime unanimous
unidad *f.* unit; unity
unir(se) to join
universidad *f.* university
universitario *adj.* university, college
urgir to be urgent
útil useful

V

vacaciones (*generally f. pl.*) vacation; **irse de —** to go on vacation
vago lazy
vagón *m.* (train) car, coach
***valer** to be worth; **— la pena** be worthwhile; **—se de** make use of
valioso valuable

valor *m.* courage; value
valoración *f.* evaluation
valorar to assess; evaluate
valla enclosure, stockade
vaquero cowboy
vaso (drinking) glass
vecindad *f.* vicinity; neighborhood
vecino neighbor
vegetal *m.* vegetable
vehículo vehicle
veinte twenty
velada social evening
ven*cer* to conquer
venda bandage
vendar to bandage; **llevar vendada una oreja** to have a bandaged ear
vendedor seller
vender to sell
venidero (forth)coming
***venir** to come; **que viene** next
venta sale
ventaja advantage
ventana window
***ver** to see; **tener que — con** to have to do with
verano summer
verdad *f.* truth
verdadero real, true
verde green; **poner —** to rip the hide off (someone) (*colloq.*)
versar to deal with, treat of
Versalles Versailles
vestir (**i**) to dress; **—se** get dressed; **el —** dressing
vez *f.* (a) time, (an) instance; **a su —** in their turn; **a veces** at times; **alguna —** ever, at some time; **cada — más** more and more; **por primera —** for the first time; **tal —** perhaps; **toda — que** whenever
viajar to travel
viaje *m.* trip; **hacer un —** take a trip
víbora snake
vida life
vidrio glass (substance)
vigilar to watch over
vino wine
visado visa
vista view
visto seen; **por lo —** apparently
viuda widow
vivienda dwelling
vivir to live
vivo alive
vocación *f.* vocation, calling
volar (**ue**) to fly
voluntad *f.* will
volver (**ue**) (*past part.* **vuelto**) to return, go back; **— a** (+ *infin.*) to (do something) again
voz *f.* voice; **en — baja** in a low voice, quietly; **en — alta** aloud
vuelo flight
vuelta turn, return; short trip; **dar media —** turn half around; **dar una —** take a walk, ride, etc.

Y

y and
ya already; **— que** since, because; **— no** no longer, not any more
***yacer** to lie (at rest, near death, etc.)
yegua mare
yerra (*see* **errar** to err)

Z

zapatilla house slipper
zapato shoe

ENGLISH–SPANISH VOCABULARY

A

abandoned abandonado
abduct raptar
about sobre, de, acerca de (**concerning**): a eso de (**time**): alrededor de (**time and location**); más o menos; cerca de
abroad el extranjero
absolute absoluto
absorbed absorto; **— in each other** acaramelados
abuse *v.* abusar
accede acceder (a)
accept aceptar
accident accidente *m.*
accompany acompañar
according to según
accuse acusar
achieve lograr, alcan*z*ar
act actuar (úo), comportarse
activity actividad *f.*
actor actor
adapt adaptar
add añadir
address *n.* dirección *f.*, señas *f. pl.*; *v.* diri*g*irse a; dirigir la palabra a
adherence adhesión *f.*
administrative administrativo
admit admitir
adopt adoptar
advantage ventaja; **to take —** aprovecharse
advent advenimiento
adventure aventura
advertising propaganda comercial
advice consejo(s)
advise aconsejar, recomendar (ie)
affection cariño
afraid: to be *tener miedo, temer
after *prep.* después de; tras; *adv.* después
afternoon tarde *f.*
again otra vez; de nuevo; **to do something —** volver a hacer algo
against contra
age edad *f.*; **to be . . . years of —** tener... años de edad
agenda orden del día *m.*
agent agente
aggression agresión *f.*
ago hace (+ *period of time*)
agree *estar de acuerdo; estar conforme(s); **to — to** *con*venir* en
airplane avión *m.*
airport aeropuerto
alive vivo
along por; a lo largo de
all todo; **at —** nada; **not at —** de nada
allow permitir, dejar
almost casi
already ya
although aunque
aluminum aluminio
always siempre
American norteamericano
Amazon Amazonas *m. sing.*
among entre
ammunition municiones *f. pl.*
analysis análisis *m.*
and y, e
Andrew Andrés
anecdote anécdota
angry enojado, enfadado; **to get —** enojarse, enfadarse
animal animal *m.*
animator animador
Ann Anita
announce anunciar
annoy molestar
another otro
answer *v.* contestar, responder; *n.* contestación *f.*, respuesta
any algún, alguno, etc.; cualquier(a); ningún (*neg.*), ninguno, etc.
anybody cualquiera; cualquier persona; nadie (*neg.*)
anything cualquier cosa; nada (*neg.*)
apartment apartam(i)ento, piso
apparatus aparato
apparent aparente, evidente
appeal apelar
appear parecer (zco); aparecer (zco); mostrarse (ue)
apply apli*c*ar; **to — for** solicitar, pedir (i)
appoint nombrar
apprenticeship aprendizaje *m.*
approach *v.* acer*c*arse a; **—ing** proximo, venidero, que se acerca

appropriate *v.* apropiar
approve aprobar (ue)
architect arquitecto
Argentinian argentino
arid árido
arm *n.* brazo; arma (**weapon**); *v.* armar(se)
armchair sillón, *m.*, butaca
army ejército
around alrededor de; a eso de (**number or hour**)
arrange arreglar
arrest *v.* prender, *de*tener*
arrive llegar
artery arteria
article artículo
artist artista
as *conj.* como; *adv.* tan; **— . . . —** tan... como; **— much** tanto; **— long** mientras
ashamed avergonzado; **to be —** *tener vergüenza de
ask preguntar (**question**); pedir (i) (**request**)
asleep dormido; **to fall —** dormirse (ue)
assault asalto
astrology astrología
astronaut astronauta
astronomical astronómico
at en; a; **— home** en casa; **— night** por la noche, de noche; **— nightfall** al anochecer, al atardecer
athlete atleta
attack *v.* atacar, asaltar; *n.* ataque, asalto
attend asistir (a); **to — to** atender a
attention atención *f.*; **to pay —** prestar atención; *hacer caso de or a; **to attract —** llamar (la) atención
attract *a*traer*
austere austero
author autor, autora
avenue avenida
await esperar
awaken despertar(se) (ie)
away: to be (**a certain distance**) **—** distar

B

baby nene *m.*, nena *f.*
bachelorhood soltería
back fondo; **— door** puerta de atrás
bad mal(o)
badly mal
ball pelota
bandage *n.* venda; *v.* vendar
bankrupt insolvente, quebrado; **to be —** *estar quebrado
bargain ganga
baseball béisbol *m.*
bathe bañar(se)
bathing: — suit traje de baño *m.*
battlements almenaje *m.*; murallas almenadas
be *ser; *estar; **to — supposed to** *haber de; **to — . . . years old** *tener... años
beach playa
beam viga (**structural**)
bear llevar; soportar (**endure**)
beard barba
beautiful hermoso; bello
beauty belleza, hermosura
because porque; **— of** a causa de; por (+ *infin.*)
become *hacerse; llegar a ser; *ponerse; convertirse (ie) en; **to — of** *ser de, *hacerse de
bed cama; **to go to —** acostarse (ue)
bee abeja
before *prep.* antes de; delante de, ante; *adv.* antes; primero
beg rogar (ue)
begin empezar (ie); comenzar (ie)
beginning principio; **at the —** al principio; **at the — of** a principios de
behave *conducirse, comportarse
behavior conducta
behind detrás de
being ser *m.*
believe *creer
bell campana; **— tower** campanario
belong pertenecer (zco), *ser de
bench banca
besides además
best mejor; **to do one's —** esforzarse (ue); *hacer lo que sea de su poder
betray traicionar
better mejor
between entre
beyond más allá (de)
big grande
bill cuenta
bird pájaro, ave *f.*
bite *v.* morder (ue)
black negro
blond rubio
blood sangre *f.*

blue azul
board tabla
boat barco; buque *m.*; bote *m.*; lancha
bold atrevido, audaz
book libro; **— dealer** librero
booklet folleto
bookstore librería
boring aburrido
born nacido; **to be —** nacer (zco)
borrow pedir (i) prestado, tomar prestado
both ambos, los dos
bother molestar(se)
bottle *n.* botella
bow *n.* arco
box *n.* caja
boy muchacho, chico, niño; hijo
bracelet pulsera
branch rama
break romper (*past part.* roto); **to — down** derribar, derrumbar, echar abajo
breakfast *n.* desayuno; *v.* desayunar(se)
brick *n.* ladrillo; *adj.* de ladrillos
bridge puente *m.*
brilliant brillante
bring *traer
broken roto
bronzed bronceado
brother hermano; **—-in-law** cuñado; **little —** hermanito
brush cepillo
build *construir (uyo)
building edificio
bullfighter torero
burn quemar(se)
business negocios
businessman hombre de negocios
busy ocupado
but pero; sino; mas
butter mantequilla
buy comprar
by por; de; para (**a certain time**); **— the way** a propósito

C

cad sinvergüenza *m.*
cafe café *m.*
call *v.* llamar; **to — on the telephone** llamar por teléfono; **to be —ed** llamarse; *n.* llamada
campaign campaña
can (to be able) *poder; *saber
canteen cantina
capable capaz; **to be — of** *ser capaz de; *poder
capital capital *f.* (**city**); capital *m.* (**money**)
capture capturar
car coche *m.* auto; vagón, *m.* coche (**train**)
card tarjeta; carta (**at cards**)
care cuidado; **to take — of** cuidar de
career carrera
careful: to be — *tener cuidado; cuidarse de
carefully con cuidado
carry llevar; **to — out** realizar, llevar a cabo
cartoonist caricaturista
case caso; **in —** en caso de que
Castilian castellano, de Castilla
castle castillo
Catalonia Cataluña
catastrophe catástrofe *f.*; desastre *m.*
catch coger; prender; **to — up with** alcanzar; coger
cause causa
ceiling techo, cielo raso
center centro
century siglo
certain cierto; **a —** cierto
certainly seguramente; sí que
certainty certidumbre *f.*
chain cadena
chair silla; **big —** sillón *m.*
championship campeonato
chance oportunidad *f.*
change *n.* cambio; *v.* cambiar
character carácter *m.*
characteristic *n.* característica
charge *v.* cargar, lanzarse contra; cobrar (**money**)
Charlie Carlitos
charming encantador
chat charlar
cheap(ly) barato
cheat engañar, estafar
chest cofre *m.*, baúl *m.*
chief jefe
childhood niñez *f.*
children niños
Chilean chileno
choke ahogar, estrangular
choose escoger
church iglesia
cigarette cigarrillo
circle círculo
circumstantial circunstancial

circus circo
city ciudad *f.*
civilization civilización *f.*
class clase *f.*
clean limpio
clear claro
client cliente
climate clima *m.*
clothes ropa(s)
clothing ropa(s)
club club *m.*
cluster *v.* agruparse, apiñarse
coast costa, litoral *m.*
coffee café *m.*; **— pot** cafetera
cold frío; **to be —** *tener frío; **to be very — out** *hacer mucho frío
collaborator colaborador
collapse *n.* colapso; *v.* derrumbarse
collective colectivo
collector coleccionista
color color *m.*
colossal colosal
column columna; **relief —** columna de relevo
come *venir; **to — back** volver (ue); **to — in** entrar (en *or* a); **— what may** venga lo que venga
comfortable cómodo
command *v.* mandar
commit cometer; **— suicide** suicidarse
commoner plebeyo
company compañía; empresa
complain quejarse (de)
complement complementar
complete *adj.* completo
completely del todo, completamente
complicated complicado
conclude concluir (uyo)
concrete concreto
condemned condenado; **— man** reo (de muerte)
condition condición *f.* (often *pl.*)
conduct conducta
confess confesar
conquer conquistar; ven*c*er
consciousness conciencia
consent consentir (ie) (en)
consider considerar
consist consistir (en)
constantly constantemente
construction construcción *f.*
consume consumir
contact *n.* contacto
continually continuamente
continue se*gu*ir (i), continuar (úo)
contract contrato
contribute contribuir (uyo)
control *n.* dominio; control *m.*; *v.* dominar
conversation conversación *f.*
convict *v.* condenar
convince conven*c*er
cook *v.* cocinar, guisar
cool fresco; **to be —** *hacer fresco
cost costar (ue)
cottage casita
cotton algodón *m.*
count contar (ue); **to — on** contar con
country *n.* país; patria; campo (*opp. of* **city**); *adj.* del campo; campestre
couple pareja, matrimonio
courage valor *m.*
course curso; **of —** desde luego, claro (está), por supuesto
court tribunal *m.*
cousin primo
couturier costurero
cover *v.* cubrir; **—ed with** cubierto de
cow vaca
craft barco; embarcación *f.*
crazy loco
create crear
crime crimen *m.*
crisis crisis *f.*
cross *v.* atravesar (ie); **— each other** cru*z*arse
crowd multitud *f.*; muchedumbre *f.*
crush aplastar
cry llorar
crying llanto
cultivate cultivar
cultural cultural
culture cultura
cup taza
cure curar
curious curioso
cut *v.* cortar; **— off** cortar; **— in two** partir en dos
cypress ciprés *m.*

D

daily diario, cotidiano
damage avería; daños; **—s** daños y perjuicios (*law*); **to suffer —, be damaged** sufrir avería
dance bailar
dancer bailarina
danger peligro
dare atreverse (a)

daring atrevido
dark a oscuras; oscuro
darling amorcito, mi corazón, cielito
daughter hija
dawn amanecer *m.*; **at —** al amanecer
day día *m.*
dazzling brillante, deslumbrante
dead muerto
dean decano
dear querido
death muerte *f.*
deceive engañar
decide decidir(se a)
decision decisión *f.*
declare declarar
deep profundo, hondo
defend defender (ie)
defense defensa
delicious delicioso
delighted encantado; **to be —** complacerse (zco) en; alegrarse de
deliver entregar
demand *n.* demanda; *v.* exigir
democratic democrático
dense denso
deny negar (ie)
depend depender
depth profundidad *f.*
desert desierto
deserve merecer (zco)
design diseñar
despair desesperación *f.*
desperate desesperado; **to make —** desesperar
desperately desesperadamente
destroy destruir (uyo); destrozar
destruction destrucción *f.*
detail detalle *m.*
develop desarrollar(se)
device aparato
devote dedicar
diamond diamante *m.*, brillante *m.*
Dick Riqui
die morir(se) (ue)
diet régimen *m.*, dieta
different diferente, distinto; diverso
difficult difícil
difficulty dificultad *f.*
dimension dimensión *f.* (*often pl.*)
dinner cena, comida
direct directo
dirty sucio
discover descubrir (*past part.* descubierto)
discuss comentar; discutir
discussion discusión *f.*
distance distancia; **in the —** a lo lejos, en la distancia; **long distance (phone)** a larga distancia
district barrio, distrito
disturb molestar
ditch cuneta
do *hacer; **to have to — with** *tener que ver con; **to — with** hacer de
doctor médico; doctor (*title*)
document documento
dog perro
dollar dólar *m.*
Dominick Domingo
door puerta; **next —** la casa contigua or de al lado
doubt *v.* dudar; *n.* duda; **There is no —** No cabe duda (de)
down abajo; **— the street** calle abajo; **to go —** bajar; **to sit —** sentarse (ie)
downstairs: to go — *ir abajo, bajar
downtown en el centro; **to go —** *ir al centro
drama drama *m.*
dramatic dramático
draw dibujar (**art**)
dream *v.* soñar (ue) con
dress *n.* vestido, ropa; *v.* vestir(se) (i); **to get —ed** vestirse
drink beber
drive *ir (en coche); manejar
drop dejar caer; *caerse
dry seco
due to por; debido a, a causa de
during durante; por
dust *n.* polvo; *v.* despolvorear, limpiar

E

each cada; **— other** (*use reflexive pronouns*) + uno a otro, etc.
ear oreja; oído; **in one's —** al oído
earlier antes; más temprano
early temprano; a principios de; joven (**age**)
earn ganar
earth tierra
East *n.* este *m.*; *adj.* oriental
easy fácil
easily fácilmente
eat comer
economic económico

edge borde *m.*, orilla, margen *f.*
educate educar
education education *f.*, enseñanza; estudios (*pl.*)
effect *n.* efecto; *v.* realizar, efectuar (úo)
effective efectivo, eficaz
effort esfuerzo; **to make an — to** esforzarse por
eight ocho; **at — o'clock** a las ocho; **— hundred** ochocientos
eighteen diez y ocho, dieciocho
either o
electric eléctrico
elegant elegante
eleven(th) once; onceno
emperor emperador
employ emplear
employee empleado
empty vacío
enchant encantar
end *v.* terminar, acabar; *n.* fin *m.*; extremo, extremidad *f.*; **at the — of** a fines de; **from now to the —** de aquí hasta fines
ending terminación *f.*, conclusión *f.*
enemy enemigo
energetic enérgico
engagement compromiso, noviazgo
engineer ingeniero
English inglés
enjoy gozar de; gustarle mucho (a alguien); **— oneself** divertirse (ie)
enormous enorme
enough bastante
enter entrar en *or* a
enthrall encantar, cautivar
enthusiasm entusiasmo
entire entero
entirely completamente, enteramente
enunciate pronunciar, articular
epoch época
equality igualdad *f.*
equally igualmente
escape *n.* fuga, escape *m.*; *v.* escaparse
especially sobre todo, especialmente; **— well** sumamente bien
essential esencial
establish establecer (zco)
Europe Europa
European europeo
even hasta, aun; **not —** ni siquiera; **— though** aunque
evening noche *f.*; tarde, *f.* **(early)**
event suceso, acontecimiento
ever alguna vez; nunca (*negative implication; also after comparative or superlative*)
every cada; todos los, todas las
everybody todo el mundo, todos
everyone todo el mundo
everything todo
everywhere en todas partes
evidence evidencia
evil mal *m.*
evoke evocar
exactly exactamente
exaggerate exagerar
exam(ination) examen *m.*
examine examinar
example ejemplo; **for —** por ejemplo
execution ejecución *f.*
excellent excelente
exchange *v.* cambiar
exclaim exclamar
exhausted agotado, rendido
expect esperar, confiar (ío) (en)
expel expulsar; suspender
expensive caro, costoso
experience experiencia
expert perito
explain explicar
exploration exploración *f.*
explore explorar
explorer explorador
express *v.* expresar
expression expresión *f.*
extend extender(se) (ie)
extremely sumamente; —ísimo (*ending on adj. or adv.*)
eye ojo
eyeglasses gafas *f. pl.*

F

face *n.* cara, rostro; *v.* *dar a (**location**); encararse con (**a situation**)
fact hecho; **in —** de hecho, en efecto, en realidad; **the — that** el hecho de que; **the — is** ello es que
factor factor *m.*
fail fracasar
fair *adj.* justo
faith fe *f.*
fall *v.* *caer(se); **to — asleep** dormirse (ue); **to — down** *caerse; **to — in love** enamorarse (de)
family familia
famous famous
fare thee well adiós; hasta luego; vaya con Dios

farm granja. cortijo
fashion moda; — **house** casa de modas, modistería; **to be in** — *estar de moda
fast rápido; rápidamente; **as** — **as possible** lo más rápidamente posible
father padre
fatigue fatiga
favor favor *m.*
favorite favorito, predilecto
fear *n.* miedo; temor *m.*; *v.* temer, *tener miedo (de *or* a)
feature característica; facción *f.* (**of face**)
federal federal
feel sentir(se) (ie); **to** — **like** *tener ganas de
feeling sentimiento
fellow hombre; fulano, tío
feminine femenino
fence cerca
fertile fertil, fecundo
few pocos; **a** — unos pocos, unos cuantos
field campo
fierce feroz; encarnizado
fifteen quince
fifty cincuenta
fight *n.* lucha, pelea; *v.* luchar, pelear
fighting lucha, combate *m.*
figure figura; cifra (**number**)
fill llenar(se); desempeñar (**a position**)
filled (with) lleno (de)
final final, definitivo
finally por fin; al fin
finance hacienda
find hallar, encontrar (ue); descubrir
fine fino
finger dedo
finish acabar, terminar, concluir (uyo)
fire *n.* fuego, incendio; — **escape** escalera de salvamento; *v.* disparar (**a gun**)
firm *adj.* firme
first primer(o); **at** — al principio; **the** — **thing** lo primero
flag bandera
flat llano
flee *huir (uyo)
flight piso (**of a building**); vuelo (**air**)
floor suelo, piso; **upper** — piso de arriba
flower flor *f.*
fly *v.* volar (ue); *ir en avión
follow se*g*uir (i)
food alimento (*generally pl.*), comestibles *m. pl.*
fool tonto, necio
foot pie *m.*; **on** — a pie
footstep paso, pisada
for *prep.* por; para; *conj.* porque, pues
force *n.* fuerza; *v.* obli*g*ar; for*z*ar (ue); *hacer
foreign extranjero
forest bosque *m.*, selva
forget olvidar(se de)
forgive perdonar
form formar
former *adj.* antiguo; **the** — *pron.* aquél, aquélla, etc.
formidable formidable
forty cuarenta
forward (hacia) adelante
fountain fuente *f.*
fourth cuarto
franc franco
France Francia
fraternity fraternidad *f.*
free *adj.* libre; *v.* librar, libertar
freedom libertad *f.*
frequently con frecuencia
friar fraile; **F—** Fray
friend amigo
friendship amistad *f.*
from de; desde
front frente *m.*; **in** — **of** en frente de, delante de; ante
fulfill cumplir (con); reali*z*ar, llevar a cabo
full lleno
furniture muebles *m. pl.*
furrow sur*c*ar
further más
fury furia
future futuro

G

game juego; deporte *m.*; partida
garden jardín *m.*
gather reunir(se) (úno)
gay alegre
gaze (at) contemplar, admirar
generally generalmente
Geneva Ginebra
genius genio
gentleman señor, caballero
geographical geográfico

get *ob*tener*, conse*guir* (i); co*g*er; **to — angry** enfadarse; **to — sick** *ponerse enfermo; **to — up** levantarse; **to — to** lle*g*ar a, *ir a
ghost fantasma *m.*, espectro, aparecido
girl muchacha
give *dar; **to — out** agotarse; **to — up** renunciar; rendirse (i) (**surrender**)
glass vidrio; vaso, copa (**drinking**)
gloomy sombrío
glorious glorioso
glove guante *m.*
go *ir; **to — aboard** subir; **to — away** *irse; **to — down** bajar; **to — for a walk** ir de paseo, *dar un paseo; **to — home** ir a casa; **to — in** entrar (en *or* a); **to — into** penetrar; **to — out** *salir; **to — out on one's own** instalarse por su cuenta; **to — to bed** acostarse (ue); **to — to sleep** dormirse (ue); **to — up** subir
God Dios
gold oro
good buen(o)
Gothic gótico
government gobierno
grab (**by**) co*g*er (de)
grade nota (**school**); grado
graduate graduar(se de) (úo)
grandfather abuelo
grass hierba
grafted injertado
grave *adj.* sobrio; grave
graze pastar, pacer (zco)
great gran(de)
greater mayor, más grande
greatness grandeza
green verde
greet saludar
group grupo
grow crecer (zco); aumentar
growing *adj.* creciente
guard guarda, guardia
guest huésped, invitado
guide *n.* guía *m.*; *v.* guiar (ío); **to be —d** guiarse
guitar guitarra
gypsy gitano

H

hair pelo; cabellos *pl.* (*poetic*)
half *n.* mitad *f.*; *adj.* and *adv.* medio
hall salón *m.* (**room**); corredor *m.*
hallway pasadizo, corredor *m.*
hand mano *f.*
handsome guapo
hang col*g*ar (ue); ahor*c*ar (**a person**); **to be —ing** *estar colgado
happen suceder, pasar, ocurrir
happily feliz; felizmente
happiness felicidad *f.*
happy feliz; contento; alegre; **to be — that** alegrarse de que
hard duro; difícil; mucho; **to work —** trabajar mucho **or** fuerte; **too —** demasiado; demasiado difícil
hardworking trabajador
harmony armonía
hat sombrero
hate *v.* odiar
have *tener; **— a good time** divertirse (ie); **— left** (**over**) quedarle a alguien; **— to** tener que
head *n.* cabeza; *v.* diri*g*irse a
headquarters cuartel *m.* (**military**)
health salud *f.*; sanidad *f.* (**hygiene**)
hear *oír; oír decir; oír hablar; escuchar
heart corazón *m.*; alma (*fig.*)
heat calor *m.*
heaven cielo; **for H—'s sake** ¡por Dios!
heavy pesado; fuerte, mucho (*fig.*)
help ayudar; **not to be able to —** no *poder menos de
her su(s)
here aquí; acá (**toward me**); **— is** aquí tiene Ud.; he aquí; aquí está
hero héroe
hesitation titubeo, vacilación *f.*
hidden escondido
hide esconder(se); ocultar(se); **to be hiding** *estar escondido
high alto; subido (**price**)
higher superior; más alto
highway carretera
hill cuesta
his su(s)
historical histórico
history historia
hold *tener; guardar
holiday día de fiesta, día feriado
Holland Holanda
home casa; **at —** en casa; **to feel at —** sentirse (ie) como en casa; **to go —** *ir a casa
hope *n.* esperanza; *v.* esperar
horizon horizonte *m.*
horse caballo

hospital hospital, *m.*, sanatorio
hot caliente; **to be — out** *hacer mucho calor
hotel hotel *m.*
hour hora
house casa
how? ¿cómo?; ¿qué tal?; **— much?** ¿cuánto?; **— many?** ¿cuántos?
how! ¡qué!; ¡cómo!; **— I wish ...!** ¡ojalá...!
however sin embargo
huddle acurrucarse; **to be —d** *estar acurrucado
human humano
humanity humanidad *f.*
hundred cien(to); **five —** quinientos; **seven —** setecientos; **nine —** novecientos; **a — thousand** cien mil
hunger hambre *f.*
hungry hambriento; **to be very —** *tener mucha hambre
hunt *v.* cazar; *n.* cacería, caza
hunter cazador
hurricane huracán *m.*
hurry *darse prisa, apresurarse
hurt herir (ie); dañar, *hacer daño; **— oneself** hacerse daño
husband marido
hut choza
hydrant boca de riego (para incendios)

I

ice hielo
idea idea
ideal ideal
identical idéntico
idiot idiota *m.* and *f.*
if si
ignore no *hacer caso de *or* a, desconocer (zco); pasar por alto
ill enfermo, malo; **to take —** *ponerse enfermo, malo
imagine imaginarse
immediately en seguida, inmediatamente
impassable insuperable, insalvable
impolite descortés, grosero
importance importancia
important importante
imposing imponente
impossible imposible
impression impresión *f.*
impressive impresionante
improve mejorar(se); superar
in en; durante; por
incident incidente *m.*
include incluir (uyo)
including incluso
independence independencia
indicate indicar
indiscreet indiscreto
indispensable indispensable
industrialized industrializado
industry industria
inferior inferior
infinite infinito
influence *n.* influencia; *v.* influir (uyo) en, influenciar
information información *f.*; datos *m. pl.*, informes *m. pl.*
ingenuity ingeniosidad *f.*
inhabitant habitante
inland tierra adentro
innocent inocente
inquire (about) preguntar (por)
inside dentro
insist insistir (en); empeñarse (en)
inspired inspirado
inspiring inspirador
install instalar
instruction instrucción *f.*
intellectual intelectual
intelligence inteligencia
intelligent inteligente
intensify intensificar
interest interés *m.*
interesting interesante; **to make —** *darle interés (a algo)
interior interior *m.*
interpret interpretar
interrupt interrumpir
into en
introduce presentar (**a person**); *introducir
investigation investigación *f.* (often *pl.*)
invitation invitación *f.*
invite invitar
involved envuelto
iron *n.* hierro; *v.* planchar
island isla
its su(s)
itself mismo (*intensifying*)

J

jacket chaqueta
jaguar jaguar, tigre *m.*
Japanese japonés
Jim Diego
job empleo, puesto, trabajo

John Juan
join participar; unir(se) a *or* con; juntarse con
journalist periodista
joy alegría
judge juez
Juliet Julieta
jump saltar
June junio
jungle selva, jungla
jury jurado
just *adj.* justo; *adv.* sólo; **to have —** acabar de (+ *infin.*)

K

keep guardar, conservar; *man*tener*; **to — away** mantenerse a distancia; **to — on** seguir (+ *present part.*)
key llave *f.*
kill matar; **to be —ed** *ser muerto; morir (ue)
kind *n.* tipo, clase *f.*; *adj.* bondadoso, simpático
kindness bondad *f.*
kitchen cocina
knock llamar (a la puerta); **— down** derribar
know conocer (zco) (**to be acquainted or familiar with**); *saber (**to know a fact, know how**)
known: well — (muy) conocido

L

label etiqueta
laboratory laboratorio
lady dama, señora
lake lago
lamp lámpara
land *n.* tierra; *v.* tomar tierra, aterri*z*ar (**airplane**)
landscape paisaje *m.*
language lengua, idioma *m.*; lenguaje *m.* (**use of language**)
large grande
larger más grande; mayor
last *adj.* último; pasado; **— night** anoche; *v.* durar; tardar
late tarde
lately recientemente
later después; más tarde
Latin America Latinoamérica, Hispanoamérica
latter: the — éste, ésta, éstos, éstas
laugh *v.* reír(se) (í); **to — at** reírse de
launch lan*z*ar, botar
law ley *f.*; derecho (**profession**)
lawyer abogado
lazy perezoso, holgazán
lead *v.* diri*g*ir, *conducir
lean inclinarse; **to — out** asomarse
learn aprender; *saber (*pret.*)
least menos; menor (**slightest**); **at —** al menos, a lo menos, por lo menos
leather cuero
leave *salir (de) (**go out**); dejar (**leave behind**)
left izquierdo; **to the —** a la izquierda
leg pierna
lend prestar
less menos
lesson lección *f.*
let dejar, permitir
letter carta
level nivel *m.*
liberty libertad *f.*
library biblioteca
lie *v.* mentir (ie); **to — down** acostarse (ue), recostarse (ue)
life vida; el vivir
light *v.* prender, encender (**a cigarette, etc.**); *n.* luz *f.*; *adj.* ligero
like *v.* *querer; gustarle a uno; *prep.* como; **— that** así
limit *n.* limite *m.*; *v.* limitar
limitation limitación *f.*
line línea
lion león
list lista
listen escuchar; oír
literary literario
literature literatura
little pequeño (**small**); poco (**not much**); **a —** un poco, algo
live *v.* vivir
lock *v.* cerradura; *n.* cerrar (ie) con llave
lonely solitario
long largo (length); **as — as** mientras; **— time** mucho tiempo; **to take — to** tardar (en); tardar mucho
longer *adj.* más largo; *adv.* más tiempo; **no —** *adv.* ya no
look *n.* mirada; *v.* parecer (zco); *estar; **to — at** mirar; **to — for** bus*c*ar; **to — like** parecerse a
lose perder (ie)
loss pérdida
loud alto
love *n.* amor *m.*; *v.* amar, *querer;

to be (very much) in — *estar (muy) enamorado; **— story** idilio
lover amante
low bajo
luck suerte *f.*
lucky afortunado; **to be —** *tener suerte, *ser afortunado
lulling arrullador, adormecedor

M

made hecho; **to be — of** *ser de
magazine revista
magnificent magnífico
mail echar al correo; enviar (ío) por correo
major *adj.* mayor, principal
majority mayoría
make *hacer; ganar (**money**)
man hombre
mankind humanidad *f.*; el hombre
manly masculino, muy hombre
manufacture fabricar
many muchos
March marzo
Marian Mariana
marriage casamiento (**ceremony**); matrimonio
married casado; **to get —** casarse (con)
marry casarse con; **— off** casar
marvelous maravilloso
masterpiece obra maestra
material *adj.* material
matter *n.* asunto, cosa; cuestión *f.*; **What's the —?** ¿Qué tienes?; ¿Qué pasa?
matter *v.* importar; **What does it —?** ¿Qué importa? **no — how much** por mucho que
may *Use* poder *to mean can or is allowed to; use subjunctive of subordinate clause verb after a conjunction of uncertainty or indefiniteness*
May mayo
mean *v.* *querer decir, significar
means medio; **by no —** ni mucho menos
measles sarampión *m.*
measure *n.* medida
medieval medieval
Mediterranean *n.* Mediterráneo; *adj.* del Mediterráneo, mediterráneo
meet reunirse (reúno); encontrar (ue); conocer (zco)
meeting reunión *f.*
megaphone portavoz *m.*, bocina
member miembro
mentality mentalidad *f.*
mention mencionar
merchandise mercancía
method método
midday mediodía *m.*
middle *n.* centro; medio; **in the — of** en medio de; *adj.* medio; **— class** clase media; **M— Ages** la Edad Media
midnight medianoche; **at —** a medianoche
midst medio; **in the — of** en medio de
mile milla
milk leche *f.*
million millón *m.* (de)
millionaire millionario
mind mente *f.*; entendimiento; **to keep in —** llevar *or* *tener en cuenta
mine mío; **of —** mío
minister ministro (**government**)
ministry ministerio; **— of finance** el ministerio de hacienda
minute minuto
miracle milagro
mirror espejo
miss perder (ie), faltar a (**a function**); no acertar (ie), no *dar en (**a target**); echar de menos (**a person**); **to be —ing** faltar
mistake *n.* equivocación *f.*
mistaken equivocado; **to be —** *estar equivocado, equivocarse
mix mezclar
mobilize movilizar
modern moderno
moment momento
Monday lunes
money dinero; plata (*fam.*)
monk fraile
month mes *m.*
moon luna
more más; **— and —** cada vez más
morning mañana
most *adv.* más; *adj.* los más; *n.* los más, la mayor parte
mother madre
mount *v.* subir, montar; aumentar
mountain montaña
mouth boca
move *v.* mover (ue); moverse
movement movimiento
movies cine *m.* (**theater** *or* **art**); **movie star** estrella *or* astro de cine

moving *adj.* conmovedor
much mucho; **as — as** tanto... como; **so —** tanto
mule mulo, mula
museum museo
my mi(s)
mysterious misterioso
murder homicidio; asesinato
now ahora; **— that** ya que; **from — to the end** de aquí hasta fines
nowadays hoy (en) día
number número; **to call a —** pedir (i) un número
numerous numerosos (*genally pl.*)
nurse enfermera
nylon nilón *m.*

N

nail uña (**finger**)
name nombre *m.*
narrow estrecho
nation nación *f.*
nature naturaleza
navigate navegar
near cerca de
nearsightedness miopía
necessary necesario; **it is —** hay que (+ *infin.*)
need necesitar; *hacerle falta a uno, faltar
neighbor vecino
neither ni
network red *f.*
never nunca, jamás
new nuevo
newlyweds recién casados
news nueva(s), noticia(s)
newspaper periódico
newspaperman periodista *m.*
next próximo, siguiente; que viene; **the — day** al día siguiente; **— week** la semana que viene
nice simpático
niece sobrina
night noche *f.*; **last —** anoche
nightfall anochecer *m.*; atardecer *m.*; **at —** al anochecer
nine nueve; **—-thirty** las nueve y media
nobody nadie
noise ruido
nonintervention no intervención *f.*
nonsense tontería(s), disparate(s) *m. pl.*; **N—!** ¡Qué va!
nor ni
north norte *m.*
North African norteafricano
northwest noroeste
nose nariz *f.*
notebook cuaderno
nothing nada
notice *v.* notar, fijarse en
novel novela

O

obligation obligación *f.*
obstacle obstáculo
obtain *obtener, conse*gu*ir (i)
obvious evidente, obvio
occasion ocasión *f.*
occupy ocupar
occur ocurrir, suceder
October octubre
offend ofender
office oficina; oficio; **post —** casa de correos
official *n.* funcionario (**public**); *adj.* oficial
often a menudo, frecuentemente, muchas veces
old viejo, antiguo; **to be . . . years —** *tener... años de edad
older mayor; más viejo
oldest mayor; más viejo
olive aceituna; **— tree** olivo, aceituno
on en; sobre
once una vez; un día; **at —** en seguida
one uno; se (*impersonal*); **at — o'clock** a la una
only solamente, sólo
open *v.* abrir; *adj.* abierto
operate operar
operating room quirófano
opinion opinión *f.*
operation operación *f.*
opportunity oportunidad *f.*
oppose *o*pon*erse (a)
or o
orange naranja
order *n.* orden *m.* (**orderliness, etc.**); orden *f.* (**command**); **in — to** *prep.* para; por; **in — that** para que *v.* mandar; pedir (i), encargar
original original
other otro
our nuestro (-a, -os, -as)
ours (el) nuestro, etc.
outside fuera, afuera; **—of** fuera de
outsmart (**oneself**) pasar(se) de listo

outstanding destacado; sobresaliente
overcome superar; vencer
own *adj.* propio; **on his —** por su propia cuenta; *v.* *poseer, *tener
owner dueño, propietario

P

pack empaquetar; **to — a suitcase** *hacer una maleta
package paquete *m.*
page página
paint pintar
painter pintor
painting cuadro; pintura
pair par *m.*
palace palacio
pale pálido
panorama panorama *m.*
paper papel *m.*
pardon perdonar
parents padres
Paris *n.* París; *adj.* parisiense, de París
park *n.* parque *m.*; **to — (a car)** estacionar
part *n.* parte *f.*; **to take —** tomar parte, participar
party fiesta, reunión *f.* tertulia; partido (**political**)
pass *v.* pasar; aprobar (ue); **to — a course** *salir aprobado
passage paso; pasaje *m.*
passenger pasajero
passerby transeúnte, viandante
past pasado; **half— three** las tres y media
patience paciencia
patient *n.* paciente, enfermo
pay *v.* pagar; **to — attention** prestar atención; **to — for** pagar
peaceful tranquilo
peak pico
peasant campesino, labrador
pen pluma
people personas; gente(s) *f.*; pueblo
perfect perfecto
perform realizar; cumplir con
perhaps tal vez, quizá(s)
period periodo
perish perecer (zco), morir (ue)
permit *v.* permitir
person persona
personal íntimo; personal
personality personalidad *f.*
perspective perspectiva
persuasive persuasivo
pet protegido
Pete(r) Pedro
phone *v.* telefonear
picturesque pintoresco
piece pedazo (**bit**); pieza
pitcher botijo, jarrón *m.*
pity lástima; **It's a —** Es lástima
place *v.* colocar, *poner; *n.* lugar *m.*, sitio, paraje *m.*, **in the first —** en primer lugar
plain *n.* llano, pampa
plan *n.* plan, proyecto; *v.* planear
plane avión *m.*; **by —** *en* o por avión
plant *n.* planta; *v.* plantar; sembrar (ie) (**seed**)
plastic plástico; **— surgery** cirugía estética
plateau meseta
play *n.* comedia, drama *m.*; *v.* jugar (ue); tocar (**an instrument**); **to — a role** *hacer un papel
plea ruego
please por favor, haga el favor de; *v.* gustar
pocket *n.* bolsillo; *adj.* de bolsillo
poem poema *m.*
poet poeta *m.*
poetess poetisa
point punto; **— of view** punto de vista; **on the — of** a punto de
police (**force**) policía *f.*
policeman policía, guardia
politics política
poor pobre
popular popular; **to be very —** *estar de moda, *ser popular
populated poblado
population población *f.*
portable portátil
porthole ventanilla
position posición *f.*; puesto, cargo (**job**)
possessions posesiones *f. pl.*, propiedad *f.*
possessive posesivo
possibility posibilidad *f.*
possible posible
postpone aplazar
pot olla
power poder *m.*
powerful poderoso
pray rezar, orar
prearranged predeterminado
precarious precario
precaution precaución *f.*

precisely precisamente
prediction predicción *f.*
prefer preferir (ie)
preferable preferible
premeditated premeditado
preparation preparativos *m. pl.*, preparación *f.*
prepare preparar(se)
presence presencia
present *adj.* actual; presente; *n.* regalo; *v.* presentar
preservation preservación *f.*
president presidente
pretend fingir
pretty bonito, hermoso
prevent impedir (i)
price precio
pride orgullo
prince príncipe
princess princesa
principal *n.* director; *adj.* principal
principle principio
prisoner prisionero
private privado, particular
prize premio
problem problema *m.*
probably probablemente (*or future of probability*)
produce *v.* *pro*ducir*
product producto
professional profesional
professor profesor
profit provecho; **to make — from** sacar ventaja de; aprovecharse de
profound profundo
program programa *m.*
project *n.* proyecto; *v.* proyectar
promise prometer
proposition propuesta, proposición *f.*
prosaic prosaico
protect proteger
proud orgulloso; **to be —** enorgullecerse (zco); *estar orgulloso
provided that con tal que; si
province provincia
provisions provisiones, abastos
prudently con prudencia
psychological psicológico
psychology psicología
public público; oficial
publish publicar
pupil alumno
pure puro
purify purificar
pursue perseguir (i)
put *poner, colocar; **— on** ponerse; **— out** apagar (**a light, etc.**); extender (ie) (**one's hand, etc.**)

Q

quarrel riña
quarter cuarto; **at a — to seven** a las siete menos cuarto; **a — after nine** las nueve y cuarto
question *n.* pregunta; cuestión *f.* (**issue**); **to be a — of** tratarse de; *v.* preguntar; dudar de
quite bastante

R

radio radio *f.* (*Spain*); *m.* (*South America*)
rain llover (ue)
rainy lluvioso
raise levantar
rapt sumo (**attention**)
rare raro
rather bastante; algo; más bien; **— than** antes que
reach *n.* alcance *m.*; **out of —** fuera de alcance; *v.* alcanzar, llegar a
read *leer
ready listo; preparado
real verdadero
realize *darse cuenta de; realizar; efectuar (úo)
really de veras, verdaderamente; ¿verdad? ¿de veras?
reason razón *f.*
recall recordar (ue) (**remember**)
receive recibir
receiver receptor *m.*
recent reciente
reception recepción *f.*
receptive receptivo
recognize reconocer (zco)
recommend recomendar (ie)
record disco (**phonograph**)
red rojo
reddish rojizo
reflect reflejar
refrigerator nevera, refrigerador *m.*
refuse *v.* rehusar; rechazar; **— to** negarse (ie) a, no *querer (*pret.*)
region región *f.*
reiterate reiterar
rejoin reintegrarse a
relative *n.* pariente, parienta; *adj.* relativo
remain quedar(se)

remember recordar (ue); acordarse de (ue)
remind (**of**) recordar (ue)
rent renta, alquiler *m.*
repeat repetir (*i*)
reply *v.* responder, contestar
represent representar
representative *n.* representante; *adj.* representativo
repulse rechazar
reputation fama
require requerir (ie), necesitar
reserve reservar
resist resistir
resort *n.* recurso (**recourse**)
respect *n.* respeto; *v.* respetar
rest *n.* resto; lo demás; los demás (**others**); descanso; *v.* descansar
restaurant restaurante *m.*, restorán *m.*
result resultado
resume reanudar
retract *desdecirse, retractarse
return volver (ue); devolver
reunion reunión *f.*
reveal revelar
reward *n.* premio, galardón *m.*
rhythm ritmo
rich rico
Richard Ricardo
ridiculous ridículo
right derecho; razón *f.*; **to be —** *tener razón; *ser justo *or* correcto; **— there and then** en el acto; **to the —** a la derecha; **that's —** es verdad
ring *n.* anillo; *v.* sonar (ue)
rise subir; levantarse
river río
road camino
robe bata
role papel *m.*; **to play a —** *hacer un papel
romantic romántico
roof techo
room cuarto; **dining —** comedor *m.*; **living —** salón *m.*
root raíz *f.*
roommate compañero de cuarto
rough turbulento (**sea**); áspero (**land, etc.**)
round redondo
royal real
rubber caucho
rule *v.* gobernar (ie)
run *v.* correr; **— over** atropellar; **— out** *salir corriendo; *n.* recorrido

S

sad triste
safety seguridad *f.*
sail *v.* navegar
sailboat bote de vela *m.*
salient saliente
salvation salvación *f.*
same mismo
satisfied (**with**) satisfecho, contento (de)
save salvar; ahorrar
say *decir
school escuela
science *n.* ciencia; *adj.* científico, de ciencia
scientific científico
scientist hombre de ciencia, científico
scold reñir (i), regañar
scream grito
sea mar *m.*
searchlight reflector *m.*
seasick mareado; **to get —** marearse
seat asiento
second segundo
secret secreto
secretary secretario, a
section sección *f.*; parte *f.*; región *f.*
securities valores *m. pl.*
see *ver
seek buscar
seem parecer (zco); **— like** parecerse a; parecer
seize coger
selection surtido; selección *f.*
self-determination autodeterminación *f.*
selfish egoísta
sell vender
send enviar (ío), mandar
sensation sensación *f.*
sentence *v.* sentenciar; condenar; *n.* frase *f.*, oración *f.*
separate *adj.* separado; distinto
September septiembre
serious serio
servant criado
serve servir (i)
service servicio
set out *salir para, encaminarse
set up montar
settler colono
seven siete
seventy setenta
several algunos, varios
severity severidad *f.*, rigor *m.*
shake *v.* sacudir, menear

share *v.* compartir, dividir
sharp agudo; cortante; en punto (**time**)
shave afeitar(se)
shimmer rielar
shine relucir (zco), brillar
ship *n.* barco, vapor *m.*; **by —** por mar, en barco
shirt camisa
shoe zapato; **— store** zapatería
short bajo, pequeño; corto, breve; poco; **a — time ago** hace poco tiempo, no hace mucho
shot tiro, disparo
should deber
shout gritar
show *v.* mostrar (ue), enseñar
showcase mostrador *m.*
shrub arbusto
sick enfermo, malo
side lado
sight vista; **at first —** a primera vista
sign *v.* firmar; *n.* letrero (**poster**); señal *f.*, signo
silent silencioso
silk seda
silly tonto, necio
silver *n.* plata; *adj.* de plata
similar semejante, parecido
simply sencillamente, simplemente
since *prep.* desde; *conj.* ya que, puesto que, pues (**because**); desde que (**time**)
sing cantar
singer cantante *m.*, cantatriz *f.*
single solo; **not a — word** ni una sola palabra
siren sirena
sister hermana; **—-in-law** cuñada
sit (down) sentarse (ie); **sitting, seated** sentado
situated situado
situation situación *f.*
six seis; **— year old** de seis años
skirt falda
sky cielo
sleep *v.* dormir (ue); **to go to —** dormirse; **—ing** *adj.* dormido, que duerme; *n.* sueño
sleepy soñoliento; **to be —** *tener sueño
slight ligero
slightest menor
slim delgado
slope cuesta, falda, ladera
slowly lentamente, poco a poco
small pequeño
smart inteligente, listo
smile *n.* sonrisa; *v.* sonreír (i)
smoke fumar
smooth liso, igual, llano; suave; tranquilo (**water**)
snow *n.* nieve *f.*; *v.* nevar (ie)
so *adv.* tan; así; *conj.* de modo que, de manera que; **— as not to** para no; **— that** para que, a fin de que, de modo que; **— much** *adv.* tanto; *adj.* tanto, -a; **— many** tantos, -as
soak empapar
soccer sóquer *m.*, fútbol *m.*
social social
society sociedad *f.*
soil *n.* suelo, terreno
soiled sucio, manchado
soldier soldado
solitary solitario
so-long hasta pronto, hasta luego
solvent solvente
some algún, alguno; *pl.* algunos, unos, unos cuantos
somebody alguien, alguna persona
someone alguien; **— else** otro; otra persona
something algo
sometimes a veces
somewhat algo
somewhere en algún lugar, en alguna parte
son hijo
soon pronto; **as — as** tan pronto como, así que, luego que, en cuanto; **as — as possible** cuanto antes, tan pronto como sea posible
sorry: to be — sentir (ie); arrepentirse (ie) de
sound *v.* sonar (ue)
south sur, sud
space *n.* espacio; plaza (**a place**); *adj.* espacial, del espacio
Spanish español; de español; **—speaking** de habla española
spank dar una paliza
sparsely apenas; aquí y allá, a grandes trechos
speak hablar
speaker orador, conferenciante
special especial
specialist especialista
specialize especializarse
species especie *f.*
spectacle espectáculo
spend gastar (**money**); pasar (**time**)

spirit espíritu *m.*
spite: in — of a pesar de; **in — of the fact that** no obstante que, a pesar de que
splendor esplendor *m.*
sporting deportivo
spring primavera (**season**)
spy espía *m.* and *f.*
stability estabilidad *f.*
stagnation estancamiento
stain *v.* manchar
staircase escalera
stamp sello
stand *estar de pie; levantarse; **to — out** destacarse; **to — up** *ponerse de pie, levantarse
standard nivel *m.*; criterio; **— of living** nivel de vida
star estrella; astro
start *v.* empe*z*ar (ie), comen*z*ar (ie)
state *n.* estado; *v.* afirmar, *decir, manifestar (ie)
station estación *f.*
statistics estadísticas
stay quedar(se)
steal robar
steamship vapor *m.*; **— line** compañía de vapores
steel acero
step paso; peldaño (**of staircase**); **to take a —** *dar un paso
Steven Esteban
still *adv.* todavía; no obstante, sin embargo
stimulate estimular
stocking media
stop *de*tener*(se), parar(se); parali*z*ar(se)
store tienda; **department —** bazar *m.*; almacén *m.*
storm tormenta
story cuento
stout gordo; vigoroso, recio; **—hearted** de recio corazón, intrépido
strange extraño; extranjero (**foreign**)
straw paja
street calle *f.*; **down the —** calle abajo, por la calle
stretch estirar(se); **to — out to** extenderse (ie) hasta
strong fuerte
structure estructura
struggle lucha
student estudiante, estudianta
studious estudioso
study *n.* estudio; *v.* estudiar
subject *n.* sujeto; materia
submarine submarino
submission sumisión *f.*
submit someter; entregar
suburbs afueras *f. pl.*
subversive subversivo
succeed lograr, *tener éxito
success éxito
successful: to be — *tener éxito
such (a) *adj.* tal, tales; *adv.* tan
suddenly de repente
sue levantar pleito contra demandar
suffer sufrir
suicide suicidio; **to commit —** suicidarse
suit traje *m.*
suitcase maleta
sum suma
summer verano
sun sol *m.*
sunny: to be — *hacer sol; *haber sol
superior superior
supermarket supermercado
supper cena; comida
supposed supuesto; **to be — to** *haber de
sure seguro (de)
surely seguramente
surface superficie *f.*
surgeon cirujano
surgery cirugía; **plastic —** cirugía estética
surpass superar
surprise *n.* sorpresa; *v.* sorpender; **to be —d** sorprenderse (de)
surrender rendirse (i)
surround rodear (de)
suspend suspender
swear jurar
swim nadar
Swiss suizo
sword espada
system sistema *m.*

T

table mesa
take tomar; coger; llevar; **to — advantage of** aprovecharse de; **to — a trip** *hacer un viaje; **to — a walk** *dar un paseo; **to — away** quitar; llevarse; **to — long** tardar en; **to — off** quitarse (**clothing, etc.**); despe*g*ar (**an airplane**); **to — out** sa*c*ar; **to — sick** *ponerse enfermo; to — (**time**) **to** tardar . . . en

tale cuento
talk *v.* hablar
tall alto
task tarea
taste *n.* gusto; sabor *m.*; *v.* probar (ue)
tavern taberna, venta
tax *n.* impuesto
tea té *m.*
teach enseñar (a)
tear *n.* lágrima
technical técnico
technique técnica
teeming pululante
telephone *n.* teléfono; *v.* telefonear, llamar por teléfono
television televisión *f.*
tell *decir; contar (ue), narrar
ten diez
tension tensión *f.*
tenth décimo
term semestre *m.* (**school**)
territory territorio
than que; de; del que, etc.
thank *v.* agradecer (zco); **— goodness** gracias a Dios; **to — for** agradecer
that *dem.* ese, esa; eso; aquel(la); aquello; *conj.* que; **— one** ése, etc.
theater teatro
their su(s)
then luego; entonces; después
there allí; ahí (**near you**); allá (**yonder**); **— is, are** hay
therefore por eso, por lo tanto
these *adj.* estos, estas; *pron.* éstos, éstas
thief ladrón
thing cosa; artículo
think pensar (ie); creer; **to — of, about** pensar en; **what do you — of that?** ¿qué le parece a Ud. eso?
third tercer(o)
thirst sed *f.*
thirsty: to be — *tener sed
thirty treinta
this este, esta; esto
thorough cuidadoso, completo, cabal
those *adj.* esos, esas, aquellos, aquellas; *pron.* ésos, ésas, aquéllos, aquéllas
thousand mil
threat amenaza
throat garganta
through por
throughout por (todo)
ticket billete *m.*; entrada, localidad *f.* (**theater, etc.**)
tie corbata
time tiempo; hora; vez *f.*; época; **on —** a tiempo; **at all —s** a todas horas; **at this — of day** a esta(s) hora(s) (del día); **to have a good — (good —s)** divertirse (ie)
tiptoe: on — de puntillas; **to walk on —** *andar de puntillas
tired cansado
tiring fatigoso, cansado
to a; para
today hoy
together junto(s)
tomorrow mañana
tongue lengua; idioma *m.*
too también; demasiado
tooth diente *m.*; **— brush** cepillo dental *or* para los dientes
top cima; **on —** (por) encima
touch *v.* tocar
tour recorrido, circuito
toward hacia
tower torre *f.*
town pueblo, población *f.*; **in —** en la ciudad, de la ciudad (*after superlative*)
toy juguete *m.*
track carril *m.*; viarieles *m.* (**railroad**) (*generally pl.*)
trade comercio
train tren *m.*; **mail —** tren estafeta
transfer trasladar
transmitter transmisor *m.*
trap trampa
travel viajar
tree árbol *m.*
tremble temblar (ie)
trip viaje *m.*; **to take a —** *hacer un viaje
tropical tropical
trouble pena, pesar *m.*; dificultad *f.*
truck camión *m.*
true verdadero; **it is not —** no es verdad
truly verdaderamente
trunk baúl *m.*
truth verdad *f.*
try tratar; ensayar, probar (ue); **— on** probarse; **— to** tratar de, esforzarse (ue) por; **— out** ensayar
turn volver(se) (ue); doblar (**a corner**); **— around** volverse; **— into** *hacerse, convertirse (ie) en; **— on the radio** *poner la radio; **— off the radio** apagar, la radio; **— out (to be)** resultar, *salir

twenty veinte
type tipo, clase *f.*
typewriter máquina de escribir

U

unable: to be — no *poder
unarmed sin armas; desarmado
uncle tío
under bajo; debajo de
undersea submarino
understand comprender; entender (ie)
undertaking empresa
undress desnudar(se), desvestir(se) (i)
unfortunately desafortunadamente, por desgracia
unhappy infeliz; descontento
unique único, singular
unit unidad
United Nations Naciones Unidas
United States los Estados Unidos
university universidad *f.*
unless a menos que, si no
unpleasant desagradable
unpleasantness disgusto
unrealistic poco realista
until *prep.* hasta; *conj.* hasta que (+ *clause*)
unusual raro, extraordinario
up arriba; **— the street** calle arriba; **to eat —** comerse
upon en, sobre; **— hearing, seeing, etc.** al oír, ver, etc.
use *n.* uso; **to make — of** *valerse de; *hacer uso de, emplear; *v.* usar, emplear
useless inútil
usual acostumbrado, de siempre; **as —** como de costumbre

V

vacation *n.* vacaciones *f. pl.*; **to be on — *v.*** *estar de vacaciones; **to go on —** *irse de vacaciones
vain vano; **in —** en vano
Valencian valenciano
valley valle *m.*
valuable valioso, precioso
vehicle vehículo
velocity velocidad *f.*
verge: on the — of a punto de
very muy; **— early in the morning** muy de mañana
via por
victim víctima (*always f.*)
victory victoria
view vista
villa quinta, casa de campo, villa
village pueblecito
virtue virtud *f.*
visit *v.* visitar
voice voz *f.*; **in a loud (soft) —** en voz alta (baja)
vote *n.* voto; sufragio; *v.* votar
voyage viaje *m.*

W

wait (for) esperar
walk *andar, pasear(se), caminar
want *querer
warm caliente, caluroso; **to be very — out** *hacer mucho calor
warn amonestar, advertir (ie), avisar
wash *v.* lavar; lavarse
waste perder (ie); echar a perder; **to — time** perder tiempo
watch *n.* reloj (de pulsera); *v.* vigilar
water *n.* agua; *v.* regar (ie)
way modo, manera
wealth riqueza
wealthy rico, riquísimo
weapon arma
wear llevar
weather tiempo, clima *m.*
wedding boda
week semana
well *adv.* bien; **(both) as — as** (tanto) como; *exclam.* pues bien; **— -known** (muy) conocido
well *n.* pozo
west oeste *m.*
Western occidental
what *rel pron.* lo que
what? ¿qué?, ¿cuál?
what! ¡cómo!
what for? ¿para qué?
whatever cualquiera (que), cualquier cosa que; **any —** cualquiera
wheat trigo
when cuando
when? ¿cuándo?
where donde; a donde
where? ¿dónde?, ¿a dónde?
wherever (a)dondequiera
whether si (*not followed by subjunctive*); que (*may be followed by subjunctive*)
which *rel. pron.* que, el cual
which? *pron.* ¿cuál?; *adj.* ¿qué?
while *conj.* mientras (que); *n.* rato; **a long —** mucho tiempo

white blanco
who *rel. pron.* quien, que, el que, el cual
who? ¿quién(es)?
whole entero
whose *rel. pron.* cuyo
whose? ¿de quién?
why? ¿por qué?
wide ancho; **to open —** abrirse de par en par
wife mujer, esposa
will *n.* voluntad *f.*; *v.* *querer
willing dispuesto (a)
win ganar
winding tortuoso
window ventana
wine vino
wing ala
winter invierno
wish *n.* deseo; *v.* desear
with con
within dentro de; en
without *prep.* sin; *conj.* sin que
wolf lobo
woman mujer; señora; **a young —** una joven, una señorita
wonder preguntarse (*or use future of probability*)
wonderful maravilloso
wood madera
wood(s) bosque *m.*
wool lana
word palabra
work *n.* trabajo; obra (**of art, etc.**); *v.* trabajar; funcionar, marchar, *andar
worker obrero, trabajador
world mundo; **all over the —** (de) todas partes del mundo
worry *v.* preocupar
worse peor
worst peor
worth *n.* valor *m.*; *adj.* **to be —** *valer; *prep.* **to be — the trouble** valer la pena
worthwhile: to be — *valer la pena
wrinkle *n.* arruga; *v.* arrugar; **full of —s** muy arrugado
write escribir
written escrito
wrong incorrecto, equivocado; injusto; **to be —** no *tener razón, *estar equivocado
wrongly mal

X

Xavier Javier

Y

yard yarda
year año
yearning ansia
yesterday ayer
yet todavía; ya; **not —** todavía no; **— to be** por
young joven
your tu(s), vuestro (-a, -os, -as), su(s)
yours (el) tuyo, vuestro, suyo, etc.
youth juventud *f.*
Yugoslavia Yugoeslavia

Z

zone zona

INDEX

References are to sections, except where page numbers (p.) *are indicated.*